Economics and Ethics 1

Springer
Berlin
Heidelberg
New York
Hong Kong
London
Milan
Paris
Tokyo

Wilhelm E. Krelle

Economics and Ethics 1

The Microeconomic Basis

With 56 Figures and 7 Tables

Springer

Professor Dr. Wilhelm E. Krelle
Universität Bonn
Rechts- und Staatswissenschaftliche Fakultät
Adenauerallee 24–42
53113 Bonn
Germany
wilhelm.krelle@wiwi.uni-bonn.de

ISBN 3-540-44318-5 Springer-Verlag Berlin Heidelberg New York

Cataloging-in-Publication Data applied for
A catalog record for this book is available from the Library of Congress.
Bibliographic information published by Die Deutsche Bibliothek
Die Deutsche Bibliothek lists this publication in the Deutsche Nationalbibliografie; detailed bibliographic data is available in the Internet at <http://dnb.ddb.de>.

Springer-Verlag Berlin Heidelberg New York
a member of BertelsmannSpringer Science+Business Media GmbH

http://www.springer.de

Hardcover-Design: Erich Kirchner, Heidelberg

SPIN 10894508 42/3130-5 4 3 2 1 0 – Printed on acid-free paper

Preface

When one gets older, one looks at the science in which one has been working for a long time from a certain distance such that the general approach, the contours of the whole and the connections to other parts of the social sciences come to the foreground whereas the elaboration of the details must be left to younger colleagues. This applies also to this book: details are left to younger colleagues – if they find it worthwhile to try this new approach. I know quite well that the ideas presented here are incomplete and more in the spirit of a research program than a final product in itself. But time runs out. I personally think that this new road is worthwhile trying, but, of course, I, as the author, am not unprejudiced. On the other hand, after a certain age one is not so sensible to be torn to pieces by his critics, nature will do that anyway.

I present here only the basic ideas, the "hard core" of the theory and leave out most of the definitional relations which close the system. I leave that to the interested reader and to the scholar who wants to work with the system.

There are some repetitions in the book. This is done in order to make the single sections of the book as much self contained as possible and in order not to compel the reader to read the whole book to understand some points he is interested in. Notations are only consistent in each section, but not between sections.

In this book only the building blocks of a general dynamic disequilibrium system are considered: the theory of households, firms, banks, of the educational system, the government, and the formation of prices, wages, and interest rates. The different systems are not always compatible. They must be specified and simplified to a certain degree to form a consistent general theory. This will not be done here.

After these general remarks, I should like to come to the special principles that underlie this "new" approach – not totally new, of course, each scientist today stands on the shoulders of giants of the past.

1. The Walrasian System is to a large extent the theoretical base of the leading neoclassical school in economics as far as the static approach is concerned. But the work of Sonnenschein (1972) and Debreu (1974) showed that this system does not restrict the possible outcomes under the realistic assumptions that there are more households than commodities in the economy, and (following Popper) a theory which admits everything cannot be accepted as a scientific theory. The theory needs more structure to become meaningful. But this means that the theory has to be tailored to certain types of economies, e.g. to the economies of special western industrialized countries.

   The background of the model is a European type economy. More structure means inevitably: concentrating on special features which may not be characteristic for other economies.

2. The Walrasian general equilibrium system is static. It does not consider the monetary system, the government and foreign countries. We present a model where the monetary system and the government are fully included. But (for simplicity) we neglect foreign countries.

3. The assumptions of utility maximization of households and (to a smaller degree) of profit maximization of firms which underlie the "normal" neoclassical theory came lately under heavy attack, often connected with criticism of the high degree of abstraction used in the economic theory, see e.g. Mark Blaug "The disease of formalism in economics, or bad games that economists play", lectiones jenenses, Jena 1998, and the literature cited in this paper.

   Substantial criticism came also from the sociological as well as from the psychological point of view, confer Renate Mayntz "Rationalität in sozialwissenschaftlicher Perspektive", lectiones jenenses number 18, Jena 1999; from the point of view of experimental economics the work of Reinhard Selten may be cited. This criticism is mainly directed against the existence of utility functions for the households and the assumption of maximizing this function in order to derive demand and supply functions. In an analogous way though to a smaller degree the assumption of maximizing profits by firms has been criticized.

   In our approach there is no utility function. The person which has to decide on something (e.g. the household on consumption expenditures) does it by considering different points of view (e.g. the satisfaction of wants, possible situations in the future, moral obligations) and weighing them. The weights change under the influences of other persons and of ideologies, philosophies and theologies. This approach allows to include the influence of the spiritual side of life in economic analysis and conversely shows the influence of economics on the spiritual side.

   The suggested decision criteria are somehow in line with the corresponding theories in sociology and psychology: there are almost always different points of view or principles of judgement to be taken into account when a person or an institution wants to reach a decision. The decision makers try to find a solution to their problem which somehow considers all different points of view which he or she finds relevant in this case. The optimal decision comes out as a result of compromise between these principles.

4. The Walrasian system is constructed to demonstrate the economic situation in a fictitious state of general equilibrium which will never be reached in practice. In our approach the system is always in disequilibrium, expectations will (almost) never come true, but there is an (always frustrated) tendency to come to an equilibrium. The situation is like that of a dog chasing a hare: if the dog comes near to the hare, the hare makes some unexpected turn, and the dog stays again far behind its target.

5. The Walrasian system states the theoretical result of the economic interdependence of many households and firms under the assumption of perfect competition, but it cannot show how this result may be reached in practice. The auctioneer who announces prices and prohibits all transactions till a general equilibrium is reached is an unrealistic construct which has no equivalence in practice. In our approach, all prices are made by decisions of persons (given their information); there is no impersonal apparatus which determines prices or other economic variables.

6. The "normal" economic theory assumes continuity of all functions which implies that choices have to be made between infinitely many alternatives – which is impossible in practice. We do not make this abstraction: everything is finite in our approach – as the number of particles in the whole universe is finite. In the computer age we should not be afraid of large numbers, though in our approach the person has to choose only between few known alternatives. This is not always mentioned explicitly. Thus we also use normal analysis but only the integers (in general: the nearest integer, if the solution is not discrete) have a meaning.

The microeconomic system gives an insight into the functioning of a market economy, but it is not operational in the sense that it can be used as guide for economic policy. One needs a macroeconomic system for this purpose. But it is hopeless to derive a macroeconomic system directly from the microeconomic one. The macroeconomic system which I have in mind depends on the distribution of the characteristics of households and firms which are put forward in the microeconomic system. The derivation of the macroeconomic system is an econometric problem. Some suggestions can be made on the structure of this system. They must be checked. Unfortunately, I cannot do that myself. But perhaps some scholars may find the system suggested in this book interesting and promising enough to complete it formally and to test the macroeconomic version.

Finally I want to thank Werner Hildenbrand, Speaker of the Special Research Center (Sonderforschungsbereich) 303 at Bonn University, and Peter Schönfeld, head of one of the projects of this Research Center, for accepting this reserach as part of the work of this center and providing the necessary office space and the means for employing student assistants (studentische Hilfskräfte); I only name a few: cand. rer. pol. Menten, Schmitz, Dirlenbach, Zimmermann, Richter, Heinrichs, Radermacher, Klar, Claßen who prepared the manuscript from my hand writing. Markus Richter put the manuscript in a shape which made it publishable at Springer. I also wish to thank Dr. Müller from the Springer Verlag. Without his encouragement and promise to publish the manuscript it would not have been written. And finally I want to thank all friends and relatives who by their love and friendship gave me the force to write this book.

Wilhelm Krelle Bonn, March 2003

Table of Contents

List of Figures

List of Tables

CHAPTER 1
The Theory of the Household

1.1 Introduction

Ethics, where economics started from in classical antiquity, has reentered economics. There are more and more articles to be found in the literature which deal with ethical problems in a market economy (see the literature cited at the end). Thus, I think, it is time to analyze the relation of ethics and economics in general, i.e. to show where ethics influences economics (and vice versa), and how this can be taken into account in economics. In this book we deal with the microeconomic links of ethics and economics. Ethics addresses human beings to think and to act in a certain way. This may be brought into the form of evaluations of ideas and acts. In each case the single person is the addressee, also where social relations are concerned. This is the basic approach in microeconomics (as in the Walrasian system). The transition to macroeconomics represents a difficult task and will not be treated here.

The influence of ethics on economics is the main topic of this book. But we shall also shortly deal with the inverse relation: the influence of economics on ethics. As to the influence of the economic order on moral behavior, there are people like Roepke (1958) who think that a market economy will eat up the moral capital built up during non–capitalistic centuries, and there are opposite views. E.g. Albert O. Hirschman writes: "There is here ... the insistent thought that a society where the market assumes a central position ... will not only produce considerable new wealth ... but generate as a by–product ... a more "polished" human type — more honest, reliable, orderly and disciplined, as well as more friendly and helpful ... ". The criminal statistics seem to indicate a rising trend of criminal acts, but it is not clear how much of this is due to a larger extent of prosecution. There is a whole literature on the economics of crime, starting with Gary S. Becker (1968), which also indicates the rising interest in ethical problems.[1]

We shall explain the relations of economics to ethics, where ethics is conceived as the science of evaluating possible human ideas and actions. A moral evaluation is an immaterial reward or punishment of a certain size connected with a certain perceived or real act of a person that — if positive — comprises respect, esteem, reverence and the like by others and good conscience, and — if negative — contempt, disdain, breaking off relations and the like by others

---

[1] In Krelle (1996) I showed that a market economy does not necessarily induce people to cheat or lie or take other immoral actions, though one cannot prove this for all possible situations. Güth (1998) comes to a similar conclusion.

and/or pricks of conscience by the person himself. Often these reactions of society or of the "super–ego" to an act of a person is of much greater importance for the person than any sort of physical reward or punishment. But be that as it may: we assume that with each decision of a person which is of ethical importance[2] there is a "moral evaluation" connected with it. We explain the origin and the change of these moral evaluations and their influence on economics (this is the main topic of this paper), and vice versa: the influence of economics on these moral evaluations.

In the whole book we assume that a person is able to state his evaluation of a certain phenomenon numerically on a scale of discrete numbers, e.g. as $-\bar{z}, -\bar{z}+1, \ldots, 0, 1, 2, \ldots, +\bar{z}$, $\bar{z}$ an integer ≥ 1, where a valuation of $-\bar{z}$ means the largest possible dislike, 0 means: no judgement or indifference, and $+\bar{z}$ means the largest possible appreciation.[3] Of course, the grading may be coarse ($\bar{z}$ may be a small, positive number). Such grading is done permanently in politics and economics, also at the university level (e.g. in the economics department of Bonn University only 12 numbers between 1 and 5 (these numbers included) are admissible in rating an examination paper; and all professors do this without complaint). A reader who refuses to accept the possibility of "rating" a phenomenon in this sense according to the preference of a person may stop here and save his time.

1.2 Classification of Decisions and of Principles to Rate Them

We divide all situations where a moral evaluation may appear into the following large groups:

1. Private decision problems of moral importance in personal life,

2. Public issues of the general political and economic order and of the current policy,

3. Normal decisions of economic agents, i.e. households, enterprises, organizations in education and research, banks and the government.

---

[2] There are many acts without moral importance, e.g. whether I like apples or pears. For these acts the corresponding morality figure is zero.

[3] Each conception and each act causes an emotion which may be positive, zero or negative. It is assumed that there is an upper and a lower bound of the force of these emotions. This is in the spirit of Galileo Galilei who should have said as the device for science: to measure what is measurable and to make measurable what (till now) is not measurable.

There are different points of view[4] a person may have to evaluate a certain decision. We group them into the following categories:[5]

1. Economic advantage of the person considered or profit in the case of a firm ($= G$)
2. Expectation of punishment if the action is illegal ($= H$)
3. Emotional attraction of the act ($= EM$)
4. Force of imitation (or repudiation) of the behavior of others ($= IM$)
5. Judgement on the economic performance of a political and economic system ($= E$)
6. In the case of a firm:
   - 6a. Profits ($= G$); already considered in 1.
   - 6b. Production ($= X$)
   - 6c. Employment ($= L$)
   - 6d. The distribution of profits ($= D$)
   - 6e. The risk of bankruptcy ($= R$)
7. Moral evaluation ($= M$)

Not all of these categories are applicable for each type of decision, and perhaps there might be still other principles of importance for an individual. But those mentioned above seem to be the most important ones. We illustrate the working of these principles of decision first by looking at situation 1: private decision problems in personal life where some decisions might be punishable or immoral.

1.3 Private Decisions of Moral Importance

We assume that there are h possible private situations of moral importance with which the person may be confronted (see Table 1.1). We call them B_1, ... , B_h.[6] In each of these situations the person has two possible decisions: a

---

[4] Instead of "point of view" we shall also use the word "criterion" or "judgement".

[5] These categories are to be taken as example. There might be others as well. In section 1.9 we shall generalize the approach.

[6] If one is content with a crude approximation one could identify the h situations of moral importance for a person with the classification in criminal statistics, see e.g. the "Hauptdeliktsgruppen" in the Statistical Yearbook for the FRG, 1995, p. 376. But our theoretical concept goes much further.

"good" one B_{i1} and a "bad" one B_{i2}, $i = 1, \ldots, h$, where "good" or "bad" is determined by law or (if the law is silent) by the ethics which the majority of the population accepts.[7] In many cases the economic and the moral evaluation of a decision of a person run parallel, in others not. E.g. when passing by a store which exhibits some of its merchandise openly outside the shop the person may not touch it (the good act) or may steal (the bad act).[8] The figures $G_{i1}^{(p)}, G_{i2}^{(p)}$ in Table 1.1 indicate the economic advantage or disadvantage to the person p caused by the decision B_{i1} or B_{i2}, respectively; in our example: $G_{i1}^{(p)} = 0$ (if one does not steal, one does not have an economic advantage by not touching the merchandise), but $G_{i2}^{(p)} > 0$: the value of the loot for the thief is positive; this value measures the internal attraction; it is not an actual flow of money. The figure $G_{i2}^{(p)}$ represents the immediate advantage as well as all expected future advantages for person p which result from the theft. It is measured by an index of satisfaction which is normalized to lie between $-\bar{z}$ and $+\bar{z}$, $\bar{z} > 0$, a positive integer. $-\bar{z}$ indicates the highest possible dislike (a very large loss), $+\bar{z}$ the highest possible satisfaction. In our example: $0 \leq G_{ij}^{(p)} \leq +\bar{z}$.

The figures $EM_{ij}^{(p)}$ in Table 1.1 indicate the emotional ("irrational") attraction of the decisions B_{ij}. In our example of a possible theft of merchandise the person might be a kleptomaniac and cannot resist the urge to steal. Sexual offenses might fall under this category, also insults, assaults and other acts.[9] Here: $-\bar{z} \leq EM_{ij}^{(p)} \leq +\bar{z}$.

The next column $IM_{ij}^{(p)}$ in Table 1.1 indicates the attractive or repulsive force of the observed actual behaviour of other people. $IM_{ij}^{(p)}$ is (if positive) the "force of imitation" of the behavior of others on person p or (if negative) the "force of repudiation of common behavior", always with reference to a certain decision. These are "external effects" of the behavior. If many people act in a certain way (e.g. trespass against moral or state laws) there is an inducement to do the same (imitation and conformism are widespread in the population). But for a minority the effect may be opposite: there are people in the society who principally object to the opinion or acts of all others and want to impress other people just by doing the opposite of what other people do (snobs are an example). These "external effects" are well known in consumption theory.[10]

---

[7] This ordering is a matter of convenience of notation and has no importance with regard to the substance.

[8] Of course, that there are only two possible decisions is a simplification. It is not difficult to extend the approach to a finite number of possible decisions. But this will complicate the approach without any new insights into our problem.

[9] Of course, there are many kinds of emotional and instinctive impulses. Textbooks of psychology list them. But they are also known since long time from philosophy; see e.g. Spinoza (1665).

[10] cf. Corneo (1997).

Table 1.1. Decision Table; Private Ethical Problems for Individuals[1)]

possible situations of a person	possible punishments $S_0 = 0$	S_1	…	S_m	Math. expectation of punishment	Subjective evaluation of punishment	Immediate advantage for person p	Emotional attraction	Force of imitation[2)] of others	Moral valuation by person p	Proportion of persons choosing B_{ij}	Frequency of occurrence of B_i	Morality rate, criminal rate, resp[3)]	Elasticity of GDP with respect to $\overline{v}_{ij}$	Total valuation by person p
B_1: "good" decision B_{11}	$w_{11,0}$	$w_{11,1}$	…	$w_{11,m}$	$E(S_{11})^{(p)}$	$H_{11}^{(p)}$	$G_{11}^{(p)}$	$EM_{11}^{(p)}$	$IM_{11}^{(p)}$	$M_{11}^{(p)}$	v_{11}	β_1	$\overline{v}_{11}$		$V_{11}^{(p)}$
B_1: "bad" decision B_{12}	$w_{12,0}$	$w_{12,1}$	…	$w_{12,m}$	$E(S_{12})^{(p)}$	$H_{12}^{(p)}$	$G_{12}^{(p)}$	$EM_{12}^{(p)}$	$IM_{12}^{(p)}$	$M_{12}^{(p)}$	v_{12}		$\overline{v}_{12}$	$\epsilon_{Y,\overline{v}_{12}}$	$V_{12}^{(p)}$
⋮															
B_h: "good" decision B_{h1}	$w_{h1,0}$	$w_{h1,1}$	…	$w_{h1,m}$	$E(S_{h1})^{(p)}$	$H_{h1}^{(p)}$	$G_{h1}^{(p)}$	$EM_{h1}^{(p)}$	$IM_{h1}^{(p)}$	$M_{h1}^{(p)}$	v_{h1}	β_h	$\overline{v}_{h1}$		$V_{h1}^{(p)}$
B_h: "bad" decision B_{h2}	$w_{h2,0}$	$w_{h2,1}$	…	$w_{h2,m}$	$E(S_{h2})^{(p)}$	$H_{h2}^{(p)}$	$G_{h2}^{(p)}$	$EM_{h2}^{(p)}$	$IM_{h2}^{(p)}$	$M_{h2}^{(p)}$	v_{h2}		$\overline{v}_{h2}$	$\epsilon_{Y,\overline{v}_{h2}}$	$V_{h2}^{(p)}$

1) This includes decisions to act against moral and civil laws as well as decisions to act against the public order.–We assume that all probability distributions $w_{ij} = (w_{ij,0}, w_{ij,1}, \ldots, w_{ij,m})$ are taken from a finite set W of probability distributions. The situations $B_1, \ldots, B_h$ depend on the general political and social order and the actual political and economic decisions of the government, which we collect in the vector $\bar{\mathcal{O}}$ (to be explained later). Thus $B_1(\bar{\mathcal{O}}), \ldots, B_h(\bar{\mathcal{O}})$. At the beginning of a period a person can only be in one decision situation, though several persons may be in the same decision situation.

2) if negative: non–conformity to others

3) The observed criminal rate $\overline{v}_{i2} = v_{i2} \cdot \beta_i$ may be found in the criminal statistics. The morality rate $\overline{v}_{i1}$ is defined as $\overline{v}_{i1} = v_{i1} \cdot \beta_i$.

They are included in this approach. A formula for estimating IM is suggested in section 1.10 for the case of private households. A similar approach may be used here in the case of personal decisions.

The figures $M_{i1}^{(p)}, M_{i2}^{(p)}$ in Table 1.1 connected with the decisions B_{i1}, B_{i2} constitute the moral evaluation of these decisions by person p.[11] They are also normalized to lie between $-\bar{z}$ and $+\bar{z}$. A value of $-\bar{z}$ for $M_{ij}^{(p)}$ means the highest possible moral condemnation of decision j in the situation B_i, a value of $+\bar{z}$ the highest possible moral distinction of that act, and $M_{ij}^{(p)} = 0$ means moral indifference.

The $G_{ij}^{(p)}, EM_{ij}^{(p)}, IM_{ij}^{(p)}$ and $M_{ij}^{(p)}$ in Table 1.1 refer to a specific person p and are in general different from person to person. The following two columns in Table 1.1 refer to the set of all persons in the society. v_{i1} indicates the

11 Details will be given below, see section 1.4.

proportion of all persons who, if confronted with problem i, would choose the good alternative B_{i1}, the proportion $v_{i2} = 1 - v_{i1}$ would choose the bad alternative B_{i2}[12] . The β_i in the next column are the frequencies with which the problems B_i occur in the society. The $\bar{v}_{i1}$ in the following column in Table 1.1 are equal to $v_{i1} \cdot \beta_i$ and may be called the *morality rates* for the different decision problems.[13] The $\bar{v}_{i2} = v_{i2} \cdot \beta_i$ are the *observed criminal rates.*

The second–last column shows the elasticities of real GDP with respect to $\bar{v}_{i2}$: e.g. $\epsilon_{Y,\bar{v}_{12}} = \frac{\partial Y}{\partial \bar{v}_{12}} \cdot \frac{\bar{v}_{12}}{Y}$; it indicates by which percentage GDP per capita changes if $\bar{v}_{12}$ (i.e. the criminal rate in situation i) is changed by 1%.[14] This measures the economic consequences of the bad actions $B_{12}, \ldots, B_{h2}$. Of course, other measures (e.g. the effect on the distribution of income) may also be taken into account.

The last column of Table 1.1 gives the total valuation $V_{ij}^{(p)}$ of a decision B_{ij} by person p. Since valuations are crude estimations we admit only positive or negative integers or zero as valuation figures. We shall derive these valuations later (see equation (1.1) below). These total valuations $V_{ij}^{(p)}$ are also normalized to lie between $-\bar{z}$ and $+\bar{z}$. Of course, if we want to consider the society as a whole and if there are N persons in the society ($p = 1, \ldots, N$), each column in Table 1.1 is really a matrix of N columns.

Now we come to the first two columns of Table 1.1. The decision to move from B_i to B_{ij} may be illegal. There are $m + 1$ possible punishments in the society; each of them will be rated by the person by a figure $S_\mu^{(p)}$ between $-\bar{z}$ and zero, $\mu = 0, \ldots, m$, where $\mu = 0$ means: no punishment and $\mu = m$ the highest possible punishment. There will be probabilities $w_{ij,\mu}$ of being caught and sentenced to a punishment μ, a situation which is evaluated as $S_\mu^{(p)}$ by person p. Thus person p by choosing B_{ij} is confronted with the probability distribution ("in utiles") of punishment:

---

[12] It will be shown below how the v_{i1}, v_{i2} are determined, see section 1.7.

[13] The v_{ij} are theoretical figures. Actually, only the proportion β_i of the population is confronted with problem B_i.

[14] The reactions of other agents on the change of $\bar{v}_{12}$ are taken into account. E.g. if the percentage of people who do not steal rises, one needs less policemen, less judges, less prisons, and the money saved may be used for more productive purposes. — The approach above assumes that the GDP, called Y, is a function of all criminal rates $\bar{v}_{12}, \ldots, \bar{v}_{h2}$ (as well as other variables):

$$Y = Y(\bar{v}_{12}, \ldots, \bar{v}_{h2}). \text{ In general: } \frac{\partial Y}{\partial \bar{v}_{i2}} < 0.$$

Thus

$$\frac{\partial Y}{Y} = \epsilon_{Y,\bar{v}_{12}} \cdot \frac{d\bar{v}_{12}}{\bar{v}_{12}} + \cdots + \epsilon_{Y,\bar{v}_{h2}} \cdot \frac{d\bar{v}_{h2}}{\bar{v}_{h2}},$$

where $\epsilon_{Y,\bar{v}_{i2}} = \frac{\partial Y}{\partial \bar{v}_{i2}} \cdot \frac{\bar{v}_{i2}}{Y} < 0$, in general: a rise in the criminal rate will reduce GDP. Thus given these elasticities one only needs to know the relative changes of the criminal rates in order to know the effect on GDP.

$$W(S_{ij})^{(p)} := ((w_{ij,0}, S_0^{(p)}), (w_{ij,1}, S_1^{(p)}), \dots, (w_{ij,m}, S_m^{(p)})), \quad w_{ij,k} \geq 0,$$

$$\sum_{k=0}^{m} w_{ij,k} = 1, \quad -\bar{z} \leq S_\mu \leq 0, \quad \mu = 1, \dots, m$$

This is equivalent to a lottery ticket with losses instead of prizes (a soldier who goes to war carries such a ticket: with probability $w_{ij,0}$ he comes back unharmed, with probability $w_{ij,m}$ he will be dead, and with the probabilities in between he comes back with some more or less bad injuries; a person that runs the risk of performing an illegal action is in a similar situation). We may form the mathematical expectation of the disutility of punishment:

$$E(S_{ij})^{(p)} = \sum_{\mu=0}^{m} w_{ij,\mu} S_\mu^{(p)} \leq 0, \quad -\bar{z} \leq E(S_{ij})^{(p)} \leq 0, \quad \text{see Table 1.1},$$

but this may not have a meaning for the person; his risk behavior will come into view. Thus we assume that a person in this situation is able to state a figure $H_{ij}^{(p)}$ between $-\bar{z}$ and 0 which reproduces its "degree of dislike of this probability distribution":

$$H_{ij}^{(p)} \leftarrow W(S_{ij})^{(p)}, \quad -\bar{z} \leq H_{ij}^{(p)} \leq 0,$$

where $\leftarrow$ means "evaluation of".

There is a special section, section 1.8, which deals with this problem of evaluating probability distributions[15].

---

[15] One may think of another approach which takes into account the time preference (or the economic horizon) of the person explicitly. Let us assume that the punishments start in the next period and stay the same in each future period. Then each alternative B_{ij} is connected with probabilities $w_{ij} = (w_{ij,0}, w_{ij,1}, \dots, w_{ij,m})$ of punishments evaluated as $S_0, S_1, \dots, S_m$. Let the future (as far as punishment is concerned) be discounted by the person by a rate $d \geq 0$. Then, assuming neutral behavior with respect to risk the disutility of punishment would be evaluated by the person as

(∗) $H_{ij}^{(p)} = E(S_{ij})^{(p)} \cdot h$, where $h = \sum_{t=1}^{\infty} \left(\frac{1}{1+d}\right)^t$ and $-\bar{z} \leq H_{ij}^{(p)} \leq 0$;
in general: $h = h^{(p)}$;

$h = \frac{1}{d} \geq 0$ is the "economic horizon" of the person. The following table presents some possible values for d and h:

d	0	.01	.05	.33	.5	1	...	∞
$h = \frac{1}{d}$	∞	100	20	3	2	1	...	0

But not all of these values h are admissible. Since $-\bar{z} \leq E(S_{ij})^{(p)} \cdot h \leq 0$ we get $h \leq \frac{-\bar{z}}{E(S_{ij})^{(p)}}$. E.g. for $\bar{z} = 10$ and $E(S_{ij})^{(p)} = -5$ we get $h \leq 2$, for $\bar{z} = 10$ and

This explains the first two columns of Table 1.1.

A pure economic theory would consider only $G_{ij}^{(p)}$ and $H_{ij}^{(p)}$ as determinants of a decision of person p. But, as shown above, there are other influences to be taken into account, namely the emotional attraction EM, the force of imitation (or repudiation) IM of others, and the moral evaluation M which codetermine the decision. Other points of view in our list (the judgement on the economic performance of a political and economic system and the points of view relating to a firm) do not apply in this context. Thus we have 5 determinants for the evaluation of a decision B_{ij} by a person: the economic gain G_{ij}, the subjective evaluation of the punishment H_{ij}, if the action is illegal, the emotional attraction EM_{ij}, the force of imitation IM_{ij} and the moral evaluation M_{ij}. These influences are weighed by factors $\alpha_{ij,k}$ which are in general different for different persons. Thus we finally get for the evaluation $V_{ij}^{(p)}$ of a decision B_{ij} by the person p:[16]

$$V_{ij}^{(p)} = n.i.(\alpha_{ij,1}^{(p)} \cdot G_{ij}^{(p)} + \alpha_{ij,2}^{(p)} \cdot H_{ij}^{(p)} + a_{ij,3} \cdot EM_{ij}^{(p)} + \alpha_{ij,4}^{(p)} \cdot IM_{ij}^{(p)} + \alpha_{ij,5}^{(p)} \cdot M_{ij}^{(p)}), n.i. = \text{nearest integer}^{17} \tag{1.1}$$

$E(S_{ij})^{(p)} = -1$ we get $h \leq 10$. Higher values of h are possible, but they cannot degrade the valuation of punishment below the limit of $-\bar{z}$. The assumption that the punishment stays forever is a simplifying assumption in order to keep the expressions simple. If the punishments S_{ij} were only imposed for h periods we would get

$$H_{ij}^{(p)} = E(S_{ij})^{(p)}[1 - (\frac{1}{1+d})^h] \cdot \frac{1}{d}.$$

If the punishments were different in time we would get

$$H_{ij}^{(p)} = d \cdot \sum_{t=1}^{h} E(S_{ij,t})^{(p)}(\frac{1}{1+d})^t.$$

A person with $h > 1$ may be called risk averse, a person with $h < 1$ a risk lover. In our approach (see also section 1.7) the risk aversion or love of risk is used instead of discounting the future.

16 We always use integer approximations in this paper, but do not indicate that explicitly, in general.

17 In this formula it is supposed that the person has a sense for evaluation of phenomena (measured by the size of $\bar{z}$) which is a personal characteristics of the person and equal for all phenomena. This might not be true for all persons. It is possible that a person may be able to judge certain phenomena very accurately but other only very crudely (e.g. for one phenomenon it could only state: I like it, or I have no judgement, or I do not like it; for others it could state: I am very much in favor of it, or: it is sympathetic to me, but not very much, or: I have no judgement and accordingly for the negative side). The different scales have to be made equal before using formula (1). (I thank Werner Hildenbrand for hinting at that problem.) This can be done in different ways. We suggest a very simple one. Let

$$\bar{z}_1 < \bar{z}_2 < \ldots < \bar{z}_n, \quad \text{all numbers discrete,}$$

The $\alpha_{ij,k}^{(p)}, k = 1, \ldots, 5$ are subjective weights for the values G, H, EM, IM and M, with $0 \leq \alpha_{ij,k}^{(p)}$ and $\sum_{k=1}^{5} \alpha_{ij,k}^{(p)} = 1$.[18] The weights depend on the personal characteristics of the person, which are taken as given here. For G, H, EM, IM, M and α only finitely many values are admissible, e.g. all integer values between $-\bar{z}$ and $+\bar{z}$ for $G, H, EM, IM, M, \bar{z}$ a positive integer, and $\frac{\tilde{z}_k}{\tilde{z}}$ for $\alpha_{ij,k}^{(p)}$, $\tilde{z}$ and $\tilde{z}_k$ non–negative integers, where $\tilde{z}_k \leq \tilde{z}$ and $\sum_{k=1}^{5} \tilde{z}_k = \tilde{z}$. The upper index p indicates that this figure is "private" to the person, i.e. different from person to person.

The person p chooses that decision $B_{ij}^{(p)}$ which is most attractive for him (or her)[19], namely that with the maximum value of $V_{ij}^{(p)}$:

---

be the extreme evaluations of phenomena $1, 2, \ldots, n$ by a person. The actual evaluations may be discrete numbers z_i^* between $-\bar{z}_i$ and $+\bar{z}_i$, $i = 1, 2, \ldots, n$. Now the smaller scales are enlarged by a number $\beta_i > 1$ such that

$$\bar{z}_i \cdot \beta_i = \bar{z}_n, \quad i = 1, \ldots, n-1.$$

The actual evaluation z_i^* of a phenomenon i on the scale $\bar{z}_i$ can now be transferred to an evaluation z_i^{**} on the scale $\bar{z}_n$ by:

$$z_i^{**} = \beta_i z_i^*$$

(actually, to z_i^{***} where this is the nearest integer to z_i^{**}). In all following variants of equation (1.1) always equal $\bar{z}$ are supposed to be valid for all phenomena.

18 If the $\alpha_{ij,k}^{(p)}$ are given by nature there will be no freedom of will left for the individual. He will not be responsible for his valuations and decisions. But we assume that the person has some influence on the weights $\alpha_{ij,k}^{(p)}$. It may resist emotional or imitational drives, see section 1.4.

19 This theory of decision is constructed on a "medium level of abstraction" and in a way to fit into economic theory. It is not identical to the decision theory used in psychology, which is more detailed, but it may be conceived as a type of aggregated version of this theory. For a review of the development of the behavioral theory in psychology, see: Icek Ajzen "Attitudes, Traits and Actions: Dispositional Prediction of Behavior in Personality and Social Psychology", in L. Berkowitz (ed.): *Advances in Social Psychology*, Vol. 20, 1987, pp. 1–6; Julius Kuhl and Jürgen Beckmann: "Action Control: From Cognition to Behavior", Springer–Verlag Berlin, 1985; Mark Conner and Christopher J. Armitage: "Extending the Theory of Planned Behavior: A Review and Avenues for Future Research", in: *J. of Appl. Social Psychology*, No. 28, 1998, pp. 1429–1464; Stephen Sutton: "Predicting and Explaining Intentions and Behavior: How Well are we Doing?" in: *J. of Appl. Social Psychology*, No. 28, 1998, pp. 1317–1338. Following this literature the current state of the psychological decision theory may be sketched as follows. The theory is called TPB (= theory of planned behavior) or (in an extended version): TRA (= theory of reasoned action), and mainly developed by Icek Ajzen. The *behavior* of a person is explained by his behavioral *intentions*. The intentions are basically explained by three factors:

$$B_{ij}^{(p)} \leftarrow \max(V_{i1}^{(p)}, V_{i2}^{(p)}), \qquad j \in \{1, 2\}, \tag{1.2}$$

We may infer from equation (1.1):

1. The larger the M_{ij}, i.e. the clearer and the stiffer the moral rules are, the more likely is a behavior according to these rules.

2. A larger economic horizon (or: a smaller future discount rate) leads, as usual, to more moral decisions in the case where G_{ij} and M_{ij} are inversely related.

3. Higher punishments for crimes and deviations from moral behavior yield less crimes in general, i.e. if $h > 0$.

4. The more people give a bad example by breaking moral and legal rules, the more people will choose the "bad" decision.

5. Usually moral laws do not contradict criminal laws, i.e. for all $M_{ij} > 0$ we have $E(S_{ij}) = 0$. Conflicts arise if $E(S_{ij}) < 0$ for $M_{ij} > 0$.

6. For finite $E(S_{ij})$ and finite h, EM_{ij}, IM_{ij} and M_{ij} and sufficiently small weights $\alpha_{ij,k}$ for these values there always exists a number G_{i2} such that V_{i2} is positive and the largest among all V_{i1}, V_{i2}. This means: since there are almost no limits for evaluations of a situation by different persons, there will always be persons who take any possible criminal or immoral action if the economic incentive is large enough. From the individual point of view: everything is possible. We are, however, finally not interested in individual behavior but in the behavior of large groups of people.

---

1. Attitudes. These are conceived as the overall evaluation of the behavior, an expectation value of the outcome of the decision. (This may be identified with our figures G and H.)
2. Subjective norms. These are norms internalized by the person. (This may be identified with our value M.)
3. Perceived behavioral control. These are conceptions of the person whether it will be able to perform the task, whether the necessary resources will be available etc. (This is in our approach taken into account at the definition of the initial state B_i and the attainable state B_{ij}. Only actions which can be carried out by the person are considered in our approach.)

The list of determinants is not considered to be exclusive. Conner and Armitage suggest six additional determinants, among them: belief salience (which may be identified with EM), past behavior and habits (which is similar to our IM), moral norms (which are M in our approach). All these determinants may influence the intentions directly or indirectly via the attitudes or other variables. According to Sutton, p. 1333 this theory could explain between 40 and 50% of the variance in intentions and between 19 and 38% of the variance in behavior. That means, we have to be modest in our demands on the theory.

Table 1.1 illustrates the assumptions on private decisions and their consequences. In the relevant cases we have

$$G_{i1} < G_{i2} \quad \text{and } M_{i1} > M_{i2}.$$

If G_{ij} and M_{ij} run parallel and $E(S_{i1}) = 0$ there is no moral problem, we are in the best of all worlds as far as moral behavior is concerned. One should try to find a political, social and economic order where this comes true. But this does not seem possible for all issues.

1.4 Moral Standards and the Determination of Moral Evaluations of a Decision

Equation (1.1) in section 1.3 shows the determinants of the evaluation of a decision by person p. These are: the immediate economic advantage $G_{ij}^{(p)}$ (which follows from the specific decision), the expectation $E(S_{ij})$ of being punished if the decision is illegal (this expectation is treated as common knowledge), the size $h^{(p)}$ of the economic horizon (specific for each person, since $H_{ij}^{(p)} = E(S_{ij})^{(p)} \cdot h$, *see* (*) in note 15 above), the emotional attraction $EM_{ij}^{(p)}$, the force of imitation $IM_{ij}^{(p)}$ and the moral evaluation $M_{ij}^{(p)}$ of the decision by person p. We want to explain the moral evaluations $M_{ij}^{(p)}$. First, there is an interdependence of moral judgments within each society. Value judgments are discussed and transferred from person to person either personally or by the information system. Thus, in principle, everyone is influenced by the value judgments of everyone else though usually only to a relatively small amount so that one keeps one's convictions by and large for a longer time and changes only slowly (as a rule).

But there are also theologies and philosophies (including ideologies and economical, sociological and other theories) from which moral standards (also in the form of an optimal behavior) can be derived. The word "philosophy" has to be interpreted in the broadest sense. It also includes economic theories with implications for optimal behavior. Thus Marxism is a "philosophy" in this sense, and Keynesianism or neoclassical economics as well. They influence the "moral standards", i.e. the evaluation of personal decisions, also the evaluation of collective decisions (to be treated later, see section 1.16). The theologies and philosophies are passed on in the form of books, by the teaching in schools, by oral tradition etc.[20] They change only slowly. They influence the evaluations

[20] There is a reason to differentiate between theologies and philosophies. If moral standards are derived from the commandments of God revealed in the scriptures, they cannot be debated by the faithful. And if the majority of people believe in God and his commandments and therefore accept the ethics which follows from it, there will be a

of persons but are in turn not largely influenced by these evaluations. Usually many philosophies with different moral standards for each possible decision exert their influence in a society. It might happen that a decision B_{i1} which is best from the economic point of view is bad from the point of view of a certain philosophy k.[21]

We assume that each theology or philosophy k postulates or favors moral standards

$$\bar{M}^{(k)} = (\bar{M}_{11}^{(k)}, \bar{M}_{12}^{(k)}, \dots, \bar{M}_{h1}^{(k)}, \bar{M}_{h2}^{(k)}),$$

i.e. each possible decision B_{ij} is morally evaluated by a positive or negative figure $\bar{M}_{ij}^{(k)}$ or, if the theologies or philosophies are silent or indifferent in this issue, by $\bar{M}_{ij}^{(k)} = 0$. The evaluations may be rather different in the different theologies and philosophies (e.g. entrepreneurship may be positively evaluated in one philosophy and discriminated as exploitation in another).[22] These "moral standards" $\bar{M}_{ij}^{(1)}, \dots, \bar{M}_{ij}^{(K)}$ (if there are K theologies and philoso-

---

higher and more stable moral standard than in a secularized society, where many sometimes short–lived "philosophies" with different ethics fight for recognition. Moreover, all theologies and philosophies are handed down in the form of books which are written by persons under certain cultural conditions, and the words must be interpreted in the light of these conditions. The interpretation of religious traditions changes slowly, as far as the ethical consequences are concerned. The interpretation and the acceptance of philosophies and their moral implications change faster, since there is no "authority" behind the ethical valuations. In this section we keep the ethics of different theologies and philosophies as given and constant.

21 Let $Y = \tilde{Y}(B_{11}^{(1)}, B_{21}^{(1)}, \dots, B_{h1}^{(1)}, \dots, B_{11}^{(N)}, B_{21}^{(N)}, \dots, B_{h1}^{(N)}) =: \tilde{Y}(\bar{B}_1)$ be the size of GDP per capita if all persons $1, \dots, N$ take the "best" decision from the economic point of view, and $\tilde{Y}(\bar{B}_1) > \tilde{Y}(\bar{B}_2)$, where $\tilde{Y}(\bar{B}_2)$ is the size of GDP per capita, if all persons use a "bad" decision from the economic point of view. Then there may exist a philosophy k which does not care about GDP per capita but instead about some type of welfare or salvation W, where

$$W = \tilde{W}(\bar{B}_j), \quad j \in \{1, 2\},$$
$$\text{and } \tilde{W}(\bar{B}_2) > \tilde{W}(\bar{B}_1).$$

Our theory deals also with this case.

22 Our approach does not judge the different types of ethics. It allows an "ethics of responsibility" (Verantwortungsethik) as well as an "ethics of conviction" (Gesinnungsethik). A person is equipped with an intellect by which he is able to judge the consequences of his actions, and that implies: he may be kept responsible for these consequences. Some examples may illustrate this. From the point of view of the "ethics of conviction" it is not allowed to kill a person irrespective of the consequences. Thus according to this ethics it would not be allowed to kill Hitler in order to save the lives of hundred thousands or more persons. Or it is not allowed to kill a person that has taken hostages and threatens to kill them (if there are no other means to free the hostages); it is not allowed to form catholic advisory boards for pregnant women and to give them a certificate of having consulted such a board (because this certificate would allow the women to procure an abortion), irrespective of how many abortions are avoided and lives are saved because of this consultation. The ethics of conviction is based on the

phies) influence (in general) each person directly or indirectly (via other persons). These relations may be modeled as a Markov chain. This means that the moral evaluation $M_{ij,t}^{(p)}$ of a decision M_{ij} by person p in period t is to a proportion $p_{ij,p}^{(p)}$ determined by his own moral evaluation in the period before and with other proportions $p_{ij,p}^{\nu}$ by the moral evaluation of other persons ν, $\nu = 1, \ldots, N$, $\nu \neq p$ and again with other proportions $\overline{p}_{ij,p}^{\kappa}$ by the moral evaluation of a theology or philosophy κ.[23,24] Let there be N persons and K doctrines in the society. Then we assume:

$$
\begin{aligned}
(M_{ij,t}^{(1)}, \ldots, M_{ij,t}^{(N)}, \bar{M}_{ij}^{(1)}, \ldots, \bar{M}_{ij}^{(K)}) = \quad & (M_{ij,t-1}^{(1)}, \ldots, M_{ij,t-1}^{(N)}, \\
& \bar{M}_{ij}^{(1)}, \ldots, \bar{M}_{ij}^{(K)}) \cdot P_{ij}, \\
i = 1, \ldots, h, \quad j = 1, 2, & \\
\text{or:} \quad \tilde{M}_{ij,t} = \tilde{M}_{ijt-1} \cdot P_{ij}, & \qquad (1.3) \\
\text{where} \quad \tilde{M}_{ij,t} = (M_{ij,t}^{(1)}, \ldots, M_{ij,t}^{(N)}, \ \bar{M}_{ij}^{(1)}, \ldots, \bar{M}_{ij}^{(K)}) &
\end{aligned}
$$

---

conception that a person is responsible for his acts, and the acts are classified into "good" and "bad" ones irrespectable of the consequences for which God is responsible. I personally do not share this opinion, and I think a modern society and economy cannot be run under this principle. From the point of view of an "ethics of responsibility" not the act itself but its consequences are of primary importance. Our approach leaves it to the person which type of ethics he accepts.

23 We do not go into the details of this transfer of moral values. It may be accomplished by formal individual contracts, see e.g. Urs Schweizer, Vertragstheorie, Tübingen (Mohr Siebeck) 1999, or by some sort of social contract, see Wolfgang Kersting, Die politische Philosophie des Gesellschaftsvertrages, Darmstadt (Wiss. Buchgesellschaft) 1994. In economics this subject is partly covered under the headline of preference and choice or by Welfare economics, see e.g. the text book Andrew Mas-Colell, Michael D. Whinston and Jerry R. Green, Microeconomic Theory, New York, Oxford (Oxford University Press) 1995, ch. 1-3 and 21-23. We think more on the hundreds of informal contacts of a person to other persons where views are exchanged and moral values are revealed and to a certain degree adjusted. The way how these influences are exerted in detail is difficult to analyze, but the final effect may be revealed by repeated inquiries and interviews similarly as the yearly polls of the Allensbach Institut on the hopes and fears of the German population with respect to the situation in the next year.

24 This book is not concerned with the contents of different ethics. This may be found in the text books of ethics. I only mention Jan Rohls "Geschichte der Ethik", 2.Aufl., Tübingen (Mohr Siebeck) 1999 who presents the development of ethics from prehistoric ages up to the 20th century. Theological ethics with special reference to economics are presented in Arthur Rich, Wirtschaftsethik, Vol.I and II, Gütersloh (Gerd Mohn),1990, from the protestant point of view and in a more general context in Franz Böckle, Fundamentalmoral, München (Kösel) 1977 and in the encyclicals of the popes from the catholic point of view. In this book we deal with the influence of any ethics on the behavior of a person, especially on the economic behavior, and (to a smaller degree) on the opposite relation: the influence of the economic situation on ethics.

$$
\text{and } P_{ij} = \left(\begin{array}{ccc|ccc}
p_{ij,1}^{(1)} & \cdots & p_{ij,N}^{(1)} & 0 & \cdots & 0 \\
\vdots & & \vdots & \vdots & & \vdots \\
p_{ij,1}^{(N)} & \cdots & p_{ij,N}^{(N)} & 0 & \cdots & 0 \\
\hline
\bar{p}_{ij,1}^{(1)} & \cdots & \bar{p}_{ij,N}^{(1)} & 1 & & 0 \\
\vdots & & \vdots & & \ddots & \\
\bar{p}_{ij,1}^{(K)} & \cdots & \bar{p}_{ij,N}^{(K)} & 0 & & 1
\end{array}\right),
$$

$$\text{and } p_{ij,\mu}^{(\nu)} \geq 0, \bar{p}_{ij,\nu}^{(\kappa)} \geq 0 \text{ and } \nu = 1, \ldots, N, \quad \mu = 1, \ldots, N,$$

$$\text{and } \sum_{\nu=1}^{N} p_{ij,\mu}^{(\nu)} + \sum_{\kappa=1}^{K} \bar{p}_{ij,\mu}^{(\kappa)} = 1,$$

$$\text{and } -\bar{z} \leq M_{ij,t-1}^{\nu}, \quad \bar{M}_{ij,t-1}^{\kappa} \leq +\bar{z}, \quad \bar{z} > 0, \text{integer}$$

The $M_{ij,t}^{(\nu)}$ stay for all t in the limits $-\bar{z}$ and $+\bar{z}$. The system converges to $\bar{M}_{ij}$ with:

$$\bar{M}_{ij} := (\tilde{M}_{ij}^{(1)}, \ldots, \tilde{M}_{ij}^{(N)}, \bar{M}_{ij}^{(1)}, \ldots, \bar{M}_{ij}^{(K)}) \text{ and } \bar{M}_{ij} = \bar{M}_{ij} \cdot P_{ij}.$$

The solution of this system of equations gives the value $\tilde{M}_{ij}^{(\nu)}$ of the final moral evaluation of a decision B_{ij} by each person ν. It depends on the influence of the theologies and philosophies $1, \ldots, K$ and of the convictions of other people.

The convergence values $\bar{M}_{ij}$ may be derived as follows. Let $x = (y, z)$ be the column vector

$$x = \begin{pmatrix} y \\ z \end{pmatrix} = \begin{pmatrix} x_1 \\ \vdots \\ x_m \\ x_{m+1} \\ \vdots \\ x_n \end{pmatrix} = \begin{pmatrix} M_{ij}^{(1)} \\ \vdots \\ M_{ij}^{(N)} \\ \bar{M}_{ij}^{(1)} \\ \vdots \\ \bar{M}_{ij}^{(K)} \end{pmatrix} \text{ and } Q = P' = \begin{pmatrix} Q_0 & Q_1 \\ O & I \end{pmatrix}, \quad x_t = Qx_{t-1},$$

$$\text{where } Q_0 = \begin{pmatrix} p_{11} & \cdots & p_{m1} \\ \vdots & & \vdots \\ p_{1m} & \cdots & p_{mm} \end{pmatrix}, \quad Q_1 = \begin{pmatrix} p_{m+1,1} & \cdots & p_{n1} \\ \vdots & & \vdots \\ p_{m+1,m} & \cdots & p_{nm} \end{pmatrix}$$

$O =$ the $(n-m) \times m$ null matrix and $I =$ the $(n-m) \times (n-m)$ unit matrix

The stationary solution:

$$y = Q_0 y + Q_1 z$$

yields $y = (I - Q_0)^{-1}Q_1 z$, i.e. all stationary solutions are:[25]

$$x = \begin{pmatrix} (I - Q_0)^{-1}Q_1 z \\ -------- \\ z \end{pmatrix}, \quad z \in R^{n-m}, \tag{1.4}$$

and for all initial values $x_0^{'} = (y_0^{'}, z_0^{'})$ we have

$$\lim_{t\to\infty} x_t = \begin{pmatrix} (I - Q_0)^{-1}Q_1 z_0 \\ -------- \\ z_0 \end{pmatrix} = \begin{pmatrix} y \\ z_0 \end{pmatrix}$$

independent of the initial values $y_0^{'}$. Thus the asymptotic values of the moral convictions in a population depend essentially on the theologies and philosophies which are valid in the society, but also on the transition probabilities given in the matrix Q_0, i.e. on the mutual influence that the persons exert on each other — but not on the initial conditions of the personal moral values. If governments have some influence on the information system (influence on journals, books, radio, television) they will endeavor to reduce the influence (i.e. the $\bar{p}_{ij,\nu}^{\kappa}$) of all theologies and philosophies κ which the leading group does not like and to increase the influence of a philosophy it likes (e.g. a certain religion or a certain philosophy like Marxism). We do not model this explicitly.

If the relative influence $p_{ij,\nu}^{(\nu\prime)}$ which person $\nu\prime$ exerts on person ν with respect to the moral evaluation of a decision B_{ij} and the relative influence $\bar{p}_{ij,\nu}^{(\kappa)}$ which the philosophy κ exerts on person ν are given by nature or by social and political influences beyond the control of the person, the person would not be responsible for his actions. The person would be a sort of robot that is programmed by nature or by society for which the person is not responsible; there would be no freedom of will and thus no responsibility for misdeeds. A person would be like an animal with some more intelligence.

But this is not necessarily implied by system (1.3) above. The relative influences $p_{ij,\nu}^{(\nu\prime)}$ and $\bar{p}_{ij,\nu}^{(\kappa)}$ are subject to the decisions of person ν: a person is not forced to join a group of bandits or to accept a certain philosophy. The person chooses his groups of friends and his position in the society, of course within certain limits. But in almost all cases these limits leave enough room for personal decisions such that we may say: person ν is responsible for choosing the $p_{ij,\nu}^{(\nu\prime)}$ and $\bar{p}_{ij,\nu}^{(\kappa)}$. We do not go into these details of this process of forming

[25] I thank Dr. Christopeit for all these calculations. The inverse $(I-Q_0)^{-1}$ exists, since we assume that $\sum_{i=1}^{m} p_{ij} < 1, j = 1, \ldots, m$, i.e. : that some doctrines always influence the moral standards $\bar{M}_{ij}^{(\kappa)}, \kappa = 1, \ldots, K$. In this case all eigenvalues of Q_0 have modulus strictly smaller than one (cf. Murata (1977), p. 23, theorem 1.19). Hence $Q_0^t \Rightarrow 0$. Moreover, since $\lambda = 1$ is not an eigenvalue of Q_0, $I - Q_0$ is regular and its inverse $(I - Q_0)^{-1}$ is a nonnegative Matrix admitting the representation $(I - Q_0)^{-1} = \sum_{t=0}^{\infty} Q_0^t$.

the preferences of a person and determining the degree of responsibility for his actions; the criminal law in all countries implies that "normal" persons are responsible for their decisions, and that means in our approach: that they have an influence on the $p_{ij,\nu}^{(\nu\prime)}$ and $\bar{p}_{ij,\nu}^{(\kappa)}$, which allows us to treat these parameters as exogenous[26] .

The $M_{ij,t}^{(\nu)}$ and $\bar{M}_{ij}^{(\kappa)}$, $\nu = 1, \ldots, N$, $\kappa = 1, \ldots, K$, are (as explained before) figures between $-\bar{z}$ and $+\bar{z}$. After each round t of the Markov chain calculation the results $M_{ij,t}^{(\nu)}$ have to be enlarged or lowered to the next integer value which we call $\hat{M}_{ij,t}^{\nu}$. Let there be n_1 persons with equal evaluation: $\hat{M}_{ij,t}^{1} = \hat{M}_{ij,t}^{2} = \ldots = \hat{M}_{ij,t}^{n_1} =: \hat{M}_{ij,t}(1)$, n_2 persons with evaluation $\hat{M}_{ij,t}(2)$, $\ldots$, n_s persons with evaluation $\hat{M}_{ij,t}(s)$ such that $n_1+n_2+\ldots+n_s = N$. Thus from the Markov chain of equation (1.3) we get the distribution $D(\hat{M}_{ij,t})$ of the valuation of decision $B_{ij,t}$ for all t by

$$
\begin{aligned}
&D(\hat{M}_{ij,t}) = (\hat{v}_{ij,t}(1), \ldots, \hat{v}_{ij,t}(s)) \\
&\text{where} \quad \hat{v}_{ij,t}(\sigma) = \frac{n_\sigma}{N}, \quad \sigma = 1, \ldots, s
\end{aligned}
\tag{1.5}
$$

The foregoing analysis demonstrates the importance of theologies and philosophies (as far as they imply ethics) for the coherence and stability of the moral convictions in a society. They are a kind of anchors which keep the society together and prevent it from falling apart. But what happens if these "anchors" lose their power, as it seems to be the case now, at least in the western world? The number of agnostics rises, who acknowledge no moral authority. To realize the consequences of it we go to the extreme and assume that there is no religion and no philosophy or (if they exist) they have no moral influence on people, only the influence of other people exists. In this case the Markov matrix P_{ij} in equation (1.3) assumes the form

$$
P_{ij} = \left(\begin{array}{ccc|ccc}
p_{ij,1}^{(1)} & \cdots & p_{ij,N}^{(1)} & 0 & \cdots & 0 \\
\vdots & & \vdots & \vdots & & \vdots \\
p_{ij,1}^{(N)} & \cdots & p_{ij,N}^{(N)} & 0 & \cdots & 0 \\
\hline
0 & \cdots & 0 & 1 & & 0 \\
\vdots & & \vdots & & \ddots & \\
0 & \cdots & 0 & 0 & & 1
\end{array}\right)
\tag{1.6}
$$

where now

[26] If one is not content with stopping the analysis at this point one may go a step further, see section 1.5. But we do not pursue these routes here.

$$\sum_{\nu=1}^{N} p_{ij,\mu}^{(\nu)} = 1, \qquad \mu = 1,\dots,N, \quad p_{ij,\mu}^{(\nu)} \geq 0$$

This implies that the influence of theologies and philosophies which may have existed before is now distributed to the other members of the society. The society is "left alone", all changes of moral convictions are endogenously determined. What will be the result? The system may now be written in the former notation:

$$y_t = Q_0 \cdot y_{t-1},$$

where

$$y_t = \begin{pmatrix} y_{1t} \\ \vdots \\ y_{mt} \end{pmatrix} = \begin{pmatrix} M_{ij,t}^{(1)} \\ \vdots \\ M_{ij,t}^{(N)} \end{pmatrix}, \; Q_0 = \begin{pmatrix} p_{11} & \dots & p_{m1} \\ \vdots & & \vdots \\ p_{1m} & \dots & p_{mm} \end{pmatrix} = \begin{pmatrix} p_{ij,1}^{(1)} & \dots & p_{ij,1}^{(N)} \\ \vdots & & \vdots \\ p_{ij,N}^{(1)} & \dots & p_{ij,N}^{(N)} \end{pmatrix}$$

and $\quad p_{ij} \geq 0, \qquad \sum_{\nu=1}^{m} p_{\nu\mu} = 1, \quad \mu = 1,\dots,m.$

The matrix Q_0 is called a stochastic matrix. The character of the solution of the Markov chain $y_t = Q_0 \cdot y_{t-1}$ is well known[27]. The solution may be written as

$$y_t = \sum_{\mu=1}^{m} \bar{A}_\mu \cdot \lambda_\mu^t \cdot \bar{y}_\mu$$

where $\lambda_1,\dots,\lambda_m$ are the eigenvalues of the matrix $(Q_0 - I\lambda)$, the $\bar{y}_\mu$ are the eigenvectors and the $\bar{A}_\mu$ depend on the initial conditions. We may assume that the matrix Q_0 is irreducable[28] because a society does not fall apart in different sub–societies which do not communicate with each other. We may also assume that Q_0 is aperiodic[29]. If it were periodic, the flow of influence

---

[27] I thank Dr. Werner for the discussion of the solutions. For the definitions of reducible and aperiodic matrices and their influence on the solution see also Krelle (1988 a).

[28] A matrix A is reducible if it is possible to reorder the lines and the adjoined columns of A such that it takes the form $A = \begin{pmatrix} A_{11} & A_{12} \\ A_{21} & A_{22} \end{pmatrix}$, where A_{11} and A_{22} are quadratic matrices whereas A_{21} and/or A_{12} are zero.

[29] A matrix A is periodic (or cyclic) if it is possible to reorder it by changing the lines and the adjoined columns such that it takes the form:

$$A = \begin{pmatrix} 0 & A_{12} & 0 & \dots & 0 \\ 0 & 0 & A_{23} & \dots & 0 \\ \vdots & \vdots & \vdots & \vdots & \vdots \\ 0 & \dots & \dots & 0 & A_{n-1,n} \\ A_{n1} & 0 & \dots & \dots & 0 \end{pmatrix}.$$

on moral convictions would always circle around certain groups of people; the influence goes from group A to group B ... to group Z and then back to group A. This seems to be very unlikely. If Q_0 is neither periodic nor reducible, Q_0 has an eigenvalue 1 with multiplicity 1, say : $\lambda_1 = 1$. All other eigenvalues are smaller than 1 in absolute value. They might be conjugate complex or real. This proves that the system of moral convictions of the population may converge, but the convergence value depends completely on the initial conditions. There may be fluctuations (if there are negative real or conjugate complex eigenvalues). Since the initial conditions are to a certain degree arbitrary, the same is true for the convergence values. Anything may happen.

1.5 A Digression: Explanation of the Transfer Probabilities

In equation (1.3) the transfer matrix P appears which contains the transfer coefficients $p_{ij,\mu}^{(\nu)}$ and $\bar{p}_{ij,\nu}^{(\kappa)}$. We treated them as exogenous, which leaves room for the freedom of will of the person. We may go one or more steps further but naturally have to stop somewhere. We do not pursue this line of approach further but we may suggest two lines of thought to explain the transfer probabilities.

Explanation 1. The sizes of the transfer probabilities depend on the position of the persons within the society, where "position" describes the geographical location of the person as well as the position in the social hierarchy. Let there be N persons $P_1, \ldots, P_N$ in the society and Z possible positions $POS_1, \ldots, POS_Z$, where $Z > N$. Thus $Z - N$ positions remain empty. E.g., if there are 2 persons in the society and 3 positions we get 6 possible combinations. Each combination may be given a certain probability of being realized in the future. The person we consider may disregard combinations with very low probability of realization. The following table illustrates the approach for this example:

	Positions in the Society			probability of realization
	POS_1	POS_2	POS_3	
1	P_1	P_2		π_1
2	P_2	P_1		π_2
3	P_1		P_2	π_3
4	P_2		P_1	π_4
5		P_1	P_2	π_5
6		P_2	P_1	π_6

Allocation of 2 persons P_1, P_2 to 3 positions = combination 1,...,6

$\pi_i \geq 0$

$\sum_{i=1}^{6} \pi_i = 1$

Let $D(POS_\eta, POS_\xi)$ be a measure of the distance of position η to position ξ. the larger the distance the smaller the influence of POS_ξ to POS_η and thus the smaller p_η^ξ in the transition matrix P.

Explanation 2. Another approach consists of repeating the Markov procedure for the parameters p and $\bar{p}$ in the following way. Rewrite equation (1.3) by

(∗) $\boxed{x_t = x_{t-1} \cdot P_{t-1}}$

where $x_t := (M_t^{(1)} \cdots M_t^{(N)}, \bar{M}^{(1)} \cdots \bar{M}^{(K)})$

$$P_{t-1} = \begin{pmatrix} p_1^{(1)}(t-1) & \cdots & p_N^{(1)}(t-1) & | & 0 & \cdots & 0 \\ \vdots & & & | & \vdots & & \vdots \\ p_1^{(N)}(t-1) & \cdots & p_N^{(N)}(t-1) & | & 0 & \cdots & 0 \\ -- & -- & -- & -- & -- & -- & -- \\ \bar{p}_1^{(1)}(t-1) & \cdots & \bar{p}_N^{(1)}(t-1) & | & 1 & & \\ \vdots & & & | & & \ddots & \\ \bar{p}_1^{(K)}(t-1) & \cdots & \bar{p}_N^{(K)}(t-1) & | & & & 1 \end{pmatrix}$$

The first column in P_{t-1} may be written as a row vector:

$$y_{t-1} := (p_1^{(1)}(t-1) \cdots p_1^{(N)}(t-1) | \bar{p}_1^{(1)}(t-1) \cdots \bar{p}_N^{(K)}(t-1))$$

Now we put: $y_{t-1} = y_{t-2} \cdot P_{t-2}$ and repeat that for columns 2 to N in P_{t-1}. This means we get Markov chains of the type

$$y_{t-1}^{(1)} = y_{t-2}^{(1)} \cdot P_{t-2}^{(1)}, \ldots, y_{t-1}^{(N)} = y_{t-2}^{(N)} \cdot P_{t-2}^{(N)}$$

Let $y_{t-1}^{(1)'}, \ldots, y_{t-1}^{(N)'}$ be the corresponding column vectors. We may reformulate the matrix P_{t-1} in equation (∗) as

$$P_{t-1} = \begin{pmatrix} & & & | & & 0 & \\ & & & | & -- & -- & -- \\ y_{t-1}^{(1)'} & \cdots & y_{t-1}^{(N)'} & | & 1 & & \\ & & & | & & \ddots & \\ & & & | & & & 1 \end{pmatrix}$$

where $y_{t-1}^{(\nu)} = y_{t-2}^{(\nu)} \cdot P_{t-2}^{(\nu)}, \quad \nu = 1 \ldots, N$

We could continue that way and stop if $y_{t-T}^{(\nu)} \approx y_{t-T-1}^{(\nu)}$ for some $T \geq 2$ or (if this does not happen) if information on x_t is lacking for $t \leq t - \tau \quad, \tau \geq 2$.

1.6 The Length of the Economic Horizon

Besides depending on $M_{ij}^{(p)}$ the value $V_{ij}^{(p)}$ of a decision B_{ij} depends on the subjective expectation of punishment $H_{ij}^{(p)} = E(S_{ij})^{(p)} \cdot h^{(p)}$. The mathematical expectation $E(S_{ij})^{(p)}$ is given to the individual person. But $H_{ij}^{(p)}$ is also a function of the economic horizon $h^{(p)}$ of the person p. We assume that the length of the foresight follows a relatively stable distribution in the society: relatively few people live only from day to day (i.e. the length of their horizon is zero), relatively more have a bit more foresight, but above a certain size the relative number of persons with rather large foresight declines. Fig. 1.1 gives an example of such a distribution. It may be explained as the convergence value of a Markov chain with respect to the length h of the economic horizon, which is a measure for the risk aversion. We assume that the risk aversion or love of risk is a personal attribute which applies to all decisions; thus: $h^{(p)}$. There is a mutual influence on it, and the theologies and philosophies may not be silent either on this subject. Thus, similar to equation (1.3), we get the equations

$$(h_t^{(1)}, \ldots, h_t^{(N)}, \bar{h}^{(1)}, \ldots, \bar{h}^{(K)}) = (h_{t-1}^{(1)}, \ldots, h_{t-1}^{(N)}, \bar{h}^{(1)}, \ldots, \bar{h}^{(K)}) \cdot P \quad (1.7)$$

$$P = \left(\begin{array}{ccc|ccc} p_1^{(1)} & \cdots & p_N^{(1)} & 0 & \cdots & 0 \\ \vdots & & \vdots & \vdots & & \vdots \\ p_1^{(N)} & \cdots & p_N^{(N)} & 0 & \cdots & 0 \\ \hdashline \bar{p}_1^{(1)} & \cdots & \bar{p}_N^{(1)} & 1 & & 0 \\ \vdots & & \vdots & & \ddots & \\ \bar{p}_1^{(K)} & \cdots & \bar{p}_N^{(K)} & 0 & & 1 \end{array} \right)$$

with the constraints as in equation (1.3). This system converges to values according to equation (1.4). If we consider the distribution $(h^{(1)}, \ldots, h^{(N)})$ as constant, this implies that the Markov process has already converged to its asymptotic value. But we may as well consider the $h^{(p)}$ as variable and explain it by equation (1.7). This is an empirical question.

1.7 The Relative Frequencies of Personal Decisions

Let

$$v_{i1} = \frac{\#(p|V_{i1}^{(p)} \geq V_{i2}^{(p)})}{\#(p)}, \quad 0 \leq v_{i1} \leq 1, \quad \text{where: } \#p = N \quad (1.8)$$

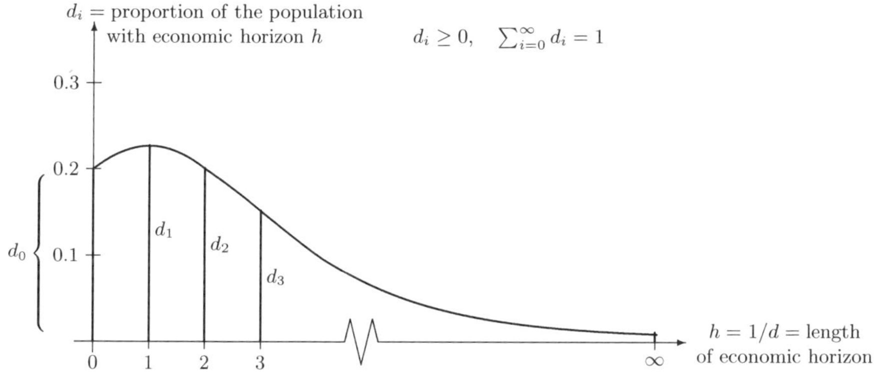

Figure 1.1. Distribution of Economic Foresight in the Society

be the relative number of persons that in a situation B_i would choose B_{i1}, and accordingly

$$v_{i2} = 1 - v_{i1} = \frac{\#(p|V_{i1}^{(p)} < V_{i2}^{(p)})}{\#(p)}$$

the relative number of persons who would choose B_{i2}. E.g. in our example of the theft of merchandise exhibited outside the shop v_{i1} is the proportion of the population who in such a situation would stay honest and $v_{i2} = 1 - v_{i1}$ the proportion who would steal. If our theory of decision is (at least approximately) right, the v_{i1} or v_{i2} may be derived from the personal distributions of the values of $G_{ij}^{(p)}, H_{ij}^{(p)}, EM_{ij}^{(p)}, IM_{ij}^{(p)}, M_{ij}^{(p)}$ and of the $\alpha_{ij,k}^{(p)}, k = 1, \ldots, 5$ which determine the valuation $V_{ij}^{(p)}$ of the decision B_{ij}, see equation 1.1. All these distributions may be obtained by public polls where persons have to assign integer values between $-\bar{z}$ and $+\bar{z}$ to the magnitudes $G_{ij}^{(p)}, H_{ij}^{(p)}, EM_{ij}^{(p)}, IM_{ij,0}^{(p)}$ and $M_{ij}^{(p)}$ and non–negative integer values $\tilde{z}_1, \ldots, \tilde{z}_5$ where $\sum_{k=1}^{5} \tilde{z}_k = \tilde{z}$ to the weighing factors such that $\alpha_{ij,k}^{(p)} = \frac{\tilde{z}_k}{\tilde{z}}$, where $\tilde{z}$ is a given positive integer, e.g. 10. By using equation 1.1 one gets the valuations of the situation in question and by using equation (1.8) the relative number v_{i1} of persons who would prefer B_{i1} and accordingly of those who would prefer B_{i2}. If the relative frequencies β_i of occurrence of the decision situation B_i would be known, the morality and criminal rates $\bar{v_{i1}}, v_{i2}$ could be estimated and compared with the actual values, which would be a test of the theory. Of course, one could also ask the persons directly whether they prefer B_{i1} (which is valued as V_{i1}) over B_{i2} (which is valued as V_{i2}) but one may not be sure to get the right answer (few people would like to reveal themselves as criminals). But from the values of $G_{ij}, H_{ij}, EM_{ij}, IM_{ij}$ and M_{ij} and their weights $\alpha_{ij,k}$ one may infer the preferences of the person with respect to B_{i1} or B_{i2}, if one has some confidence in the decision theory suggested above. In any case we assume that the valuations of $G_{ij}, H_{ij}, EM_{ij}, IM_{ij}$ and M_{ij} on an integer scale of $-z$ to $+z$ for each decision B_{ij} can be done by each person or (in a short cut) each person could indicate directly his valuation V_{ij} of this alternative.[30] Fig. 1.2 illustrates the case. B_{i1} is chosen if $V_{i1} \geq V_{i2}$. On the axes the values V_{i1} and V_{i2} are measured with $-\bar{z} \leq V_{ij} \leq +\bar{z}$ and the adjoined relative frequencies $w_{ij,-\bar{z}}, \ldots, w_{ij,+\bar{z}}$ are listed for these coordinates[31]. Each integer point in the square $-\bar{z}, \ldots, +\bar{z}$ has the probability (= relative frequency) of the product of the two adjoined relative frequencies; e.g. the point P in Fig. 1.2 appears with the relative frequency of $w_{i1,\bar{z}-1} \cdot w_{i2,2}$. In all situations indicated by the thick dots in the dotted triangle ABC the decision B_{i1} is taken, and the relative frequency v_{i1} of this decision in the society equals the sum of the products $w_{i1,\xi_1} \cdot w_{i2,\xi_2}$ for points (ξ_1, ξ_2) lying in the dotted area. Thus, the relative frequencies v_{i1} and v_{i2} may be derived from the distribution of the basic entities $G_{ij}, H_{ij}, EM_{ij}, IM_{ij}$ and M_{ij} (weighted by $\alpha_{ij,k}$) which cause these decisions, see equation (1.8).

It follows that the relative frequencies of "bad" decisions can be reduced by lowering the temptation G_{i2} for a "bad decision", by raising the expectation of punishment H_{i2} (e.g. by enlarging the "economic horizon" h), by curbing emotional instincts EM_{i2} which lead to immoral acts, by influencing people to imitate good acts, but not bad ones ($IM_{ij} \uparrow$ if $\bar{v}_{i1} \uparrow$) and by building up a morale M_{i2} which "punishes" the offender by his own conscience and by social disdain.

1.8 Uncertainty on the Consequences of Decisions

Till now we assumed that the consequences of decisions are known to the decision maker and that he evaluates a decision by taking into account the consequences. But there are many cases where these consequences are not known because they depend on nature (e.g. weather conditions) or on the unknown acts of other people which in turn may depend on the own action, a game–theoretic situation which we consider in the next section. In this section we assume that the person knows the probability distribution of the outcomes of his action. The situation may be sketched as follows:

---

[30] Unfortunately one needs, in general, the complete personal distribution of G, H, EM, IM, and M in the population in order to derive the v_{ij}. Indices like mean and variance of the personal distribution of these values do not suffice to determine v_{ij}. I thank Professor Schürger for this hint.

[31] Of course $w_{ij,\xi} \geq 0$ and $\sum_{\xi=-\bar{z}}^{+\bar{z}} w_{ij,\xi} = 1$.

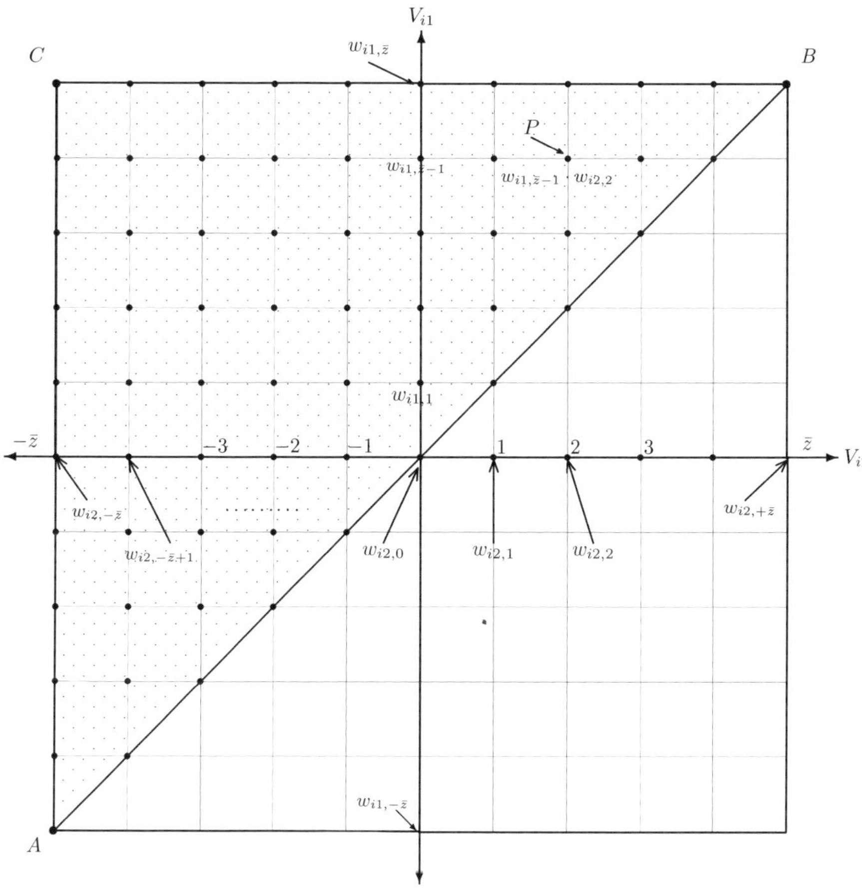

Figure 1.2. Probabilities of Choosing V_{i1} or V_{i2}

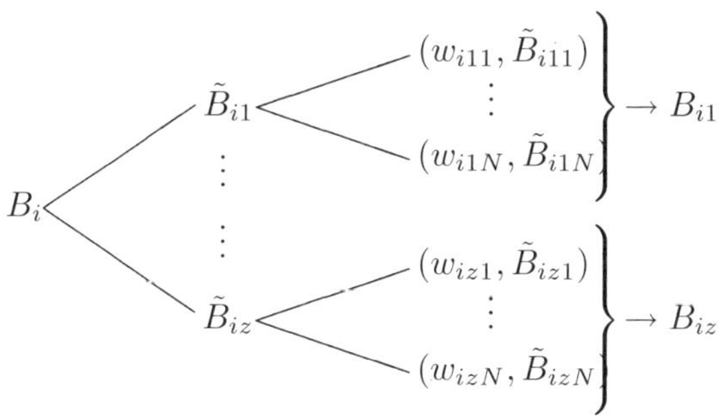

We assume that the person is in situation B_i and has the possibilities to move to $\tilde{B}_{i1}, \ldots, \tilde{B}_{iz}$, where these are probability distributions on the possible situations $\tilde{B}_{i\zeta 1}, \ldots, \tilde{B}_{i\zeta N}$, $\zeta = 1, \ldots, z$. As shown in equation 1.1 in section 1.3 the person p evaluates his situations in $\tilde{B}_{i\zeta\nu}$ by $V_{i\zeta\nu}^{(p)}$, $\zeta = 1, \ldots, z$, $\nu = 1, \ldots, N$. Now the person has to consider the probability distributions $V_{i\zeta}^{(p)} := ((w_{i\zeta 1}, V_{i\zeta 1}^{(p)}), \ldots, (w_{i\zeta N}, V_{i\zeta N}^{(p)})), \zeta = 1, \ldots, z$ and to evaluate them in order to find out which decision is the best for him. The probability distribution is equivalent to a lottery ticket with payoffs $V_{i\zeta 1}^{(p)}, \ldots, V_{i\zeta N}^{(p)}$ with probabilities $w_{i\zeta 1}, \ldots, w_{i\zeta N}$. We assume that the person is able to evaluate the lottery tickets $V_{i\zeta}^{(p)}$, $\zeta = 1, \ldots, z$, or in other words: to imagine a situation $B_{i\zeta}$ which he could reach with certainty and which is equivalent in his opinion to the actual situation $\tilde{B}_{i\zeta}$ he is confronted with[32]. We leave it to the person which rule he will apply to determine this certainty equivalent. There are several suggestions how this choice could (or should) be made, see the foregoing note. It seems that in most cases an evaluation rule which only considers the arithmetic mean (or mathematical expectation) and the variance would be a good approximation of the procedure. Let $V_{i\zeta\nu}^{(p)}$ be the evaluation of the state $\tilde{B}_{i\zeta\nu}$ by person p as stated in equation 1.1 in section 1.3, $i = 1, \ldots, h$, $\zeta = 1, \ldots, z$, $\nu = 1, \ldots, N$. Then

$$E(V_{i\zeta})^{(p)} = \sum_{\nu=1}^{n} w_{i\zeta\nu} V_{i\zeta\nu}$$

is the mathematical expectation and

$$VAR(V_{i\zeta})^{(p)} = \sum_{\nu=1}^{n} w_{i\zeta\nu} (V_{i\zeta\nu} - E(V_{i\zeta})^{(p)})^2$$

is the variance.

Then it seems reasonable to assume that a person in his evaluation of uncertain outcomes of his decision looks at the mean (or expectation) of the possible outcomes and corrects it according to his behavior against risk, i.e. we may assume that it evaluates the distribution $V_{i\zeta(p)}$ by

$$V_{i\zeta}^{*(p)} = E(V_{i\zeta})^{(p)} + d^{(p)} VAR(V_{i\zeta})^{(p)}$$

where $d^{(p)} < 0$ if it is risk averse

$d^{(p)} = 0$ if it is risk neutral

$d^{(p)} > 0$ if it loves risk

---

[32] Let $V_{i\zeta}^{*}$ be the evaluation of $B_{i\zeta}$ and $V_{i\zeta 1}, \ldots, V_{i\zeta N}$ the evaluation of $\tilde{B}_{i\zeta 1}, \ldots, \tilde{B}_{i\zeta N}$ and let all evaluations be given in monetary units. Then $V_{i\zeta}^{*}$ is the amount of money the person is willing to pay for a lottery ticket with the probability distribution $((w_{i\zeta 1}, V_{i\zeta 1}), \ldots, (w_{i\zeta N}, V_{i\zeta N}))$ of prizes. There is a whole literature on this subject, see e.g. Krelle (1968), pp. 171, Weber and Camerer (1987) and the literature quoted there. We do not go into details here.

The person chooses d freely. If after this choice $V_{i\zeta}^{*(p)}$ does not lie within the limits $-\bar{z},\ldots,+\bar{z}$ the valuation will automatically be reduced to the next limit. As already said, the person may choose another rule. In any case we are now back to the case of decision under certainty according to equation 1.1 in section 1.3.

1.9 Evaluations in Case of Interdependent Decisions

Now we consider the case that the consequences of a decision of a person depend on the decisions of other persons who in turn are influenced by the decision of the person considered. There are many possible interdependencies, according to different assumptions on the information, on the repetitions of the situation, on the intelligence of the decision makers etc. In this section we show that in almost all cases our formulation of the decision problem of a person covers also the situation of interdependence of the decisions of different persons. Our theory comprises all cases where the game-theoretic solution suggests an unequivocal strategy of a person, because all other strategies would yield a lower payoff. This applies for all solution concepts assumed by the players and all situations of information and possibilities of enforcement of contracts. All types of agreements stay behind the scene. They may influence the definition and the evaluation of the situation B_{ij} which may be reached after the decision but not the principle so that finally the person has to consider the available alternatives and to take a decision. The outcome may be a probability distribution, a case considered in the foregoing section 1.8, but the decision is unique and not a probability distribution. There are game-theoretic solutions of certain situations where the theory suggests that the person chooses a probability distribution of his strategies: his decision is subject to chance. This case is not covered by our theory. It is hardly possible to advise somebody to throw a dice to determine what to do in an essential situation (as opposed to a social game), with the exception of the case of indifference.

After all, everything which that exists is the result of decisions of persons and (or) the result of nature (which may be subject to chance, at least as we understand it now). This is what we want to model.

In the following we give some examples how game-theoretic solutions may be put into our framework. For simplicity we consider only the interdependence between the decisions of two persons and we assume that for each person only two alternatives are available.

Consider a person i who is in situation B_i and a person j in the situation B_j. Each person has two alternatives B_{i1}, B_{i2} or B_{j1}, B_{j2}, respectively. Let $V_{i,kl}$ be the evaluation of the situation $B_{i,kl}$ of person i, if it chooses B_{ik} and person j chooses B_{jl}, $k \in \{1,2\}$, $l \in \{1,2\}$, and similarly $V_{j,kl}$. Then the situation is represented by the double payout matrix person j: B_j

person i: B_i

	B_{j1}		B_{j2}	
B_{i1}	$V_{i,11}$	$V_{j,11}$	$V_{i,12}$	$V_{j,12}$
B_{i2}	$V_{i,21}$	$V_{j,21}$	$V_{i,22}$	$V_{j,22}$

Thus far the approach is quite general: it covers all possible cases of a two person–two strategy–game (to use the game theoretical vocabulary) as seen by a neutral observer with full information. But now the problems arise: the state of information of both players may be different, the game may be repeated several times (perhaps an infinite or undefined number of times), there might be cooperation between the players or not et cetera. Also the concept of the solution of this game may be debated. There exists a lot of literature on this subject. We deal here only with the case of non–cooperative repeated games with full information of both players[33] and we accept an equilibrium point as the solution of the game. We may interprete it as the strategy of each player whom we would observe in the long run in case of rational players[34] We consider the following four cases:

1. There exists a unique unterminated equilibrium point in pure strategies. This is the solution, and this determines the payoff of each player. The following example demonstrates this case:

	B_{j1}		B_{j2}	
B_{i1}	3	3	4	2
B_{i2}	2	4	2	2

[33] For a detailed analysis of two person games see, e.g. Krelle (1968).

[34] Of course, persons are not always rational, thus the actual behavior of persons may deviate from this "solution". We have to consider the *actual* behavior of people. In most cases this can be described by our approach, also in the case of interdependent decisions. We show this for the case of a 2-person, 2-strategy game, but it is also valid for an arbitrary number of persons and strategies.

The only equilibrium point is (B_{i1}, B_{j1}) which is in pure strategies. Player i (having the choice between B_{i1} and B_{i2}) will choose B_{i1} and player j B_{j1}.

2. It might happen that there are more than one equilibrium points in pure strategies and in addition an equilibrium point in mixed strategies. The following game is an example of it:[35]

B_i \ B_j		v_j: B_{j1}	$1 - v_j$: B_{j2}
w_i	B_{i1}	$-2 \quad -3$	$2 \quad 3$
$1 - w_i$	B_{i2}	$3 \quad 2$	$-2 \quad -4$

This game has the two equilibrium points $(B_{i2}, B_{j1}), (B_{i1}, B_{j2})$ in pure strategies and the equilibrium point $w_i = \frac{1}{2}$, $v_j = \frac{4}{9}$ in mixed strategies, where w_i is the probability with which player i plays B_{i1} (and $1 - w_i$ the probability with which he plays B_{i2}), and v_j, $1 - v_j$ the same for player j. The payout expectation for player i in the case that the mixed equilibrium point is chosen is $\frac{2}{9}$, that of player j is $-\frac{1}{2}$; that means that each equilibrium point in pure strategies dominates the equilibrium point in mixed strategy. Thus this point will not be chosen. Instead, one of the two equilibrium points in pure strategies will be chosen. But which one? There is a whole literature on this problem of equilibrium selection. We shall not go into it. There may be a "strong" and a "weak" player. The equilibrium point will be chosen which is most advantageous to the strong player (the game is known under the name: "battle of sexes").

3. The following game has one equilibrium point in pure strategies which is dominated by a non–equilibrium point in pure strategies (the game is known as "prisoners dilemma"):

[35] For these and the following games, see Krelle (1968), pp. 217.

	B_{j1}		B_{j2}	
B_{i1}	3	4	0	5
B_{i2}	4	2	2	3

The only equilibrium point is (B_{i2}, B_{j2}), but this point is clearly dominated by the point (B_{i1}, B_{j1}) which is not an equilibrium point. If we stick to the definition of the solution (that it must be an equilibrium point) the players are caught in the "prisoners dilemma", i.e. they must choose (B_{i2}, B_{j2}), because another choice of one person alone would only deteriorate his position. Persons who are caught in the prisoners dilemma are those who do not trust the other person and are not able to learn that there might be persons who can be trusted and who show that through their behavior. They always think: if I move to the dominant non–equilibrium point, the other will not do so whatever he says and promises before and thus will put me in a worse situation than the one in which I anticipate that he will do that. Thus in case that the persons mistrust each other the decision situation for the two players looks like this:

$$B_i \begin{cases} B_{i1} \to V_{i1} = 0 \\ B_{i2} \to V_{i2} = 2 \end{cases} \qquad B_j \begin{cases} B_{j1} \to V_{j1} = 2 \\ B_{j2} \to V_{j2} = 3 \end{cases}$$

It is clear that the point (B_{i2}, B_{j2}) will be realized which is the prisoners dilemma.

But there might be another extreme which also leads to a situation which conforms to our approach. Let person i and j be those who have known each other for a long time and trust each other unconditionally. They know: the other will never cheat his companion. To cheat the other person is evaluated by both as the largest evil, a shame which gets the highest possible negative weight, say $-\bar{z}$. In this case the payoff matrix changes to

	B_{j1}		B_{j2}	
B_{i1}	3	4	0	$-\bar{z}$
B_{i2}	$-\bar{z}$	2	$-\bar{z}$	$-\bar{z}$

The decision situation for the two players is now:

$$B_i \begin{cases} B_{i1} \rightarrow V_{i1} = 3 \\ B_{i2} \rightarrow V_{i2} = -\bar{z} \end{cases} \qquad B_j \begin{cases} B_{j1} \rightarrow V_{j1} = 4 \\ B_{j2} \rightarrow V_{j2} = -\bar{z} \end{cases}$$

Now the solution is the dominant point (B_{i1}, B_{j1}) which is the best which could be reached by the persons in this situation. That means: "confidence" (or "trust") comes in and makes it possible to come to a better solution than under mistrust. This idea has to be generalized to cover the cases between absolute mistrust and absolute trust. We assume that the two persons have the opportunity to talk to each other in the sense that each may promise to the other to use a certain strategy though it is not obliged to do so. The basic assumptions are the following. If person i promises to use a certain strategy B_{ik} ($k \in \{1, 2\}$ in our example) and does it afterwards it gets a moral gain $M_i(T) \geq 0$ independent of the outcome of the game. This moral gain covers the internal satisfaction of being a trustworthy person (T stands for trustworthiness) as well as the future advantages in dealing with that person again or with other persons or alternatives which originate from his reputation of being trustworthy. If it uses the other strategy B_{il}, $l \in \{1, 2\}$, $l \neq k$, it gets a moral loss $M_i(BT) \geq 0$ where BT stands for "break of trust". This figure $M_i(BT)$ comprises its own remorses as well as the loss of goodwill at future deals. For person j the same applies: his morality numbers are $M_j(T)$ and $M_j(BT)$. Thus if both players promise to use the strategy B_{i1} and B_{j1} respectively (which would lead to the dominant point) our original game of the type "prisoners dilemma" changes to

	B_{j1}		B_{j2}	
B_{i1}	$3 + M_i(T)$	$4 + M_j(T)$	$0 + M_i(T)$	$5 - M_j(BT)$
B_{i2}	$4 - M_i(BT)$	$2 + M_j(T)$	$2 - M_i(BT)$	$3 - M_j(BT)$

Person i would keep his promise if

$$3 + M_i(T) \geq 4 - M_i(BT).$$

Person j would keep his promise if

$$4 + M_j(T) \geq 5 - M_j(BT).$$

In general, person i and j would know only the own value figures $V_{i,kl}$ or $V_{j,kl}$, respectively, as well as the evaluations $M_i(T), M_i(BT)$ or $M_j(T), M_j(BT)$, respectively. But each person may have (subjective) probability distributions on the evaluation figures of the other person. In our case this amounts to the following:

- Person i knows the probability β_{j1} that $4 + M_j(T) \geq 5 - M_j(BT)$, i.e. that person j would use his strategy B_{j1}, $0 \leq \beta_{j1} \leq 1$, and thus use his strategy B_{j2} with probability $1 - \beta_{j1}$.
- Person j knows the probability β_{i1} that $3 + M_i(T) \geq 4 - M_i(BT)$, i.e. that person i would use his strategy B_{i1}, $0 \leq \beta_{i1} \leq 1$, and thus use his strategy B_{i2} with probability $1 - \beta_{i1}$.

Now if person i decides to move to B_{i1} he gets the expected value:

$$V_{i1}^{exp} := \beta_{j1}[3 + M_i(T)] + (1 - \beta_{j1})[0 + M_i(T)],$$

and if he decides to move to B_{i2} he gets:

$$V_{i2}^{exp} := \beta_{j1}[4 - M_i(BT)] + (1 - \beta_{j1})[2 - M_i(BT)].$$

Thus his decision situation is:

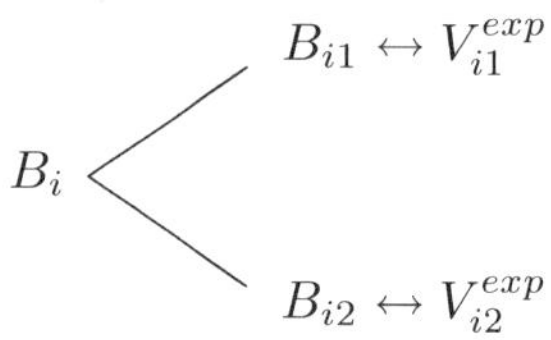

In a similar way we get for person j the decision situation

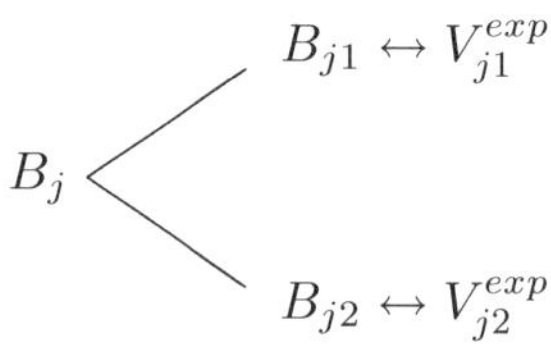

Thus under the assumption made above our theory may also be applied in cases of interdependent decisions, in this example: in prisoners dilemma–situations.[36]

[36] The $M_i(T)$ and $M_j(T)$ as well as the $M_i(BT)$ and $M_j(BT)$ are moral values which are explained by a Markov chain as all other moral evaluations, see equation (1.3) in section 1.4. The β_{i1} and β_{j1} are not constant but change according to the observations of the actual behavior of the other person. If B_{i1} is observed, β_{i1} goes up in the next period, if B_{i2} is observed, it goes down, always in the limits $0 \leq \beta_{i1} \leq 1$. The same

But there are cases where our theory cannot be applied (at least not as it is interpreted here). This comes true in the case where the situation modeled by a game matrix has only an equilibrium point in mixed strategies, but none in pure strategies. The following game matrix gives an example:

4.

B_i \ B_j	B_{j1} (v_j)	B_{j2} ($1 - v_j$)
B_{i1} (w_i)	$5 \quad -3$	$-4 \quad 4$
B_{i2} ($1 - w_i$)	$-5 \quad 5$	$3 \quad -4$

The only equilibrium point is $w_i = \frac{9}{16}$, $v_j = \frac{7}{17}$ which gives a payoff of $-\frac{5}{17}$ for player i and of $\frac{1}{2}$ for player j (w_i is the probability with which player i uses strategy B_{i1}, and v_j the probability with which player j uses B_{j1}). This case is not covered by our theory. It seems to be an exception.

1.10 The General Theory of Household Behavior

In the foregoing sections special cases and aspects of a theory of household behavior have been considered[37]. At the beginning of period 0 (or the end of

---

applies for β_{j1}: if B_{j1} is observed, it goes up, if B_{j2} is observed, it goes down. Thus we assume the existence of function F such that

$$\beta_{i1}(t) = F_i(\beta_{i1}(t-1), B_{ik}), \quad k \in \{1,2\}, \text{ and } 0 \leq \beta_{i1(t)} \leq 1$$

$$\text{and } \beta_{j1}(t) = F_j(\beta_{j1}(t-1), B_{jl}), \quad l \in \{1,2\}, \text{ and } 0 \leq \beta_{j1(t)} \leq 1$$

[37] This section extends and generalizes the approach of sections 1.1 to 1.9. In former sections we assumed that the actions themselves are always neutral and are not subject to evaluations, only the results of the actions count. We also specified the criteria $CR_{B1}, \ldots, CR_{BL}$ for judging the results of the decision as G,H,EM,IM,M and gave them the weights α. In this section the criteria $CR_{B1}, \ldots, CR_{BL}$ are not specified (with the exception of some examples), and their weights are $\beta_1, \ldots, \beta_L$. Moreover, the actions themselves (independent of the results) are subject to evaluation – a case we did not consider in sections 1.1 to 1.9.

period –1) there are h private households (or non producing decision units) in the society. A household may comprise several persons, but we treat it as one person. Each household i, $i = 1, \ldots, h$ is in a situation B_i which is special to this household: not two households are in the same situation, and all households are different. Thus there is a 1 to 1 relation between household i and situation B_i where the household is in. Of course, there are many "empty" situations, where no household is in.

A situation B_i is characterized by objective features B_i^{obj} and subjective features B_i^{sub}:

$$B_i = (B_i^{obj}, B_i^{sub})$$

B_i^{obj} is a vector of parameters which describe the objective situation of household i:

1. the location of the household, including its apartment and the environment
2. the political, economic, judicial and social order valid in that region
3. the composition of the household (adult persons, children of different ages etc.)
4. employment, income, wealth of the members of the household
5. knowledge and the capabilities of the members of the household
6. other objective features of the household

The household i has z possible actions (or decisions) $A_{i1}, A_{i2}, \ldots, A_{iz}$ at its disposal by which it reaches the situations $B_{i1}, B_{i2}, \ldots, B_{iz}$, respectively. These actions comprise

1. change of location of the household
2. actions to change the political, economic and social order
3. demand of consumption goods of different kinds
4. change of composition of the household, including the forming of new households and the end of the old household i[38]
5. change of employment, income and allocation of wealth
6. change of knowledge and capabilities (e.g. by attending schools)
7. other changes which are under the control of the household.

---

[38] Death and birth of households will be considered later in detail.

The subjective features B_i^{subj} of the household form the base for choosing a certain action which yields $B_{ij}, i = 1, \ldots, h, j = 1, \ldots, z$ by providing the evaluations of the alternatives. Thus B_i^{subj} is a vector of parameters which describe the subjective characteristics of household i. They consist of criteria $CR_{A1}, CR_{A2}, \ldots, CR_{AM}$ to evaluate the household decisions $A_{i1}, A_{i2}, \ldots, A_{iz}$ themselves. Furthermore, they consist of criteria $CR_{B1}, CR_{B2}, \ldots, CR_{BL}$ to evaluate the situations $B_{i1}, B_{i2}, \ldots, B_{iz}$ which will be reached by the decisions or in other words: which are the consequences of the decisions. We shall see later that the household needs also weights to combine these criteria, namely

1. $\alpha_1, \ldots, \alpha_M$ to determine the relative weights of the criteria CR_{A1}, $CR_{A2}, \ldots, CR_{AM}, \alpha_\mu \geq 0, \sum_{\mu=1}^{M} = 1$;
2. $\beta_1, \ldots, \beta_L$ to determine the relative influence of the criteria CR_{B1}, $CR_{B2}, \ldots, CR_{BL}, \beta_\lambda \geq 0, \sum_{\lambda=1}^{L} = 1$
3. γ, the relative weight of the judgement of the consequences of an action compared to the relative weight $(1 - \gamma)$ given to the action itself, $0 \leq \gamma \leq 1$. The judgement of the consequences is called "ethics of responsibility" (Verantwortungsethik in German), the judgement of the actions is called "ethics of persuasion" (Gesinnungsethik in German).

The situation may be illustrated as in Fig. 1.3. The basic assumption is that a household or person p is able to evaluate all actions A_{ij} as well as all the situations B_{ij} which follow from A_{ij} according to the criteria $CR_{A1}, CR_{A2}, \ldots$, CR_{AM} (as far as the actions $A_{i1}, A_{i2}, \ldots, A_{iz}$ are concerned) and according to the criteria $CR_{B1}, CR_{B2}, \ldots, CR_{BL}$ (as far as the consequences $B_{i1}, B_{i2}, \ldots$, B_{iz} are concerned[39]). "Evaluation" means grading the actions or situations on an integer scale which runs from $-\bar{z}$ to $+\bar{z}$, $\bar{z}$ an integer > 1, where $-\bar{z}$ is the largest possible dislike, $+\bar{z}$ the largest possible appreciation; zero means indifference or no judgement. All integers between $-\bar{z}$ and $+\bar{z}$ are admitted, but not uneven figures. Thus the evaluation can only be stated by one of the figures $-\bar{z}, -\bar{z}+1, \ldots, 0, 1, 2, \ldots, +\bar{z}, \bar{z} \geq 1$. The size of $\bar{z}$ indicates the fineness of the power of judgement of the person and will be different from person to person (it is chosen by the person and is part of his characteristics).

The person p evaluates the decisions (or actions) $A_{ij}, i = 1, \ldots, h$; $j = 1, \ldots, z$, according to criterion (or principle) $CR_{A\mu}, \mu = 1, \ldots, M$, by

$$V_{ij,\mu}^{(p)} = V^{(p)}(A_{ij} \mid CR_{A\mu})$$

---

[39] This does not imply that a person carries out all possible evaluations. This is impossible. But it implies that the person is able to form the evaluations of a small set of alternatives (which he considers as essential) in time. Another person would consider other alternatives. But seldom the number of 2 or 3 alternatives is exceeded. A certain period of time is needed to form the evaluations on which the final decision is based. We do not go into these details.

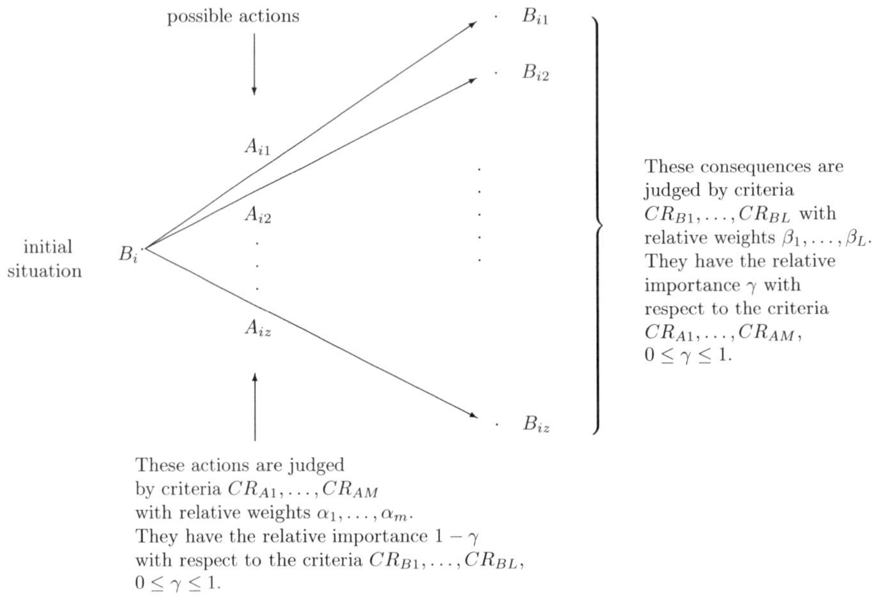

Figure 1.3. Evaluation of Actions and of the Consequences of Actions

where $-\bar{z} \leq +\bar{z}$. The person is free to choose $V_{ij,\mu}^{(p)}$. This evaluation is part of his character. The valuations will be different (in general) for different criteria $CR_{A\mu}$.

The person has to evaluate these criteria itself by allocating weights $\alpha_1^{(p)}, \ldots, \alpha_M^{(p)}$ to the criteria which state the importance which the person attributes to them, where $\alpha_\mu^{(p)} \geq 0, \sum_{\mu=1}^{M} \alpha_\mu^{(p)} = 1$. Now we postulate that the person p evaluates the action A_{ij} by

$$V_{ij}^{(p)} = n.i.(\sum_{\mu=1}^{M} \alpha_\mu^{(p)} \cdot V_{ij,\mu}^{(p)})$$

where n.i. = next integer, and $-\bar{z} \leq V_{ij}^{(p)} \leq +\bar{z}$. Similarly, the person evaluates the consequences $B_{i1}, \ldots, B_{iz}$ according to the criteria $CR_{B1}, \ldots, CR_{BL}$ by

$$W_{ij,\lambda}^{(p)} = W^{(p)}(B_{ij} \mid CR_{B\lambda})$$

where $-\bar{z} \leq W_{ij,\lambda}^{(p)} \leq +\bar{z}$.

The person gives weights $\beta_1^{(p)}, \ldots, \beta_L^{(p)}$ to these criteria, $\beta_\lambda^{(p)} \geq 0, \sum_{\lambda=1}^{L} \beta_\lambda^{(p)} = 1$. Now we postulate that person p evaluates the result B_{ij} of an action A_{ij} by:

$$W_{ij}^{(p)} = n.i.(\sum_{\lambda=1}^{L} \beta_\lambda^{(p)} \cdot W_{ij,\lambda}^{(p)})$$

where $-\bar{z} \leq W_{ij}^{(p)} \leq +\bar{z}$.

To come to a final decision the person has to make up his mind which weight to give to the evaluations of the consequences of his actions (call it γ, where $0 \leq \gamma \leq 1$) and which weight to give to the evaluation of the action itself (call it $1-\gamma$). Now the total evaluation of a decision $A_{ij}^{(p)}$ becomes

$$U_{ij}^{(p)} = n.i.(\gamma^{(p)} W_{ij}^{(p)} + (1-\gamma) V_{ij}^{(p)}),$$

and again $-\bar{z} \leq U_{ij}^{(p)} \leq +\bar{z}$.

Thus a person is characterized by the vector

$$(V_{ij,1}, \ldots, V_{ij,M}, \alpha_1, \ldots, \alpha_M, W_{ij,1}, \ldots, W_{ij,L}, \beta_1, \ldots, \beta_L, \gamma).$$

We shall illustrate this approach by two examples. Let B_i be the situation of a household with moderate income and small wealth. Let us assume that the household could choose between action

A_{i1} := to spend income and wealth for personal amusement, not caring for illness or old age

A_{i2} := saving for emergency and pension, spending for social purposes and reducing consumption expenditure accordingly

The results of these decisions would be:

B_{i1} := lots of fun at young age, destitution and misery at old age

B_{i2} := unpretentious, simple modest life without highlights, satisfaction by helping others who are in a worse situation, decent life at old age.

Let there be only two criteria for judging the actions:

CR_{A1} := propagation of joy of living

CR_{A2} := to perform a good action in the sense of the catholic ethics.

Let there also be only two criteria to judge the consequences B_{i1} and B_{i2}:

CR_{B1} := to become known in the public, to appear in the boulevard press

CR_{B2} := to get the inner satisfaction to have helped others and to conform to an inherited moral code

Now assume that person 1 and 2 are in the same situation but would evaluate the actions A_{i1}, A_{i2} with respect to the criteria CR_{A1}, CR_{A2} differently and the same for the results B_{i1}, B_{i2} with respect to the criteria CR_{B1}, CR_{B2}. Similarly, the criteria themselves would be evaluated differently: the α_1, α_2, β_1, β_2 would be different for person 1 and 2. Assume that the following table would represent the evaluations of the two possible actions according to the two criteria defined above:

Table 1.2. Evaluations. First example

Evaluation of actions according to criteria 1 and 2	$V_{i1,1}$	$V_{i1,2}$	$V_{i2,1}$	$V_{i2,2}$	α_1	α_2
by person 1	2	–1	–1	–1	.9	.1
by person 2	0	–2	1	2	.1	.9

Evaluation of the consequences of the actions according to criteria 1 and 2	$W_{i1,1}$	$W_{i1,2}$	$W_{i2,1}$	$W_{i2,2}$	β_1	β_2
by person 1	–1	–1	1	–1	0	1
by person 2	–2	2	2	1	.9	.1

With the above formulas we get for the evaluation of the actions A_{i1} and A_{i2} and the consequences B_{i1} and B_{i2}:

$$\text{by person 1: } V_{i1}^{(1)} = 1,\ V_{i2}^{(1)} = -1,\ W_{i1}^{(1)} = -1,\ W_{i2}^{(1)} = -1$$

$$\text{by person 2: } V_{i1}^{(2)} = -2,\ V_{i2}^{(2)} = 2,\ W_{i1}^{(2)} = -2,\ W_{i2}^{(2)} = 2$$

Let us put $\gamma = 1/2$ for both persons (each person gives equal weights for the judgement of the action and for its consequences). Now we could state the total evaluation of the moves to B_{i1} and B_{i2} by person 1 and 2. We get

$$\text{for person 1: } U_{i1}^{(1)} = 1,\ U_{i2}^{(1)} = -1;\ \text{thus person 1 chooses } A_{i1}$$

$$\text{for person 2: } U_{i1}^{(2)} = -2,\ U_{i2}^{(2)} = 2;\ \text{thus person 2 chooses } A_{i2}$$

Person 1 prefers the life as a playboy, person 2 the life of a modest, law abiding, inconspicuous, honest citizen. The evaluations of the Table 1.2 define the characteristics of person 1 and 2 as far as the decision situation at point B_i is concerned.

The V,W,α, β of all persons are simultaneously determined by a Markov-Chain, similarly as the $M_{ij,t}^{(1)}, \ldots, M_{ij,t}^{(N)}$ are determined in equation (1.3) in section 1.4.

The second example reproduces the German situation in 1944. At this date the defeat of Germany in the Second World War could be foreseen by the generals in the German headquarter. They had two options: to let things go as they are, i.e. not to try to kill Hitler (action A_1). The consequence B_{i1} would be that the war will be continued up to the complete destruction of Germany. Many persons on both sides would lose their lives. The other option (A_2) was to kill Hitler and to end the war immediately. The consequence

B_{i2} would be the complete occupation of Germany, but very many lives and cultural treasures could have been saved. For these actions two criteria could be assumed to be valid:

CR_{A1}: the commandment of the Bible: Thou shalt not kill[40].

CR_{A2}: the ethical command for a soldier: he has to obey orders (if they are not criminal), even if this costs his life, and not interfere with politics.

For the evaluation of the consequences only one criterion could have been applied at that time:

CR_B: to save as many lives and cultural treasures as possible.

Let there be two persons (2 generals in the headquarter) who have the same evaluations of the situation with respect to all criteria, as reproduced in Table 1.3.

Table 1.3 Evaluation of actions according to criteria 1 and 2 and evaluation of the consequences according to one criterion. Second example

$V_{i1,1}$	$V_{i1,2}$	$V_{i2,1}$	$V_{i2,2}$	α_1	α_2	W_{i1}	W_{i2}	β
2	2	-2	-2	.5	.5	-2	0	does not exist

This means: these generals accept the commandment not to kill fullheartedly and the soldier's ethics to follow orders as well. Thus they evaluate not to kill Hitler very positive from the point of view of both criteria ($V_{i1,1} = V_{i1,2} = 2$), but the action A_{i2} to kill Hitler very negative $V_{i2,1} = V_{i2,2} = -2$ from the point of view of both criteria. Both criteria are considered by them as having the same weight in their judgement ($\alpha_1 = \alpha_2 = .5$). As to the evaluation of the outcome of the actions the consequence of A_1 (not to kill Hitler) would be disastrous ($W_{i1} = -2$). The outcome of decision A_2 would be preferable, but still not good. Let us assume an evaluation of $W_{i2} = 0$. This explains Table 1.3.

According to our theory the total evaluation of action A_1 (not to kill Hitler) would be

$$V_{i1} = n.i.\ (\alpha_1 V_{i1,1} + \alpha_2 V_{i1,2}) = 2,$$

the total evaluation of action A_2 (to kill Hitler)

$$V_{i2} = n.i.\ (\alpha_1 V_{i2,1} + \alpha_2 V_{i2,2}) = -2.$$

---

[40] In the interpretation: it is not allowed to commit murders.

Now the evaluation of the outcome of both actions has to be added. The evaluations of the results of action A_1 and A_2 are

$$W_{i1} = n.i.\, W_{i1} = -2 \qquad W_{i2} = n.i.\, W_{i2} = 0$$

Let us assume that the two persons with identical evaluations of the situation nevertheless differ in their ethical conviction: person 1 only considers and evaluates the actions ($\gamma^{(i)} = 0$ in our theory). It thinks that one has to act rightly; God procures the consequences and carries the responsibility for them. Person 2 only considers the consequences ($\gamma^{(2)} = 1$). God gave the intellect to men not to disregard it but to use it. Every person is responsible for the consequences of his acts, as far as it could foresee them. The acts themselves do not count, the results are of importance. These are the intuitive justification for the different decisions on γ.

In general the total evaluation U_{i1} of a move from B_i to B_{i1} by the decision A_{i1} is:

$$U_{i1} = n.i.\, (\gamma W_{i1} + (1-\gamma)V_{i1}) = n.i.\, (\gamma(-2) + (1-\gamma)2) = n.i.\, (2-4\gamma).$$

The total evaluation U_{i2} of a move from B_i to B_{i2} is:

$$U_{i2} = n.i.\, (\gamma W_{i2} + (1-\gamma)V_{i2}) = n.i.\, (\gamma \cdot 0 + (1-\gamma)(-2) = n.i.\, (2\gamma - 2).$$

Thus person 1 (with $\gamma = \gamma^{(1)} = 0$) evaluates $U_{i1}^{(1)} = 2,\ U_{i2}^{(1)} = -2$ and will never kill Hitler.

Person 2 (with $\gamma = \gamma^{(2)} = 1$) evaluates $U_{i1}^{(2)} = -2,\ U_{i2}^{(2)} = 0$ and would try to kill Hitler.

If a person gives equal weights to the ethics of responsibility (Verantwortungsethik) and the ethics of persuasion (Gesinnungsethik), i.e. if $\gamma = 1/2$, one would get

$$U_{i1} = 0, \quad U_{i2} = -1,$$

that means: also in this case the decision would be not to kill Hitler. Only for $\gamma = 2/3$ (i.e.:substantial more weight to the consequences of the decision) the person would be indifferent between the two actions. I personally hold the view of the ethics of responsibility: we got intelligence to use it and not to disregard it in case of a conflict.

1.11 Some Further Remarks on Household Theory

In this section we gather all remarks and notes which would have interrupted the line of thought in the last sections.

a. One may ask where technical progress and the change of number and composition of households is considered. The "normal" change of products (e.g. the model of the year 2000 compared to the model of the year 1999) is taken care of by the time index: $x_{i,2000}$ versus $x_{i,1999}$. There is always a "small" technical progress involved which does not change the product substantially, as a rule. Absolutely new products (as the railway, the steam boat, the airplane, the telephone, the radio and so on at the time of their introduction into service) get a new current number in the list of products and firms which they produce. But the product must be ready and on the market, that means: these products are part of the situation $B_{i1}, \ldots, B_{iz}$ of the household i. The theory of technical progress is offered in the sectors of the firm. Thus there is no uncertainty on the side of the firms with respect to the products available for demand.

b. The same applies for labor. A person is described by his characteristics $\kappa_1^{(p)}, \ldots, \kappa_z^{(p)}$,[41] some of them (call them $\kappa_1^{(p)}, \ldots, \kappa_n^{(p)}$) indicate the amount of knowledge and abilities of the person in different fields in period t, also called: human capital. Let $\bar{\kappa}_w$ be the maximum amount of knowledge or ability in field w available in the society at period t.

   At the beginning of period 0 there are n different capabilities of economic importance which a person may have, or: n different types of labor which a person may offer. Each type of labor may be available "at the best level", to which we give the number 1, and to a less perfect degree, between zero (no ability) and 1. A person may be very skillful in one activity, but less skillful in another. There is an upper limit for the ability of a person for each type of labor. An unmusical person will never become a great musician, it may get as much lessons as possible. There are natural endowments $end_\nu^{(p)}$ for each person p for each type of labor $\nu = 1, \ldots, n$; the actual capabilities $cap_\nu^{(p)}$ of the person stay behind the limits:

$$end_\nu^{(p)} \geq cap_\nu^{(\nu)}, \quad \nu = 1, \ldots, n,$$

   see Fig. 1.4. A person acquires capabilities by schooling, education and training, but his maximum performance is fixed by his endowments. Moreover, the finite life time and the (at least gradually) with age declining capability of learning limit the exploitation of all gifts of a person. Thus we have a situation as in Fig. 1.4. The person in Fig. 1.4 stays behind his maximum capabilities in all fields. By some misfortune or error of his education he did not develop in the field where he could be most effective (labor of type 4) but got education and training mostly for

---

[41] Some of these characteristics have already been specified before: the evaluations G,H,EM,IM,M, the evaluations $V(p)(A_{ij}|CR_{A\mu})$ of action A_{ij} under the criterion or point of view μ, the evaluations $V^{(p)}(B_{ij}|CR_{B\lambda})$ of the final state B_{ij} under the criterion $CR_{B\lambda}$. Other specifications will follow.

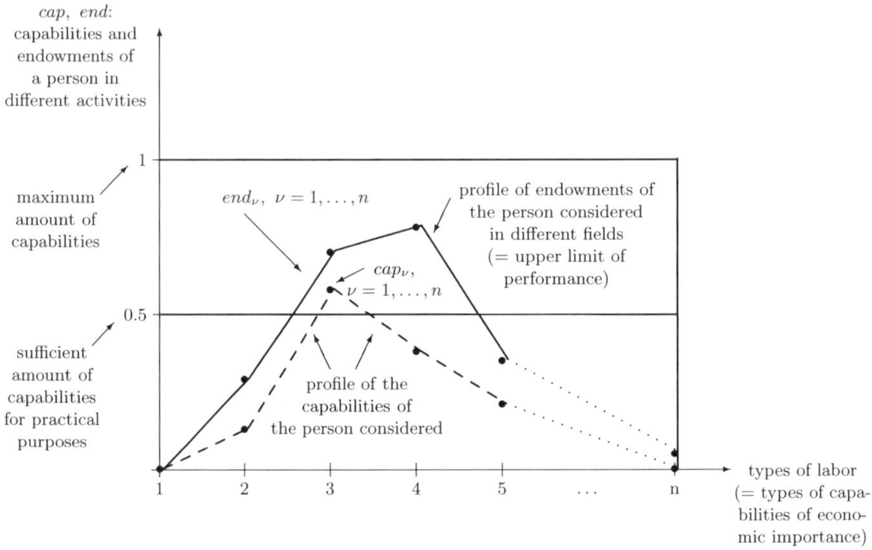

Figure 1.4. Endowments and Capabilities of a Person

labor of type 3, and he just succeeded in reaching a sufficient performance in this field (if we assume that a firm accepts labor of a special kind only if the actual performance of the person in this type of employment equals or exceeds $\frac{1}{2}$ of the maximum capability, see Fig. 1.4). Of course, any other profile of capabilities which does not exceed the profile of endowments is possible, but as already said, lack of time is the reason that the development of capabilities in one field goes to the expense of the development in other fields.

In our approach, the profile of endowments $end_\nu^{(p)}$ and capabilities $cap_\nu^{(p)}$, $\nu = 1, \ldots, n$ of a person is given at the initial situation B_i, $i \in \{1, \ldots, h\}$, where the person finds himself at the beginning of period 0, and it stays to same for the whole period. We deal with the problem of education and learning later on as well as with the extension of "types of labor" by opening up new fields of knowledge in the way of technical progress.

c. The income Y of a household comes from labor and capital. Here we are concerned with labor income Y_L which is the product of the wage rate l_ν of the kind of labor ν and the amount L_ν of employment. We assume that the wage rate is determined essentially by the trade union for the next period and employment by the entrepreneurs, also in advance for the next period.[42] Thus the household is in the beginning of period 0 informed on its labor income during that period.

---

[42] In former times this was the normal procedure in agriculture in Germany: the contracts for "Knechte und Mägde" run from Michaelis to Michaelis (Michaelis = Michaelmas).

d. Similarly, the household is (in principle) informed on the prices of all commodities (since the entrepreneurs fix them for the next period) and on the interest rates (which are fixed by the banks). But it is not informed on the value of its assets which results from the conditional demand and supply of all economic agents. A single household has (in general) a non measurable influence on the value of its assets. The household has to decide on its behavior in the next period in ignorance of the future value of its assets.

e. The government may change the laws. This is supposed to take place at the end of the former period such that the household knows the new laws valid for the next period. Thus new probabilities $w_{ij,\mu}(t+1)$ of punishment for an action A_{ij} which is now illegal will be effective in the next period. This is known to the household before it takes its decision.

f. Almost all acts of a person have some economic consequences i.e. they influence his future economic position which in the simplest case is described by income, wealth of different kinds and debts. We describe the economic situation of household i at the beginning of period 0 by EC_i and by EC_{ij} in period 0, after the decision A_{ij} has been taken. Let $G_{ij}^{(p)}$, $i = 1, \ldots, h$, $j = 1, \ldots, z$, $p = 1, \ldots, N$, be the evaluation of the economic situation EC_{ij} in the state B_{ij} by person p who is in the situation B_i. Only integer numbers are admitted for $G_{ij}^{(p)}$, which lie between $-\bar{z}$ and $+\bar{z}$, $\bar{z}$ an integer ≥ 1. Similarly as moral values are transferred from person to person, also judgements on economic states are interrelated, and they are influenced by inherited, "natural" drives: more is better than less (up to a certain amount); first look after your own economic welfare, but do not forget those in need; consider also the interest of the next generation, and other "natural principles" like that. They are not invented by men and written in books but seem to be written in the genes to a larger or smaller degree. Let us call them $\bar{G}_{ij}^{(1)}, \ldots, \bar{G}_{ij}^{(K)}$. In this case we may formulate the interrelationships between the evaluations of economic states by all persons in the society as a Markov chain:

$$(G_{ij,t}^{(1)}, \ldots, G_{ij,t}^{(N)}, \bar{G}_{ij}^{(1)}, \ldots, \bar{G}_{ij}^{(K)}) = (G_{ij,t-1}^{(1)}, \ldots, G_{ij,t-1}^{(N)}, \bar{G}_{ij}^{(1)}, \ldots, \bar{G}_{ij}^{(K)}) \cdot P_{ij} \quad (1.9)$$

or: $\tilde{G}_{ij,t} = \tilde{G}_{ij,t-1} \cdot P_{ij}$

Now the normal time of employment is different in different employments (from 3 years for an assistant at the university level to one month for unskilled labor). For simplicity we put it to one period for all kinds of labor.

where P_{ij} is the transition matrix, see equation (1.3) in section 1.4. The solution of this system of difference equations may also be found there[43] . The dynamics on the path to the convergence of the distribution of valuations of economic situations may be reproduced by the Markov chain. But after the convergence is accomplished (at least approximately), the story is not finished.

In addition to the interdependence of evaluations the phenomenon of habituation has to be taken into account. If a person stays long enough in the same economic situation (also with respect to the economic situation of others) it takes the situation as "normal", as "nothing special", as some type of "natural environment"; it does not cause a positive or negative emotion. The person is indifferent with respect to this economic situation.[44] We model that as follows.

Habituation starts if the same situation has prevailed for a certain number of decision "rounds", say: if n.i. $G^{(p)}_{ij,t-2}$ = n.i. $G^{(p)}_{ij,t-3}$ = n.i. $G^{(p)}_{ij,t-4}$, in case that after 3 "rounds" of equal integer valuations of the same situation G_{ij} habituation starts.[45] Habituation means that all future evaluations $G_{ij,t-1}, G_{ij,t}, \ldots$ of the economic situation G_{ij} are $G_{ij} = 0$. After a while the millionaire is used to his situation and rates it as more or less "normal"; similarly, a person at the lower side of economic fortune gets used to it as well and compares himself mostly to persons of the same or of a poorer economic fate. We may model this as follows for the case that after 3 rounds of equal economic outcome habituation

---

[43] In this approach the evaluation vector

$$U_i^{(p)} = (G_{i1}^{(p)}, \ldots, G_{iz}^{(p)})$$

takes the place of the utility function

$$\tilde{U}_i^{(p)} = F_i^{(p)}(Y^{real}, L_1, \ldots, L_n, c_1^{real}, \ldots, c_M^{real}, S_1, \ldots, S_z) =: F_i^{(p)}(EC^{(p)})$$

to be maximized under the budget constraint, where Y^{real} is the real income, $L_1, \ldots, L_n$ types of labor offered, $c_1^{real}, \ldots, c_M^{real}$ real consumption, $S_1, \ldots, S_z$ the different possible types of saving. Thus our approach assumes much less information on the part of the person and on the other hand considers not only the economic side of a decision but also other sides.

[44] This attitude has a long tradition and is of great personal and social importance. Horaz writes in his ode to Leuconoë: "Ut melius, quidquid erit, pati" (whatever happens, take it as if it would be better). In the Bible similar statements are found: To accept a bad fate which one cannot change as "normal" for the person is a precondition for leading a fruitful life in the limits of the fate. And on the other side it is a sort of "compensatory justice": those who are privileged by nature or by fate will be "downgraded" by habituation. A millionaire draws not necessarily more satisfaction out of his position than a person with moderate income.

[45] Recall that all numbers have to be "rounded" to the nearest integer value (n.i.). Thus convergence "in integers" occurs at a finite t, not asymptotically for $t \to \infty$. The rounding of the results of the Markov chain to integers yields an early convergence.

starts. Here we leave the process of habituation behind the scene[46] and assume (for simplicity) that this process is finished in one period and that the degree of habituation is a personal characteristic of the person and given. That means for person p:

$$\text{if n.i. } (G^{(p)}_{ij,t-4}) = \text{n.i. } (G^{(p)}_{ij,t-3}) = \text{n.i. } (G^{(p)}_{ij,t-2}) = \text{n.i. } (G^{(p)}_{ij,t-1})$$

and the same does not apply for other persons than p, then the initial condition $\tilde{G}_{ij,t-1}$ in equation (1.9) is substituted by

$$\begin{aligned}\tilde{\tilde{G}}_{ij,t-1} =&(G^{(1)}_{ij,t-1}, \ldots, G^{(p-1)}_{ij,t-1}, \hat{G}^{(p)}_{ij,t-1}, G^{(p+1)}_{ij}, \ldots, G^{(N)}_{ij},\\ &\bar{G}^{(1)}_{ij}), \ldots, \bar{G}^{(K)}_{ij})\end{aligned} \tag{1.10}$$

where $\hat{G}^{(p)}_{ij,t-1}$ is the valuation of $G_{ij,t-1}$ by person p after the process of habituation is finished. If $G^{(p)}_{ij,t-1} < 0$ (the person does not like the economic situation EC_{ij}) habituation leads to a more favorable situation, which we call $\hat{G}^{(p)}_{ij,t-1}$ where

$$G^{(p)}_{ij,t-1} \leq \hat{G}^{(p)}_{ij,t-1} \leq 0, \quad \hat{G}^{(p)}_{ij} \text{ an integer}$$

If $G^{(p)}_{ij,t-1} > 0$ habituation leads to a less favorable evaluation:

$$0 \leq \hat{G}^{(p)}_{ij,t-1} \leq G^{(p)}_{ij,t-1}, \quad \hat{G}^{(p)}_{ij,t-1} \text{ an integer}$$

The vector $\tilde{\tilde{G}}_{ij,t-1}$ in equation (1.10) is formulated under the assumption that the process of habituation in period $t-1$ is only finished for person p; if this is also true for other persons the vector $\tilde{\tilde{G}}_{ij,t-1}$ has to be adapted similarly.

This surely is a simplified approach to intertwine the two effects on the evaluation of economic phenomena: the social effect of interdependence of valuations and individual effect of habituation. But it may suffice as first approximation.

g. A certain action (a move from B_i to B_{ij}) may be illegal. There are punishments $0, 1, \ldots, m$ in the society (where 0 means no punishment and m the highest punishment). The person p evaluates the punishments by $S^{(p)}_0, S^{(p)}_1, \ldots, S^{(p)}_m$, $-\bar{z} \leq S^{(p)}_\mu \leq 0$. The probabilities to get punished after the move from B_i to B_{ij} are $(w_{ij,0}, w_{ij,1}, \ldots, w_{ij,m})$, $w_{ij,\mu} \geq 0$, $\sum_{\mu=0}^{m} w_{ij,\mu} = 1$. The person is supposed to be able to evaluate the probability distribution $W(S)^{(p)}_{ij}$ of disutilities by figures $H^{(p)}_{ij}$, where

[46] There is a literature on this process, see e.g. Banerjee (1992).

$-\bar{z} \leq H_{ij}^{(p)} \leq 0$. How the person does it, is a problem which he has to solve for himself. One possibility to accomplish this is to evaluate the punishment distribution by its arithmetic mean and the variance, where the variance is weighted by a figure $d^{(p)}$ which is the measure of risk behavior of the person. This parameter $d^{(p)}$ is a characteristic for person p and will be used whenever the consequences of a decision are only known in the form of a probability distribution. For details, see section 1.8.

h. Each situation B_i and each consequence $B_{i1}, \ldots, B_{iz}$ of the decision of a person might be connected with emotional feelings of the person. To buy drugs has the highest value for a drug addict, a kleptomaniac must steal, to see a naked person of the other sex may induce sexual feelings etc. If there are h possible situations $B_1, \ldots, B_h$, there are h emotions $EM_1^{(p)}, \ldots, EM_h^{(p)}$ connected with them for person p, where $-\bar{z} \leq EM_k^{(p)} \leq +\bar{z}$, $k = 1, \ldots, h$, where $-\bar{z}$ signifies the large possible aversion and $+\bar{z}$ the highest possible attraction. We treat these emotions as innate, different in size from person to person, but with some general tendencies. We do not elaborate this.

i. Imitation is the simplest type of learning, already existing at the higher animals, and surely of great importance. IM_{ij} is the drive to imitate with respect to the move of person p from B_i to B_{ij} (if positive – and we formulate the theory for this case), where $0 \leq IM_{ij} \leq \bar{z}$. The person will imitate what the majority of other people did in the same or in a similar initial situation. Also "similar decisions" will be taken as inducement to imitations. To formulate this correctly we have to define which situations B_j are "similar" to the initial situation B_i that the person is in.[47] There are measures of distance in mathematics, but we will leave it to the person which situations (known to him) he will consider as "similar". We specify this general idea in the following way.

   Let $\{\hat{B}_i\}$ be the set of initial situations which (as judged by the person p) are "similar" to the initial situation B_i where the person is in. They are "in the neighborhood" of B_i. After appropriate renumbering of these initial situations we could define

$$\{\hat{B}_i\} = \{B_{i-\Delta}, B_{i-\Delta+1}, \ldots, B_{i-1}, B_{i+1}, \ldots, B_{i+\Delta}\}, \quad \Delta > 0, \text{ integer}$$

   We assume that each initial situation in the set $\hat{B}_1$ has the same number z of decision possibilities $B_{i1}, \ldots, B_{iz}$ and has been occupied in the last

[47] In section 1.14 we shall present a variant of this theory where the "similarity" of households is defined by the similarity of consumption behavior and where also "snobbism" is considered – an attitude to do the opposite of that what other people do. It is up to empirical research to determine which variant fits better to the observations.

T periods by one person (or household). That implies that the person in situation B_i has $\bar{N}_i = T \cdot 2\Delta$ observations of decisions of other persons in similar situations. Let $\bar{N}_{ij}$ be the number of decisions for the alternative B_{ij}. Now it is natural to define a relative drive $I\tilde{M}_{ij}$ to imitate by the relative number of persons who took this decision, being in a similar initial situation:

$$I\tilde{M}_{ij} = \frac{\bar{N}_{ij}}{\bar{N}_i},$$

where $0 \leq I\tilde{M}_{ij} \leq 1$, $i = 1, \ldots, h$, $j = 1, \ldots, z$. We normalized all "drives" to lie between $-\bar{z}$ and $+\bar{z}$, $\bar{z} \geq 1$, integer; in case of the drive to imitate we may disregard negative "drives"[48] , so that we may normalize the relative drive to a "normal" one:

$$I\hat{M}_{ij} = \bar{z} \cdot I\tilde{M}_{ij}$$

The capability and (or) the willingness to imitate may differ from person to person. Let λ be an index of this capability and (or) willingness, where $0 \leq \lambda \leq 1$. Then finally the drive to imitate for a person p may be written as

$$IM_{ij}^{(p)} = \lambda^{(p)} I\hat{M}_{ij}^{(p)}$$

(if we reintroduce the upper index p which has been suppressed at the earlier equations).[49] Table 1.4 illustrates these definitions.

Let $\hat{D}$ be an index of deviation of the behavior of other persons in a similar situation from the "original" behavior of person h. Then the force of imitation IM is a function $f_1(\hat{D})$, $f' > 0$ for a conformist and $f' < 0$ for a snob, see Fig. 1.5 for the case of consumption behavior.

k. Moral convictions influence the decision to move from B_i to B_{ij}. This is already explained in section 1.4 (the M_{ij} are explained by a Markov chain) and need not be repeated here.

l. The weights $\alpha_{ij,1}^{(p)}, \ldots, \alpha_{ij,5}^{(p)}$ which a person p attributes to the five different criteria of evaluating a move from B_i to B_{ij} (if we accept the approach of section 1.2) are not constant. They are subject to moral judgements quite analogous to the moral judgements on the moves themselves which we analyzed in section 1.4. There are only finitely many

---

48 Surely there are persons who just want to show off by doing the opposite of what the majority of other people do. For these people we get $I\tilde{M}_{ij} = -\frac{\bar{N}_{ij}}{\bar{N}_i}$

49 There is a literature on the problem of imitation, see e.g. Bikhchandani, Hirshleifer, Welch (1992), and Ellison, Fudenberg (1997).

Table 1.4. Illustration to the Definitions Related to "Imitation"

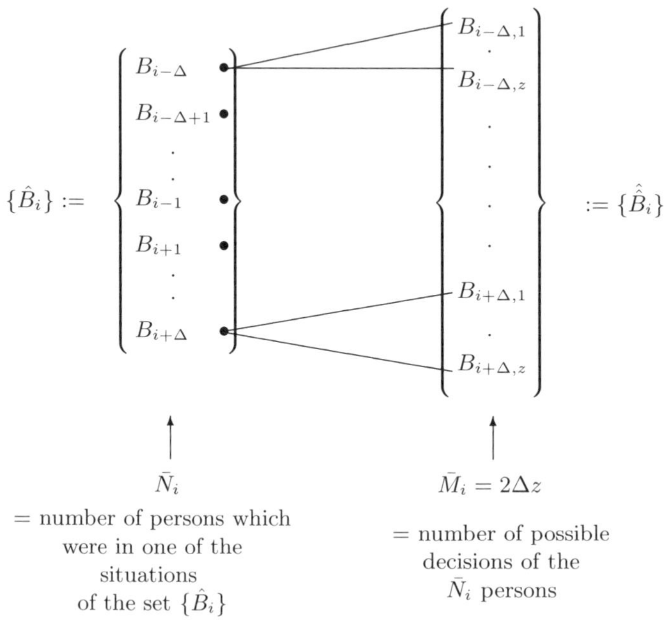

Set of decisions "similar" to B_{i1}: $\{\hat{B}_{i1}\} \subset \{\hat{\hat{B}}_i\}$

$\vdots$

Set of decisions "similar" to B_{iz}: $\{\hat{B}_{iz}\} \subset \{\hat{\hat{B}}_i\}$

$\bar{N}_{i1}$ = number of persons (contained in $\bar{N}_i$) which took a decision contained in $\{\hat{B}_{i1}\}$

$\vdots$

$\bar{N}_{iz}$ = number of persons (contained in $\bar{N}_i$) which took a decision contained in $\{\hat{B}_{iz}\}$

Relative drive to imitate: $I\tilde{M}_{ij} = \frac{\bar{N}_{ij}}{\bar{N}_i}$,

$0 \leq I\tilde{M}_{ij} \leq 1, \quad i = 1, \ldots, h, \quad j = 1, \ldots, z, \quad \sum_{j=1}^{z} I\tilde{M}_{ij} \geq 1$

$I\hat{M}_{ij} = I\tilde{M}_{ij} \cdot \bar{z} =$ absolute drive to imitate

$IM_{ij} = \lambda \cdot I\hat{M}_{ij}, \quad 0 \leq \lambda \leq 1,$

$\lambda =$ index of capability and willingness to imitate. All relations refer to a person p.

(say: H) different distributions $(\alpha_1, \ldots, \alpha_H)$ which we need to consider, where

$$\alpha_h = (\alpha_{h1}, \ldots, \alpha_{h5}), \quad h = 1, \ldots, H,$$

$$\text{and } 0 \leq \alpha_{h\nu} \leq 1, \quad \nu = 1, \ldots, 5, \quad \sum_{\nu=1}^{5} \alpha_{h\nu} = 1.$$

The set of these "feasible" weight distributions is the same for all persons. The person p evaluates these probability distributions by a figure $W_h^{(p)}$ where $-\bar{z} \leq W_h^{(p)} \leq +\bar{z}$. E.g., to ignore moral completely ($\alpha_{h5} = 0$) is a special case to which many persons would attribute a negative evaluation. Be that as it may, the evaluation of the distribution α_h by persons 1 to N in the society in period t is given by the vector $(W_{h,t}^{(1)}, \ldots, W_{h,t}^{(N)})$. But philosophies and theologies are not silent on the judgement of these distributions. If there are $\mathcal{K}$ philosophies and theologies we may reproduce their judgements by the vector $(\bar{W}_h^{(1)}, \ldots, \bar{W}_h^{(\mathcal{K})})$ which is constant in the period considered. Now the evaluation of the distribution of the α's by a person depends on his own and other people's evaluation a period before and on the evaluation by philosophies and theologies. We may assume that these influences can also be described by a Markov process:

$$\tilde{W}_{h,t} = \tilde{W}_{h,t-1} \cdot P_h$$

where

$$\tilde{W}_{h,t} = (W_{h,t}^{(1)}, \ldots, W_{h,t}^{(N)}, \bar{W}_h^{(1)}, \ldots, \bar{W}_h^{(\mathcal{K})})$$

and

$$(*) \qquad P_h = \left(\begin{array}{ccc|ccc}
P_{h,1}^{(1)} & \ldots & P_{h,N}^{(1)} & 0 & \ldots & 0 \\
\vdots & & \vdots & \vdots & & \vdots \\
P_{h,1}^{(N)} & \ldots & P_{h,N}^{(N)} & 0 & \ldots & 0 \\
\hline
\bar{P}_{h,1}^{(1)} & \ldots & \bar{P}_{h,N}^{(1)} & 1 & & 0 \\
\vdots & & \vdots & & \ddots & \\
\bar{P}_{h,1}^{(\mathcal{K})} & \ldots & \bar{P}_{h,N}^{(\mathcal{K})} & 0 & & 1
\end{array}\right),$$

$h = 1, \ldots, H$. The system is equivalent to system (1.3) in section 1.4. All constraints as well as the solution may be taken over from this section by putting $h = ij$, $W_h^{(\nu)} = M_{ij}^{(\nu)}$, $\nu = 1, \ldots, N$, $\bar{W}_h^{\kappa} = \bar{M}_{ij}^{(\kappa)}$, $\kappa = 1, \ldots, \mathcal{K}$.

m. A person is also characterized by personal traits which indicate (among others) his social behavior like reliability, ability to cooperate with others, leadership etc. Let there be r "traits of personality" of this kind

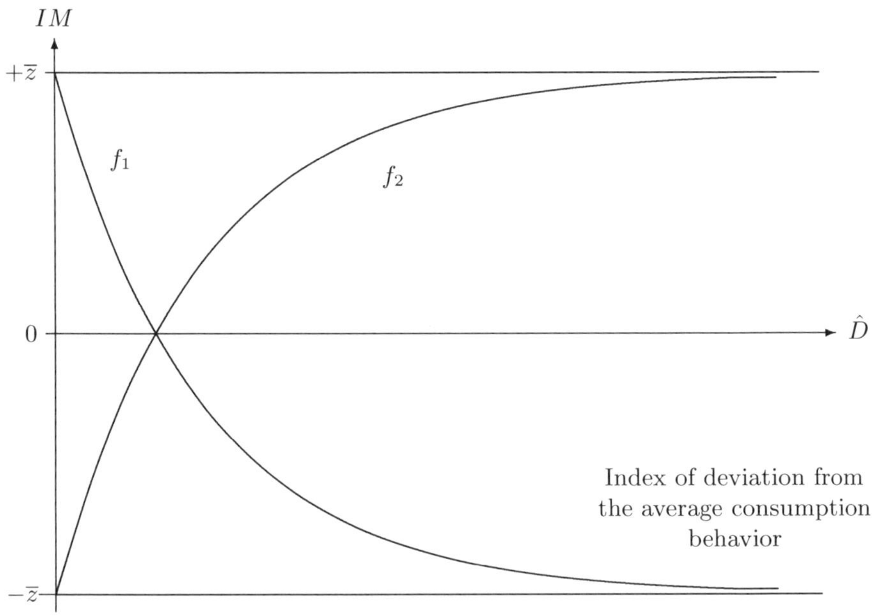

Evaluation of deviating behavior $\hat{D}$ of other person:

$$IM = f_1(\hat{D}) \text{ for a conformist}$$

$$IM = f_2(\hat{D}) \text{ for a snob}$$

Figure 1.5 The Force of Imitation as a Function of the Deviation from Average Behavior

which may be present to a certain degree or lacking. We enumerate them for person p by the vector

$$\kappa^{(p)} = (\kappa_1^{(p)}, \ldots, \kappa_r^{(p)}),$$

$$\text{where } 0 \leq \kappa_\rho^{(p)} \leq +\bar{z}, \quad \rho = 1, \ldots, r, \quad \bar{z} \geq 1$$

We consider them as inborn and independent of the other characteristics of a person.[50] They influence the productivity of a firm whereof the person is a member. We shall deal with some of these personal characteristics in the next section.

[50] For simplicity we follow here the rules for a certificate for employees who leave a firm: it is forbidden to mention negative characteristics of the person. Only by the lack of positive remarks the next employer may infer a negative trait of the person.

1.12 Entrepreneurship, Confidence and Trustworthiness

As explained earlier we assume that a person may have one or more capabilities (or qualifications) out of a finite set $g := \{g_1, \ldots, g_n\}$ of possible capabilities[51] . These capabilities may be well defined and simple to check (e.g. whether the person knows a certain field or business, which may be checked by examinations and diplomas). But there are other capabilities which are of a more subtle character, such as perspective in complicated situations, the capability of influencing other persons, the possibility of carrying through his own will against the resistance of other persons, intuition on other persons behavior, imagination on the "state of the world" in the future, and all this connected with a thorough knowledge of a certain field. This capability cannot be checked by examinations. Past behavior may give some hints but no guarantee on future performance of the person, since the future situations may (and usually will) be different from those in the past. These capabilities may have different names, one of them may be called "entrepreneurship" or "leadership" in a certain field, a latent variable[52] included in the set g of possible capabilities.

Each capability $g_\nu^{(p)}, \nu = 1, \ldots, n$, of a person p may be realized to a certain degree which is reproduced by an integer between zero (no capability for this kind) and $+\bar{z}, z$ an integer ≥ 1, (this capability is present at the highest possible degree). Thus we have

$$0 \leq g_\nu^{(p)} \leq +\bar{z}, \quad g_\nu^{(p)} \quad \text{an integer.}$$

For simplicity, we may assume that all directly measurable capabilities $g_\nu^{(p)}$ are known to everybody who cares for them, of course to the person himself and also to an employer who wants to hire the person for his firm or institution. If he (or she) does not trust the declaration or the diplomas of the person that seeks employment he (or she) may find it out soon by tests or a short term employment "at trial". This is not the case with latent variables such as "entrepreneurship" or "leadership" in a certain field. They could be ascertained only in the long run and by the actual performance in the future. But if these qualities are lacking, the firm or the institution may be ruined by the person. Only reality will unveil the actual "entrepreneurship" or "leadership" of a person.

This is where "confidence" comes in. A person p that is interested in the capability $g_\nu^{(p\prime)}$ of a person $p\prime$ in a field ν where no direct tests of the capability

[51] See e.g. Grossweischede und Grewe (Ed.), Glaubwürdigkeit in Ökonomie und Politik, Institut für Genossenschaftswesen der Westfälischen Wilhelms-Universität Münster,2000; especially the last chapter by Holger Bonus" Über Glaubwürdigkeit in der Politik".

[52] There are different methods of estimating latent variables; see e.g. Krelle, Latent Variables in Econometric Models, Disc. Paper B-104, SFB 303, Bonn, Oct. 1988.

are available forms an index $cf_\nu^{(p,p\prime)}$ called "confidence" of person p, that person $p\prime$ has the capability $g_\nu^{(p\prime)}$ in the field ν, where

$$0 \leq cf_\nu^{(p,p\prime)} \leq +\bar{z}.$$

Thus $cf_\nu^{(p,p\prime)}$ is the estimation of the unknown capability $g_\nu^{(p\prime)}$ of person $p\prime$ in the field ν by person p. The person p may overrate or undervalue the actual capability of person $p\prime$ in the field ν, which is only revealed in practice. For short we may call $cf_\nu^{(p,p\prime)}$ the "confidence of person p in person $p\prime$" with reference to the field ν.

Let $\mu = 1, \ldots, m$ be the index of capacities of a person p' which are known (or will be known with a little effort to everybody interested in it). Let $\nu = m+1, \ldots, n$ be the index of latent variables which cannot be measured directly but nevertheless may be of great importance (such as "entrepreneurship" or "leadership" or "reliability" and the like). The unknown capabilities $g_\nu^{(p\prime)}$ of person $p\prime$ in the field $\nu = m+1, \ldots, n$ are estimated as $cf_\nu^{(p,p\prime)}$ by person p on the base of that what is known by his performance in the past and presence in related fields where the capacities can be measured.

For simplicity we assume that all persons agree on what are related fields $\nu^{rel}(\nu)$ to a field $\nu = m+1, \ldots, n$, where the performance is not directly observable. Now we may assume that the confidence $cf_\nu^{(p,p\prime)}$ of person p in person $p\prime$ in the field ν is a function of the actual performance of person $p\prime$ in the related fields $1, \ldots, m'$:

$$cf_\nu^{(p,p\prime)} = F^{(p)}(g_1^{(p\prime)}, \ldots, g_{m\prime}^{(p\prime)}), \; \nu = m+1, \ldots, n$$

(all latent variables), where the "related fields" (related to ν)[53] are the fields $1, \ldots, m\prime$ and m' may be a function of ν.[54] The functions $F^{(p)}$ may be different from person to person. In the simplest case a weighted average may do:

$$cf_\nu^{(p,p\prime)} = \sum_{\nu=1}^{m\prime} \alpha_\nu^{(p)} \cdot g_\nu^{(p\prime)}, \quad 0 \leq \alpha_\nu^{(p)} \leq 1, \; \sum_{\nu=1}^{m\prime} \alpha_\nu^{(p)} = 1$$

The $\alpha^{(p)}$ may be different from person to person such that different persons p put different degrees of confidence in a person $p\prime$ in spite of equal information on the person. The measures $g_\nu^{(p)}$ of the capability of a person in field ν are supposed to be unequivocal but, of course, different in the different fields (e.g. picces produced, profits attained, papers accepted for publication in one period).

---

[53] It must be defined which fields are "related" to the field ν. A possible definition may be the following. A field μ is related to the field ν if the same basic forces of the body or of the intellect are used in μ as in ν.

[54] Other variables may also come in (see the literature on latent variables).

Thus the definition of the initial position B_i of a person i must be enlarged by the indexes of confidence in persons 1 to N (if these are the persons where the capabilities cannot be measured directly) with respect to the pertinent performances $(1, \dots, n)$:[55]

$$B_i = (\dots, cf_1^{(p\prime=1)}, \dots, cf_n^{(p\prime=1)}, \dots, cf_1^{(p\prime=N)}, \dots, cf_n^{(p\prime=N)}, \dots,)$$

The confidence figures belong to the characteristics of a person. They are of great practical importance. A large part of the decisions concerning the personnel in the leading positions of an institution depends on it.

There is another latent variable which characterizes a person: the estimates of the *trustworthiness* of other persons. Whereas the confidence in other people refers to their estimated performance in different fields, the trustworthiness refers to the degree of belief of a person p in assertions of a person p'. This is of importance for the agreements reached (or not reached) in the negotiations to coordinate the decisions of different persons. Section 1.8 deals with this problem; it is not central for our approach. Thus we only hint at this problem but do not go into the details.

1.13 Income and Expenditure of a Household. Some Definitional Relations

Till now not much of traditional economics has entered the scene. But this will change now. In this section we provide the definitional relations. Consider a household which consists of two ablebodied adults p_1 and p_2 (usually mother and father) and a number of children and (perhaps) pensionaries. The two adults are characterized as far as their capabilities to work are concerned in situation B_i by the vector

$$cap^{(p_i)} = (cap_1^{(p_i)}, \dots, cap_n^{(p_i)}),\ i = 1, 2,\ cap_\nu^{(p_i)} = g_\nu^{(p)} \quad \text{in section 1.12}$$

and (as far as their personal characteristics are concerned) by the vector

$$\kappa^{(p_i)} = (\kappa_{i1}^{(p_i)}, \dots, \kappa_{ir}^{(p_i)}), \quad i = 1, 2$$

In addition, the situation of the household as a whole is characterized by *common features* like: marital status, number and age of children, location, relation to neighbors and so on, which we describe by the vector[56]

$$\Lambda = (\lambda_1, \dots, \lambda_z)$$

---

[55] We leave out the notation $p = i$.

[56] Many of these variables may be 0-1 variables, where 0 means that the household does not have that characteristics and 1 that it has it.

Thus the situation of a household before any decision, at point B_i, is as far as the labor supply and the household characteristics are concerned described by the vector

$$B_i = (K_i, \Lambda_i, \dots)$$

$$\text{where } K_i = (cap_i^{(p_1)}, cap_i^{(p_2)}, \kappa_i^{(p_1)}, \kappa_i^{(p_2)})$$

$$\text{and } \Lambda_i = (\lambda_{i1}, \dots, \lambda_{iz})$$

Now we come to the *economic situation* of a household at the initial point B_i which we shall describe in an annex to this section in some detail.Here we only give an overview. The economic situation of a household is reproduced by a vector EC_i the elements of which indicate the value of the state variables at the beginning of period 0 whereas the flow variables refer to the period before (therefore they get the index −1). As already said the income earned in one period is spend in the next period. Thus the length of the period should not be too large. But also other flow variables in the last period codetermine the situation of the household in the beginning of period 0, not only income: the consumption goods bought at this period (whether they are durables or not), tax payments, transfer payments and receipts and other flow variables. Thus the economic situation EC_i of household i in state B_i is (as far as its own variables are concerned) determined by the vector EC_i^{state} of the value of the state variables at the beginning of period 0 and by the vector $EC_{i,-1}^{flow}$ of flow variables in the period before:

$$EC_i = (EC_i^{state}, EC_{i,-1}^{flow})$$

Finally the decisions $\overline{DEC}_i$ of other economic agents or states of nature referring to the next period 0 but known to the household before it takes its d ecision for the next period constitute a feature of the decision point B_i of the household. Thus a household in the decision situation B_i is characterized by:

$$B_i = (K_i, \Lambda_i, EC_i, \overline{DEC}_i), \quad i = 1, 2, \dots, H, \tag{1.11}$$

if there are H households.

All elements of the vectors K_i, Λ_i and EC_i and $D\bar{E}C$ are discrete and finite. Thus there is a finite number of situations where a household could be in.

Annex to Section 1.13: Some Details on Income and Expenditure of a Household

The foregoing definition of the situation B_i of a household i gives the general idea. But for practical tests and econometric estimations more details are necessary. They are presented in this annex which may be skipped by persons who are only interested in the general approach.

The economic situation of a household at the beginning of period 0 is described by the vector EC (index i of the initial situation and of the household omitted):

$$EC = (Y_{-1}^{net}, c_{-1}, \bar{c}, TR_{-1}^{-}, CA, KSt, W_{KSt}^{mv}, SEC, W_{SEC}^{mv}, TD, \\ DE, L^{(s)}, L, TR_{-1}^{+}, p, l, d, r, v_{KSt}, v_{SEC}) \tag{1.12}$$

where:

- Y^{net} = net income $= lL + KSt \cdot d_{KSt} + SEC \cdot r_{SEC}^{+} + TD \cdot r_{TD} + TR^{+} - T - DE \cdot r_{B}^{-}$
- c = $(c_1, \ldots, c_M)$ = consumption of commodities $1, \ldots, M$ bought in the former period. Durable consumption goods survive more than one period.
- $\bar{c}$ = $\bar{c}_1, \ldots, \bar{c}_M$ = amount of durable consumption goods.
- TR^{-} = transfer payments of the household.
- CA = amount of cash.
- KSt = $(KSt_1, \ldots, KSt_M)$ = capital stock of firms $1, \ldots, M$ owned by the household, in nominal value (e.g. number of shares of a certain nominal value). Thus $KSt \cdot d_{KSt} = \sum_{i=1}^{M} KSt_i \cdot d_{KSt,i}$ = income from distribution of dividends on shares, where $d_{KSt,i}$ = distribution of profits on share KSt_i per unit of capital stock.[57]
- W_{KSt}^{mv} = $(W_{KSt,1}^{mv}, \ldots, W_{KSt,M}^{mv})$ = market values of capital stocks, where $W_{KSt,i}^{mv} = KSt_i \cdot v_{KSt,i}$, $v_{KSt,i}$ = market value per unit of KSt_i.
- SEC = $(SEC_1, \ldots, SEC_M, SEC_B, SEC_G)$ = securities issued by firms $1, \ldots, M$, by banks (index B) or by the government (index G) in nominal terms (e.g. number of securities of a certain kind) and owned by the household. $SEC \cdot r_{SEC}^{+} = \sum_{i=1}^{N} SEC_i \cdot r_{SEC,i}^{+}$ = income from securities, $r_{SEC,i}^{+}$ = interest rate on SEC_i.
- W_{SEC}^{mv} = $(W_{SEC,1}^{mv}, \ldots, W_{SEC,M}^{mv}, W_{SEC,B}^{mv}, W_{SEC,G}^{mv}$ = market value of securities, where $W_{SEC,j}^{mv} = SEC_j \cdot v_{SEC,j}$, $j = 1, \ldots, M, B, G$, $v_{SEC,j}$ = market value of securities of type j.

---

[57] The household does not only own capital stock in form of shares and other types of ownership of firms, but also land of different size and houses. They are included in $KSt_1, \ldots, KSt_M$. For simplicity we assume (as did v. Thünen) land of equal quality. There is a fixed amount LA of land available on earth, and the whole land is owned by households, firms (and other institutions) or the government. We do not model this in detail.

TD = time deposits at banks, r_{TD} = interest on time deposits.

DE = debts of the household at the banks (we assume that a household could borrow money only from the banks), r_B^- = interest rate on debts.

$L^{(s)}$ = $(L_1^{(s)}, \ldots, L_n^{(s)})$ = maximum amount of labor of type $1, \ldots, n$ supplied by the household.

L = $(L_1, \ldots, L_n)$ = labor of types $1, \ldots, n$ offered by the household. We assume that all labor contracts are concluded at the beginning of a period and valid for that period.

TR^+ = transfer receipts of the household.

T = taxes paid by the household.

p = $(p_1, \ldots, p_M)$ = price of commodities.

l = $(l_1, \ldots, l_n)$ = wage rate for all types of labor.

d = $(d_1, \ldots, d_M)$ = profits distributed by firms $1, \ldots, M$ per unit of capital stock.

r = $(r_{SEC,1}^+, \ldots, r_{SEC,M}^+, r_{SEC,B}^+, r_{SEC,G}^+, r_B^-)$ = interest rates paid for securities issued by firms $1, \ldots, M$, by banks($r_{SEC,B}^+$) and by the government ($r_{SEC,G}^+$), and interest rate r_B^- to be paid to the banks by the debtors (firms and households)[58].

v_{KSt} = $(v_{KSt,1}, \ldots, v_{KSt,M})$ = market value of one unit of capital stock of firms $1, \ldots, M$ (e.g. for shares which are traded at the exchange: the value at the exchange).

v_{SEC} = $(v_{SEC,1}, \ldots, v_{SEC,M}, v_{SEC,B}, v_{SEC,G})$, analogously.

Thus the economic situation at the beginning of period 0 is determined by the value of the state variables CA, KSt, SEC, DE at that point of time as well as by the flow variables $Y^{net}, c_1, \ldots, c_M$ and TR^- of the period before. L, TR^+, p, l are valid for the period 0 and known to the household whereas the variables d, r, v_{KSt}, v_{SEC} valid for period 0 are not known to the household at the beginning of period 0. All elements of EC are discrete and finite.

---

[58] Actually, the $r_{SEC,j}^+$ are weighted averages of the interest rates $r_{SEC,j}^{+(t)}$ of securities issued at the beginning of period t by sector j. We may go back to these more basic concepts and define $r_{SEC,j}^+$ as a vector $(r_{SEC,j}^{+(0)}, r_{SEC,j}^{+(-1)}, \ldots, r_{SEC,j}^{+(-\bar{T})})$

1.14 Normal Economic Decisions of Private Households and the Budget Constraint

This is where "normal economics" comes in, though with some variation. This theory goes to a large part parallel to the theory of private decisions (section 1.3), but not completely. As far as decisions of the households are concerned we treat the household as a person, i.e. we do not go into the "inner life" of the household. But as to the description of the possible situation B_i of a household, $i = 1, \ldots, H$, we have to consider also the non–economic characteristics of the household. As explained in the foregoing section they consist of the personal characteristics $K_i = (\kappa_{i1}, \ldots, \kappa_{ir})$ of the adult and ablebodied persons within the household as well as the characteristics of the household as a whole, $\Lambda_i = (\lambda_{i1}, \lambda_{i2}, \ldots, \lambda_{iz})$, e.g.: marital status, number of children, age, profession, location etc. (where $\lambda_{i\zeta} \in \{0, 1\}$, where 0 means that the household does not have that characteristic and 1 means that it has it). Of course, the economic situation EC_i at the decision point B_i is most important. It refers to the beginning of period 0.

There exists a definitial relation called budget constraint between these variables which we shall derive now by defining receipts and expenditures of a household in a period and taking their difference. Since this is nothing new, we shall proceed as in the foregoing section: first to state the general principle and in an annex go into the details.

Let REC be the receipts of a household in one period and EXP the expenditure. Then the change ΔCA of cash is

$$REC - EXP = \Delta CA$$

Let CA $\geq$ 0 be the cash at the beginning of period 0. In order to avoid bankruptcy the condition

$$\Delta CA \geq -CA$$

must be fulfilled. All decisions of the household concerning the real and the financial side must keep this relation, called the budget constraint. Unfortunately neither CA nor ΔCA are known with certainty when the household has to decide on buying consumption goods and on investing in different fields. The future price of financial assets which may be liquidated is not known. Thus CA is only known as a probability distribution. The same applies for ΔCA: the employer may go bankrupt, a debtor may not pay etc.

The following approach assumes that the household knows almost all data which are relevant for its decision, but only "almost". As already said, the household does not know the values v_{KSt} and v_{SEC} of its assets which are formed at the exchange on the base of the demand and supply of capital stock and securities. The household contributes to this evaluation by its portfolio decision but does not know other people's portfolio decisions and the resulting price. Moreover, the household does not know the interest rates r^+_{SEC} and the size d of dividends and the interest rate r^-_B it has to pay for debts because this depends on the monetary and fiscal policy of the central bank and the government which is not known in advance. This concludes the general description of the decision point B_i of a household. Details are given in the following annex.[59]

The decision of the household which finds itself at the decision point B_i is based on the evaluation of the alternatives $B_{i1}, \ldots, B_{iz}$. We shall come to this later.

Annex to Section 1.14: Some Details on Normal Economic Decisions of Private Households and on the Budget Constraint

Total net receipts REC of a household in one period are defined by

$$REC = Y^{net} + T + DE \cdot r_B^- - \Delta KSt \cdot v_{KSt} - \Delta SEC \cdot v_{SEC} + \Delta DE \tag{1.13}$$

where: $\Delta KSt \cdot v_{KSt} = \sum_{i=1}^{M} \Delta KSt_i \cdot v_{KSt,i}$ = income from selling capital stock (if ΔKSt_i is negative) and cost of buying capital stock (if ΔKSt_i is positive). Capital stock includes land and houses.

$\Delta SEC \cdot v_{SEC} =$ similarly for securities

$\Delta DE =$ income by borrowing from the banks (if ΔDE = change of the size of debts is positive), and expenditure if debts are repaid (ΔDE negative)[60]

---

[59] These assumptions on the state of information of a household do not imply that a specific household actually knows all prices, interest rates etc. It knows those where it is interested in and disregards all others. These prices etc. form (together with its income) the base of its consumption and saving decisions. Uncertainty comes in by the valuation of the assets by the capital markets. Saving and investment decisions have to be taken under ignorance of the valuation of its assets by the exchange.

One may object and suggest that the same uncertainty prevails with respect to prices etc. But this is not true. For most consumer goods the (real) prices vary only in relatively small ranges, whereas the asset prices may fluctuate substantially. Thus we may simplify the approach by assuming that the household knows the commodity prices of the next period exactly (because the firm, which produces the commodity, announces its price and keeps it for the whole period) whereas it does not know the future prices at the exchange which determine the value of its assets.

[60] The following notations are used: Total cash CA in circulation is held by households i, firms f, banks B or the government G:

$$CA = \sum_{i=1}^{H} CA^{(i)} + \sum_{f=1}^{M} CA^{(f)} + CA^B + CA^G$$

Total capital stock KSt_f of firm f is held by households, banks and the government:

$$KSt_f = \sum_{i=1}^{H} KSt_f^{(i)} + KSt_f^{(B)} + KSt_f^{(G)},$$

where $KSt_f = KSt_{f,-1} + \Delta KSt_f, \quad f = 1, \ldots, M$

If we want to include the change of net wealth into the definition of income we would have to add the expression

$$\sum_{i=1}^{M}[(\Delta KSt_i)\ v_{KSt,i} + KSt_i\ \Delta v_{KSt,i}] +$$

$$\sum_{j\in J}[(\Delta SEC_j)\ v_{SEC,j} + SEC_j\ \Delta v_{SEC,j}],$$

$$J = \{1, \ldots, M, B, G\}.$$

But we shall not do that. There is a time dimension of the capital stock KSt_i and of the securities (SEC_j) which we did not consider in detail till now but which must be considered, since the interest rate paid on securities differs for securities issued at different periods. Let us assume that the eldest capital stock and the eldest security of a firm or an institution i dates back to T periods before. Let $KSt_{i,t}$ be the capital stock of firm i issued at the beginning of period t. Accordingly, $SEC_{j,t} \cdot r_{SECj,t}$ is the interest on securities of institution j issued at the beginning of period t. Then we have:

$$KSt_i\ d_i = (\sum_{t=-T}^{0} KSt_{i,t}\ )d_i \quad \text{and}$$

$$SEC_j\ r^+_{SEC,j} = \sum_{t=-T}^{0} SEC_{j,t}\ r^+_{SEC,j,t}$$

We define $SEC_j = \sum_{t=-T}^{0} SEC_{j,t}$. These are all securities issued from $-T$ to 0 by institution j.[61] Then $r^+_{SEC,j}$ is a weighted average of all interest rates for securities of that institution:

$$r^+_{SEC,j} = \frac{\sum_{t=-T}^{0} SEC_{j,t}\ r^+_{SEC,j,t}}{\sum_{t=-T}^{0} SEC_{j,t}}$$

There are certain relations between TR^+ and TR^-. Let $TR^+(B_i)$ be the receipts of transfer payments of a household in the situation B_i and analogously

---

Similarly for securities:

$$SEC_{f,\nu} = \sum_{i=1}^{H} KSt^{(i)}_{f,\nu} + SEC^{(B)}_{f,\nu} + SEC^{(G)}_{f,\nu}$$

where $SEC_{f,\nu}$ = securities issued by institution f at time ν, $f \in \{1, \ldots, M, B, G\}$ and $\nu = 0, -1, -T$, if securities have a term of T periods. The interest rates for the different vintages of securities may be different.

[61] All the securities have the same dimension (e.g. DM), thus they may be added though the associated rates of interest may be different.

$TR^-(B_i)$ its transfer payments. Let there be H households which are in the situation $B_1, \ldots, B_H$: Let $TR^-_{Fh}, TR^-_{Bh}, TR^-_{Gh}$ be the transfer payment of all firms, banks and the government respectively to households. Then in a closed economy the following relation must hold:

$$\sum_{i=1}^{H} TR^+(B_i) = \sum_{i=1}^{H} TR^-(B_i) + TR^-_{Fh} + TR^-_{Bh} + TR^-_{Gh} \tag{1.14}$$

In the definition of the decision point B_i the nominal values KSt and SEC of the capital stocks and the securities (respectively) appear, see equation (1.11) and (1.12). If the market values $v_{KSt,i}$ and $v_{SEC,j}$ of these assets are known, we get also the market values W^{mv}_{KSt} and W^{mv}_{SEC} of these assets:

$$W^{mv}_{KSt,i} = KSt_i \cdot v_{KSt,i}, \quad i = 1, \ldots, M \quad \text{and}$$

$$W^{mv}_{SEC,j} = SEC_j \cdot v_{SEC,j}, \quad j = 1, \ldots, M, B, G$$

Of course, all these variables may change in time.

In equation (1.13) we defined the net receipts of a household. Similarly we may define its total net expenditure EXP:

$$EXP = cp + DE \cdot r^-_B + T + TR^- \tag{1.15}$$

where:

$cp = \sum_{i=1}^{M} c_i p_i =$ the consumption expenditures

$DE \cdot r^-_B =$ the interest payments for the debts of the household

$T =$ tax payments

$TR^- =$ transfer payments to other households or institutions

All variables are assigned to the beginning of period 0. If they are state variables like KSt, SEC, DE there are no problems. If they are flow variables (like $l, c, T, \ldots$) they refer to the total flow of the period before, here the period -1.

Now we may state the *budget constraint* of a household:

$$REC_0 - EXP_0 = \Delta CA: \tag{1.16}$$

the difference of receipts and expenditures in period -1 is the change of cash at the beginning of period 0 compared to the beginning of period -1. Since $\Delta CA = CA_1 - CA_0$ and CA_1 cannot be negative (then the household is bankrupt, a case which we do not consider here), we have for the budget constraint:

$$\Delta CA \geq -CA_0, \quad CA_0 \geq 0 \tag{1.17}$$

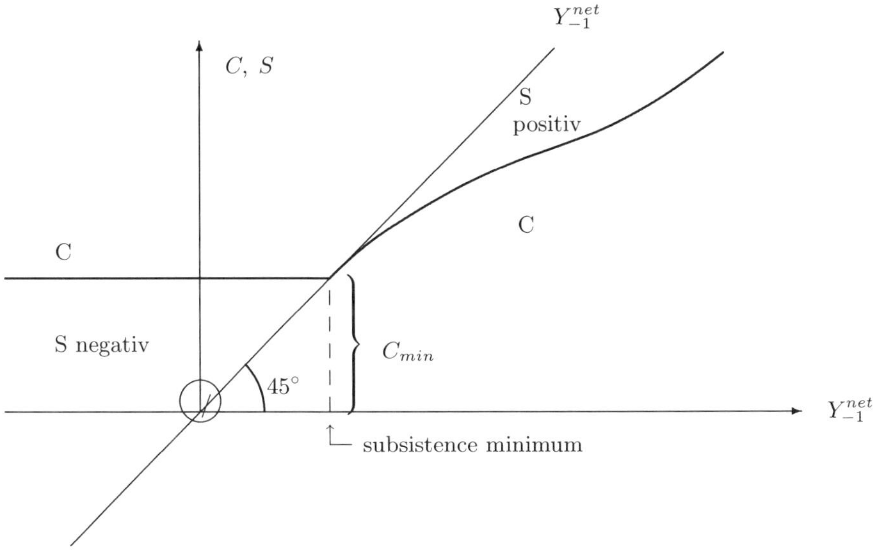

Figure 1.6 Net Income Y_{-1}^{net} (Including Transfer Receipts) divided in Consumption C and Saving S; the General Shape

We may now define consumption C and saving S. For simplicity, we include transfer payments in consumption:

$$C = c \cdot p + TR^{-} \tag{1.18}$$

$$S = \Delta KSt \cdot v_{KSt} + \Delta SEC \cdot v_{SEC} + \Delta TD + \Delta CA - \Delta DE \tag{1.19}$$ [62]

such that

$$Y_{-1}^{net} = C + S \tag{1.20}$$ [63]

---

[62] S may be negative, since $\Delta KSt, \Delta SEC, \Delta TD$ and ΔCA may be negative (the person could sell all his assets) and DE may be positive (the person could encumber himself with debts).

[63] Y_{-1}^{net} may also be negative, see the definition in section 1.13 above: taxes T might be higher than all receipts (T might also include all losses by robbery, pillage, looting, etc.) and (or) interest payment on debts $DE \cdot r_B^{-}$ may be excessive. But consumption C must be positive and larger or equal as the subsistence minimum, otherwise the person would not exist.

Kuznets has shown that in the theory in the long run (with higher net income) collective saving tends to be a more or less constant part of income. Thus the familiar Keynesian consumption or saving function for the economy as a whole must be modified as shown in Fig. 1.6. We may assume that individual saving and consumption does not deviate fundamentally from this scheme.

Total wealth of the person (not included durable consumption goods) is

$$WE = KSt \cdot v_{KSt} + SEC \cdot v_{SEC} + TD + CA - DE$$

Unfortunately, the budget constraint (1.17) cannot be guaranteed by the household to hold in all circumstances, even not in our model where we assumed that all commodity prices are known in advance for the whole period. The household may determine C and S but ΔCA is determined by solving equation (1.19) for ΔCA:

$$\Delta CA = S + \Delta DE - \Delta KSt \cdot v_{KSt} - \Delta SEC \cdot v_{SEC} - \Delta TD \qquad (1.21)$$

In this equation v_{KSt} and v_{SEC} are not known by the household since they are determined by the brokers on the base of conditional demand and supply of capital stock and securities by all households. If v_{KSt} and v_{SEC} are not known, the actual demand and supply ΔKSt and ΔSEC are not known either (the household orders ΔKSt and ΔSEC only conditioned upon the values v_{KSt} and v_{SEC}, see section 1.25)[64] Thus, since the expressions $\Delta KSt \cdot v_{KSt}$

---

[64] Consider a person at the beginning of period 0. It may own money M_0 (including short term deposits at the banks), time deposits DEP_0 at a fixed bank rate z_B, different securities with nominal value $W_{10}, \ldots, W_{n0}$ (if there are n securities) and real wealth $RV_{10}, \ldots, RV_{m0}$ (in natural units, there are m types of real wealth). The securities have a price of $v_{10}, \ldots, v_{n0}$ at the exchange, and the pieces of real wealth have a selling price of $w_{10}, \ldots, w_{m0}$ at the beginning of period 0. Then the wealth of the person at time 0 consists of money and of invested capital K_0:

$$V_0 = M_0 + K_0$$

$$\text{where } K_0 = DEP_0 + \sum_{\nu=1}^{n} W_{\nu 0} \cdot v_{\nu 0} + \sum_{\mu=1}^{m} RV_{\mu 0} \cdot w_{\mu 0}$$

The wealth at the end of period 0 (the beginning of period 1) is (we omit some expressions of higher order and define for a variable x: $\Delta x_0 = x_1 - x_0$):

$$V_1 = V_0 + \Delta M_0 + \Delta DEP_0 + \sum_{\nu=1}^{n} [v_{\nu 0} \Delta W_{\nu 0} + W_{\nu 0} \cdot \Delta v_{\nu 0}] + \sum_{\mu=1}^{m} [w_{\mu 0} \Delta RV_{\mu 0} + RV_{\mu 0} \cdot \Delta w_{\mu 0}]$$

The person decides on $\Delta W_{\nu 0}, \Delta RV_{\mu 0}$ and ΔDEP_0, it cannot decide on the price changes $\Delta v_{\nu 0}$ and $\Delta w_{\mu 0}$. The person has to decide on $\Delta W_{\nu 0}$ *before* knowing $\Delta v_{\nu 0}$ since the price of an asset at the exchange will be found by total offer and demand which is not known to the person. That means: the person has to give *conditional* orders to the broker, conditioned on the price of the asset which is only known ex post, at the end of period 0. Thus the value of the expression $W_{\nu 0} \cdot \Delta v_{\nu 0}$ is not known to the person when it has to decide on $\Delta W_{\nu 0}$. This leads to the fact that the person cannot decide on the change ΔM_0 of cash: the change of cash depends on all buying or selling decisions of the person, partly at prices which are not known at the time of the decision.

This is (as we assume) not so with respect to ΔDEP_0 (the person decides on it, and the actual value equals its nominal value) as well as with respect to change of the value of real wealth $RV_{11}, \ldots, RV_{m1}$, namely $\Delta w_{10}, \ldots, \Delta w_{m0}$. The real wealth of a person (or household) consists of agricultural land, forests, houses, long term consumption goods like automobiles, furniture and so on.

and $\Delta SEC \cdot v_{SEC}$ are not known at the beginning of the planning period, the household cannot plan and predict ΔCA, and that means: the budget constraint (1.17) may not hold: the household may go bankrupt. We do not pursue this case here.

The change of wealth equals saving plus the change of the valuation of assets:

$$\Delta WE = S + KSt \cdot \Delta v_{KSt} + SEC \cdot \Delta v_{SEC} \tag{1.22}$$

We now come to the expression $\overline{DEC}_i$ in equation (1.11), the vector of the decision of other economic agents referring to the next period and known to the household before it has to decide on its own behavior in the next period. We define

$$\overline{DEC}_i = (L_i, TR_i^+, l, p, T_i) \tag{1.23}$$

That means:

1. The firms decide at the beginning of period 0 (and valid for this whole period) on the employment L_i of persons belonging to a household i which is in situation B_i. They decide also on the price p of the commodities. Their decisions are known to the household at the beginning of period 0. But it does not know the interest rates $r_{SEC,1}^+, \ldots, r_{SEC,M}^+$ which firms $1, \ldots, M$ would pay for newly issued securities and the amounts $d_1, \ldots, d_M$ they will distribute as profits per unit of capital stock.

2. The trade unions decide on the wage rates $l_1, \ldots, l_n$ for period 0, and the household knows them.[65]

3. The banks decide on the interest rate r_B^- a household has to pay for a loan and on the interest rate $r_{SEC,B}^+$ they will pay for newly issued securities. The household does not know that before.

4. The government decides on taxes T_i the household in situation B_i should pay and on transfer payments TR_i^+ a household in situation B_i will receive, and the household knows that.

The decisions L, TR, l, p, T are announced at the beginning of period 0 and are valid till the beginning of period +1. They are known to the household before it takes its own decisions.

---

[65] This may exaggerate the union power. But in many countries, e.g. in Germany, the union power is very strong and still becoming even stronger because highly automatized firms without large inventories (with deliveries "just in time") become very sensitive to strikes and are "on the mercy" of the trade unions.

1.15 Consumption and Saving of Private Households

The household inherits the net income Y_{-1}^{net} from the last period and decides *in the first step* how to divide it between consumption (including transfer payments) and saving:

$$Y_{-1}^{net} = C + S,$$

see Fig. 1.6, a variant of the picture familiar to all economists.[66] For the reason given earlier there are only finite many subdivisions of Y_{-1}^{net} into consumption and saving feasible, and there are different considerations or points of view relevant for the choice of the household:

- the real net income per capita of the family (if it is small, higher proportions of consumption will be preferred)
- the prospects of support in case of disease and old age
- the expectation of income in the future
- the interest which may be earned by saving
- the willingness to "keep up" with the neighbors, to indicate a high income if in the society the person is judged by his income
- certain instincts and drives (like alcoholism, drug addiction, sexual urges) which can only be satisfied by certain expenditures which are counted as consumption.

But there are also motives for consumption expenditures which get a better note from ethics:

- to shield the children from hunger and cold
- to help others who are in need directly or indirectly (by supporting relief organizations); note that transfer payments are part of consumption
- moral obligations.

Let there be n points of view in judging the consumption ratio $\gamma = \frac{C}{Y_{-1}}$, $0 \leq \gamma \leq 1$, or equivalently the savings ratio $1 - \gamma$. There are only finite many γ, say N, e.g. $\gamma \in= \{0; 0.05; 0.1; \ldots, 1\}$. Each γ gets a note $u_i(\gamma)$ from the point of view i, $i = 1, \ldots, n$, where $-\bar{z} \leq u_i(\gamma) \leq +\bar{z}$, $\bar{z} > 0$, integer. Let α_i be the weight the person gives to the point of view i, $0 \leq \alpha_i$, $\sum_{i=1}^{n} \alpha_i = 1$. Then our theory says that the person evaluates γ from the point of view

[66] Cf. the remarks on C, S and Y made in section 1.13 and 1.14.

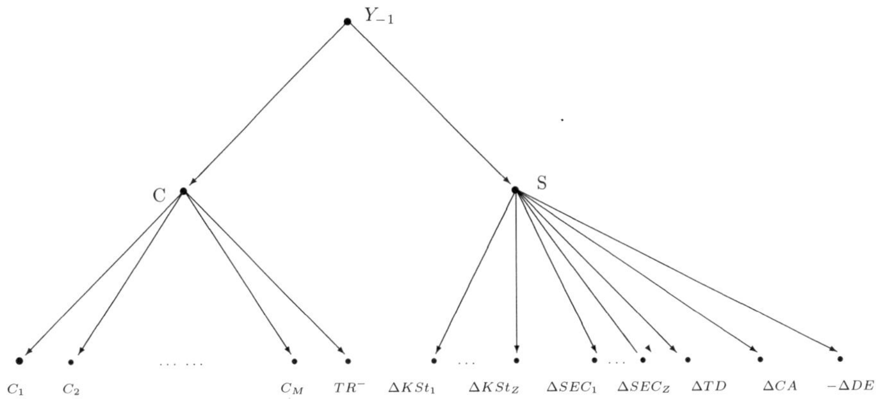

Figure 1.7 General Outline: Household Decisions, Use of Income. The Case of Known Asset Prices.

i by $u_i(\gamma)$ which lies between $-\bar{z}$ and $+\bar{z}$. Total evaluation of γ would be $u(\gamma) = \sum_{i=1}^{n} \alpha_i v_i(\gamma)$, and the person chooses γ^* which maximizes $u(\gamma)$:

$$\gamma^* \Leftarrow \max(u(\gamma_1), \ldots, u(\gamma_N)).$$

This yields $C^* = \gamma^* Y_{-1}$ and $S^* = (1 - \gamma^*)Y_{-1}$.

Now we come to the *second step* (see Fig. 1.7): the household has to allocate C^* to the purchase of consumption goods $c_1, \ldots, c_M$ and to transfer payments TR such that

$$\sum_{i=1}^{M} c_i p_i + TR = C^*$$

Only finite many $C_i \geq 0$ and $TR \geq 0$ are admissible, C^* and $p_1, \ldots, p_M$ given. Thus only finite many vectors $C_\mu = (c_{\mu 1}, \ldots, c_{\mu M})$ and finite many TR_μ are eligible, say: $\mu = 1, \ldots, z$, such that the above equation is (approximately) fulfilled. Each admissible combination (C_μ, TR_μ) gets a mark $v_i(C_\mu, TR_\mu)$ between $-\bar{z}$ and $+\bar{z}$ from the point of view i. Such points of view may be:

- the normal needs for subsistence in the geographical region
- the special interests of the person in the household (music, sport, literature, communication etc.)
- certain instincts and drives like smoking, alcohol, moral considerations of different kinds and so on.

There are some general rules on the allocation of total consumption expenditure C on the main categories of consumption goods, see Fig. 1.8. At the subsistence minimum almost all expenditure is used for food. Dwelling and clothes follow next in an order which depends on the climate and other living

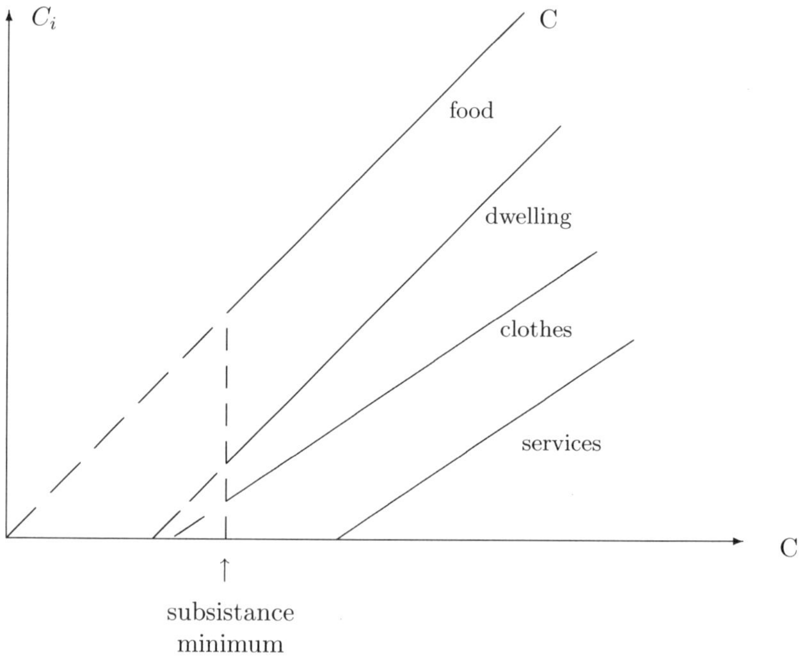

Figure 1.8. Consumption Expenditures; the General Shape

conditions. The proportion of the expenditure for food in total consumption expenditure declines eventually. Finally the services get the upper hand (which is called "Fourastier's Law"). Of course, there will be individual deviations from this general shape.

Let there again be n points of view by which the person evaluates the vector (C_μ, TR_μ) and let β_i be the weight which the person attributes to the points of view, $i = 1, \ldots, n$, $0 \leq \beta_i \leq 1$, $\sum_i \beta_i = 1$. Similarly as in the first step a combination (C_μ, TR_μ) is evaluated by

$$U(C_\mu, TR_\mu) = \sum_{i=1}^{n} \beta_i v_i(C_\mu, TR_\mu)$$

The household chooses that combination $\mu^* = (C_{\mu^*}, TR_{\mu^*})$ where

$$\mu^* \longleftarrow \max(U(C_1, TR_1), \ldots, U(C_z, TR_z))$$

Now we come to the *third step*: the allocation of total saving S^* to capital stock which yields ΔKSt, to securities ΔSEC,to time deposits ΔTD, to cash ΔCA and to the reduction of debts $-\Delta DE$. After suitable renumbering we may formulate this as:

$$\sum_{\zeta=1}^{z}(\Delta KSt_\zeta \cdot v_{KSt_\zeta} + \Delta SEC_\zeta \cdot v_{SEC_\zeta}) + \Delta TD + \Delta CA - \Delta DE = S^*,$$

if there are z "types" of capital stock and securities, given total savings S^* and the prices v_{KSt} and v_{SEC} of capital stock and securities, respectively, in the next period. But this is an oversimplified approach: actually the prices v_{KSt} and v_{SEC} valid for period 0 are not known to the person because they depend on supply or demand ΔKSt and ΔSEC of *all* persons, and this is unknown when the person orders sales or purchases of capital stock or securities. Thus the change of cash ΔCA in equation 1.21 cannot be determined in advance, in general, and this approach, illustrated in Fig. 1.7 is only the ex post view, at the end of the planning period 0. We come to the ex ante view later in section 1.25. Here some comments on the meaning of ΔKSt and ΔSEC are in order.

$\Delta KSt_\zeta \cdot v_{KSt_\zeta}$ and $\Delta SEC_\zeta \cdot v_{SEC_\zeta}$ are sums of values of capital stock and securities issued by M different firms or institutions. We assume that all capital stock (whatever may be the date of issue) is issued at a nominal value of 1 DM and that the profit payments d_ζ of firm ζ are equal for capital stock of all dates of issue. In this case the value v_{KSt_ζ} is equal for all capital stocks of firm (or institution) ζ, irrespective of the time of issue.

$$\text{Thus } \Delta KSt_\zeta \cdot v_{KSt_\zeta} = \sum_{t=-T}^{0} \Delta KSt_{\zeta,t} \cdot v_{KSt_\zeta}$$

This is not so with securities. Different issues of securities of the same firm or institution may be endowed with different interest rates and will therefore have different prices. Thus:

$$\Delta SEC_\zeta \cdot v_{SEC_\zeta} = \sum_{\zeta=1}^{M} \sum_{t=-T}^{0} \Delta SEC_{\zeta,t} \cdot v_{SEC_\zeta,t}$$

This approach to consumption and saving of households is very detailed. For many purposes it may be advisable to aggregate some of the "points of view" of the household in evaluating the possible decisions into more general categories as it is done in Table 1.1.

A state $B_{ij} = (K_{ij}, \Lambda_{ij}, EC_{ij}, \overline{DEC}_{ij})$[67] which may be reached from B_i (i.e. where the budget constraint is fulfilled with a probability accepted by the household) may be judged by the household h by four different aggregate perspectives which include the "points of view" given above:[68]

---

[67] The decision $\overline{DEC}_i$ of other economic agents are supposed to be formally independent of the decision of the household h (which we consider now) to move to B_{i1} or $B_{i2}, \ldots,$ or B_{iz}, see section 1.9.

[68] This approach takes into account the criticism of sociologists on the usual assumption of economic theory that household decisions are basically determined by economic considerations, see e.g. Mayntz (1999). E.g.: Max Weber differs between "zweckrationalem Handeln" (here covered by G), "wertrationalem Verhalten" (here covered by M) "emotionalem" und "intuitivem Handeln" (here covered by EM), and decisions which are

$G_{ij}^{(h)}$ = an index of the economic well being of the household h in the state B_{ij}, judged by household h. It will be related to real net receipts $REC^{real} = REC/\bar{p}$, $\bar{p}$ = price index of consumer goods; but also to the difference of real net receipts of period 0 to that of period -1 may be relevant.The household is free in its evaluation, but has to state it on a discrete integer scale between $-\bar{z}$ and $+\bar{z}$, $\bar{z} > 0$. This index $G_{ij}^{(h)}$ conforms to the same index in the theory of private decisions, see section 1.3.

$EM_{ij}^{(h)}$ = emotional evaluation of the state B_{ij} by household h. This follows from instinct, blind habits, animal spirits, addiction, prejudice etc., without any rational basis. This evaluation has also to be stated on a scale between $-\bar{z}$ and $+\bar{z}$. The index $EM_{ij}^{(h)}$ conforms to the same index in the theory of private decisions, see section 1.3. The index H in section 1.3 which indicates the attitudes to punishment is not applicable here, since there is no punishment involved in these decisions.

$IM_{ij}^{(h)}$ = an index of imitation (or repudiation) of the behavior of other households. This index catches conformism or repulsion and snobbism in the society: people behave in a certain way because other people do so (what may be called conformism), or on the contrary: people want to differentiate themselves from the crowd and behave in a way which contradicts the "normal", accepted behavior (what may be called snobbism). This may be formalized as follows.[69] A household h with receipts REC compares itself with households of similar receipts, say: with households of receipts $REC(1 \pm \alpha)$, $0 \leq \alpha \leq 1$. The receipts of these households in detail are not directly observable by household h, but the average consumption vector $c_{1,-1}^{(\bar{h})}, \ldots, c_{M,-1}^{(\bar{h})}$ of the last period of "similar" households $\bar{h}$ (which may be in other states) is observable. The average consumption of commodity j of these households is

$$\bar{c}_{j,-1}^{(\bar{h})} = \frac{1}{N^{(\bar{h})}} \sum_{\bar{h} \in \{N^{(\bar{h})}\}} c_{j,-1}^{\bar{h}}, \quad j = 1, \ldots, M; \tag{1.24}$$

where

governed by "Tradition, blinde Gewohnheit, automatische Routine" (here covered by IM). Thus our approach takes into account some sociological points of view which seem to be justified.

[69] This is a variant of the theory of imitation suggested in section 1.11. In section 1.11 we considered only conformism and left it to the judgement of the household which initial conditions it would classify as "similar". Here we deal with the special case where "similarity" is defined by deviation of consumption behavior, but enlarged the admissible region by covering also the case of snobbism.

$N^{(\bar{h})}$ = the number of other households which fall into the range of households with which household h compares itself; $\{N^{(\bar{h})}\}$ is the set of these households. Then an index of deviation of a possible consumption behavior $c_{ij}^{(h)}$ of household h from the average behavior of similar households if it moves to the point B_{ij} is:

$$\hat{D}_{ij}^{(h)} = \sum_{j=1}^{M} \bar{p}_j (\bar{c}_{j,-1}^{(\bar{h})} - c_{ij}^{(h)}), \tag{1.25}$$

where $\bar{p}_j = \frac{p_j}{\bar{p}}$ is the real price of commodity j and $\hat{D}_{ij}^{(h)}$ is positive, if the consumption of commodity j by household h is "too small" (compared to the consumption of similar households) and negative, if it is "too large". Now the household has to evaluate this deviation as usual within the limits $-\bar{z}$ and $+\bar{z}$, which gives the index $IM_{ij}^{(h)}$ of the evaluation of the situation B_{ij} with respect to the realized behavior of comparable households. $IM_{ij}^{(h)}$ is a function of $\hat{D}_{ij}^{(h)}$ and lies in the limits $-\bar{z}$ and $+\bar{z}$. If h is a conformist, $IM_{ij}^{(h)}$ has his highest value if $\hat{D}_{ij}^{(h)} = 0$ and his lowest (a negative one) if $\hat{D}_{ij}^{(h)}$ is highest in absolute value. If h is a nonconformist or snob[70], $IM_{ij}^{(h)}$ has his lowest (negative) value if $\hat{D}_{ij}^{(h)} = 0$ and his highest if $\hat{D}_{ij}^{(h)}$ is highest in absolute value. Fig. 1.5 shows possible shapes of the function

$$IM_{ij}^{(h)} = f(\hat{D}_{ij}^{(h)}) \tag{1.26}$$

As usual, only integer values count.

$M_{ij}^{(h)}$ = moral evaluation of the state B_{ij} by household h. This is equivalent to the moral evaluation of personal acts. We refer to section 1.4.

Thus the household has four principles to evaluate a possible move from B_i to B_{ij}:

$$(G_{ij}^{(j)}, EM_{ij}^{(h)}, IM_{ij}^{(h)}, M_{ij}^{h}), \tag{1.27}$$

where each element of this vector takes an integer value between $-\bar{z}$ and $+\bar{z}$.

[70] For a more detailed analysis see: Corneo (1997).

Each principle is given a certain weight α such that the final evaluation of B_{ij} by household h is:

$$
\begin{aligned}
& V_{ij}^{(h)} = \alpha_{ij,G}^{(h)} \cdot G_{ij}^{(h)} + \alpha_{ij,EM}^{(h)} EM_{ij}^{(h)} + \alpha_{ij,IM}^{(h)} IM_{ij}^{(h)} + \alpha_{ij,M}^{(h)} M_{ij}^{h}, \\
& 0 \leq \alpha_{ij,k}^{(h)} \leq 1, \quad \sum_{k \in \{K\}} \alpha_{ij,k}^{(h)} = 1, \quad k \in \{G, EM, IM, M\} = \{K\}, \\
& j = 1, \ldots, z
\end{aligned}
\tag{1.28}
$$

Now the household in a situation B_i chooses that alternative B_{ij}which it likes most, i.e. : where the valuation figure $V_{ij}^{(h)}$ is maximal:[71]

$$
B_{ij}^{*} \longleftarrow \max(V_{i1}^{(h)}, \ldots, V_{iz}^{(h)}) \tag{1.29}
$$

This comprises purely economic utility maximizing behavior where "utility" is interpreted as G_{ij} but also purely emotional, adaptive and moral motivations of a decision of a household. In general, all four points of view will be present. The weights $\alpha_{ij,k}^{(h)}$ are supposed to be given in the short run. They may follow a distribution which is rather fixed in the society in the short run.

Only a small percentage of the population will act according to one principle alone, be it the economic, the emotional, the imitational or the moral. The majority will take into account two or more of these principles (this, of course, is a guess). Households which find themselves in the same or a similar decision situation might show similar demand behavior. For the long run the development of the $\alpha_{ij,k}^{(h)}$ may be explained by a Markov chain, similarly as the $h_t^{(\nu)}$ in section 1.6.

1.16 Morality and Criminality in a Society and Their Effect on the Economy

The internal situation of a society in a given period as far as personal morality is concerned may be reflected by the vector

$$
\mathcal{M} = (v_{11}, v_{21}, \ldots, v_{h1})
$$

of the proportions of persons acting according to the moral rules, if confronted with decisions of moral importance. This vector may be called the "basic degree of personal morality" in the society. Conversely, the vector

---

[71] This is a theoretical concept. Actually (as already said before) no household has time and can put in enough effort to evaluate all alternatives. Only few alternatives in the neighborhood of the realized situation are considered and evaluated. This means: there are limitations $j \in \{J\}$ to be considered where $\{J\}$ is the set of alternatives which household h takes into account if his actual situation is that of B_i.

$$\mathcal{K} = (v_{12}, v_{22}, \ldots, v_{h2})$$

indicates the "basic degree of personal criminality". From the criminality vector $(v_{12}, v_{22}, \ldots, v_{h2})$ we may infer the frequency of violations of moral and criminal laws. Let $\beta = (\beta_1, \beta_2, \ldots, \beta_h)$ be the average number of decision problems of the kind encountered in the $B_1, \ldots, B_h$ per unit of time which a person will be confronted with,[72] or in other words: the frequency of occurrence of the choice problem B_i. Let $N_{i2} = v_{i2} \cdot N$ be the number of persons who in situation B_i would choose the bad alternative B_{i2}, where $N =$ the number of persons in the society. Then the observed number $\bar{N}_{i2}$ of violations of moral obligations or of criminal laws is given by the vector

$$\bar{N_{\bullet 2}} = \quad (\bar{N}_{12}, \bar{N}_{22}, \ldots, \bar{N}_{h2}), \quad \text{where} \quad \bar{N}_{i2} = \beta_i \cdot v_{i2} \cdot N, \quad i = 1, \ldots, h. \tag{1.30}$$

$\bar{N}_{\bullet 2}$ may be called the *actual criminality*. We define

$$\bar{V} = (\bar{v}_{12}, \ldots, \bar{v}_{h2})$$

the *vector of observed criminal rates* in the society, where $\bar{v}_{i2} = \frac{\bar{N}_{i2}}{N} = \beta_i \cdot v_{i2}$ is the relative number of persons taking the "bad" decision B_{i2}. It may be called the *observed criminal rate* for situation B_i and may be found in the criminal statistics. The vector

$$\bar{N}_{\bullet 1} = (\bar{N}_{11}, \bar{N}_{21}, \ldots, \bar{N}_{h1}), \text{where } \bar{N}_{i1} = \beta_i v_{i1} \cdot N,$$

gives the number of persons who actually choose the "good" decision; $\bar{v}_{i1} = \frac{\bar{N}_{i1}}{N} = \beta_i v_{i1}$ may be called the *observed morality rate* in the society with respect to situation B_i; of course, $v_{i1} + v_{i2} = 1$ and $\bar{v}_{i1} + \bar{v}_{i2} = \beta_i$. In case of $\beta_i = 0$ the decision problem B_i does not occur, thus the $\bar{N}_{i1}$ and $\bar{N}_{i2}$ do not exist: how persons act in this situation cannot be observed.

The β_i,v_{ij} and the $\bar{v}_{ij}$ are also reproduced in Table 1.1. The effect of a change of the observed criminal rate on the economy may be measured by the elasticities $\epsilon_{Y,\bar{v}_{i2}} = \frac{\partial Y}{\partial \bar{v}_{i2}} \cdot \frac{\bar{v}_{i2}}{Y}$ which will be negative if criminal acts reduce GDP, or the other way round: if "good" behavior increases GDP. This does not always hold true; e.g. following the principle: "Give all you have to the poor", will certainly not increase GDP.

The figures v_{ij} and therefore also the figures $\bar{v}_{ij}$ depend (among others) on the ethical rules $\bar{M}_{ij}^{(1)}, \ldots, \bar{M}_{ij}^{(K)}$ which have influence in the society, on the size of these influences on all persons of the society, and on the mutual influence of people with regard to moral standards, see equation (1.3): the moral state $M_{ij,t}^{(p)}$ of a person p in period t with respect to a decision B_{ij} is a

[72] For simplicity we assume that the probability of being confronted with a moral problem is equal for all persons.

function of $M_{ij,t-1}^{(1)}, \ldots, M_{ij,t-1}^{(N)}$ and of $\bar{M}_{ij}^{(1)}, \ldots, \bar{M}_{ij}^{(K)}, p \in \{1, \ldots, N\}$. $M_{ij}^{(\nu)}$ codetermines the evaluation $V_{ij}^{(p)}$ of a decision B_{ij} of person p (see equation 1.1 in section 1.3), and the relation of $V_{i1}^{(p)}$ and $V_{i2}^{(p)}$ determines the decision $B_{ij}^{(p)}$ (see equation 1.2. As already said, the variable v_{i1} is defined as the relative number of persons whose evaluations are $V_{i1}^{(p)} \geq V_{i2}^{(p)}$. Thus finally the $\bar{v}_{ij}$ are also functions of the moral standards $\bar{M}_{ij}^{(1)}, \ldots, \bar{M}_{ij}^{(K)}$ which have influence in the society. Since the decisions $B_{ij}^{(p)}$ influence the GDP per capita, we have defined the influence of ethics on economics as far as the personal morality is concerned.

All the magnitudes appearing in the foregoing sections depend on the general political and economic order and the actual political and economic policy in the society. We shall come to this in the next section. Some concluding remarks may be appropriate. The simplest way to reduce crime is to reduce β_i, i.e. to reduce the opportunities to commit crime and to enlarge the expectation $E(S_{ij})$ of being punished. Raising the morals M_{ij} is a much more difficult and time consuming task. One has to increase the influence of ethics, i.e. to increase the $\bar{p}_{ij,\nu}^{(\kappa)}$ in equation (1.3) — surely the best way from the moral as well as from the economic point of view (less police, less prisons etc.), if moral and economic requirements run parallel.

1.17 Private Valuations of Collective Issues

Now we come to a second type of moral evaluations. Besides the private problems which lead to a decision of a person, there are issues where the judgment of a person is required. This refers to all public issues where the person as a member of the society is involved though it may not be among the members of the leading group (called government) which decides on the issues. We may differ between the following social states SST to be evaluated by a person p:

1. Political constitution SST_1 of the society with the alternatives

   - SST_{11} (e.g. a fully centralized government, a certain method of determining the government, a well defined set of civil rights (if any), ...)

     ⋮

   - $SST1z$ (e.g. a decentralized government, a certain method of elections of local governments, another set of civil rights, ...)

   All possible alternatives are listed here. They are judged by person p with respect to different criteria $CR_{SST_{11}}, \ldots, CR_{SST_{1M}}$ (e.g. administrative efficiency, degree of personal freedom, degree of equality of the citizen, degree of interior peace, chance of economic development, degree of power at the international scene; but also moral aspects are of importance). "Judgement" means: allocating an order of preference, an integer between $-\bar{z}$ and $+\bar{z}, \bar{z} \geq 1$ to each alternative $SST_{1\zeta}$ from the point of view of the criterion $CR_{SST_{1\mu}}$. Similarly as in section 1.10 we write this evaluation as:

$$V^{(p)}_{SST_{1\zeta,\mu}} = V^{(p)}(SST_{1\zeta}|CR_{SST_{1\mu}}), \quad \zeta = 1, \ldots, z, \quad \mu = 1, \ldots, M,$$

where $-\bar{z} \leq V^{(p)}_{SST_{1\zeta,\mu}} \leq +\bar{z}$.

Now the overall evaluation $V^{(p)}_{SST_{1\zeta}}$ of a political constitution ζ must be arrived at by person p, an evaluation which takes into account all different points of view of judgement. As in section 1.10 the person has to state the relative importance $\alpha^{(p)}_{SST_{11}}, \ldots, \alpha^{(p)}_{SST_{1\mu}}$ of the criteria of judgement, where $\alpha^{(p)}_{SST_{1\mu}} \geq 0$ and $\sum_{\mu=1}^{M} \alpha^{(p)}_{SST_{1\mu}} = 1$

Now the total evaluation may be taken as a weighted average of all different evaluations:

$$V^{(p)}_{SST_{1\zeta}} = \sum_{\mu=1}^{M} \alpha^{(p)}_{SST_{1\mu}} \cdot V^{(p)}_{SST_{1\zeta,\mu}} \quad ,$$

which also lies between $-\bar{z}$ and $+\bar{z}$.

2. The second social state SST_2 refers to the economic order where the alternatives $SST_{21}, \ldots, SST_{2z}$ are to be judged by person p under the criteria $CR_{SST_{21}}, \ldots, CR_{SST_{2M}}$ The extremes in the possible economic orders are a totally planned economy and an absolutely free market economy. But, of course, of more interest are the alternatives in between. The criteria may be the GDP per capity, the distribution of income, the rate of growth of GDP and the stability of the growth path and other economic and non-economic indicators; here also moral considerations come in. Similarly as in 1. above one gets

$$-\bar{z} \leq V^{(p)}_{SST_{2\zeta,\mu}} = V^{(p)}(SST_{2\zeta}|CR_{SST_2}, \mu) \leq \bar{z}$$

and the total evaluation

$$V^{(p)}_{SST_{2,\zeta}} = \sum_{\mu=1}^{M} \alpha^{(p)}_{SST_{2\mu}} \cdot V^{(p)}_{SST_{2\zeta,\mu}}$$

3. This way one continues with other social states $SST_3, \ldots SST_Z$ which comprise public law, civil law, criminal law etc. But also actual policy moves may be included in this evaluation procedure.

We may ask where the evaluation V and the weights α which a person p applies come from. The answer is: they are the product of history and interpersonal influences which are modeled as a Markov Chain, see equation (1.3) in section 1.4 as far as the evaluations V are concerned[73] and equation (∗) in section 1.11 for the weights α. This need not be repeated here.

Some final remarks concerning this section are in order. Among the criteria by which the alternatives are judged there are some economic ones, see above. Thus economic theory is needed to determine the economic consequences of a specific economic order. In a free society all sorts of nonsense may be published and given the name of economic theory. If persons who believe it reach decisive positions in the society the result may be a catastrophe for the nation. The best way to avoid this is to teach all children in school the basic economic relations and facts in a simple way, but always according to the latest results of the generally accepted economic theory.

Here as well as in the foregoing approaches one may argue that no person will be able to evaluate these billions of alternatives. This, of course, is right, but no person is supposed to do so. For almost all alternatives a person will have no judgement, and that means $V = 0$. As a rule only for some adjacent alternatives the person will be able or willing to take over the effort and pains to make up his mind. But there might be exceptions. Sometimes an idea spreads in the population (according to the rules of the Markov chain), where persons evaluate alternatives high which are far off from reality and which are incompatible with other evaluations; e.g. romanticists of the 19th century who idealize the medieval political and economic order, or communists today who do the same with a planned economy and state property. The actual political and economic order is decided by the leading group called government (see section 1.20 and 1.21). Their decisions on all public issues constitute the political and economic order of the next period.

1.18 Transition to the Next Period: Change of Issues

The collective issues which are subject to personal evaluations may change: in the next period new collective issues may have come up which could not be considered in the last period because they did not exist or were of no interest. The decision to build atomic energy plants or not makes only sense after the physical and the engineering knowledge has been accumulated to an amount which makes these plants possible.

Decentralization of production depends on the existence of a fast and reliable information system and of a transportation system which in turn requires the accumulation of knowledge and investment in different fields. The

[73] Substitute $V^{(p)}_{SST_{1\zeta,\mu}}$ for $M^{(p)}_{ij}$ in equation (1.3), $p = 1 \ldots, N$.

knowledge and the ability of a society in period t is the set of all productive capabilities $cap_{1,t}^{(p)}, \ldots, cap_{n,t}^{(p)}$ of all persons $p = 1, \ldots, N$ available at period t (see section 1.11). They change according to the organization of the learning process in the society. We shall come to this later. Moreover, the personal characteristics $\kappa_{1,t}^{(p)}, \ldots, \kappa_{r,t}^{(p)}$ of all persons (see section 1.11) codetermine the productive abilities and thus the relevant issues in the society. Here we assume that this accumulation of knowledge continues in the period considered such that in the next period new collective issues arise with new possible decisions. These new possible decisions have to be evaluated in the same way as the old ones. The evaluation of the "old" decisions may change if new ones become feasible. E.g. new knowledge may make it possible to construct economically effective power plants on the base of sunlight or other practically non–exhaustable resources. It might even be that some old alternatives will never become attractive after new ones become feasible; in that case we may cancel them.

1.19 Collective Decisions

Up to now we have considered only personal decisions and personal valuations which may have effects on other people but are valid only for that person. Now we shall turn to decisions which are valid for the whole society.[74] As a rule, they are taken by a relatively small group of people called government (or by a small number of groups of people, the relations between them being fixed by the constitution or by some other convention). We must differentiate between decisions taken with respect to the basic political and economic order (usually in the form of constitutional laws) and those with respect to current issues within this order (usually in the form of ordinary laws). In this context we shall

[74] Collective decisions cannot simply be derived from individual preferences, except in special cases (only two alternatives, or single–peakedness of a one-dimensional utility function if majority voting is the decision procedure). The voting paradox of Condorcet shows this in the latter case. The general result is the famous impossibility theorem of Arrow (1963): if there are three or more alternatives, then the only social preference order which satisfies a set of quite natural conditions is the dictatorial one: the social preference is determined by the preference of one person. We cannot present this well known result in detail. For a discussion and evaluation of this theorem see e.g. Mas–Colell et al. (1995). The consequence of this theorem is that one has to specify the decision process in detail and that the result, i.e. the social preference, depends on this specification. Thus social welfare depends on the social and political order which determines the decision process. The final decision on collective issues has no immediate relation to the valuation of the alternatives by persons in the society, in general. Democracy tries to constitute a tie between these evaluations and the decision of the government which finally defines the social preferences, but this tie is very loose; moreover, the individual preferences are not constant and may be influenced by the government. We come back to this in section 1.20.

only consider decisions within the limits of the constitution. Constitutional changes are dealt with in chapter 5: "The Theory of the Government".

If there were a dictator p^* (the leading group consists of one person), the decisions would be easily determined: for each issue B_i the decision $B_{i\zeta}$ is chosen for which $V_{i\zeta}^{(p^*)}$ is maximal. But usually there is a group decision. There is a whole literature on the problem of the existence of a social preference ordering.[75] In this approach we assume measurability and interpersonal comparability of preferences — surely restrictive assumptions, but not unreasonable ones in our context.[76] Then we may assign a certain relative weight $g_i^{(p^*)}$ to each person p^* which is member of the leading group with respect to the issue i. It indicates his (or her) influence within the group. Then by informal compromising within the leading group (assumed to have N^* members) a valuation

$$\bar{V}_{ij} = \sum_{p^*=1}^{N^*} g_i^{(p^*)} \cdot V_{ij}^{(p^*)}, \quad g_i^{(p^*)} \geq 0, \quad \sum_{p^*=1}^{N^*} g_i^{(p^*)} = 1^{77} \tag{1.31}$$

of a decision B_{ij} emerges.

If the capacity of compromising and reaching a decision within the leading group were unlimited and if there were no differences in the decision process between basic decisions on the general political and social order and current and more short term decisions within this order, the political and economic order $\mathcal{O}$ of the next period would be determined by

$$\mathcal{O}_i^* \Leftarrow \max(\bar{V}_{i1}, \ldots, \bar{V}_{iz}) \tag{1.32}$$

---

75 For a survey see e.g. Krelle (1968), pp. 85 ff. There are new results, see Mas-Colell, Winston, Green (1995): Strategic voting must be excluded, i.e. voting against the own preferences. This implies that the preferences of a person are common knowledge.

76 In our context these assumptions are not so strange as it is sometimes depicted in the literature. For many parts of economics one does not need these restrictive assumptions. But for other purposes one needs them. E.g. the normal utilization of public polls depends on them, and (to my knowledge) nobody has objected to this until now. E.g. each year the Institut für Demoskopie Allensbach asks a representative sample of the German population: Sehen Sie dem neuen Jahr mit Hoffnungen oder Befürchtungen entgegen? It offers four answers: „Mit Hoffnungen, mit Befürchtungen, mit Skepsis, Unentschieden“ and forms the difference of the percentage of answers of this year compared to those of the last year, which implies measurable and interpersonal comparable preferences. Of course, there will be a certain degree of uncertainty connected with these figures; we take that into account by considering only integer values. In this book we assume that a person can state his largest possible affection or his largest possible aversion or his indifference to a phenomenon and that it is able to interpolate between these values in a coarse way similar to a professor who grades the examination papers of his or her students.

77 If all $g_i^{(p*)}$ are assumed to be equal, the median of all evaluations is usually taken as the collective preferred decision. This is surely right if one assumes a majority voting procedure. We suggest the arithmetic mean instead of the median for the case of different personal weights and informal bargaining. But this is an empirical question.

But the capacity of processing issues is limited, and decisions on the basic political and economic order are usually much more difficult than decisions on the current policy. But we disregard this difference here. We may assume that in one period only a small number γ of issues can be treated and solved by the leading group, and these are the *most urgent* ones. *Most urgent* are those, where the possible new state $B_{i\zeta}$ gives a value $\bar{V}_{i\zeta}, \zeta \neq 1$ which in the opinion of the leading group is very much larger than the value $\bar{V}_{i1}$ of the present state. We reorder the issues according to the possible gains which they promise if the *best* decision $B_{i\zeta}$ (according to the opinion of the leading group as stated above) is taken. If there are n issues in the collective domain we get:

$$\begin{aligned} \Delta\bar{V}_{1\zeta_1} &= \bar{V}_{1\zeta_1} - \bar{V}_{11}, \\ &\vdots \\ \Delta\bar{V}_{n\zeta_n} &= \bar{V}_{n\zeta_n} - \bar{V}_{n1}, \end{aligned} \tag{1.33}$$

where $\Delta\bar{V}_{1\zeta_1} \geq \Delta\bar{V}_{2\zeta_2} \geq \cdots \geq \Delta\bar{V}_{n\zeta_n}$. Changes in the basic political and economic order are only made for issues $1, \ldots, \gamma$, where the advantage of a change exceeds a certain threshold value $\Delta\bar{V}$. Thus, only if $\Delta V_{i,\zeta_i} > \Delta\bar{V}, i = 1, \ldots, \gamma$, where $\Delta\bar{V}$ is a rather large number, i.e. only in the case of a rather large advantage, changes in the basic order and in the current policy are made, and this only for a small number γ of issues.

1.20 Determination of the Leading Group and of the Influence of Each Person within the Group

The problems of selection of the persons p^* which form the leading group (the government) and of the determination of their relative influence g within the group have still to be solved. In the feudal system this problem is solved in a very simple way: the family into which one is born decides on the political and economic position of a person. In a democracy there are elections which directly or indirectly determine the composition of the leading group and thus the political and economic order of the society.

There are many different election systems. We assume here a system which is a simplified form of the German election system.[78] For each issue i we reorder the possible alternatives $B_{i1}, \ldots, B_{iz}$ according to the amount of freedom which they give to the individual: the more freedom, the larger the chance of scientific and technical progress, but also: the larger the risk of personal

[78] This should be taken as an example.

failure, of distress, misery, insecurity, crime. In this new order[79] the realized alternative lies somewhere between B_{i1} and B_{iz}, as a rule. As already stated, all valuations $V_{i1}^{(p)}, \ldots, V_{iz}^{(p)}$ of a person p are integers between a maximum $\bar{z} > 0$ and a minimum $-\bar{z} < 0$, where a valuation of zero means: no judgment, or indifference.

As an example we consider four basic types of moral valuations of the alternatives B_{ij} for the possible solution of an issue B_i if one orders the alternatives according to the degree of freedom that they grant to the persons: increasing (the liberal line), decreasing (the communist line), first increasing and after a while decreasing (the social market policy line) or the opposite (the idea that a pure market economy and a pure planned economy may function but not a mixture). These types may be the possible "party lines" or "platforms" of four different parties, see Fig. 1.9. A "party line" of a party $P_\rho, \rho = 1, \ldots, 4$ in our example, is a set of (in general moral) valuations $M_{i1}(P_\rho), \ldots, M_{iz}(P_\rho)$ of the alternative decisions for each collective issue i. As a rule, the valuation $M_{ij}^{(p)}$ of a person p will not coincide with any party line $M_{ij}(P_\rho)$.

The distance $D(i, p, P_\rho)$ of the moral valuations of an issue i by a person p to the party line of party P_ρ can be measured by the quadratic deviation of the two valuations:

$$D(i, p, P_\rho) := \sum_{j=1}^{z} [M_{ij}^{(p)} - M_{ij}(P_\rho)]^2.$$

Summed up over all issues this yields the *total distance* of person p from the party line of party ρ:[80]

$$D(p, P_\rho) := \sum_i D(i, p, P_\rho).$$

Person p elects that party to which his total distance $D(p, P_\rho)$ is smallest. Let $V(P_\rho)$ be the number of votes for party ρ (by persons with minimum distance to party ρ) and let there be R parties. Then the relative votes for party ρ are

$$v(P_\rho) = \frac{V(P_\rho)}{\sum_{\rho=1}^{R} V(P_\rho)}.$$

If there are H seats in the parliament, $n_\rho := v(P_\rho) \cdot H$ seats are won by party ρ[81] , and these are taken by the n_ρ first ranking members of party ρ. Let us

---

[79] The one–dimensional order of the alternatives is a simplification, of course. A more–dimensional approach would be more appropriate. But we choose here the simplest case.

[80] For simplicity we do not take into account possible different weights of the issues. For a certain person a certain issue may be of great importance, for another negligible. But on average this may balance out.

[81] We do not state the change to integer values and a possible lower bound for votes in order to obtain a seat in parliament.

reorder the persons according to their distance to the party line and assume that those persons whose distance to the party line is minimal are members of the party and that their ranking depends on this distance to the party line and on personal characteristics.

Thus for party ρ we have for persons $p_1, p_2, \ldots$:

$$D(p_1, P_\rho) \leq D(p_2, P_\rho) \leq \ldots$$

and the persons $p_1, p_2, \ldots, p_{n_\rho}$ are elected. Let us assume that party ρ (or a coalition of some parties) has the majority, then persons $p_1, p_2, \ldots, p_{n_\rho}$ form the *leading group* $p_1^*, \ldots, p_{n_\rho}^*$ in the society. Their valuation of collective issues decides on the actual political and social order, after the relative influence $g_i^{(p^*)}$ of each person p^* on decisions of type i has been determined. The influence of each person p^* depends on his personal characteristics such as eloquence, capability to convince others, knowledge in different fields, ability to present himself or herself in television and interviews etc.. We called them $\kappa_1^{(p)}, \ldots, \kappa_r^{(p)}$, see section 1.12. They will be different for different persons. They could assume any integer value between 0 and $\bar{z}$: $0 \leq \kappa_\rho \leq \bar{z}, \rho = 1, \ldots, r$. The value $\bar{z}$ is the maximum amount of a capability, a value of 0 means that these characteristics are lacking. These personal characteristics follow a certain distribution in the society as well as in the group of persons who are elected. In case of a binomial distribution with a basic probability of $0,5$ (which is a reasonable assumption)[82] and e.g. $\bar{z} = 5$ one gets the relative frequencies $w(\kappa_\rho)$ of persons p having a size K_ρ of the personal characteristics κ_ρ as follows

size K_ρ of the personal characteristics κ_ρ	0	1	2	3	4	5
relative frequency $w(\kappa_\rho)$	0,03	0,16	0,31	0,31	0,16	0,03

where: $\sum_{\kappa_\rho} w(\kappa_\rho) = 1$

The weight $g_i^{(p^*)}$ of a person p^* in determining the party valuation $\bar{V}_{ij}$ of the alternative B_{ij} is a function of all of these characteristics. For simplicity we assume a simple additive formula. Let $\kappa_\rho^{(p^*)}$ be the size of a personal characteristic κ_ρ of person p^* and let $\gamma_{i\rho}$ be the importance of the characteristic κ_ρ for problem i, $\quad 0 \leq \gamma_{i\rho} \leq \Gamma$, $\quad \Gamma$ a positive integer. In this context we take $\gamma_{i\rho}$ as given. Then an index of the absolute influence of person p^* on the party evaluation $\bar{V}_{ij}$ of a decision B_{ij} would be

[82] Of course, other figures are possible. This is an empirical question.

$$G_i^{(p^*)} = \sum_{\rho=1}^{r} \gamma_{i\rho}\kappa_\rho^{(p^*)} > 0, \text{ and the relative influence:}$$
$$g_i^{(p^*)} = \frac{G_i^{(p^*)}}{\sum_{p^*} G_i^{(p^*)}} \tag{1.34}$$

This surely is a simplified approach. An alternative would be to assume that there is a predetermined order of ruling a country: a president, a prime minister, ministers, secretaries of state, party chiefs, chairmen of parliamentary groups etc., and their influence is given by the constitution or by the rules of procedure (subject to earlier decisions). Now the distribution of persons p^* of the ruling group over these positions determines the influence $g_i^{(p^*)}$ of each person p^*. This distribution depends on the personal characteristics of these persons, so that we are back at the first approach.

1.21 Transition to the Next Period: Change of Government

The issues which necessitate decisions may change in time, but also the people who decide on the alternative change.

The first phenomenon has already been dealt with (see section 1.18). We now turn to the second problem: change of the personal composition of the leading group (the government). This implies a change of decisions also on the old issues, since the preferences of different people are different in general, and this keeps the society moving.

Let there be l parties in the beginning of the period with different party lines (or party platforms). We assume that they mainly differ in their attitude towards personal freedom of the citizens or (inversely) in their attitude towards (organized and enforced) solidarity. How much personal freedom should a person give up in order to comply with solidarity as perceived by the leading group? Or to put it in popular terms: how much liberalism and how much socialism should be realized in the society?[83] Fig. 1.10a-c show (as an example) the party lines of 4 parties. Let us assume that party 1 (= P_1 in Fig. 1.10a, a

[83] This seems to be the basic issue now. In former times other issues were predominant: feudal system versus democracy or church power versus secular power. — Of course, liberalism should not be confused with egoism. A liberal society as it is conceived here does not hinder anybody to give all it owns to the poor but it does not compel him to do so. It lets the system determine the distribution of income and wealth but does not take away something from the rich to give it to the poor. In this sense, the "Soziale Marktwirtschaft" in Germany is a mixture of liberal and socialist features; the German parties have more or less the profile of P_3 in Fig. 1.9 and Fig. 1.10b.

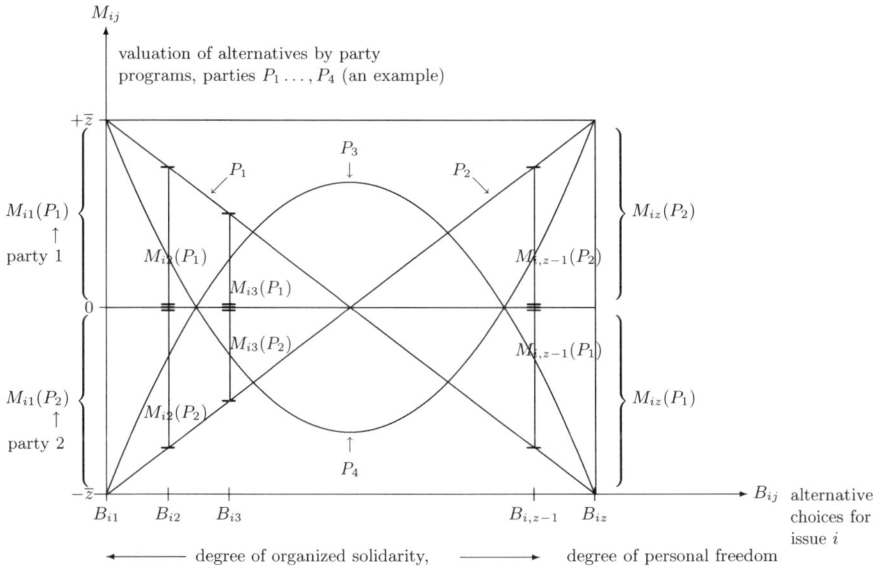

Figure 1.9. Possible Party Lines

socialist party) won the election at the beginning of the period.[84] Then this party presents the government out of its leading personalities, as shown in an example in the foregoing section. Now the other parties $P_2, \ldots, P_4$ in Fig. 1.10 see where the trend of the political convictions in the population is going and they adapt to a certain degree to the political line of the winning party P_1. This may be formalized as follows.

Let the difference in the party line of a party π to the winning party 1 in terms of the moral valuation $M_{ij} - M(B_{ij})$ of the alternative B_{ij} be:

$$D_{1,\pi}(B_{ij}) = \left[M^{(1)}(B_{ij}) - M^{(\pi)}(B_{ij})\right] \tag{1.35}$$

Then party π corrects its line in the direction of the line of the winning party 1 in order to win the next election or at least to improve the result of the election. This correction may be modeled as

$$\Delta M_{ij}(P_\pi) = \gamma_{1,\pi} \cdot D_{1,\pi}(B_{ij}), \quad 0 < \gamma_{1,\pi} < 1 \tag{1.36}$$

$\gamma_{1,\pi}$ must be empirically determined.

Fig. 1.10a-c illustrate this change of the party lines of parties $P_2, \ldots, P_4$.

This correction takes place in the interval between the last and the new election. In our model we may (for simplicity) put this next election in the

[84] The "winning" of elections may have different meanings, according to the specific electoral law. We do not go into these details.

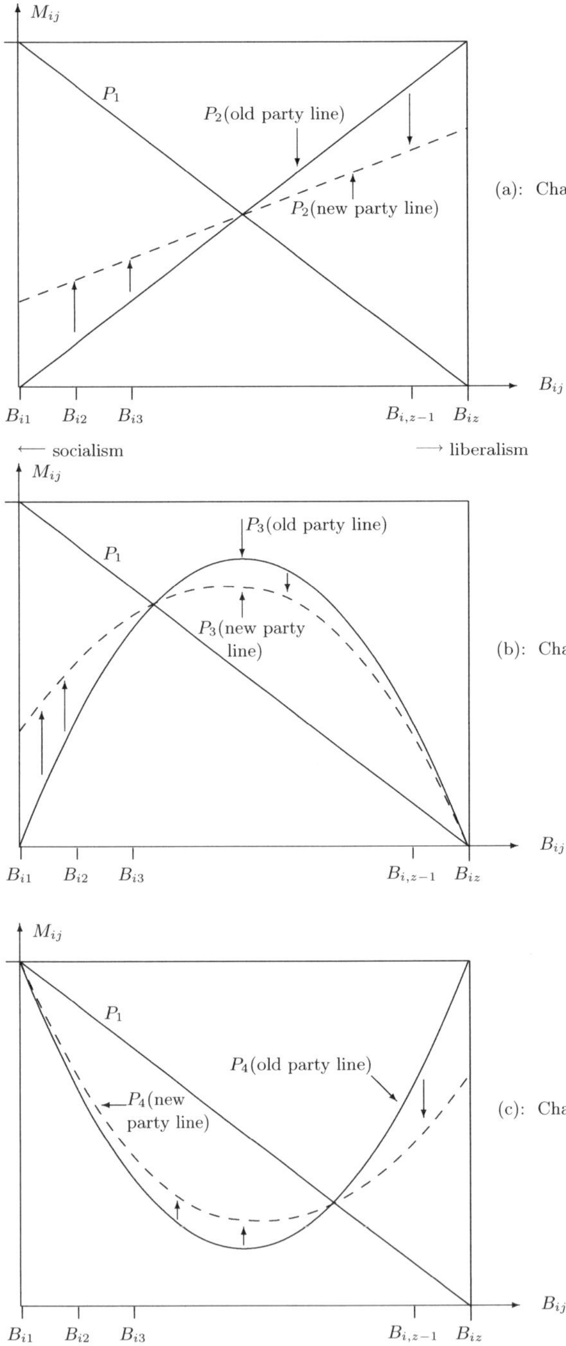

(a): Change of party line, party P_2

(b): Change of party line, party P_3

(c): Change of party line, party P_4

Figure 1.10 Change of Party Lines of Parties $P_2, \ldots, P_4$ after P_1 has won Elections

beginning of the next period. Then at the beginning of the next period there are different party lines with different leading persons who want to be elected by persons whose preferences have changed and where additional issues appear.

1.22 Digression 1: The Interaction of the Spiritual Domain and Economics

In this section we want to show how in our theory the philosophies (this word taken in the broadest sense, including theologies, ideologies etc.) influence the decisions of persons (in particular: the economic decisions) and how in turn the situation of persons (in particular: the economic situation) influences the philosophies. The first direction may be identified with the name of Hegel, the second with the name of Marx.

Let there be K philosophies documented in books known in the society. A book is an arrangement of symbols which may have different meanings and is open to different interpretations. Take the Bible as an example. The words (in Hebrew or Greek) are fixed (through there might be different versions, but we neglect this feature). Thus a philosophy $\bar{\Phi}^{(k)}$ is given by an assembly of symbols which we call words $w_1^{(k)}, \dots, w_z^{(k)}$:

$$\bar{\Phi}^{(k)} = (w_1^{(k)}, \dots, w_z^{(k)}).$$

Somebody has to give a meaning to the symbols. Person p in situation B_i in period t converts the symbols to a set of understandable propositions $\Sigma_{i,1,p,t}^{(k)}, \dots, \Sigma_{i,z,p,t}^{(k)}$. Thus

$$\bar{\Phi}^{(k)} \longrightarrow \Phi_{i,p,t}^{(k)} = \{\Sigma_{i,1,p,t}^{(k)}, \dots, \Sigma_{i,z,p,t}^{(k)}\}.$$

This set of propositions is a subjective interpretation of a text by person p. But person p is not an empty page: it is shaped by traits as described in section 1.10–1.12 which are adjoined to the initial condition $B_{i,t}^{(p)}$ where the person is in at time t. Thus the interpretation $\Sigma_{\zeta,p,t}^{(p)}$ is a function of the situation of person p at $B_{i,t}^{(p)}$:

$$\Sigma_{i,\zeta,p,t}^{(k)} = \Sigma_{\zeta,p,t}^{(k)}(B_{i,t}^{(p)}), \quad k = 1\dots,K,\ i = 1,\dots,h,\ \zeta = 1,\dots,z.$$

It implies also moral evaluations of possible decisions:

$$\Phi_{i,p,t}^{(k)} \longrightarrow \bar{M}_{i,j,p,t}^{(k)}$$

In equation (1.3) in section 1.4 we neglected the variables p and t as arguments of $\bar{M}_{ij}^{(1)}, \dots, \bar{M}_{ij}^{K}$ which is possible in the very short run and if we consider the situation of a specific person. Thus the sequence

$$\bar{\Phi}^{(k)} \longrightarrow \Phi_{p,t}^{(k)} \longrightarrow \bar{M}_{i,j}^{(k)}(p,t)$$

describes the influence of philosophies on the evaluation of alternatives in general (the Hegel direction). But, as explained in section 1.4, the actual evaluation of an alternative depends not only on moral judgements coming from philosophies, but also on judgements of other persons. In section 1.4, equation (1.3), we described that relation by

$$\tilde{M}_{ij,t} = \tilde{M}_{ij,t-1} \cdot P_{ij} \tag{1.37}$$

where P_{ij} is the matrix of the influences $p_{ij,\nu}^{(\nu')}$ of person ν' on person ν and of the influences $\bar{p}_{ij,\nu}^{(\kappa)}$ of philosophy κ on person ν. These influences $p_{ij,\nu}^{(\nu')}$ and $\bar{p}_{ij,\nu}^{(\kappa)}$ were taken as given. But they depend on the information system, and now we turn to the derivation of this dependence. We now take the philosophies as given.

We start by explaining the influence $p_{ij,\nu}^{(\nu')}$ of person ν' on person ν in judging the decision ij. There are two types of determinants: personal relations and those exerted by the information system. A person $\nu' \in \{N\}$ knows persons $\nu \in \{N\}$ because they are members of the same family, neighbors or friends, and it communicates with them. Let $\{N_\nu^{(\nu')}\} \subset \{N\}$ be the set of all persons ν' which communicate with person ν and let $\hat{p}_{ij,\nu}^{(\nu')}$ be the influence which person $\nu' \in \{N_\nu^{(\nu')}\}$ exerts on person ν in the context ij.

Moreover, there exists an information system (newspapers, periodicals, circular letters, radio, television, schools, universities, churches, etc.) which transfers information and valuation of some persons (which are in a leading position either in government of in the information system) to a large number of others. Consider an information system $I \in \{\bar{I}\}$, where $\{\bar{I}\}$ is the set of all information systems. Let $\{N_\nu^{(I)}\}$ be the set of all persons ν which receive messages by the information system I. There is an editorial staff for each system I. We assume that the chief editorial manager, call him $\nu^*(I) \in \{N\}$, determines the general political and philosophical line. Let $\hat{\hat{p}}_{ij,\nu}^{\nu^*(I)}$ be the influence of person $\nu^*(I)$ on person ν via the information system I with respect to the decision ij. Then the $p_{ij,\nu}^{(\nu')}$ in equation (1.3) are explained by

a. the personal relationships to other persons:

$$p_{ij,\nu}^{(\nu')} = \begin{cases} \hat{p}_{ij,\nu}^{(\nu')}, & \text{if } \nu' \in \{N_\nu^{(\nu')}\} \\ 0, & \text{if } \nu' \notin \{N_\nu^{(\nu')}\} \end{cases}$$

b. the influence of those who control the information system:

$$p_{ij,\nu}^{(\nu')} = \begin{cases} \hat{\hat{p}}_{ij,\nu}^{(\nu')}, & \text{if } \nu' = \nu^*(I) \text{ and } \nu \in \{N_\nu^{(I)}\}, I \in \{\bar{I}\} \\ 0, & \text{if } \nu' \neq \nu^*(I) \text{ and(or) } \nu \notin \{N_\nu^{(I)}\}, I \in \{\bar{I}\} \end{cases}$$

The size $\hat{p}_{i,j,\nu}^{(\nu')}$ or $\hat{\hat{p}}_{i,j,\nu}^{(\nu')}$ depends on the personal characteristics of the person and are taken as given.

Now it is very important which person ν' is the chief editorial manager $\nu^*(I)$ in one of the information systems I. This is different in different economic, social and political systems. The person may be determined by the owner of the information system, if there is private property, by the government (in dictatorships), by the political parties, by organizations like churches. This is part of the general order of the society which is subject to collective decisions, see section 1.17 to 1.20.

We now turn to the direct influence of philosophies, measured by the parameters $\bar{p}_{ij,\nu}^{(\kappa)}$ in equation (1.3). We differentiate between two classes of persons:

a. persons ν which know theologies and philosophies and are familiar with the moral rules which follow from them; these persons form the "educated class", a subset $\{N^{**}\} \subset \{N\}$ of all persons in the society: $\nu \in \{N^{**}\}$. Each person $\nu \in \{N^{**}\}$ is influenced, as far as the judgement on a decision ij is concerned, by a philosophy κ, $\kappa = 1, \dots, K$ to the degree $\bar{p}_{ij,\nu}^{**(\kappa)}$:

$$\bar{p}_{ij,\nu}^{(\kappa)} = \begin{cases} p_{ij,\nu}^{**(\kappa)}, & \text{if } \nu \in \{N^{**}\}, \kappa = 1, \dots, K \\ 0, & \text{if } \nu \notin \{N^{**}\} \end{cases}$$

This is a distribution of the influences $p_{ij,\nu}^{**(\kappa)}$ in the society which depends on the school curriculum, on the courses of instruction at the different levels of education which in turn depend on the general political order of the society.

b. There are person ν which do not belong to the "educated class" in the above sense, but nevertheless may be well informed on the moral consequences of philosophies through the influences of other persons (parents, friends, teachers, ...). This influence has already been considered under the headline of personal relationships.

Thus the $p_{ij,\nu}^{(\nu')}$ and the $\bar{p}_{ij,\nu}^{(\kappa)}$ are explained by the general political and economic order of the society. We do not go into the details here.

This comprises the Hegel type relation: the influence of the spiritual side of the society on the actual decisions of persons.

Now we come to the opposite causal relation: the influence of the actual situation of persons on philosophies which we may call: Marx type relations. There are two types of influences:

1. the always new interpretation of existing philosophies in the light of the actual situation $B_i^{(p)}$ in which the person p is in, which cares for the interpretation. This has already been considered and will be repeated here:

$$\bar{\Phi}^{(k)} \longrightarrow \Phi^{(k)}_{i,p,t} = \{\Sigma^{(k)}_{i,1,p,t}, \ldots, \Sigma^{(k)}_{i,z,p,t}\},$$

$$\text{where } B^{(p)}_{i,t} \longrightarrow \Sigma^{(k)}_{i,\zeta,p,t}, \quad \zeta = 1, \ldots, z, \; i = 1, \ldots, h$$

$$\text{and } \Phi^{(p)}_{i,p,t} \longrightarrow \bar{M}^{(k)}_{i,j,p,t},$$

The moral judgement on a move from B_i to B_{ij} depends on the interpretation of philosophy k by person p in situation B_i at time t.

2. But philosophies do not fall from heaven, they are invented by persons p^* under the influence of their situation $B^{(p^*)}_{i,t}$ at time t. Only few people are able to develop a new philosophy. Thus the appearance of a new philosophy is a rare event. We may model this as follows. There is an urn with lots of lottery tickets. Nature draws one ticket per period from that urn. 95 % or more are zeros: if nature draws one of those tickets, there will be no new philosophy developed in that period: nature does not give the necessary inspiration to a person. Let us say: 5 % of the tickets carry the name of a person $p^* \in \{p_n, p_{n+1}, \ldots, p_N\}$ which may receive the basic idea of a new philosophy as inspiration from heaven (or from hell, thus we better say: from nature). Thus if nature draws the ticket of a person that means: it inspires that person to a new philosophy which, of course, is influenced by the personality of the person and his situation B_i. A certain degree of knowledge and education is necessary to be able to receive that inspiration; thus only a certain partial set $\{p_n, p_{n+1}, \ldots, p_N\}$ of all persons $\{p_1, \ldots, p_N\}$ is represented in the urn.

As pointed out earlier, a philosophy in the sense this word is used here does not need to be a "philosophy" in the sense of Kant[85] . Here we mean by

---

[85] According to Kant (1787), p. 818 ("Von dem Ideal des höchsten Gutes als einem Bestimmungsgrunde des letzten Zweckes der reinen Vernunft"). The following three problems should be dealt with in a philosophy

1. What can I know? (the problem of the theory of cognition: What is truth?)
2. What should I do? (the problem of individual and social ethics)
3. What may I hope for? (This comprises the questions: Where do I come from, and where do I go? What will be after my death? What is the sense of my life? Where does the evil of this world come from? ... and related formulations)

There are many different possible answers to these questions, and each combination of the answers defines a philosophy or a theology. We do not go into details, but shall only hint at the possible contents of a philosophy. Of course, there is no agreement as to these possible contents. In the encyclical "Fides et Ratio" (1998), pope Jean–Paul II complains that the modern philosophies do not try to give answers to the metaphysical question (c) above, or in other words: they are concerned with problems (a) and (b). He wants to encourage the philosophers to live up to their name ("lovers of wisdom") and close the gap to theology. Faith and reason are "the two ails of human mind", and he treats them as having equal rights. I think that there is a fundamental difference between the first two types of problems and the third one. One can well understand "philosophy" a set of coherent and consistent propositions which describe parts of the world and thus give some orientation for decisions and behavior. Thus part of economics is a philosophy in this sense.

1.23 Digression 2: The Connection to Sociology and Political Science

As pointed out in section 1.17 a person has to judge the political, social and economic order of the society it is living in as well as alternatives which are realized elsewhere or exist only as project or draft. Of course, nobody will know all alternatives of social orders which existed at some time or are suggested in the literature. This does not matter, they get the evaluation figure 0. The social orders are judged with respect to the following principles:

a. Degree of freedom and possibility of development which they grant to a person

b. Degree of safety and invulnerability which they guarantee to a person. This refers to the internal legal order and protection against crime as well as the protection against assaults and raids from outside.

c. Degree of economic success compared to other societies in a similar situation, and compared to other, non-realized alternatives.

d. Degree of the justice of income and property distribution and of the justice of intergenerational distribution

e. Degree of possible political influence

f. Possibility of an advancement in the social pyramid.

⋮

There may be still other principles to judge a social order, but these seem to be the most important ones.

A person evaluates the social orders with respect to the point of view i by a figure v_i between $-\bar{z}$ and $+\bar{z}$:

$$-\bar{z} \leq v_i \leq +\bar{z}, \quad \bar{z} \geq 1, \text{an integer}, \ v_i \text{ also an integer}, \ i \in A = \{a, b, \dots\}$$

The person weighs all points of view $i \in A$ by a figure $\gamma_i \geq 0, \sum_{i \in A} \gamma_i = 1$ to get the total valuation of the social order under consideration by:

$$v = \sum_{i \in A} \gamma_i v_i, \quad \text{where } -\bar{z} \leq v_i \leq +\bar{z}$$

---

why the modern philosophers shy away from dealing with these metaphysical problems and leave them to the theologians.

This valuation will be different from person to person, in general.

Actually, things are a bit more complicated: The points of view $i \in A$ may be disintegrated further. We show this for the principle a: the degree of freedom. For the other principles things are analogous. We may distinguish between

a_1 : freedom of expression, freedom of the press

a_2 : freedom of assembling and of demonstration

a_3 : freedom to form political parties

a_4 : freedom of economic activities

$\vdots$

and other freedoms along this line. All these freedoms are (in general) limited. E.g. the freedom a_1 of expression is subdivided into freedoms $a_{11}, \ldots, a_{1z}$ with different limitations; e.g.: a_{11} = freedom without any limitation; a_{12} = only invitations to murder are forbidden; a_{13} in addition: pornography is forbidden and so on. The person evaluates the alternatives $a_{11}, \ldots, a_{1z}$ by $v_{a11}, \ldots, v_{a1z}$ where

$$-\bar{z} \leq v_{a1\zeta} \leq +\bar{z}, \quad \zeta = 1, \ldots, z$$

Most people would prefer some limitations of the freedom of the press to keep some privacy in the society and to prevent the press to become a school of crime. Now we assume that the persons weigh the $a_{11}, \ldots, a_{1z}$ by figures $\alpha_{a11}, \ldots, \alpha_{a1z}$, $0 \leq \alpha_{a1\zeta}, \sum_{\zeta=1}^{z} \alpha_{a1\zeta} = 1$ such that the total index of preference for "freedom of expression" by the person considered becomes

$$v_{a1} = \sum_{\zeta=1}^{z} \alpha_{a1\zeta} \cdot v_{a1\zeta}, \quad \text{where } -\bar{z} \leq v_{a1} \leq +\bar{z}$$

Similarly we get the valuation figures $v_{a2}, \ldots, v_{az}$. There are weights for the $a_1, \ldots, a_z$, say $\beta_{a1}, \ldots, \beta_{az}, 0 \leq \beta_{ak}, \sum_{k=1}^{z} \beta_{ak} = 1$ such that the total evaluation of the social order under consideration with respect to freedom (which forms the "point of view a") becomes

$$v_1 = \sum_{k=1}^{z} \beta_{ak} \cdot v_{ak}$$

The valuations $v_2, \ldots$ with respect to other points of view are attained in a similar way.

But how arise the weights $\alpha, \beta, \gamma, \ldots$ for the different points of view and the evaluations v of the alternatives? They are not simply inventions of the person but are to a large extent socially determined: one person influences the other, and there are influences by books and tradition. A Markov Chain as in equation (1.3) in section 1.4 is the right instrument to analyze and reproduce these interrelations. The M in equation (1.3) has to be substituted by α, β, γ, or v, respectively. We do not repeat this approach.

But this shifts the unknown from the α, β, γ and v to the transition probabilities p in equation (1.3). And this is where sociology comes in.

There are n types of work. Some of them are intimately related and form trades (or occupations, jobs, professions). The names of people still reflect these medieval groups: Smith, Miller, shepherd, shoemaker, weaver and so on. The economic activities form the social groups. In the 19th century this is simplified to the groups of workers, employees, entrepreneurs, and capitalists and land owners. Now a process of diversification has taken place. In the "Statistisches Jahrbuch 1999 für die Bundesrepublik Deutschland", p. 587 ff. one finds 42 sections of the German economy. Each sector forms a group of persons who communicate almost daily and influence each other more intensively than they are influenced by persons of other professions.

The second principle of forming groups are common hobbies: sports, music, theater, mountain climbing, sailing etc. There are thousands of clubs which unite people of the same hobby. They are communicating much more among themselves than with other people. The same applies for people with common political convictions – they form the rank and file of the parties – and for people with strong religious convictions. In former times the family connections have also been strong, but now they are rather weak, as a rule. The ties between persons of the same group are much stronger, and that means: the p_{ij} in equation (1.3) in section 1.4 are much larger for people of the same group as for people belonging to different groups.

The number of the groups increases with technical progress which produces new sectors of the economy and thus new occupations and new groups. The number of clubs also increases with income per capita because this leaves more spare time and increases the vacation time and thus leaves room for developing otherwise hidden capabilities and dispositions outside of the main occupation.

This may suffice to indicate how the connection to sociology may be constructed. But this is not our topic here.

1.24 The Direct Influence of Ethics on Normal Economic Decisions. A Short Review and Preview

The cases which we have considered hitherto are personal decisions of economic or noneconomic character where a "bad" decision may possibly lead to punishment (situations $B_{12}, \dots, B_{h2}$ in Table 1.1). Moreover, we have considered personal evaluations of different possible political and economic states of the society. But normal economic decisions in the field of consumption, investment, exports, imports, portfolio composition etc. are not of this kind.

There is a broad field of admissible lawful decisions, limits as far as the law is concerned are rather broad, and the normal decisions fall within these limits. But ethics is not silent in these cases: it influences the economic decisions directly.

The general approach is the same in the foregoing sections. We enumerate all possible situations where an economic agent may find himself and has to decide on certain economic actions. Since all economic evaluations appear in discrete numbers between a lower limit $-\bar{z}$ and an upper limit $+\bar{z}$, $\bar{z} \geq 1$, an integer, there are only finite many combinations of all these variables, that means: finite many possible situations, where an economic agent has to choose an alternative, and only finite many alternatives. Thus we have for economic decisions the same basic approach which may be illustrated as follows:

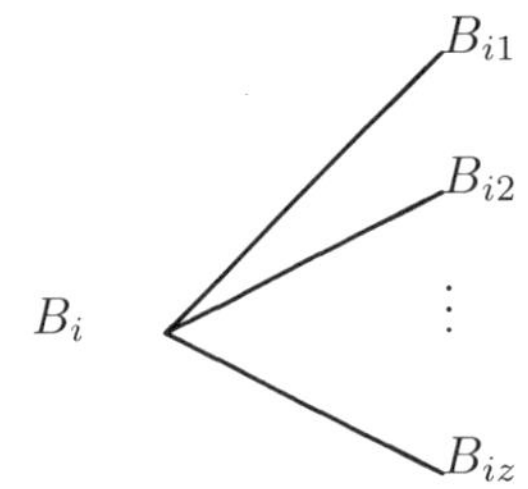

Of course, the initial situation B_i has to be described exactly and the possible moves to $B_{i1}, \ldots, B_{iz}$ as well. Both are different in different economic situations. We have specified the situations and possible moves (or decisions) for private households and we shall do that for firms, banks including the central bank, the government, the education and research system. For simplicity, we leave out foreign countries. Moreover, we have indicated or shall indicate the decision criteria for each of these economic and noneconomic agents. This defines the dynamics of the system, i.e. the rules of transition from one period to the next. In all of these decisions economics as well as ethics are involved.

1.25 The Conditional Sales or Purchases of Capital Stock and Securities

As already stated in the foregoing sections, the asset prices are not known, when the person has to put his sale or purchase orders. Let there be H capital stocks $KSt_1, \ldots, KSt_H$, all traded at the exchange. Their prices at the end of period -1 (i.e. on the beginning of period 0) are $v_{KSt,1,-1}, \ldots, v_{KSt,H,-1}$. For period 0 the prices $v_{KSt,h,0} = v_{KSt,h,-1} + \Delta v_{KSt,h,-1}$, $h = 1, \ldots, H$, are valid.[86] Similarly for securities. Let there be K securities with prices $v_{SEC,k,-1}, k = 1, \ldots, K$ at the end of period -1 and prices $v_{SEC,k} = v_{SEC,k,-1} + \Delta v_{SEC,k,-1}$ during period 0 till the beginning of period 1. To simplify the notation we put $(W_1, \ldots, W_n) = (KSt_1, \ldots, KSt_H, SEC_1, \ldots, SEC_K)$ and $(v_1, \ldots, v_n) = (v_{KSt,1}, \ldots, v_{SEC,K})$ and we call W a "security" or an "asset".

If all prices for goods as well as for securities would be known to the person before it decides on consumption, saving and the composition of his portfolio, there would be no uncertainty problem for the person which makes it difficult to come to a decision. In Fig. 1.7 and 1.11 this situation is illustrated. First the person chooses how to divide his net income between consumption and saving. Then it decides which commodities to buy for consumption purposes and which transfer payments to make. In a third step[87] it decides on the allocation of saving, i.e. on the portfolio composition – always by grading the alternatives according to different points of view and by weighting these points of view as shown in equation 1.1. We shall not repeat that here. But, unfortunately, things are not so easy. The commodity prices may be fixed in advance and known to the person because the producer fixes them in advance. We come to that later on. But the security prices are fixed by brokers on the base of *total* conditional demand and supply of securities; that means: the person's demand and supply must be decided upon before the prices of securities are known but may be conditioned upon these prices. This means in our model: for sales or purchases of securities the prices in the future period 0 are unknown to the person when it has to order his sales or purchases of assets. The person may put in some money and effort by the amount CO to reduce the uncertainty of future prices. Unfortunately, the costs have to be paid before one gets the result, i.e. it is uncertain to which extent the information enables the person to choose a better composition of his portfolio and thus improve the wealth at the end of period 0. But the person may guess that the advantage may be estimated by a rate δ by which his wealth will be improved compared to the wealth without that (inside) information. δ is an expectation value with a variance $Var(\delta)$. Thus it may happen that actually (ex post) the result obtained with information may be worse than without it.[88] But this will be an exception.

The person will decide to get the additional information by paying the price CO (in general) if $WE(1+\delta)-CO \geq WE$, i.e. if the expected wealth WE and the rate of advantage δ of buying the information are large enough and the cost CO of this information is small enough: $WE \geq \frac{CO}{\delta}$. The additional inside information consists of expectation and variance of the profits $d_1, \ldots, d_H$ to

[86] As usual we shall omit the index 0 in the following.

[87] Of course, it is possible to throw all three steps together into one simultaneous decision. But the three step procedure is much nearer to reality and easier to handle. Thus we stick to it.

[88] The situation is similar to that of a person who has to decide to read a book or not. After it has read it it knows whether it was worthwhile reading – but his time is lost.

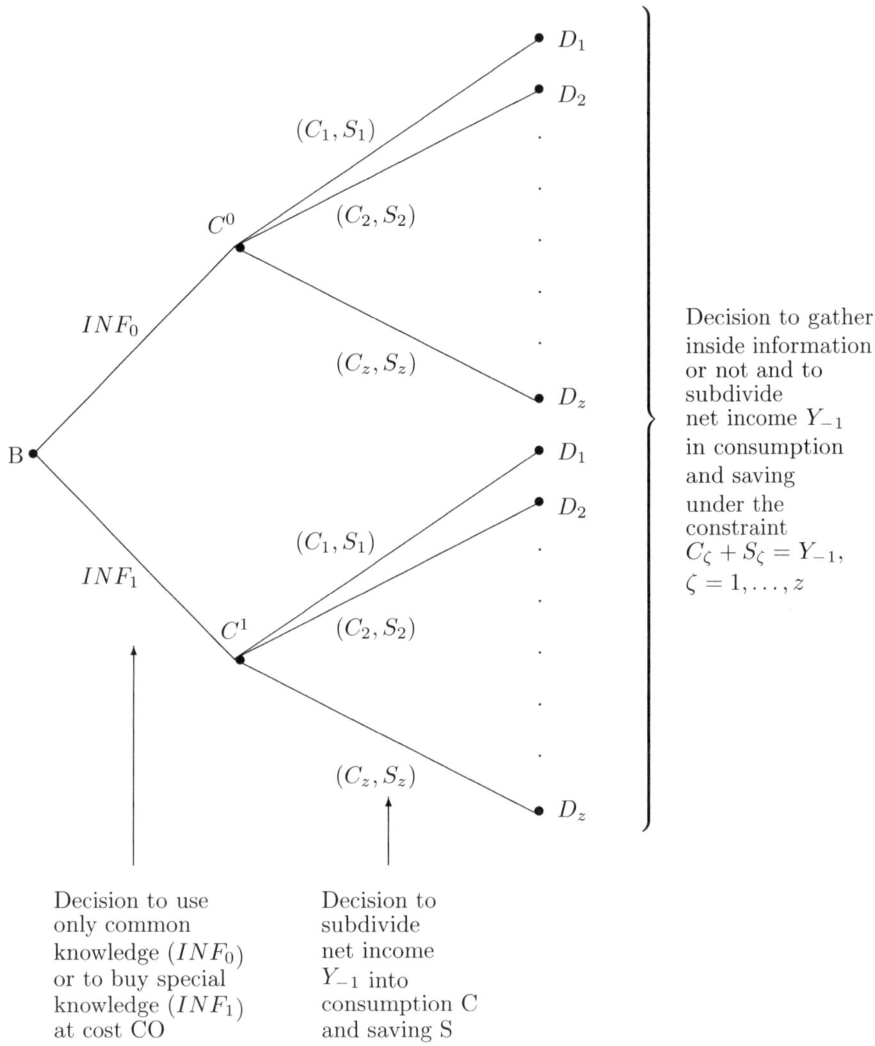

Figure 1.11 Household Decisions. Use of Income. The Case of Unknown Asset Prices

be distributed in period 0 on the capital stock and on the expectation and variance of the prices of all kinds of capital stocks and securities. Of course, the person is also provided with that information which is common knowledge and consists of the distributed profits, of the prices of the assets and of GDP in the past. This is the only information which the person has if it chooses to stay uninformed (as most of the small capital owners do, since they have neither time nor money nor the necessary knowledge in business administration).

Before we come to the decision criteria and decision rules of a person we have to specify the model, i.e. the conceptual framework in which we want to treat the problem. We do that with the help of Fig. 1.11.

1. The initial situation is symbolized by the point B in Fig. 1.11 and specified in section 1.15. First the person has to decide whether to be content with the "common knowledge" on the economic situation of the firm the assets of which it owns or considers to purchase or whether to try to get more detailed, specific, "inside" knowledge. The common knowledge consists of the past development of the prices of the assets (Fig. 1.13a-c shows as an example the prices of the shares of Siemens, Allianz and General Electric), of GDP and of other indicators of economic activity. To get more detailed "inside" information on the prospects, plans and chances of the firms the person is interested in needs a lot of inquiries, interviews, research on the economic environment, competition of other firms – information which is not easy to get. Thus in Fig. 1.11 and 1.12 the person moves from B to C^0 or C^1 by choosing INF_0 (= no special information) or INF_1 (= additional information). The following concepts do not depend on this choice (the decisions do depend on it, of course).

2. The next step is to decide how income is divided between consumption and saving, C and S. There are z possibilities to do that. Thus the person moves from C^0 or $C^{(1)}$ to D_1, D_2 or D_z in Fig. 1.11 and 1.12.

3. Now the person decides which commodities to buy and how much to spend for other purposes (transfer payments) – a move from D_ζ to $E_{\zeta 1}$ or $E_{\zeta 2} \ldots$ or $E_{\zeta y}$. These and the following decisions may be illustrated by similar graphs as Fig. 1.12.

4. Now comes the decision on financial allocations – a move from E_ζ to $F_{\zeta 1}$ or $F_{\zeta 2} \ldots$ or $F_{\zeta x}$. That means: total saving S will be allocated to the purchase of different securities $(\bar{F}_1, \ldots, \bar{F}_n)$, to the change ΔTD of time deposits, of cash ΔCA or of the debt position ΔDE.

5. The final step consists of conditional orders to the brokers concerning buying or selling orders for each security, conditioned on the price of the security. The expenditures for a security i should not exceed the financial allocation $\bar{F}_i$ in order to avoid bankruptcy. The prices of all securities result from the conditioned orders of all economic agents (see section 1.26) and are not known when the person has to state his orders.

We assume that a broker accepts only buying or selling orders ΔW_i of a security $i \in \{1, \ldots, n\}$ conditioned upon the price v_i of that security and upper financial limits but not orders conditioned on the prices of other securities or

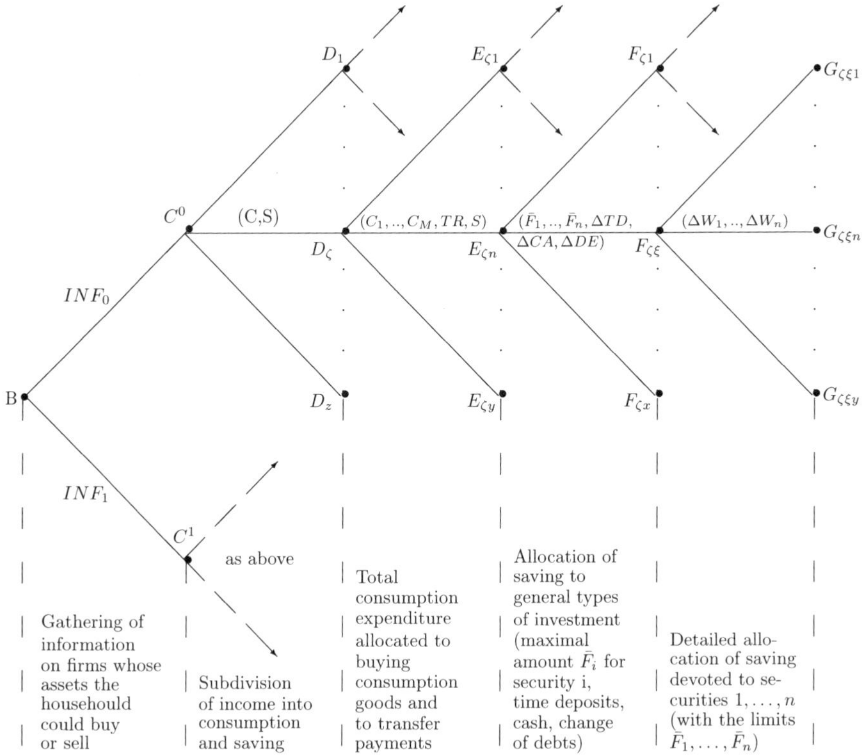

Figure 1.12 Some Details: Household Decisions, Use of Income. The Case of Known Asset Prices

upon general "states of the nature".[89] If he would accept other conditions he would come into the position of a Walrasian auctioneer: trading must be

[89] This assumption has far reaching consequences. It allows the immediate fixing of the asset price according to demand and supply of that specific asset without considering other asset prices and thus avoiding the artifact of an auctioneer à la Walras – a positive consequence. But there is a cost; a person that wants to realize an optimal portfolio cannot do this in general by giving only these types of conditional orders, because the optimal supply or demand of one specific asset depends on the prices of *all* assets, not only on the price of this asset. Thus the person that gives these types of conditional orders to brokers cannot be sure to end up with a portfolio which is considered as "optimal". We shall show this for the case where the person that wants to optimize his portfolio accepts the von Neumann–Morgenstern axioms of rational behavior under risk, see e.g. Krelle (1968),p. 138 ff. (Axiomensystem A); Breuer, Gürtler, Schumacher (1999), p. 9 ff. call it the Bernoulli principle. In this case the utility U of a risky investment with a payoff of x_i with probability π_i can be expressed by

$$U = \sum_i \pi_i \varphi(x_i), \quad \pi \geq 0, \quad \sum_i \pi_i = 1, \quad \varphi' \begin{cases} > 0 \leftrightarrow \text{risk loving} \\ = 0 \leftrightarrow \text{neutral behavior against risk} \\ < 0 \leftrightarrow \text{risk aversion} \end{cases}$$

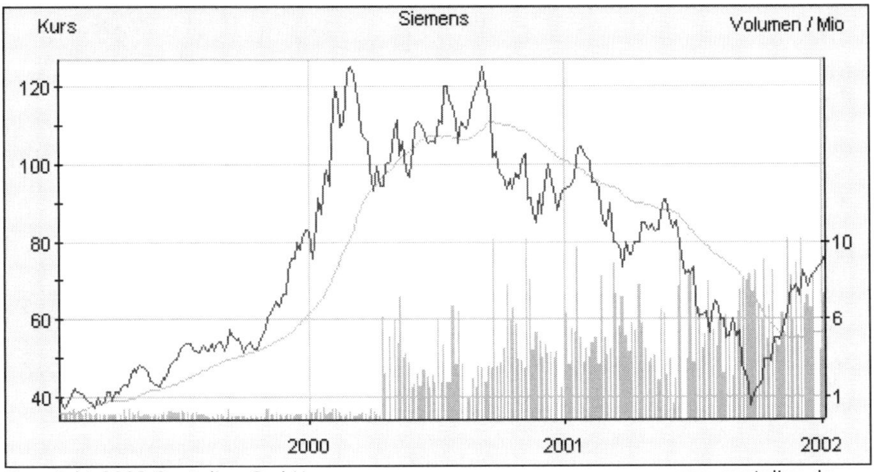

a) Siemens-Share, WKN:723610, 100-day-Moving Average

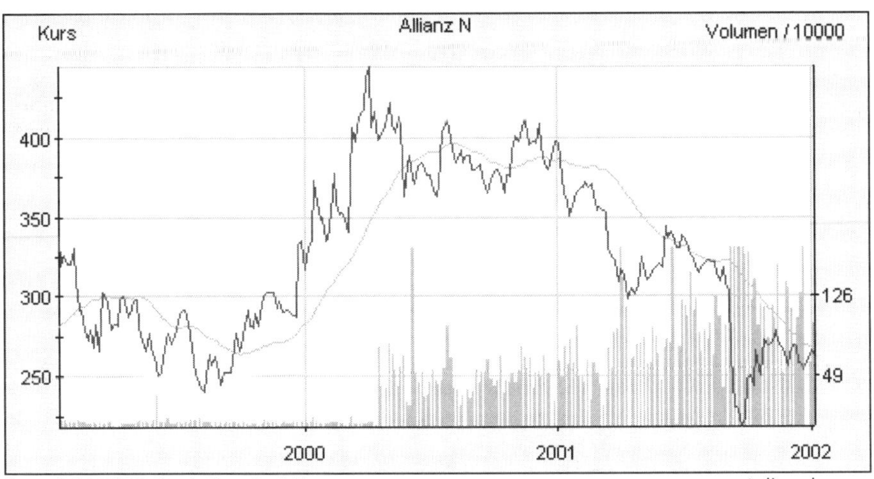

b) Allianz Share, WKN 840400, 100-day-Moving Average

Figure 1.13. Prices of Different Stocks at the Frankfurt Exchange

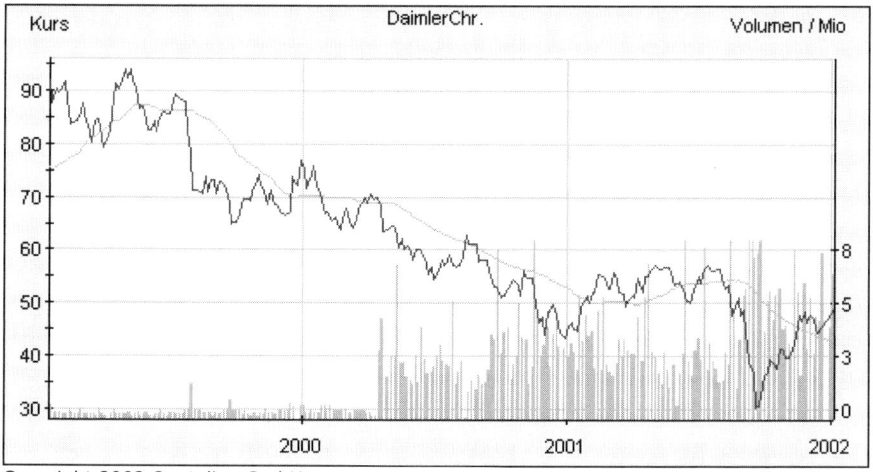

 www.quoteline.de

c) Daimler-Chrysler-Share, WKN 710000, 100-day-Moving Average

Figure 1.13 (continued). Prices of Different Stocks at the Frankfurt Exchange

---

The total utility U of different risky investments is the sum of the utilities of the single assets. Thus if there are N assets:

$$U = \sum_{j=1}^{N} U_j = \sum_{j=1}^{N} \sum_{i} \pi_{ji} \varphi(x_{ji})$$

In our case the payoffs x_{ji} take the form $x_{ji} = \frac{\alpha_j}{v_j^*} d_{ji}$, where d_{ji} = dividend payments per unit of share j in case i (which comes true with probability π_{ji}), v_j^* = price of share j in the period to come, unknown to the person; but it conditions his buying or selling orders on this price. α_j is that part of his wealth (calculated with the prices v_j^*) which the person devotes to asset j:

$$V^* = A_1^d v_1^* + \ldots + A_N^d v_N^* \text{ and } \alpha_j = A_j^d v_j^*, \quad \alpha_j \geq 0, \quad \sum_j \alpha_j = 1,$$

where A_j^d is the number of assets j in the portfolio. The d_{ji} are given to the person (or estimated by the person on the base of his information); the v_j^* are unknown to the person when he takes his decision on the composition of his portfolio, but the person may condition his demand or supply order on the v_j^*; the α_j are decision variables. The normal assumption is that the person wants to maximize his utility and uses the α_j as instruments to achieve this purpose:

$$U = \sum_{j=1}^{N} U_j = \sum_{j=1}^{N} \sum_{i} \pi_{ji} \varphi(\frac{\alpha_j}{v_j^*} d_{ji}) \longrightarrow \max_{\alpha_1, \ldots, \alpha_N}!$$

$$s.t. \; \alpha_j \geq 0, \quad \sum_j \alpha_j = 1$$

This yields the following system:

$$\frac{\partial U}{\partial \alpha_1} = \underbrace{\sum_i \pi_{1i}\varphi'(\frac{\alpha_1}{v_1^*}d_{1i})\frac{d_{1i}}{v_1^*}}_{=:U_1'} - \underbrace{\sum_i \pi_{Ni}\varphi'(\frac{1-\alpha_1-\ldots-\alpha_{N-1}}{v_N^*}d_{Ni})\frac{d_{Ni}}{v_N^*}}_{=:U_N'} = 0$$

$$\vdots$$

$$\frac{\partial U}{\partial \alpha_{N-1}} = \underbrace{\sum_i \pi_{N-1,i}\varphi'(\frac{\alpha_{N-1,i}}{v_{N-1}^*}d_{N-1,i})\frac{d_{N-1,i}}{v_{N-1}^*}}_{=:U_{N-1}'} -$$

$$\underbrace{\sum_i \pi_{Ni}\varphi'(\frac{1-\alpha_1-\ldots-\alpha_{N-1}}{v_N^*}d_{Ni})\frac{d_{Ni}}{v_N^*}}_{=:U_N'} = 0$$

This means that the $\alpha_1, \ldots, \alpha_N$ (where $\sum_{j=1}^N \alpha_j = 1$) have to be chosen such that the marginal utilities U_j' are equal for all investments $j = 1, \ldots, N$. But the solutions $\alpha_1^*, \ldots, \alpha_N^*$ depend on the asset prices $v_1^*, \ldots, v_N^*$:

$$\alpha_j^* = f_i(v_1^*, \ldots, v_N^*), \quad j = 1, \ldots, N,$$

which are determined by demand and supply of *all* persons. If the person we consider could give the conditional order

$$A_j^d = \frac{\alpha_j^*}{v_j^*}, \quad \alpha_j^* = f_j(v_1^*, \ldots, v_N^*),$$

to the broker and all other persons equivalently and if all brokers could find prices $v_1^*, \ldots, v_N^*$ where total supply and demand are equal for all assets, all persons could realize their optimal portfolio simultaneously. But this is not so, because the broker accepts only orders of the type

$$A_j^d = \frac{\alpha_j^{**}}{v_j^*}, \quad \alpha_j^{**} = F_j(v_j^*)$$

That means the person has to approximate α_j^* by α_j^{**}. This could be done by linearization of the function f_i:

$$\hat{\alpha}_j = a_{j0} + a_{j1}v_1^* + \ldots + a_{jN}v_N^*.$$

Then

$$A_j^d \approx \frac{\hat{\alpha}_j}{v_j^*} = \frac{a_{j0}}{v_j^*} + a_{j1}\frac{v_1^*}{v_j^*} + \ldots + a_{jj} + \ldots + a_{jN}\frac{v_N^*}{v_j^*}$$

The relations $\frac{v_\nu^*}{v_j^*}$ have to be estimated by the person. Thus it may give the conditioned order

$$\hat{A}_j^d = a_{jj} + \frac{c_{j0}}{v_j^*} + c_j, \quad c_j = const \approx a_{j1}\frac{v_1^*}{v_j^*} + \ldots + \frac{a_{j,j-1}}{v_{j-1}^*} + \frac{a_{j,j+1}}{v_{j+1}^*} + \ldots + a_{jN}\frac{v_N^*}{v_j^*}$$

to the broker. It is clear that after all conditional orders have been carried out the person will realize that the result is not the optimal portfolio, and the game may start anew.

inhibited till a point of general equilibrium is reached, and this may take years. But if we think of one broker for each security, the broker could easily and quickly fix the price such that demand equals supply.

Thus the conditional order of the person would be: if the price of security i is v_i in period 0 buy the amount $\Delta W_i^{(+)}$. If this price is $w_i > v_i$ or higher, sell the amount $\Delta W_i^{(-)}$. The person has to fix $\Delta W_i^{(+)}$ in advance conditioned on the price v_{i0} which is determined by the brokers such that total demand equals total supply for each security, see section 1.26 below. The person is free to choose $\Delta W_i^{(+)}$ and $W_i^{(-)}$ conditioned upon v_i in the limits of his budget constraint.

This concludes the conceptual framework. Now we turn to the decision strategies of the person. There are many points of view of choosing an optimal portfolio within the financial constraint. We start with points of view of an "informed" person:

- trust in the future development of the firm or institution
- emotional links
- distribution of risks
- to exert an influence on the management of the firm

There may be "grades" given to different possible portfolios according to these points of view. After the different points of view have been weighted, the person may arrive at an ordering of these portfolios and thus find out the best one for each conditioned future price of the security.

We consider three decision strategies of the "*uninformed*" person:

- to keep the portfolio constant which comprises habit and indolence[90]
- "trend chasing"
- arbitrage.

1. To keep the portfolio constant is the simplest and cheapest decision: no work is needed, and if the portfolio represents an unbiased sample of all securities one may expect an average development of its price and of dividend payments and interest rates. If one is content with that and is

---

This result does not depend on the use of the von Neumann–Morgenstern criterion for optimal behavior under risk. In practice the μ, σ–criterion is often used (μ = expectation, σ = standard deviation) though from the theoretical point of view the von Neumann-Morgenstern approach is more plausible. The two principles are incommensurable. For the μ, σ–criterion: see e.g. Krelle (1968), p. 148 ff. or Breuer, Gürtler, Schuhmacher (1999), p. 40 ff.

[90] An asset comprises also shares of investment funds: These funds produce *one* commodity (consisting of the yield of the portfolio). Thus "keeping the portfolio constant" means to stay with one investment fund – a simple and for many persons attractive alternative.

only interested in a reasonable long term yield this is not a bad policy as it seems to be at first sight.

2. One may use trends in the observed prices of the assets in order to improve the value of the portfolio. This policy is called "trend chasing" in the literature[91]. Usually there is a trend in the time series of prices of assets, see Fig. 1.13a-c. It seems to be a reasonable policy to buy an asset, if its price v is going up and to sell it, if its price is going down. But this rule should be applied within certain limits, i.e. if the price v lies in the region $v_{min} \leq v \leq v_{max}$, where the limits are determined by the development of GDP. If v lies outside the limits, the opposite rules should be applied. If v_{min} is the lowest reasonable price of this asset (the price under most pessimistic auspices) and if the price lies below that limit one would expect that sooner or later the price would go up again. By buying this asset at a very low price one may take advantage of future price rises. If v_{max} is the highest price one could expect under most favorable conditions and if the price lies above that level it would be a good policy to sell this asset as long as the price is "too high". Thus in case of "trend chasing" the order for the broker would be: in case of a rising trend (e.g. $v_{-3} < v_{-2} < v_{-1}$, i.e. increasing prices in the last three periods)

   and if $v_{-1} \leq v_{max}$: buy the amount $\Delta W > 0$
   if $v_{-1} > v_{max}$: sell the amount $\Delta W < 0$

   in case of a falling trend (e.g. $v_{-3} > v_{-2} > v_{-1}$, i.e. decreasing prices in the last three periods)

   and if $v_{-1} \leq v_{min}$: buy the amount $\Delta W > 0$
   if $v_{-1} > v_{min}$: sell the amount $\Delta W < 0$

   Of course, the ΔW have to be in accordance with the budget constraints:

$$\begin{aligned} \Delta W \cdot v &\leq \bar{M} \quad if\ \Delta W > 0 \\ -\Delta W &\leq \bar{W} \quad if\ \Delta W < 0 \end{aligned}$$

   where $\bar{M}$ is the amount of money the broker may dispose of and $\bar{W}$ the amount of the asset the broker may sell. Fig. 1.14 illustrates the situation.[92]

---

[91] See e.g. Wang (1993), p. 259.

[92] It is interesting to note that the behavior of "trend chasing" may lead to exchange crashes or unreasonable overstatements of the value of assets. Let there be a wave of pessimism in the population of the capital owners such that v_{max} and v_{min} are very low and let there be a falling trend and $v_{-1} > v_{min}$. Then everybody wants to sell its assets as fast as possible which yields a crash of all asset prices. The opposite would happen if there is a wave of optimism, a rising trend and $v_{-1} \leq v_{min}$.

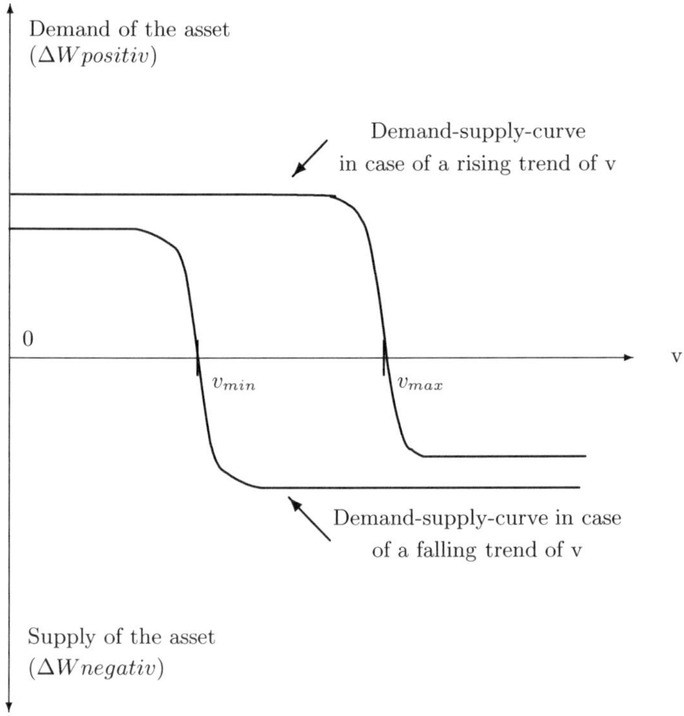

Figure 1.14 Demand of an Asset (ΔW positive) or Supply of that Asset (ΔW negative) Conditioned on the Price v of that Asset. "Chasing the Trend"-Strategy, Tendencies.

$$v_{max} = a \cdot \bar{Y}_{-1}(1+g)$$

$$v_{min} = a \cdot \bar{Y}_{-1}(1-g),$$

Within these tendencies and limits the person is free to choose its optimal demand or supply of assets conditioned upon the price v of the asset. Thus "trend chasing" does not determine supply and demand of assets unequivocally. Nevertheless, in the following we shall suggest a plausible rule for determining the size of ΔW, see Fig. 1.15, to be interpreted later. A simplified version is illustrated in Fig. 1.14. In case of a rising trend and $v > v_{max}$ the person would supply the total amount of the asset (in order to take advantage of the exceptional (and surely excessive) price of the asset). In case of a rising trend and $v < v_{max}$ the person would buy the asset up to an amount determined by the liquidity constraint (in order to participate on the increasing value of this asset). This explains the right curve in Fig. 1.14. In case of a falling trend and $v > v_{max}$ the person would sell all assets it owns in order to avoid further losses. If $v < v_{max}$ the person would buy these assets

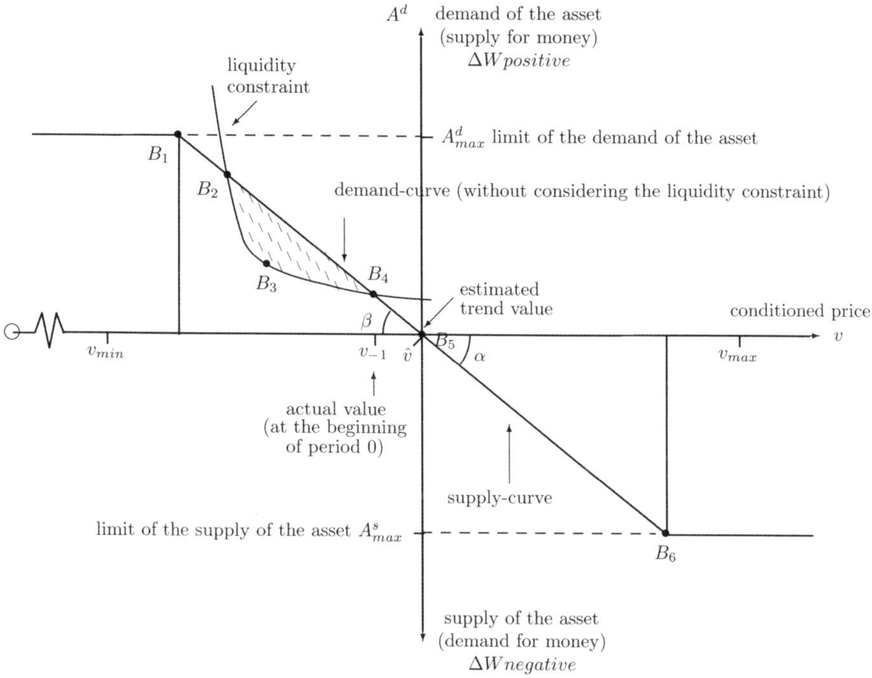

Figure 1.15 Demand and Supply of an Asset in Case of a Linear Relation between the Amount of the Asset Demanded or Supplied and the Deviation from the Supposed Long-Term Trend Price of the Asset

(since this undervaluation of the asset cannot stay for a long time), up to a level determined by the liquidity constraint.

In Fig. 1.15 a more sophisticated demand and supply behavior is illustrated. We come to this later.

3. Let there be more than one security in the market. Now *arbitrage* comes in: by changing the portfolio composition such that the differences in yield of different securities are taken into account the person may increase his wealth. We assume that the person understands the advantages of arbitrage and uses this possibility to improve the value of his portfolio. In this context we have to differ between securities (in the narrow sense) and capital stock.

Let $r^{real}_{SEC} = \frac{r_{SEC}(1-RISK)}{v^{cond}_{SEC}}$ be the real interest rate on a security conditioned upon the price v^{cond}_{SEC} of that security in period 0, taken as risk free by allowing for deducting a risk percentage $RISK$.

Let $r^{real}_{KSt} = \frac{d(1-RISK)}{v^{cond}_{KSt}}$ be the real interest rate on a capital stock of unit value conditioned upon the price v^{cond}_{KSt} in period 0, taken as risk free by allowing for a risk deduction $RISK$.

r_{SEC} and d are taken as given for the person. The risk deductions $RISK$ are determined by the person and related to the variance of the observations of r_{SEC} and d where d is the profit paid on a share of nominal 1 DM. Let r_B be the (risk free) interest rate on time deposits TD at the banks. An arbitrage policy with respect to assets i and j amounts to the following rules:

(a) If $r^{real}_i > r^{real}_j \longrightarrow \Delta W_i \geq 0, \Delta W_j \leq 0$.

(b) If $r^{real}_i < r^{real}_j \longrightarrow \Delta W_i \leq 0, \Delta W_j \geq 0$.

(c) If $r^{real}_i > r_B \longrightarrow \Delta W_i \geq 0, \Delta TD \leq 0$.

(d) If $r^{real}_i < r_B \longrightarrow \Delta W_i \leq 0, \Delta TD \geq 0, \quad i = 1, \ldots, n$ (all capital stocks and securities).

For the orders to the broker these conditions have to be changed such that the comparisons relate only to prices of the same asset. Orders conditioned on prices of other assets are not accepted. Only under these conditions all prices can be fixed simultaneously without the fictitious Walrasian auctioneer. Thus the above arbitrage rules have to be substituted by the following relations. Since $r^{real}_i = \frac{r_i(1-RISK_i)}{v^{cond}_i}$ (where $r_i = d_i$ in case of capital stock) the relation $r^{real}_i > r^{real}_j$ leads to

$$(*) \qquad v^{cond}_i < v^{cond}_j \frac{r_i(1-RISK_i)}{r_j(1-RISK_j)}.$$

But conditions on v_j $(= v^{cond}_j)$ are not accepted by a broker for asset i. Thus the person has to take the value on the right hand of the inequality $(*)$ of the last period and define

$$\hat{v}_{ij} := v_{j,-1} \frac{r_{i,-1}(1-RISK_i)}{r_{j,-1}(1-RISK_j)}$$

and give the order to the broker:

(a) If $v^{cond}_i < \hat{v}_{ij} \longrightarrow \Delta W_i \geq 0, \Delta W_j \leq 0$ and similarly for the cases (b),(c),(d) above.

These rules state tendencies. The tendencies of "chasing the trend" and of "arbitrage" my be inconsistent. Then compromises are necessary. "Do nothing" $(\Delta W_i = \Delta W_j = 0)$ is often the way out of these difficulties. Without inconsistencies the person is free to determine the amount of assets bought or sold under the price conditions.[93] As already said the tendencies stated above leave much room for specification, in general. One may ask how the person determines the amounts of an asset to be bought or sold in detail. A reasonable rule which one may guess to be followed by the person concerning the size of the conditioned orders given to the brokers would be: the larger the deviation of the price v of an asset from its "normal" price $\hat{v}$, the larger would be the amount of the asset offered or demanded. In the linear case this would lead to the following order to the broker:

---

[93] This approach gives more freedom to the portfolio policy of a person. There might be many different points of view in deciding on buying or selling securities. There is a whole literature on this subject. V. Neumann and Morgenstern (1961), pp. 24, developed an axiomatic approach based on utility maximation, see also Krelle (1968), pp. 6. Assume that a person has to decide on how to allocate his wealth between two different assets, where an asset i is characterized by a probability distribution $((x_{i1}\pi_{i1}), \ldots, (x_{in}\pi_{in}))$, $x_{i\nu}$ = profit or loss, $\pi_{i\nu}$ = probability of $x_{i\nu}$, $\pi_{i\nu} \geq 0, \sum_{\nu=1}^{n} \pi_{i\nu} = 1$, $\nu = 1, \ldots, n$, $i = 1, 2$. Assume that the person has a utility (or risk preference) function

$$u = \phi(x_{i\nu}), \quad \phi' > 0, \quad \phi'' \begin{cases} < 0, & \text{if the person is risk averse} \\ = 0, & \text{if the person is risk neutral} \\ > 0, & \text{if the person likes risk} \end{cases}$$

and he wants to determine the rate α of his wealth which it should dedicate to asset 1 and thus the rate $1 - \alpha$ to asset 2, $0 \leq \alpha \leq 1$. The utility of asset 1 is $U_1 = \sum_{\nu=1}^{n} \phi(\alpha x_{1\nu})\pi_{1\nu}$, total utility is $U = U_1 + U_2 = \sum_{\nu=1}^{n} [\phi(\alpha x_{1\nu})\pi_{1\nu} + \phi((1-\alpha)x_{2\nu})\pi_{2\nu}]$ and the optimal portfolio is given by the solution of

$$\frac{\partial U}{\partial \alpha} = \sum_{\nu=1}^{n} [\pi_{1\nu}\phi'(\alpha x_{1\nu})x_{1\nu} - \pi_{2\nu}\phi'((1-\alpha)x_{2\nu})x_{2\nu}] = 0.$$

This approach is intellectually attractive, but rather far away from the decision procedure in practice. Baumol (1952) and Tobin (1956) suggested an approach which assumed normal distributions for the profits of the assets such that the profit expectations μ and its variances σ describe the situation adequately. The theory is well represented in the textbook of Felderer and Homburg (1985), p. 210–220. A simplified version runs like this. Let $V^{nom} = \sum_{i=1}^{m} p_i y_i$ be the wealth of the person, p_i = price of asset i, y_i = amount of asset i. Let $r_{i\nu} = \frac{x_{i\nu}}{p_i y_i}$ be the profit rate in situation ν and $\bar{r}_i = E(\frac{x_i}{p_i y_i})$ be the expected profit (or loss) rate per unit of asset i, where $E(\frac{x_i}{p_i y_i}) = \sum_{\nu=1}^{n} \frac{x_{i\nu}}{p_i y_i}\pi_{i\nu}$. Let $\sigma_i^2 = E(r_i - \bar{r}_i)^2$ be the variance of the profit rate for security i, $i = 1, \ldots, m$, and let the covariance be zero. The person is supposed to have a utility function which in the case of additive utilities may be formulated as $U = \sum_{i=1}^{m} U(\bar{r}_i, \sigma_i^2, y_i)$. It will be maximized with respect to $y_1, \ldots, y_m$ under the constraint $\sum_{i=1}^{m} p_i y_i = V^{nom}$. The solution is $y_i = y_i(\bar{r}_1, \ldots, \bar{r}_m, \sigma_1^2, \ldots, \sigma_m^2, p_1, \ldots, p_m, V^{nom})$. In the 2–dimensional case graphical solutions are possible, see e.g. Feldcrer and Homburg (1985), otherwise a simultaneous equation system has to be solved. This can be done by the person if the prices are fixed. But the prices depend on the demand and supply orders of all persons, conditioned only upon the prices of the security which should be bought or sold. Breuer, Gürtler, Schumacher (1999) rely on the (μ, σ)–criterion almost completely and arrive this way at a relatively simple and coherent theory though they state the limitation of this approach very clearly. Moreover, all books on finance deal also with portfolio management. They cannot be mentioned here.

if $v > \hat{v}$: sell the amount $A^s = -\Delta W = -\alpha(v-\hat{v})$, $\alpha \geq 0$, but not more than A^s_{max} ($= \bar{W}$ above, this is the total amount of that asset in the portfolio)

if $v < \hat{v}$: buy the amount $A^d = \Delta W = \beta(\hat{v} - v)$, $\beta \geq 0$, but not more than A^d_{max} (which might be determined by the amount $\bar{M}$ of finance available for this purpose, or by considering the risk spread or by other reflections; we do not go into that problem).

if $v = \hat{v}$: do nothing

Fig. 1.15 illustrates these orders for one asset; for simplicity: $\alpha = \beta$. The supply curve (valid for $v > \hat{v}$) stops at the amount A^s_{max} available in the portfolio. The linear original demand curve (valid for $\hat{v} > v$) must be corrected according to the liquidity constraint $A^d \cdot v \leq \bar{M}$, if β is not very small. For very small β demand will always stay within the liquidity limits. Thus the order given to the broker could be: at a price $v < \hat{v}$ buy the amounts given by the curve B_1, B_2, B_3, B_4, B_5; if $v > \hat{v}$, sell the amounts given by the line $B_5\, B_6$. If the broker would follow the demand curve without respecting the liquidity constraint the person would go bankrupt in the region between B_2 and B_4: the hatched area indicates the size of the deficit.

If the person is content with a linear original demand and supply curve, it has to decide on their slope α and β and on the maximal amount A^d_{max} of demand, given the liquidity constraint and the estimate of the trend value $\hat{v}$. This does not seem to overburden the intelligence of a normal person. But, of course, these ideas have to be checked. Other, especially nonlinear demand and supply curves are possible, which are influenced by estimates of an absolute maximal value v_{max} and absolute minimum value v_{min} of the asset. We do not go into these details here.

We now turn to the "informed" person. We consider only two types of "informed" persons: those which want to *maximize their income* or the value of their assets and those which want to get the power in the firm in order to *enforce their own concepts* on the future of the firm. We start with the *first category*. A person of this kind is usually interested in the long term earnings. It puts in time and money to find out the real situation and the prospects of the firm in the future. It will estimate the earning power of the firm or institution independent of the price of their securities at the exchange and compare it with this price (which is an index of the valuation by all other persons). Now supply or demand will be based on the difference of these two evaluations. In case of a security the information consists of estimates of future profits $q_0, q_1, \ldots$ of the firm. In order to come to such estimates, the likely development of the market of the final product of the firm, the product and factor prices, the ability of the management and other items have to be considered. The results are probability distributions $\pi(q_t)$, $t = 0, 1, \ldots, T$, where T is the lifetime expectation of the firm. Let r_B be the normal bank rate which is used as time discount rate. Then the value of the firm at the beginning of period 0 is:

$$\tilde{v} = \sum_{t=0}^{T} q_t \left(\frac{1}{1+r_B}\right)^t$$

where $\tilde{v}$ is a probability distribution since q_t appears with probability $\pi(q_t)$. If $q_t = q$ =const. the result would be

$$\tilde{v} = q = \frac{1-a^{T+1}}{1-a}, \quad a = \frac{1}{1+r_B}, \quad 0 < a < 1$$

Of course, more refined methods of evaluation of a firm may be used. Let $E(\tilde{v})$ be the expectation value of $\tilde{v}$. The attitude against risk may be considered by a reduction rate $RISK$ with respect to the expectation value (if the person is risk averse) or an additive rate (if the person likes risk). Now the evaluation of the value of the firm is

$$\hat{v} = E(\tilde{v})(1 - RISK)$$

and the strategy of the informed person is:

1. If $\hat{v} > v \longrightarrow \Delta W \geq 0$.
2. If $\hat{v} < v \longrightarrow \Delta W \leq 0$.
3. If $\hat{v} = v \longrightarrow \Delta W = 0$.

The constraints are the same as for the uninformed person. The person has to choose the size of ΔW_i according to his preferences within the admissible limits. The size of the ΔW will be determined (in the linear case) as in case of an "uninformed" investor, see Fig. 1.15.

There is still another type of an "informed person" which is more interested in short term earnings. It seeks information relating to value estimations of the majority of other investors be they justified (in the persons judgement) or not. If the person is interested in short term profits it will take advantage of this information and buy the security at once if it thinks that other persons will buy it soon such that the price of the asset will rise. But this "guessing what other people think what the majority thinks" is highly risky, if one does not really have reliable inside information on the plans and estimates of the most important investors. Otherwise this procedure is a Monte Carlo game. We shall not consider it.

The last part of this section deals with investors who want to influence the decisions of a firm. Till now we considered only the case of a person who wanted to optimize his portfolio composition but did not have the power or the willingness to interfere with entrepreneurial decisions of the management which directs the firm the shares of which it owns. This is the normal situation for the great majority of small investors on the capital market. These people do not behave as owner of the firm, responsible for his management, but as a pensionary who seeks the highest income no matter where it comes from and how it is achieved. But in general there are owners, usually the majority shareholder, who consider the firm as their property, feel responsible for it and have the power to determine the management and the general line of the future development of the firm. This might be one person (as in small and or middle sized firms) or a group of persons (e.g. a family, as at BMW). We treat them also as one person. If a decisive person owns the majority of shares it could resist any threat of an unfriendly take over by other owners (who represent other firms). If it owns only a minority (but the other shareholders are split into small parts and not interested in exerting entrepreneurial influence) the firm is always endangered of being bought up by other owners who want to control the firm either to shut it down (as a nuisance to their own business) or to incorporate it into their own business which would yield more profits to the combine. In principle, each firm where the majority of shares is owned by single persons who are only interested in dividend payments, is in danger of being bought up, also by much smaller owners (or firms), if these persons could convince a bank that a takeover would be a profitable business, such that the bank would lend the necessary money to buy these "free" shares or if they could pay by own shares. Only majority owners who want to preserve their domination of the firm and sheer size are a certain protection against unfriendly take-overs.

But there is another less visible influence on the management of a firm: possible investors in shares of the firm could state conditions under which they would be willing to buy these shares. If these possible investors are large enough (as in the case of pension funds or insurance companies, etc.) and if the firm needs the money from the capital market to finance its growth (loans are not complete substitutes, because in general banks will only lend in proportions to the capital stock and reserves) the persons in charge of the portfolio of these big investors have an important influence on the decisions of the management of a firm which needs the money though hitherto (in general) they do not own one share of the company.

We may model this "fight for control of the firm" which is actually a fight for the future of the firm and its policy as follows.

Consider the situation of an owner of a firm (a person who owns a sufficient size of the shares to be able to control the firm). At the end of period -1 the person has to decide:

1. Whether to keep the control (which means in case of issuing new shares: to buy a sufficient part of them) or not. In that case the decision would be to sell the shares on the capital market or to persons or institutions which want to gain control over the firm. This leads to a shift of the demand–supply–curve for assets and to pertinent orders to the broker (see Fig. 1.16).

2. If the owner wants to keep the control:

    a. whether to try to acquire the control over another firm such that a common management of the two firms would be profitable.

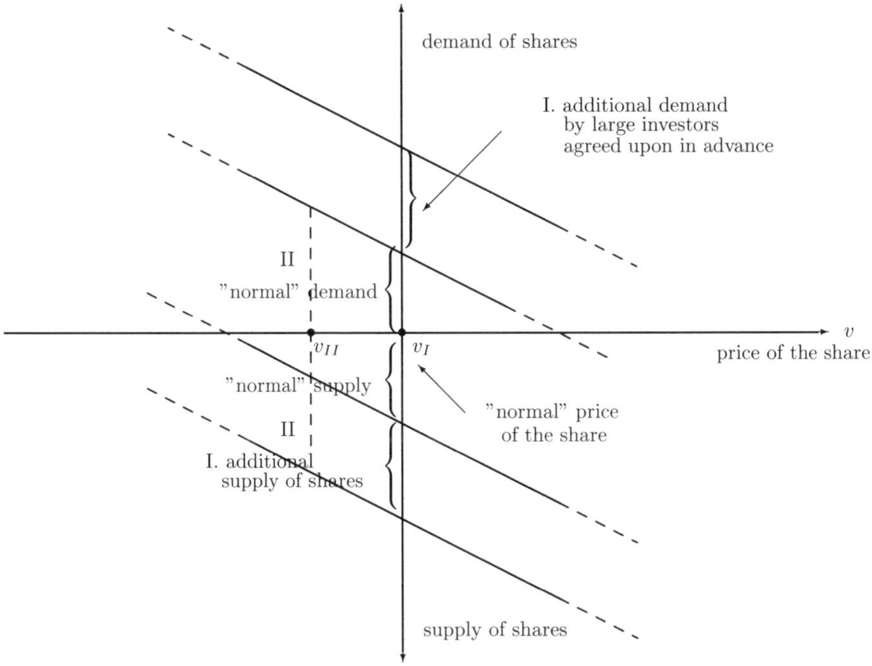

Situation on the capital market:

I: ideal case: the additional supply of newly emitted shares is compensated by additional demand of investors. The price v_I of the share is preserved.

II: without additional demand the price would drop to v_{II} where demand equals supply.

Figure 1.16. The Price Effect of Additional Supply or Demand of Shares

b. which manager (or which management) to appoint for the next period. Each manager stands for a certain general program for the future. With the choice of a manager the owner chooses a probability distribution of the future development of the firm. Actually, there are not many persons to choose from to become a manager of a large firm, in general.

Now the appointed manager has to decide:

1. on production, price, employment, inventories, investment.
2. on terms of the taking over of another firm (if the owners have agreed to this move).
3. on the financing of production, inventories and investment. If financing over the capital market is envisaged and the emission of new shares surpasses a certain amount, an agreement of the money dealers of large

investors has to be reached that they take some of these shares into their portfolio in order to avoid a drop in the price of shares. Fig. 1.16 shows the situation in the ideal case where the additional supply of shares does not lead to a drop of the price: the additional demand of big investors (e.g. by investment fonds, insurance companies, etc.) conforms to the additional supply. It also shows the drop of the price of a share from v_I to v_{II} without this additional demand.[94]

This is the end of a much too long section on conditional sales or purchases of capital stock and securities.

There is a large diversity of possible investment behavior. This leaves much room for the influence of ethics. It is not mentioned explicitly here, but the basic approach is the same as in earlier sections: All decisions, also those in investment are taken by human beings who consider the different points of view and weight them. There is nothing special in the case of investment, except the fact that uncertainty is larger compared to "normal" current business decisions.

---

[94] At the end of this section it may be appropriate to relate our approach on the behavior of a person concerning his portfolio decisions to theories to be found in the literature.

Huang and Litzenberger (1988) consider in their textbook a person that wants to maximize his consumption utility in the future where total consumption depends on the portfolio composition. The income from each asset in the portfolio depends on the state of the nature which is unknown when the person has to make his decision on consumption and on the portfolio composition; but this state becomes revealed when time goes on, till, at the end of time, the true state of nature becomes clear, see ch. 1 and ch. 7 in Huang and Litzenberger. That means that all consumption and portfolio decisions are made simultaneously and that the person is an "informed" one in our diction: it knows how "states of the nature" (future prices, demand, competition etc.) will influence the profit distributions and interest rates and it knows the probabilities of these "states of nature". In our approach there is a sequential decision process: first the person decides on the division of his net income between consumption and saving, afterwards on the demand of consumption goods and on the conditional demand or supply of securities and thus on his conditional portfolio. Demand and supply of a security are conditioned upon the price of that security (not on any other "state of the nature"). For an "informed" person this conditional demand and supply depends on future prospects. At the end of the next period only the price of the security is revealed to the person, and the whole procedure starts a new whereas at Huang and Litzenberger the decision at the beginning of the period is final, only the information changes. Huang and Litzenberger assume utility maximizing by the persons; in our approach the decision principle is left free to the person, and we also consider "uninformed" persons who decide only on the base of past experience. This will probably be the majority of investors.

Wang (1993) considers asymmetric information: there are "informed" and "uninformed" persons. Each person maximizes expected utility given its information. The information is not complete but there are aggregate supply and demand shocks and (in equilibrium) linear price functions. The uninformed persons demand a higher risk premium than the informed ones. The result is a rational expectation equilibrium of the economy which depends on the relative number of informed and uninformed persons in the market.

This approach is nearer to the one suggested above with the exception that we do not require the persons to follow a policy of maximizing expected utility conditioned upon its information, and we assume a sequential decision process.

Grossman and Stiglitz (1980) show that if arbitrage costs are not zero a market (here: the capital market) cannot be informationally efficient. This is true. All the models of the capital market treated here (including our one) neglect the transaction costs. If transaction costs are non-zero, a person would not care for differences of the price of the same asset at different markets if they are below his transaction costs. The normal excuse to this neglect is that these costs are usually very small, and "de minimis non curat praetor".

Hellwig (1980) deals with the problem whether the price reflects all available information in the market such that (as *Grossman* (1976,1978) suggests) a person needs only to look at the market price and thus can neglect his own information. Hellwig shows that this is an inconsistant proposition if there are only finite many participants in the market, because then each person actually has an influence on the price. If all persons disregard their own information, it is unclear how the price should reflect the information of all persons. The influence of the information of a person on the market price also depends on the preferences of the person – in contrast to the proposition of Grossman. In our model the market price of a security depends on the conditional demands and supplies of *all* persons. The uninformed persons influence the market price in the same way as the informed ones, and it is impossible to infer from the market price the preferences of the persons if there are more than two persons on the market. The market price of a security reflects some *average* evaluation of the asset. The estimation of the future development of a firm (and thus the future development of dividends which is the relevant information) influences the price of the security only to the extent that there are informed persons on the market.

Gennotte and Leland (1990) built a model of the capital market which could explain crashes such as that between October 16 and 19, 1987 where the security prices dropped by ca. 20% caused by the selling of ca. $6 billions of securities which amounts to ca. 0,2% of total equity value at that time. Thus small supply changes may yield catastrophic large price changes and thus catastrophic large changes of wealth of the capital owners. Gennotte and Leland explain it by a model where there is only one security, but three types of investors: uninformed ones (they only know the current prices), price informed ones (they have some idea on the future price; the model considers only one period) and supply-informed ones (they have some idea on the supply of the security), where "some idea" means knowledge of expectation and variance of the value considered. Each person within these categories maximizes a "cara" utility function (= constant absolute risk aversion) $U(W) = -exp(-\frac{W}{a})$, where W = terminal wealth. The authors calculate the rational expectation equilibrium and show that the price function is discontinuous under certain assumptions on the parameters such that small supply changes may yield large price changes.

This model is quite interesting though it rests on rather special assumptions. The villains in the play are the unobserved hedging activities which are erroneously taken as sign of information on bad news by the uninformed investors.

In our approach a similar effect is possible if the upper limits v_{max} of the price of a security are similar for a certain number of investors and the actual price exceeds v_{max}. This shifts the demand–supply curves to the left (see Fig. 1.16), the price drops, and this turning back of the trend induces all other persons to sell parts of their assets too – a crash is inevitable. Thus the same effect which Gennotte and Leland reach by their very special model is reached in our model by assuming upper and lower (subjective) bounds for the prices.

Finally I should like to hint at the book of Breuer et al. (1999) which gives good overviews over the current ideas on this subject.

I thank Martin Hellwig for his critique on an earlier version of this section and for hinting on the literature considered above.

1.26 A Digression: Fixing of the Rates by the Brokers

One may ask how on the base of these conditional orders of the households and of other economic agents the price of a security emerges. We shall come to this later in detail, but it might be good to hint at the solution of this problem by considering the simplest case. Assume that there are only two households which keep a certain amount of the same security W in their portfolio. But they evaluate the firm (or the institution) which issued the security and thus the "inner value" $\tilde{v}$ of their asset differently. Fig. 1.17 illustrates the situation of these two ("informed") persons. Person 1 evaluates the "inner value" of the security as $\hat{v}(1)$, person 2 as $\hat{v}(2)$ which is smaller than $\hat{v}(1)$ (if both persons would evaluate it identically no transactions will be possible; a market lives from different evaluations). Person 1 owns an amount of $\bar{W}(1)$ of this security, person 2 an amount of $\bar{W}(2)$ (not represented in Fig. 1.17). Portfolio considerations of person 1 would allow to buy at most the amount $\Delta W^{(+)}_{max}(1)$ of this security; for person 2 this maximum amount would be $\Delta W^{(+)}_{max}(2)$. Now the conditional order of person 1 at the proper broker could be

- buy the amount $\Delta W^{(+)}$ of the security where $\Delta W^{(+)} = \alpha[\hat{v}(1) - v]$ if this is positive, up to the amount $\Delta W^{(+)}_{max}(1)$, $\alpha > 0$ (for simplicity we assume that the liquidity constraint is not binding)[95]

- sell the amount $\Delta W^{(-)}$ of the security where $\Delta W^{(-)} = \alpha[v - \hat{v}(1)]$ if this is positive, up to the amount $\Delta W^{(-)}_{max}(1)$, $\alpha > 0$.

The conditional order of person 2 would be similar, (in Fig. 1.17 $\alpha = \beta$, for simplicity).

Now the broker puts the price of the security at v^* where $\Delta W^{(+)}(1) = \Delta W^{(-)}(2)$. At this price person 1 is willing to buy the amount $\Delta W^{(+)}(1)$ and person 2 is willing to sell this amount.

Under the assumption made above a solution v^* always exists and is unique. But this is not necessary so, if the demand–supply–curves are nonlinear. Fig. 1.18 shows an example. If the persons 1 and 2 think that at a too low market value of their securities their estimates $\hat{v}(1)$ and $\hat{v}(2)$, respectively, might be wrong and it may be better to get rid of these doubtful assets, the demand–supply–curves may bend down as shown in Fig. 1.18. In this case there are two values v where demand equals supply: v^* and v^{**}. Which value would the broker stipulate? Here stability conditions may be helpful. If, given the evaluation v^*, the broker would put the value a bit higher, the supply of the security would be larger than the demand – a sign for the broker to

---

[95] If it is binding, the order would be: buy the amounts given by the demand curve $B_1, B_2, \ldots, B_5$ in Fig. 1.15.

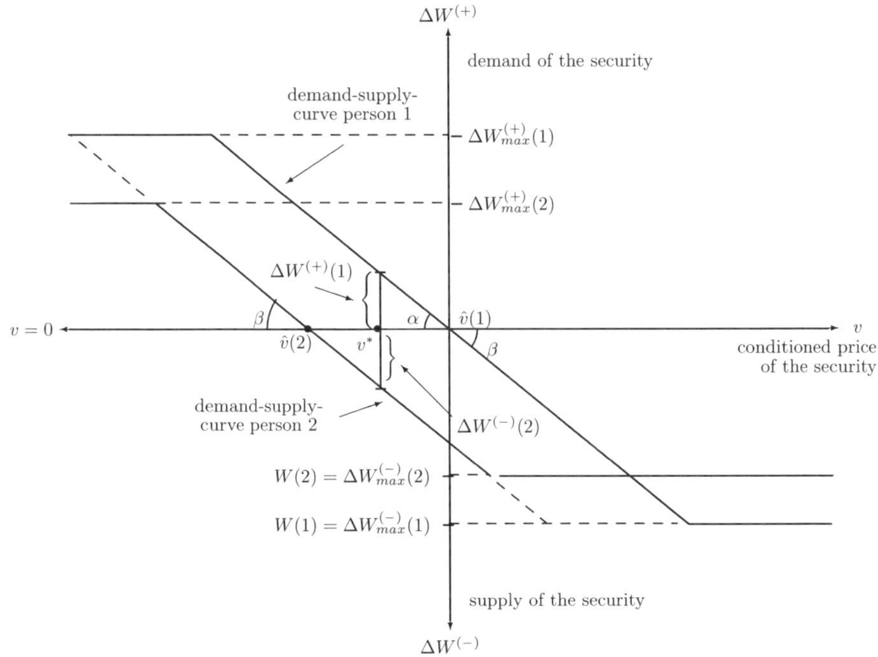

Figure 1.17. Fixing of the price v^* of a security by a broker

reduce the price; if he would put the price a bit lower, demand would be larger than supply – which would induce the broker to increase the price (see the arrows in Fig. 1.18 at v^*). But at v^{**} the opposite is true: a bit higher price would increase demand, a bit lower price would decrease it: v^{**} is an unstable equilibrium point. Thus we may conclude that the broker would choose the equilibrium price v^* which lies between the evaluations $\hat{v}(1)$ and $\hat{v}(2)$ – a reasonable result.

1.27 The Assignment of Households to Decision Situations

Let there be h different households (or persons) which are in h different decision situations $B_1, \ldots, B_h$. A household i is characterized by a vector $\Lambda_i = (\lambda_{i1}, \ldots, \lambda_{iz})$ of household characteristics, a vector $K_i = (\kappa_{i1}, \ldots, \kappa_{ir})$ of personal characteristics of the members of the household, a vector EC_i of the economic state of the household h_i and a vector $\overline{DEC}_i$ of known decisions of other economic agents, always at the beginning of period 0.

There are only finite many possible values of all the elements of the vectors K_i, Λ_i, EC_i and $\overline{DEC}_i$. The set $\{B_1, B_2, \ldots, B_n\}$ covers all possible combi-

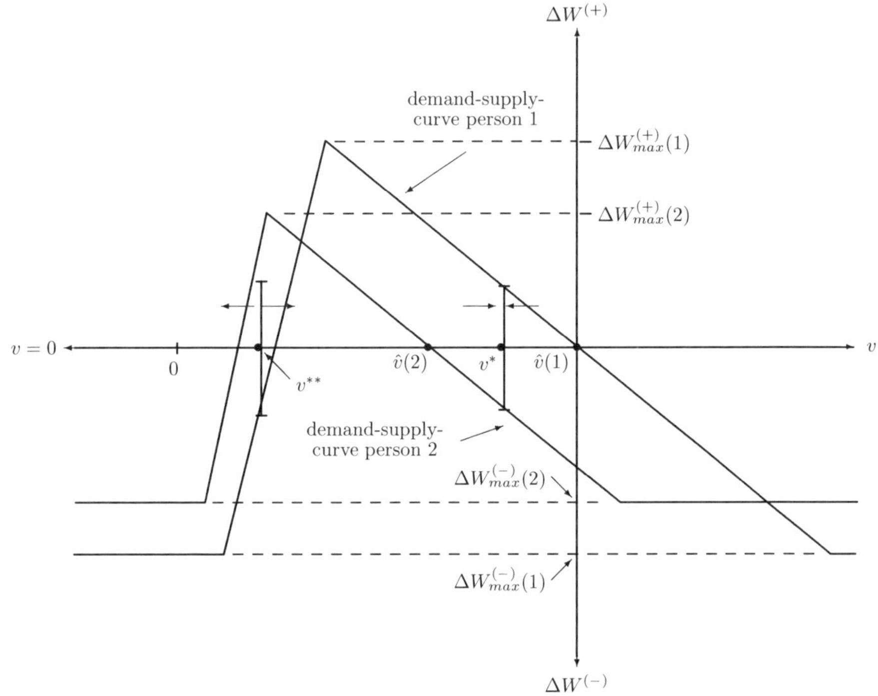

Figure 1.18. Several Prices v of a Security where Demand Equals Supply

nations of these elements, where $n > h$. Thus each household i is in exactly one decision situation B_i. We may regroup the households according to their income such that household 1 has the highest income, household 2 an equal or smaller income and so on until we reach household h with the smallest income.Accordingly we regroup the decision situations. Then, if there are no two households in the same position, the allocation of households to decision situations is as follows: In the beginning of the next period each household

$$\begin{array}{lcl}
\text{household } 1 & \longleftrightarrow & B_1 \\
\text{household } 2 & \longleftrightarrow & B_2 \\
\vdots & & \vdots \\
\text{household } h & \longleftrightarrow & B_h \\
\text{empty} & \multirow{3}{*}{$\left\{\right.$} & B_{h+1} \\
\text{decision} & & \vdots \\
\text{points} & & B_n
\end{array}$$

finds itself in another decision situation, as a consequence of own decisions and natural events (like birth, death, illness) and of changes of personal characteristics. The household may cease to exist, new households may appear on the scene and occupy new decision situations. On the microlevel this may be modeled as a stochastic process with certain transition probabilities from one state to the others including the transition to state 0 (dissolution of the household) and the transition from state 0 to a real state (a birth process). We shall not model this here but we assume that households in the same situation behave equally. Details will be found in section 1.10.

1.28 The Household Demand as a Function of the Situation of the Economy and of the Characteristics of the Household

Economists are ultimately interested in the behavior of large heterogeneous populations (the households, the investors, the banks,...). But since these populations consist of single persons they are interested in the behavior of persons as well. But it is hopeless to try to aggregate the actual behavior of all persons in the society in each period in order to arrive at the actual behavior of the population. This individual behavior is much too complicated and to a large degree unknown to an outside observer. Thus one has to make simplifying assumptions in order to arrive at the behavior characteristics of a population. *Werner Hildenbrand* (1998) dealt with this problem. His simplifying assumptions are[96]

1 There are smooth micro-relations

2 Structural stability of household characteristics

3 The standardized log income distribution is locally time-invariant

4 For two periods s and t which are close to each other the income-conditioned attribute distribution in period s is "approximately" equal to the income-conditioned attribute distribution in period t, if the income in s and t are in the same quantile position

Our basic assumption is:

Households with the same internal characteristics which are in the same external economic situation receive the same income and exert the same demand and supply. This general assumption has to be specified in order to be applicable in practice. We start with the *external situation* of the household[97].

---

[96] In order to understand the meaning of these assumptions exactly one has to read through the paper. I cannot reproduce it here in detail.

[97] In the following we present one simple (but not very realistic) interpretation of our basic assumption. One may also assume that the distribution of demand and supply within each "cube" as defined in Fig. 1.19 stays constant and that this distribution is represented by the point of gravity (e.g. the point SIT_{111} for the cube OAB ... G in Fig. 1.19)

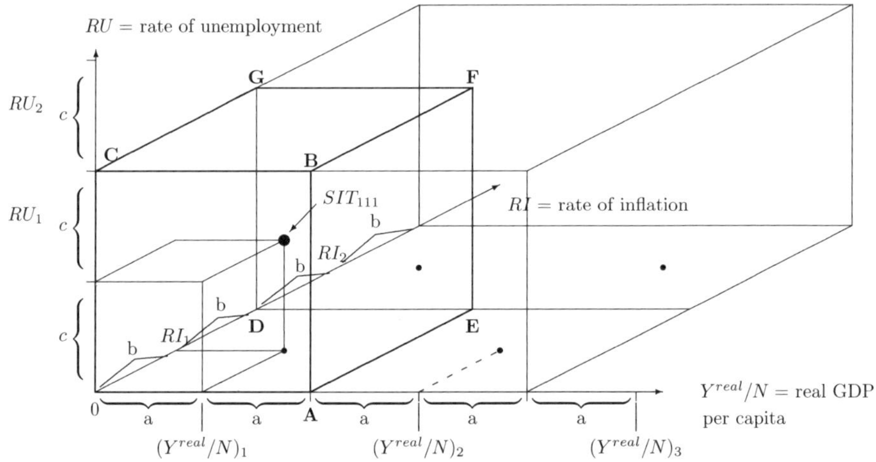

Figure 1.19 Definition of the External Situation SIT which influences the Demand and Supply Behavior of Households

Let

$(Y^{real}/N)_i$ be the real GDP per capita. Its effect on demand and supply of a household is the same as the GDP per capita between $(Y^{real}/N)_i - a$ and $(Y^{real}/N)_i + a$, see Fig. 1.19. That means: a household does not care for small differences: real incomes $(Y^{real}/N)_i \pm a$ are considered to be equal for all practical purposes

RI_j is the rate of inflation which has the same influence on household behavior as $RI_j \pm b$, see Fig. 1.19

RU_k is the rate of unemployment, where $RU_k \pm c$ is supposed to be equivalent for the household, see Fig. 1.19

Let $\{I\}$ be the set of all conceivable different real GDP per capita, $\{J\}$ the set of possible different rates of inflation and $\{K\}$ the set of all feasible different rates of unemployment. Now: $i \in \{I\}, \quad j \in \{J\}, \quad k \in \{K\}$. In Fig. 1.19 the point of gravity SIT_{111} represents all points in the cube OABCDEFG as far as their influence on income and on demand and supply of households is concerned. In other words: the household does not care for differences in Y^{real}/N, RI and RU as long as they stay in a neighborhood of SIT_{111}.

Similarly the real prices $\hat{p_1}, \ldots, \hat{p_n}$, the real wage rates $\hat{l_1}, \ldots, \hat{l_m}$, the real interest rates $\hat{r_1}, \ldots, \hat{r_k}$ are treated, where $\hat{p_\gamma} = \frac{p_\gamma}{\bar{p}}, \quad \hat{l_\mu} = \frac{l_\mu}{\bar{p}}, \quad \hat{r_\kappa} = \frac{r_\kappa}{\bar{p}}$ and $\bar{p}$ = price level, $\quad \gamma = 1, \ldots, n, \quad \mu = 1, \ldots, m, \quad \kappa = 1, \ldots, k$. Prices, wages and interest rates in a neighborhood of a certain state are treated as equal.

"De minimis non curat praetor", said the Romans. Now the *external economic situation* SIT_{ijk} at the beginning of period 0 may be defined by

$$SIT_{ijk} = ((Y^{real}/N)_i, RI_j, RU_k, \hat{p_1}, \ldots, \hat{p_n}, \hat{l_1}, \ldots, \hat{l_m}, \hat{r_1}, \ldots, \hat{r_k})$$

where $i \in \{I\}, j \in \{J\}, \ldots, k \in \{K\}$. The set SIT_{ijk} also comprises the prices of all n commodities (or groups of commodities), of all m wages for different labor and of all interest payments for all k different kinds of loans. These items are given and the same for all households. Their values are estimated on the base of economic theory by econometric methods.

The *internal characteristics* of households may be classified as follows:

a. The size of the household (1,2,...,N persons, where N is limited from above). This is characteristics 1 (Ch_1) with the possible values $Ch_{1,\gamma}$, $\gamma \in \{1, \ldots, N\}$;

b. The average age ($= Ch_2$) of the adult members of the household with the possible values $Ch_{2,\mu}$, $\mu \in \{15, \ldots, 85\}$; the second index indicates the age in years;

c. The educational status ($= Ch_3$) of the leading personality of the household[98] with possible values $Ch_{3,\omega}$, $\omega \in \{0, 1, \ldots, U\}$, where $Ch_{3,0}$ means: no education, $Ch_{3,1}$ = elementary school, ..., $Ch_{3,U}$ = the highest university degree;

d. The location of the household ($= Ch_4$). In general, the chances of income and employment are not identical in all parts of a country. For simplicity we differentiate only between 4 parts of the country: N =north, S =south, E =east, W =west. Thus we get as index of location: $Ch_{4,d}$, $d \subset \{N, S, E, W\}$;

e. The type of employment ($= Ch_5$) of the head of the household. We differentiate between the types $Ch_{5,\sigma,p,a}$, where $\sigma \in \{0, 1, \ldots, S\}$, $\sigma = 0$ means unemployed, $\sigma = 1, \ldots, S$: employed in sector $1, \ldots, S$ of the economy, $p \in \{1, \ldots, B\}, p = 1$: the lowest position, $p = B$ the highest (the boss), $a \in \{A, R\}$, A =active, R =retired;

f. Real wealth ($= Ch_6$) of the household. We may differ between $Ch_{6,w}$, where ($Ch_{6,0}$) means: no wealth, $Ch_{6,1}, \ldots, Ch_{6,W}$, where W is the highest feasible wealth; thus $Ch_{6,w}$, $w \in \{0, 1, \ldots, W\}$.

---

[98] For simplicity of the exposition of the theory we suppose households "of the old style", where only one person (usually the male) earns the money and the other person cares for the household and for the children. It is not difficult to extend the theory to cover the case of more than one money-earning person.

These categories may suffice to describe those internal characteristics of a household which could be taken from appropriate household statistics. But there are other characteristics of a more subtle type which are not so easy to get but may have also an important influence on income and expenditure. We treated them in detail in the foregoing sections. In the conceptual framework of this book the characteristics above (taken together and evaluated by the household) may be interpreted as a more-dimensional index of "economic advantage G" (see section 1.2). The other determinants in section 1.2, namely H, EM, IM, M are latent variables which may be described by appropriate indicators. If we include entrepreneurial households, we may add another latent variable, called "Spirit of Enterprise" ($= SPE$)[99]

$$
\begin{aligned}
H &= \text{evaluation of punishments connected with the situation question,}\\
EM &= \text{emotional attraction of the situation}\\
IM &= \text{force of imitation of others}\\
SPE &= \text{spirit of enterprise}\\
M &= \text{moral evaluation of the situation}
\end{aligned}
$$

There are z different moral requirements $M_1, \ldots, M_z$ which are evaluated by $v(M_1), \ldots, v(M_z)$. As characteristics of the household they form the 11th type and are written as
$Ch_{11,\xi 1}, \ldots, Ch_{11,\xi z}, \quad \xi_1, \ldots, \xi_z \in \{Z\} = \{-\bar{z}, \ldots, +\bar{z}\}$. They will be evaluated by discrete numbers between $-\bar{z}$ and $+\bar{z}$, $\bar{z} \geq 1$. H is now written as $Ch_{7,e}, \quad e \in \{E\}$, EM as $Ch_{8,f}, \quad f \in \{F\}$, IM as $Ch_{9,g}, \quad g \in \{G\}$, SPE as $Ch_{10,h}, \quad h \in \{H\}$. As already said, the index $G \quad =$ (economic) advantage introduced in section 1.2 is now substituted by six variables $Ch_1, \ldots, Ch_6$ defined above which allows to characterize a household more in detail.

Thus the *internal characteristics* of a household are described by the vector:
$Ch_{\gamma\mu\omega d\sigma pae\ldots h,\xi_1,\ldots\xi_z} := \{Ch_{1,\gamma}, Ch_{2,\mu}, \ldots, Ch_{6,w}, Ch_{7,e}, \ldots Ch_{10,h}, Ch_{11,\xi_1}, \ldots, Ch_{11,\xi_z}\}$

Thus the position POS of a household is defined by its external and internal situation which we write (by suppressing all indices) as

$$POS = (SIT, Ch).$$

Now our basic assumption says:

a. The position P of a household determines its real income Y^{real}

[99] See Krelle, "The Spirit of Enterprise as Driving Force of Technical Progress", in: Dieter Sadowski, (Ed.) *Entrepreneurial Spirits*, Wiesbaden (Gabler), 2001, p. 31-55.

b. It also determines its real demand c_i of consumption goods, $i = 1, \ldots, n$ and its allocation of financial assets and liabilities. Let $\beta_j \geq 0$ be the relative number of households which are in the position P_j. Thus

$$\sum_j \beta_j = 1 \tag{1.38}$$

Our theory implies that, if the internal characteristics and the external situation stay constant, income and expenditure of the households in this position will stay the same independent of the identity of the households. The individual households change their position and their identity (people are born, grow older and die). But they change their income and expenditures always in accordance with their position in the social and economic structure of the society. The external situation changes by economic policy and the internal situation of households changes as well (e.g. the moral convictions change, as indicated by the Markov-chain, see equation (1.3) in section 1.4). Thus the relative occupancy β_j of positions P_j change as well and may be analyzed and forecasted. E.g. let $N_{\gamma,\mu,\ldots}(t)$ be the number of households in the position $P_{\gamma,\mu,\ldots}(t)$ in period t and let $\beta_{\gamma,\mu,\ldots}(t)$ be the relative number such that $N_{\gamma,\mu,\ldots}(t) = \beta_{\gamma,\mu,\ldots}(t) \cdot N(t)$, where $N(t)$ is the number of all households. Now the household demand may be estimated as determined by the number of households in each position multiplied by the characteristic consumption demand $c_i(P_{\gamma,\mu,\ldots})$ of a household in this position. Unfortunately only very crude "positions" are recorded in the Statistical Yearbooks. Fig. 1.20 shows the number of households with monthly net income between 5000 and 7500 and 3 or more children in Germany (old territory) from 1991 to 2001. The figure shows, that this position (till now) is occupied by a number of households. Unfortunately, the statistics of household demand is not related to these "positions", thus a direct test of the validity of this theory is not possible. Now the total demand $C_i(t)$ of a consumption good i in period t is estimated by $C_i(t) = N(t) \sum_{\gamma,\mu,\ldots} c_i(P_{\gamma,\mu,\ldots}) \cdot \beta_{\gamma,\mu,\ldots}$.

This theory of consumption demand does not assume specific functional forms for the demand functions. It is flexible in the sense that it could be adapted to rather few statistical subdivisions (in that case the theory delivers only "crude" results), but it could easily be refined in case that more statistical data become available. Moreover, it includes as internal characteristics also latent variables such as moral convictions. Many features of demand are covered which are not considered in the usual approach. Thus it seems to be worthwhile to try this approach. Unfortunately, I cannot do that myself.

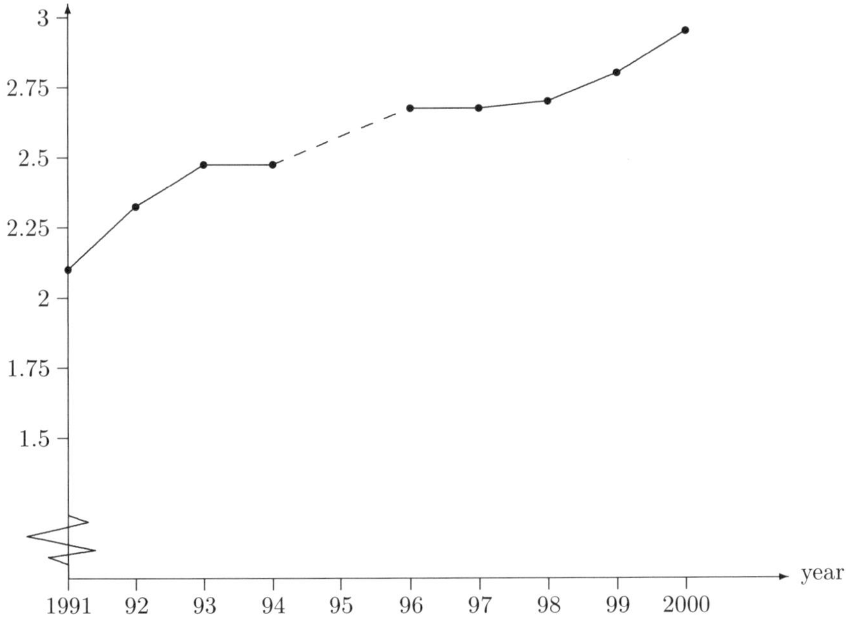

Source: Statistisches Jahrbuch für die BRD, different years, "Privathaushalte ... nach Haushaltsgröße und Haushaltsnettoeinkommen." Number for 1995 not available

Figure 1.20 Mill. households with income between 5000 and 7000 DM and 3 children or more

1.29 A Final Remark: Convergence of Evaluations

A person gets used to a situation, if he prevails long enough. A rich man is not necessarily happier than a poor man. It is only the relative change of the economic situation and the distinction between his own economic situation and that of his environment which affects the evaluation of an economic state. We may formulate this as follows:

Let $G_{ij,t}^{(h)}$ be the evaluation of the state B_{ij} by household h in the beginning of period t from the economic point of view. We measure the economic situation of the household by its real consumption $C_{ij,t}^{(h)}$ in period t. The evaluation $G_{ij,t}^{(h)}$ of the economic situation does not depend on the absolute level of real consumption, but on its rate of change $(C_{ij,t}^{(h)} - C_{t-1}^{(h)})/C_{t-1}^{(h)}$ and on the relative deviation from real consumption of comparable households: $(C_{ij,t}^{(h)} - \bar{C}_{t-1}^{(h)})/\bar{C}_{t-1}^{(h)}$, where $C_{t-1}^{(h)}$ is the actual real consumption of household h in the period before and $\bar{C}_{t-1}^{(h)}$ the average real consumption of comparable households in the period before. Let $\bar{G}^{(h)}$ be the "natural" or "inner" degree of happiness and satisfaction of household h which comes from the personal characteristics of the members of the household and from their relations, but does not depend on the size of consumption as long as the natural needs are satisfied. Then the economic evaluation $G_{ij,t}^{(h)}$ of a state B_{ij} by household h in the beginning of period t seems to follow the rule

$$G_{ij,t}^{(h)} = \bar{G}^{(h)} + \alpha_{ij,c}^{(h)} \frac{C_{ij,t}^{(h)} - C_{t-1}^{(h)}}{C_{t-1}^{(h)}} + \alpha_{ij,\bar{c}}^{(h)} \frac{C_{ij,t}^{(h)} - \bar{C}_{t-1}^{(h)}}{\bar{C}_{t-1}^{(h)}},$$

$$\bar{G}(h) \text{ a constant}, \quad \alpha_{ij,\gamma}^{(h)} \geq 0, \quad \sum_{\gamma \in \Gamma} \alpha_{ij,\gamma}^{(h)} = 1, \quad \gamma \in \{C, \bar{C}\} =: \Gamma,$$

$$\text{such that} - \bar{z} \leq G_{ij,t} \leq +\bar{z}$$

A similar approach has been suggested earlier and is in accordance with empirical results.[100]

1.30 Epilogue: The Importance of Humanities and Their Relation to the Natural Sciences

In the foregoing sections we showed how non-economic influences are introduced into economics[101] . This may give an opportunity to broaden the view and to say some words on the relation of Natural Sciences to Humanities as an epilogue which is much more personal than the statements before.

The *Natural Sciences* have a well defined object and methods of measurement to identify and characterize the object. Their main task is to find "general rules", called "natural laws", which explain the behavior of the object, at least approximately and are universally applicable. In the progress of science more and more tests become available which may clarify or rectify these "natural laws"[102] .But every person in his clear mind must accept the contemporary state of the natural sciences[103] , because one could demonstrate the validity (or at least approximate validity) by experiments in front of his

[100] See Krelle (1968), pp. 28. Empirical results may be found in: Noelle–Neumann (1999). Mrs. Noelle–Neumann shows, that the relative number of people who consider themselves as being happy in the Federal Republic of Germany has been more or less constant during a period from 1954 to 1998 (about 29% of the population). The big increase in the living standard during this period has had no influence on the happiness of people.

[101] This section is not specified on households as the former ones and thus uses partly other concepts.

[102] E.g. Einstein's Relativity Theory changed the concept of time and the explanation of a gravity field.

[103] Of course, since one finds nothing better, the contemporary state will be accepted as "truth". This "contemporary state" must be questioned and tested again and again.

eyes. One would say: The natural sciences explore the behavior of the nature (including the behavior of men) under different conditions. They do not say anything on how a person *should* behave in a certain situation.

This is not so in the *Humanities*[104] . The ultimate aim of this science is (as far as philosophy is concerned) to find an answer to existential questions like

a. Are there any laws in the spiritual development of mankind? How is the spiritual development related to the social, political and economic development?

b. Does the whole universe and my life in it have any meaning which goes beyond the immediate consequences which we observe?

c. Why do we call some actions "good", others "bad"? Could we trace that back to some general principles or holy books or to the value judgements of persons whose authority cannot be questioned?

d. If we accept some books or teachings or decisions of men as highest authority[105] , books which are written and teachings which are conceived under quite other imaginations on natural laws and economic and social conditions: do we have to accept these reports as truth? In other words: is Godfather free to switch off some natural laws if he likes it?[106] The last problem seems to be on a lower level than the other two, but many natural scientists are agnostics because of that. Thus I want to include the problem of the existence of an "eternal truth" behind the observable matters in a changing world. This takes up the old controversy of those who think along the lines of Plato (our observations only show us the shadows of the real world, the ideas behind it are the real thing) and the positivists (who think that only observations should be used to come up with a theory which is then "verified" by the facts) or the empirical rationalists (followers of Popper) who think that it does not matter where the theory comes from, but it must be possible to falsify it[107] . This should always be tried by confronting the

---

[104] We demonstrate this in this introduction by the example of philosophy.

[105] E.g. for Christians: The Bible and the decisions and confessions of the first two or four councils (Nicaea 325, Konstantinopel 381, Ephesus 431, Chalcedon 451).

[106] For Christians: Did the sun really stand still as reported in Joshua 10,13 in order to enable the Israelites to take revenge upon their foes? Since in reality the earth circles around the sun, the command "Sun stand still..." means: Earth stand still. Nobody could have survived such a sudden change of the torsional force. Did a word of Jesus change water to wine (John 2, 6-8)? Could Jesus really walk on the water (Matth. 14,25)?

[107] This is not the place to discuss methodological problems in detail. There is enough literature available, see Popper, Logik der Forschung, 8. ed. Tübingen 1984 (1.Aufl. 1935); Kuhn, Struktur wissenschaftlicher Revolutionen, 5. ed. of the German edition, Frankfurt a.M. 1981; Lakatos a) Die Geschichte der Wissenschaft und ihre rationalen Rekon-

theory with the facts. Thus each theory is preliminary. For the natural sciences (including economics) the methodological difference between a platonist and an empirical rationalist does not seem to be of practical importance because there exist measurements of the objects outside of the theory which provide the test of the adequacy of the theory. But as far as the interpretation and the "general spirit" of a theory is concerned, there is a difference[108] and this difference becomes important in the Humanities. There is no spiritual "object" outside of our thinking which could deliver "objective measurements" on the adequacy of our theories and statements to answer the questions a) – d) above (and related questions; e.g. Kant: "Was kann ich wissen? Was soll ich tun? Was darf ich hoffen?").

In the following we shall show the importance of Humanities for the individual and for social life and their interrelation with economics. We start with a general survey and come to the details and to mathematical formulas afterwards.

Fig. 1.21 illustrates the general approach. At the beginning of period 0, person i finds himself in the situation B_i, which consists of two vectors: B_i^{real}, the vector of all objective measurements of the situation of person i (such as location, family status, income) and a vector B_i^{trans} which consists of subjective statements of the person concerning his religious, philosophical and other beliefs. The person i evaluates his situation at B_i by $v_i(B_i)$, a figure between $-\bar{z}$ and $+\bar{z}$, $\bar{z} > 1$, an integer, where $-\bar{z}$ means: very bad and $+\bar{z}$: very good. In situation B_i person i has the possible decisions $DEC_{i1}, \ldots, DEC_{iz}$. The consequences of these decisions may only be known as probability distributions, called $B_{i1}^{exp}, \ldots, B_{iz}^{exp}$ (exp stands for "expected"). The B_{ij}^{exp} are evaluated by person i as $v_i(B_{ij}^{exp})$. Let DEC_{ij*} be chosen, $j* \in \{1, \ldots, z\}$ (we

---

struktionen, b) Falsifikation und die Methodologie wissenschaftlicher Forschungsprogramme, both articles in: Lakatos/Musgrave (ed.), Kritik und Erkenntnisfortschritt, Braunschweig 1974; Feyerabend, Wissenschaftstheorie, in: HdSW Vol.12, 1965; Albert, a) Plädoyer für Kritischen Rationalismus, 2.ed. München 1971, b) Traktat über Kritische Vernunft, 4.ed., Tübingen 1980.

108 This difference is very well illustrated by Stephen Hawking in: Stephen Hawking, Roger Penrose, Raum und Zeit, 3.ed. 1999 (Rowohlt). I quote from page 165: "Diese Vortragsreihe hat ganz deutlich den Unterschied zwischen Rogers und meinen Auffassungen offenbart. Er ist Platonist und ich bin Positivist. Er ist darüber bekümmert, daß sich Schrödingers Katze in einem Quantenzustand befindet, in dem sie halb lebendig und halb tot ist [Schrödinger gave the following example to question the quantum theory. There is a cat in a cage. A shot is fired which either does not hurt the cat or kills it. According to the quantum theory the cat is in a state where it is half alive and half dead. Only if somebody looks into the cage, the state of the cat is fixed]. Seiner Meinung nach kann dies nicht der Realität entsprechen. Mich dagegen kümmert das wenig. Ich verlange nicht, daß eine Theorie der Realität entspricht, da ich nicht weiß, was das ist. ... Mich interessiert nur, ob die Theorie die Ergebnisse von Messungen vorhersagen kann. Die Quantentheorie ist darin sehr erfolgreich."

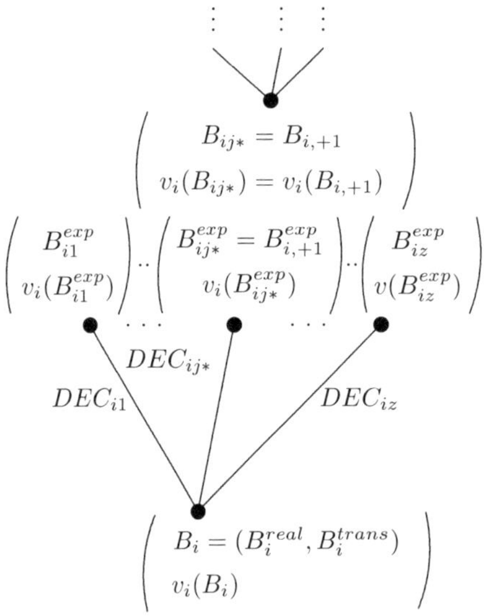

$v_i(B_i)$	=	valuation of the Situation B_i by person i at the beginning of period 0
DEC_{ij*}	=	decision of person i for period 0
D_{ij}^{exp}	=	expected situation of person i after decision DEC_{ij} has been taken and before the decisions of other persons or of nature become known (if these decisions have an influence on the situation B_i).
B_{ij*}	=	actual situation of person i, after its decision DEC_{ij*} and after the decisions of other persons or of nature become known, $j* \in \{1, 2, \ldots, z\}$. This is the initial situation $B_{i,+1}$ of person i at the beginning of period +1.
$v_i(B_{ij*})$	=	evaluation of $B_{ij*} = B_{i,+1}$ by person i

All evaluations lie in the interval $(-\bar{z}, +\bar{z})$, $\bar{z} > 1$, an integer

Figure 1.21. The General Approach

shall show below how this will be done). After DEC_{ij*} is chosen, the choice of the other persons becomes known to person i, and that means that the actual situation B_{ij*} in which the person will be in, is revealed to him which will in general be different from the expected situation B_{ij*}^{exp}. Thus also the valuation $v_i(B_{ij*}^{exp})$ will be different from the valuation $v_i(B_{ij*})$.

In general $B_{ij*} = B_{i,+1}$ will be the initial situation at the beginning of period +1 and now everything is repeated, starting with $B_{i,+1}$ and $v_i(B_{i,+1})$. The Humanities, in this approach represented by the vector B_i^{trans}, enter this process in the following way. The vector B_i^{trans} consists of elements which describe the spiritual status of person i, namely the theology $Th^{(\kappa)}$, the philosophy Ph^{λ} or the ideology ID^{μ} which the person i accepts as at least partially true; that means: which he allows some influence on his thinking and on his behavior. There are k theologies known at the beginning of period 0 as well as l philsosophies and m ideologies. Thus $\kappa \in \{1, \ldots, k\}$, $\lambda \in \{1, \ldots, l\}$, $\mu \in \{1, \ldots, m\}$. For simplicity we call them all "philosophies" and assume that the person accepts only one of them as "true". Thus the vector B_i^{trans} contains only one element, namely the "philosophy" $\Phi^{(\kappa)} \in \{\Phi^{(1)}, \ldots, \Phi^{(k)}\}$, which is accepted by person i. Let there be k theologies, philosophies and ideologies available at the beginning of period 0[109]. Each philosophy κ valuates a situation B_i and a situation B_{ij}^{exp} differently. In case that the philosophy κ is accepted we get the valuations $v_i^{(\kappa)}(B_i)$ or $v_i^{(\kappa)}(B_{ij}^{exp})$ respectively from the point of view of philosophy κ[110] , see also Fig. 1.21. We call this evaluation which results from a philosophy κ a "moral evaluation" M_i^κ and define:

$$v_i^{(\kappa)}(B_i) =: \bar{M}_i{}^\kappa \quad \text{and} \quad v_i^{(\kappa)}(B_{ij}^{\text{exp}}) =: \bar{M}_{ij}{}^\kappa \quad .$$

This term stays constant as long as the person does not change its affiliation to the philosophy κ. But this does not determine the total moral evaluation of B_i or B_{ij}^{exp}. There is the influence of the evaluation by other persons (the "public opinion") which also influences the moral evaluation. We formulated that as a Markov chain j in case of B_{ij}^{exp} as:

$$\tilde{M}_{ij,t} = \tilde{M}_{ij,t-1} \cdot P_{ij},$$

see equation (1.3) in section 1.4. Due to our assumption that person i accepts only one philosophy, the $\bar{p}_{ij,i}^{(1)}, \ldots, \bar{p}_{ij,i}^{(\kappa-1)}, \bar{p}_{ij,i}^{(\kappa+1)}, \ldots$ are zero in equation (1.3), only $\bar{p}_{ij,i}^{(\kappa)}$ is positive in this column. One sees from that equation that other philosophies, openly rejected by person i, nevertheless have indirectly an influence on it via the personal influences of other persons who in turn are influenced by these philosophies. But the moral evaluations $\bar{M}_i^\kappa$ and $\bar{M}_{ij}^\kappa$ are not the only criteria for deciding which way to go. There are others as well. B_i and B_{ij}^{exp} are many-dimensional entities, and many points of view must be considered. Let there be z possible points of view (or criteria, $Cr_1, \ldots, Cr_z$) to judge a situation B_i or B_{ij}; the moral judgement is one of them. The evaluation of B_i by person i with respect to the criterion ξ is denoted by $C_i^{(\xi)}$:

$$v_i^{(Cr_\xi)}(B_i) =: C_i^{(\xi)}, \quad -\bar{z} \leq C_i^{(\xi)} \leq +\bar{z}, \quad \xi = 1, \ldots, z$$

In section 1.2 these evaluations are specified. E.g. if i is a private household, as G, H, EM, IM, M, if i is a firm as G, X, L, D, R, M, see the explanations in section 1.2. All figures lie between $-\bar{z}$ and $+\bar{z}$. Now the total evaluation $v_i(B_i)$ of the situation B_i by person i is (as in equation 1.1 in section 1.3):

---

109 Of course, person i is free to reject all sorts of philosophies. Then there is no entry for B_i^{trans}. But we may classify this "refusal of all philosophies" as an ideology as well and thus include it into the number of philosophies.

110 If the philosophy κ is silent on a specific evaluation, we put this evaluation v_i^κ to zero

$$V_i^{(i)} := v_i(B_i) = n.i.(\alpha_{i1}^{(i)} \cdot C_i^{(1)} + \ldots + \alpha_{iz}^{(i)} \cdot C_i^{(z)}),$$
$$\alpha_{i\xi}^{(i)} \geq 0, \quad \sum_{\xi=1}^{z} \alpha_{i\xi}^{(i)} = 1 \tag{1.39}$$

A similar equation results for $V_{ij}^{(i,exp)} := v_i(B_{ij}^{exp})$, see Fig. 1.21 and equation 1.1 in section 1.3. The person selects that DEC_{ij*} for which $v_i(B_{ij})^{exp}$ is a maximum; see equation 1.2 in section 1.3. We may identify the last item $C_i^{(z)}$ with $M_i^{(i)}$, the moral evaluation of B_i by person i. All this carries over to B_{ij}, where similar equations are valid. As long as person i sticks to his philosophy $\Phi^{(\kappa)}$ the Markov chain of equation (1.3) in section 1.4 determines the actual $M_{i,t}^{(i)}$ in each period t.

In section 1.11 a theory of imitation is suggested. The emotional attraction or repulsion of a situation must be estimated separately on the basis of empirical findings. I did not look into this problem. There is a fluid transition from EM to IM. E.g. the valuation of dogs may be explained by emotion or by imitation. But that instincts and urges influence the valuation of situations and thus the behavior cannot be denied. In section 1.11 some hints are given as to the determination of H, the evaluation of illegal actions which are subject to punishment. It is a problem of empirical research to determine to what extent illegal actions are reduced by higher punishment and by faster and more complete prosecution of the criminals. The evaluation of B_i and B_{ij} from the economic point of view (called G in equation 1.1, section 1.3, if i is a private household) is of a special interest for economics, especially in our context, since the economic evaluation G competes with the moral evaluation M, see equation 1.1. Our general approach(1.39) above admits more than one point of view, e.g. (in the case that i is a household): total net income, net income per member of the household, relation of net income of this household to an average of net incomes of other households, actual employment in relation to desired employment, prospects of future income and employment, transfer payments and so on. The economic situation of a household is a many-dimensional entity, and thus many points of view should be considered. The total valuation $v_i(B_i)$ of the situation B_i is a weighted average of the different specific evaluations. In the absence of detailed empirical findings (which may be gained by public polls) we chose the simplest approach, the arithmetic mean.

Now we have to specify what the situation B_i of a person i really means. As stated above (see also Fig. 1.21) B_i is a vector $B_i = (B_i^{real}, B_i^{trans})$, where B_i^{real} is a vector of all objective determinants of the situation B_i and B_i^{trans} a vector of the "beliefs" of person i. In our simplified approach we assumed that the person i adheres only to one "philosophy" $\Phi^{(\kappa)}, \quad \kappa \in \{1, \ldots, k\}$, if there are k "philosophies" $\Phi^{(\kappa)}$ (which comprise religions and all types of ideologies). Thus in our (admittedly very simplified) approach B_i^{trans} is simply the philosophy $\Phi^{(\kappa)}$ accepted by person i. Thus we only have to specify what

B_i^{real} means in detail. In this approach B_i^{real} is a vector of very different components:

B_i^{real} $= (\Omega, SIT_i, DEC_i^{poss}, \Theta_i)$, where

$\Omega =$ a description of the actual order of the society and of the economy and a description of the knowledge in natural sciences:

$$\Omega = (\Omega^{pol}, \Omega^{jur}, \Omega^{ec}, \Omega^{ns})$$

One may imagine that Ω^{pol} is the constitution of the society and the distribution of political power among parties or social groups.

Ω^{jur} comprises all laws which regulate the private and public life and the rules of court.

Ω^{ec} is a vector which describes the economic order, i.e. all economic states from the extremes of a free market economy to the extreme of a totally planned economy; the degree of freedom of price and wage formation, the rights of the employees in a firm and so on; in short: all laws and rules which determine the economic life.

Ω^{ns} is a vector which describes the knowledge in the field of natural sciences. This delivers the natural background and the physical limitation of all decisions.

Ω is valid for all persons, thus the index i is missing.

SIT_i = a description of the personal and of the economic situation of person i: $SIT_i = (SIT_i^{pers}, SIT_i^{ec})$. SIT_i^{pers} is a vector of indicators for the personal situation of person i (family status, profession, position in the society, location ...), SIT_i^{ec} is a vector of economic indicators which characterize person i (income, employment, position in the income pyramid, ...)

DEC_i^{poss} = a vector of all possible decisions which person i could make in position B_i. In case of z possible decisions: $DEC_i^{poss} = (DEC_{i1}, \ldots, DEC_{iz})$, cf. Fig. 1.21. If i is a household, one may think of different purchases of household commodities, of different allocation of savings, of different types of advanced training, of changing the profession or the employer and so on. Of course, at each decision point $B_i, B_{i,+1}, \ldots$ only very few decisions will be considered in practice. As already said: the person has to select one out of z possible decisions, called DEC_{ij*} in Fig. 1.21. But in order to be able to do that, he has to know the consequences of his decision. This leads us to the last item of the vector B_i^{real}, namely:

Θ_i = the set of economic and social and political theories and econometric methods which allow person i to forecast an expectation value (or a probability distribution) of all components of B_{ij}, called B_{ij}^{exp}, in case that $DEC_{ij} \in \{DEC_{i1}, \ldots, DEC_{iz}\}$ is chosen. This may be formulated as $B_{ij}^{exp} = F(B_i, DEC_{ij}, \Theta_i)$. The set Θ_i changes in time, in general $\Theta_{i,+1} \neq \Theta_i$. This is where technical progress comes in at this stage. We deal with that later.

The inclusion of the general political, social and economic order Ω into the definition B_i^{real} of the real state of person i leads to the consequence that in the set DEC_i^{poss} of possible decisions also political decisions, in our context: decisions on voting have to be included. E.g. if more than a certain percentage of persons (say: 50 %) vote in favor of a change of the constitution this change will be eventually realized, and a new regime starts. The set of criteria $C_{r1}, \ldots, C_{rz}$ may also be enlarged by $C_{r,z+1}, \ldots, C_{r,Z}$, because the state B_i may also be evaluated by the degree of personal freedom, the degree of realization of the rule of law, the protection of private property, to give only some examples.

We now go back to the choice of $\Phi^{(\kappa)}$ by person i and ask:

1) will the person stick to his first decision $\Phi^{(\kappa)}$ or revise it as time passes;
2) will religion disappear from earth when time goes on and more and more features of reality may be explained by the natural sciences;
3) which service do the Humanities deliver to the society?

To 1)

Let us consider a person i which accepts a "philosophy" $\kappa \in \{1, \ldots, K\}$ at the beginning of period 0. There are adjoining philosophies $\kappa', \kappa'', \ldots$ which rest upon the same holy book (the Bible in the Christian tradition) but understand some words in another way. Goethe has characterized this fact by the translation of the first sentence of the Gospel of St. John: Faust sits in his study and reflects:

> "Geschrieben steht: 'Im Anfang war das Wort!'
> Hier stock ich schon! Wer hilft mir weiter fort?
> Ich kann das Wort so hoch unmöglich schätzen,
> ich muß es anders übersetzen,
> Wenn ich vom Geiste recht erleuchtet bin.
> Geschrieben steht: Am Anfang war der Sinn.
> Bedenke wohl die erste Zeile,
> Daß deine Feder sich nicht übereile!
> Ist es der Sinn, der alles wirkt und schafft?
> Es sollte stehen: Im Anfang war die Kraft!
> Doch, auch indem ich dieses niederschreibe,
> Schon warnt mich was, daß ich nicht dabei bleibe.
> Mir hilft der Geist! Auf einmal seh' ich Rat.
> Und schreibe getrost: Im Anfang war die Tat!"

Protestants and Catholics both recognize the Bible as their ultimate source, but they interpret some parts differently (e.g. the letter of St. Paul to the Romans and the letter of St. Jacob). The French philosopher Derrida says that nobody knows what Plato and Aristoteles really meant by their writings, because nobody knows the exact meaning of the words they used. This may be overdone, but it is a fact that the teachings of the churches as far as ethics is concerned changed a lot during the centuries.

We formulate that in the following way. A person i which accepts a philosophy $\Phi^{(\kappa)}$ really accepts a certain version of a family of philosophies $\Phi^{(\kappa)}$, $\Phi^{(\kappa')}$, $\Phi^{(\kappa)''}$, ... which all originate from the same basic source but differ in the interpretation of some words and sentences. If we accept the Markov chain of equation (1.3) in section 1.4 as an appropriate model for the change of moral convictions, the moral evaluation of a decision DEC_{ij} in period 0 is $M_{ij}^{(i)} = M_{ij,0}^{(i)}$. The average evaluation of all other members of the society (which represents the "public opinion") may be written as $\hat{M}_{ij,0} = \frac{1}{N-1} \sum_{a=1,a\neq i}^{N} M_{ij,0}^{(a)}$. If the evaluation of person i deviates too much from the public opinion, it will feel unhappy and look after another version of the same basic approach:

if $\left| M_{ij,0}^{(i)} - \hat{M}_{ij,0} \right| > F_{ij}$, person i substitutes in the next period an adjacent philosophy $\Phi^{(\kappa')}$ for the philosophy $\Phi^{(\kappa)}$, such that

$$\left| M_{ij,+1}^{(i)} - \hat{M}_{ij,+1} \right| \leq F_{ij}, \tag{1.40}$$

$F_{ij} > 0$ is a measure of tolerance of social deviations and $M_{ij,+1}^{(i)}$ the solution of equation (1.3) for the next period, if $\bar{M}_{ij}^{(\kappa)}$ which followed from $\Phi^{(\kappa)}$ is substituted by $\bar{M}_{ij}^{(\kappa')}$ which follows from $\Phi^{(\kappa')}$. If there are more than one adjacent philosophies $\Phi^{(\kappa')}$ which conform to the inequality (1.40) above that which is "nearest to" $\Phi^{(\kappa)}$ will be selected. This may be a sketch of how one could model the slow change of teaching of churches and interpretations of philosophers.

To 2)

Religion will not disappear from earth if it concentrates on its proper field and does not try to compete with the natural sciences. This is not a hindrance to the declarations of moral judgements on possible decisions DEC_{ij} based on a religious conviction, just the opposite is true.

The situation as I see it is the following. All religions originate from the writing or teaching of men who are supposed to have an access to the transcendental eternal world beyond this universe. The connection is conveyed by a unique messenger from beyond (for Christians: by Jesus Christ, son of God, whose words and sentences are the truth) or by messages received from above (like in Islam, when the archangel Gabriel transfers God's messages to

Mohammed) or by a "holy man" like Buddha or by the decisions of councils or of popes which are supposed to be inspired by the Holy Ghost or by dreams, mystical phenomena, visions and appearances (as reported in the Bible from the prophets, but also reported from persons in modern times, e.g. from Bernadette in Lourdes, who in 1858 saw the virgin Maria several times in a grotto and was canonized 1933). Now one may doubt all that and take it as psychological phenomena (the positivistic or critical rationalistic approach) or one may take it as truth and as messages from an other, the "real" world. This is the Platonic approach which sees this world and its observations as a "shadow" of the real world behind it, which is only accessible for philosophers. The Platonic view is shared by those who experienced visions and appearances and mystical connections e.g. during prayers themselves, and these events make deep impressions at the persons who experience it. Now there are persons who do not have these experiences themselves but believe in the accounts of it and others who do not and explain it by psychological conditions. The situation is the same as in the natural sciences: do we take the theories in the natural sciences as truth (or as a good approximation to truth), the Platonic approach, or as a good description and forecast of measurements without any necessary relation to reality, because nobody knows what "reality" means (the positivistic approach, cf. the remarks of Stephen Hawking in connection with the Pauly cat, cited above). There will always be people who look to this world in the sense of Plato and those who only accept the results of reproducible measurements as "real". For research in the field of natural sciences this has no consequences, but for the society as a whole it has. Judging from the statistics of the US which report that about 30% of the population are members of churches and if we deduct a rather large percentage of persons who join a church for social reasons we may estimate that about 20% of a population prefers the Platonic view. Thus religion will not die out when research goes on.

To 3)

The Humanities (here exemplified by religion and philosophy) play an important role in the development of mankind. One may infer that from the fact that they still exist and did not disappear as a hindrance to the development. But we may also understand that fact in the light of our system (1.3) in section 1.4 which shows the interdependence of moral evaluations and their relations to religions or philosophical evaluations $\bar{M}_{ij}^{(1)}, \ldots, \bar{M}_{ij}^{(K)}$. These evaluations are rather fix and thus form a sort of anchor of the system of value formation. Its convergence values depend on these fix valuations and not on the initial conditions. Thus the development of a society (though it may show cycles) is more smooth and more calculable than that of a society without these anchors. In the latter case the system may be chaotic, thus not calculable at all. On the other hand, if these anchors are really fix for a long time, the society may become totally immovable (take as an example the Egyptian society in the antiquity) – a great disadvantage in the long run. But this may be remedied if the persons revise their adherence to a special kind of religion or philosophical system and adapt their interpretation of the basic approach always in the direction of the "public opinion" if the deviation becomes too large.

Thus we see how the Humanities are fully integrated in the process of human development. Only the basic features of the integration could be shown above. The details are much more complicated.

References

[1] Albert, Hans: *Plädoyer für kritischen Rationalismus*, 2. ed., München 1971

[2] Albert, Hans: *Traktat über kritische Vernunft*, 4. ed., Tübingen 1980

[3] Banerjee, A.V.: A Simple Model of Herd Behavior, *Quarterly J. of Economics*, Vol.107, 1992, pp. 797-817

[4] Becker, Gary S.: Crime and Punishment: An Economic Approach, *Journal of Political Economics*, Vol. 76, 1968, pp. 169–217

[5] Becker, Gary, S.: Altruism, Egoism, and Genetic Fitness: Economics and Sociobiology, *Journal of Economic Literature*, Vol. 14, 1976, pp. 817–826;

[6] Beckmann, Martin: Rank in Organizations, *Lecture Notes in Economics and Mathematical Systems*, Berlin etc. (Springer), 1978, pp. 13 ff.

[7] Bergstrom, Stark: How Altruism can Prevail in an Evolutionary Environment, *American Economic Review*, Vol. 83/2, 1993, pp. 149-155

[8] Bester, Helmut / Güth, Werner: Is Altruism Evolutionary Stable?, Center for Economic Research, Tilburg University, *Discussion Paper Nr. 94103*, 1994

[9] Bikhchandani, S., Hirshleifer, D., Welch, I.: A Theory of Fads, Fashion, Custom, and Cultural Change as Informational Cascades, *Journal of Political Economy*, Vol.100, 1992, pp. 992-1026

[10] Böckle, Franz: *Fundamentalmoral*, München, 1977

[11] Cameron, Samuel: The Economics of Crime Deterrence: A Survey of Theory and Evidence, *Kyklos*, Vol. 41, 1988, pp. 301–323

[12] Cameser, Colin / Thaler, Richard: Ultimatum, Dictation and Manners, *Journal of Economic Perspectives*, Vol. 9, 1995, pp. 209–219

[13] Corneo, Giacomo / Jeanne, Oliver: Conspicuous consumption, snobbism and conformism, *Journal of Publ. Ec.*, Vol. 66, 1997, pp. 55–71

[14] Dawkins, Richard: *Das egoistische Gen* Berlin, Heidelberg, New York (Springer), 1978 pp. 83 ff.

[15] Debreu, Gerard, Excess Demand Functions, Journal of Mathematical Economics 1 (1974), S. 15-21.

[16] Delahaye, Jean–Paul / Mathieu, Philippe: Altruismus mit Kündigungsmöglichkeiten, *Spektrum der Wissenschaft*, Vol 2, 1998, pp. 8–14

[17] Dhrymes, Phoebus J.: Econometrics, New York, Evanston, and London (Harper & Row), 1970

[18] Durkheim, Emile: *Die Methode der Soziologie*, Translation of the 4. ed., Leipzig, 1908

[19] Ehrlich, Isaac: Crime, Punishment, and the Market for Offenses, *Journal of Economic Perspectives*, Vol. 10, 1996, pp. 43–67

[20] Ellison, G., Fudenberg, D.: Word of Mouth Communication and Social Learning, *Quarterly Journal of Economics*, Vol.110, 1997, pp. 93-125

[21] Engel, Gerhard: Wirtschaftsethik und pragmatische Moralskepsis. Zum Vorrang der Empirie vor der Ethik, in: Aufderheide, D. und Dabrowski, M. (ed.), *Wirtschaftsethik und Moralökonomik. Normen, soziale Ordnung und der Beitrag der Ökonomik*, Berlin (Duncker und Humboldt), 1997, pp. 71–120

[22] Engelhardt, Werner Wilhelm: Ökonomische Denktraditionen, Ökonomismus versus Ethik und die kulturellen Aufgaben der Zukunft, in: Elsner, Wolfram / Engelhardt, Werner Wilhelm / Glastetter, Werner (ed.), *Ökonomie in gesellschaftlicher Verantwortung*, Festschrift zum 65. Geburtstag von Siegfried Katterle, Berlin (Duncker und Humboldt), 1998, pp. 19–43

[23] Erling, Eide: Economics of Crime: Deterrence and the rational offender, in: *Contributions to Economic Analysis series*, Vol. 227, Amsterdam, Oxford, Tokyo (North Holland) 1994

[24] Fehr, Ernst / Tongareva, Elena: Do High Monetary Stakes Remove Reciprokal Fairness?, Experimental Evidence from Russia, *unpublished paper*, 1996

[25] Feyerabend, Paul: Wissenschaftstheorie, in: *HdSW, Vol. 12*, 1965

[26] Fiorentini, Gianluca, and Peltzmann, Sam (ed.): *The Economics of Organized Crime*, Cambridge, New York, Melbourne (Cambridge University Press), 1995

[27] Frank, Robert H.: If Homo Economicus Could Choose His Own Utility Function: Would He Want One With a Conscience?, *American Economic Review*, Vol. 77/4, 1987

[28] Gaertner, Wulf: *Wirtschaftsethische Perspektiven IV*, Schr. Ver. Soz. Pol. NF 228/IV, Berlin (Duncker und Humboldt), 1998 (see also part I-III, 1994-1996)

[29] Güth, Werner: Do Banks Crowd in or out Business Ethics — An Indirect Evolutionary Analysis, *Discussion Paper 40*, SFB 373, Humboldt–Universität at Berlin, 1998

[30] Güth, Werner / Tietz, Reinhard: Ultimatum Bargaining Behavior – A Survey and Comparison of Experimental Results, *Journal of Economic Psychology*, Vol. 11, 1990, pp. 417–449

[31] Hammerstein, Peter / Selten, Reinhard: *Game Theory and Evolutionary Biology*, Ch. 28 in: Handbook of Game Theory, Vol. 2 (ed.: Aumann and Hart), Elsevier Science, 1994, pp. 929–993

[32] Hawking, Steven: in: *Steven Hawking/ Roger Penrose, Raum und Zeit*, 3. ed., (Rowohlt), 1999

[33] Hildenbrand, W.: How Relevant are Specifications of Behavioral Relations on the Micro-Level for Modelling the Time Path of Population Aggregates?, *European Economic Review*, 1998, pp. 437-458

[34] Hirschmann, Albert O.: Rival Views of Market Society and Other Recent Essays, New York (Viking) 1986, p. 107, cited from Honk van Luijk, Rights and Interests in a Participating Market Society, Ch. 1 in: Hans de Geer, *Business Ethics in Progress*, Berlin etc. (Springer) 1994, pp. 5/6

[35] Höffe, Otfried (ed.): *Einführung in die utilitaristische Ethik*, München (Beck), 1975

[36] Höffe, Otfried: *Lexikon der Ethik*, 5. ed., München, 1997

[37] Homann, Karl: Die Rolle ökonomischer Überlegungen in der Grundlegung der Ethik, in: Helmut Hesse (ed.), *Wirtschaftswissenschaft und Ethik*, Schr. Ver. Soz. Pol. NF 171, Berlin (Duncker & Humblot) 1988, p. 218)

[38] Homann, Karl: Individualisierung: Verfall der Moral? Zum ökonomischen Fundament aller Moral, *Aus Politik und Zeitgeschichte*, Beiträge zur Wochenzeitung *Das Parlament*, 16. May 1997, pp. 23–38

[39] Homann, Karl: Sinn und Grenze der ökonomische Methode in der Wirtschaftsethik, in: Aufderheide, D. und Dabrowski, M. (ed.), *Wirtschaftsethik und Moralökonomik. Normen, soziale Ordnung und der Beitrag der Ökonomik*, Berlin (Duncker und Humboldt), 1997, pp. 11–42

[40] Homann, Karl: Normativität angesichts systemischer Sozial– und Denkstrukturen, in: Gaertner, Wulf (ed.): *Wirtschaftsethische Perspektiven IV*, Schr. Ver. Soz. Pol. NF 228/IV, Berlin, 1998

[41] Honnefelder, Ludger: Wissenschaft und Ethik: *Europa auf dem Weg zu einem Konsens*, Manuskript, Philosophisches Seminar, Abt. B, Universität Bonn, 1997

[42] Jöreskog, K.G., & Wold, H. (Eds.): Proceedings of the Conference "Systems under Indirect Observation, Causality-Structure-Prediction", Oct. 18-20, 1979 in Cartigny, near Geneve, Amsterdam (North Holland), 1980

[43] Kersting, W.: Die politische Philosophie des Gesellschaftsvertrages, Darmstadt *(wissenschaftliche Buchgesellschaft)*, 1994

[44] Kindermann, Gottfried–Karl: Außenpolitik im Widerstreit. Spannung zwischen Interesse und Moral, in: *Internationale Politik*, Sept. 1997, pp. 1–6

[45] Kliemt, Hartmut: *Antagonistische Kooperation*, Freiburg, München (Alber), 1986

[46] Kliemt, Hartmut: *Papers on Buchanan and Related Subjects*, Münster (Accedo), 1990

[47] Kluxen, Wolfgang: Perspektiven der Wirtschaftsethik, Vorträge G 353, Akademie der Wissenschaften (ed.), Opladen (Westdeutscher Verlag), 1997

[48] Koller, Peter: Rationales Entscheiden und moralisches Handeln, Kap. IX in: Julian Nida-Rümelin (ed.), *Praktische Rationalität*, Berlin (De Gruyter), 1993 pp. 281–311

[49] Krelle, Wilhelm: *Präferenz- und Entscheidungstheorie*, Tübingen, 1968, pp. 38 ff.

[50] Krelle, Wilhelm: *Theorien des wirtschaftlichen Wachstums*, 2. ed., Berlin etc. (Springer), 1988 a, pp. 751 and 758.

[51] Krelle, Wilhelm: Latent Variables in Econometric Models, *Discussion Paper B-104*, SFB 303, Bonn, 1988 b

[52] Krelle, Wilhelm: Latente Variable in ökonometrischen Prognosemodellen, in: Nikhaeizadeh und Follmer (Herausg.), Neuere Entwicklungen der angewandten Ökonometrie, Heidelberg (Physica-Verlag), p. 1-19, 1990

[53] Krelle, Wilhelm: Entwicklung und Aufrechterhaltung moralischer Standards, in: Immenga/Möschel (ed.), *Festschrift für Ernst–Joachim Mestmäcker zum 70. Geburtstag*, Baden–Baden (Nomos), 1996, pp. 227–241

[54] Krelle, Wilhelm: Ökonomische Grundlagen der Ethik, *Discussion Paper B-428*, SFB 303, Rheinische Friedrich–Wilhelms–Universität Bonn, March 1998

[55] Krelle, Wilhelm: The Spirit of Enterprise as Driving Force of Technical Progress, in: Dieter Sadowski (ed.), *Enterpreneurial Spirits*, Wiesbaden (Gabler), 2001, p. 31-55

[56] Krengel, Ulrich: *Einführung in die Wahrscheinlichkeitstheorie und Statistik*, Braunschweig/Wiesbaden (Vieweg) 1988, pp. 197 ff.

[57] Kühnel, Harry: *Alltag im Mittelalter*, 3. ed., Graz, Wien, Köln (Kaleidoskop) 1986, p. 348

[58] Kuhn, Thomas S.: *Struktur wissenschaftlicher Revolutionen*, 5. Aufl. of the German edition, Frankfurt/Main 1981

[59] Lakatos, Imre: Die Geschichte der Wissenschaft und ihre rationalen Rekonstruktionen in: *Lakatos/Musgrave (ed.), Kritik und Erkenntnisfortschritt*, Braunschweig 1974

[60] Lakatos, Imre: Falsifikation und die Methodologie wissenschaftlicher Forschungsprogramme, in: *Lakatos/Musgrave (ed.), Kritik und Erkenntnisfortschritt*, Braunschweig 1974

[61] Lorenz, Konrad: *Das sogenannte Böse*, München (dtv), 17. ed., 1992

[62] Lindstädt, Hagen: Qualität von Gruppenentscheidungen, in: *OR Spektrum*, Vol. 20/3, 1998, pp. 165–187

[63] Mas-Colell, A., Whinston, M., Green, J.R.: Microeconomic Theory, New York, Oxford, *Oxford University Press*, 1995

[64] Mayntz, Renate: Rationalität in sozialwissenschaftlicher Perspektive, *Lectiones Jenenses*, No. 18, Schriftenreihe des Max-Planck-Institutes zur Erforschung von Wirtschaftssystemen, Jena 1999

[65] Murata, Yasuo: *Mathematics for Stability and Optimization of Economic Systems*, New York, San Francisco, London (Academic Press), 1977

[66] Noelle-Neumann: Ein Museum der Irrtümer. Die Ergebnisse der empirischen Sozialforschung finden keinen Eingang in die Gesellschaft, Institut für Demoskopie Allensbach, *Disc. Paper*, 1999, Table 1; partly reprinted in Frankfurter Allgemeine Zeitung, 13. January 1999, p. 5

[67] Opp, Karl–Dieter: The Economics of Crime and the Sociology of Deviant Behavior: A Theoretical Confrontation of Basic Propositions, *Kyklos*, Vol. 42, 1989, pp. 405–430

[68] Popper, Karl: *Logik der Forschung*, 8. ed., Tübingen 1994 (1. ed. 1935)

[69] Rabin, Matthew: Incorporating Fairness into Game Theory and Economics, *American Economic Review*, Vol. 83/5, 1993, pp. 1281–1302

[70] Rich, Arthur: *Wirtschaftsethik*, Vol. I, II, Gütersloh *Gerd Mohn*, 1990

[71] Rohls, J.: Geschichte der Ethik, 2. Aufl., Tubingen *Mohr Siebeck*, 1999

[72] Röpke, Wilhelm: *Jenseits von Angebot und Nachfrage*, Erlenbach–Zürich–Stuttgart (Rentsch), 1958

[73] Roth, A.E.: Bargaining Experiments, in: J.A. Kagel / A.E. Roth (eds.), *Handbook of Experimental Economics*, Princeton (Princeton University Press), 1995

[74] Schweizer, U.: Vertragstheorie, Tübingen *Mohr Siebeck*, 1999

[75] Selten / Stoecker: End behavior in sequences of Finite Prisoner's Dilemma Supergames, *J. of Economic Behavior and Organization 7*, 1986, pp. 47–70

[76] Siep, Ludwig: *Ethik und Menschenbild*, Mauskript, Vorlesung vor der Gerda–Henkel–Siftung im Zusammenwirken mit der NRW–Akademie der Wissenschaften am 27.05.98

[77] Smith, Adam: *Theorie der ethischen Gefühle*, herausgegeben von Walther Eckstein, Leipzig 1926, Vol. I, pp. 127/128

[78] Smith, John Maynard: *Evolution and the Theory of Games*, Cambridge (Cambridge University Press), 1982

[79] Sonnenschein, Hugo, Market Excess Demand Functions, Econometrica 40, No. 3 (May, 1972), S. 549-563.

[80] Spinoza, Baruch: *Die Ethik nach geometrischer Methode dargestellt*, Hamburg (Felix Meiner), 1665, latest ed. 1994, pp. 186 ff.

[81] Taubman, Paul: The Relative Influence of Inheritable and Environmental Factors and the Importance of Intelligence in Earnings Functions, in Krelle, Shorrocks (ed.), *Personal Income Distribution*, Amsterdam, New York, Oxford (North Holland), 1978, pp. 381–394.

[82] Wieland, Wolfgang: Verantwortungsethik als Spielart des Utilitarismus, in: *Akademie–Journal*, Mitteilungsblatt der deutschen Akademie der Wissenschaften, Nr. 1/98, pp. 37–40

[83] Wright, Laurence: Double Mystery, in: *The New Yorker*, August 7, 1995, pp. 45–62

CHAPTER 2

The Theory of the Firm[1]

2.1 Introduction

The neoclassical production function is the most often used theoretical instrument when the relation between factor input and product output is analyzed. There are different versions of this theory. In the course of time the simple 2-factor static Cobb-Douglas production function is developed to a system of holothetic dynamic production functions (Sato (1999), p. 316). The static version fits into the Walrasian System. This system came under attack recently, see Sonnenschein (1972) and Debreu (1974). In the foreword to this book I gave some reasons for it.[2]

In chapter 1 I suggested a theory of the household which is nearer to reality and avoids (in my opinion) some shortcomings of the traditional theory of the household. In this chapter I do the same with respect to the theory of the firm – with some differences. In the theory of the household I took the household as a unity and did not look into the interior of the relations between the different members of the household. In other words: I identified the household with a person. This seems to be a tolerable simplification. But this cannot be done in the theory of the firm. The organization of the firm is essential for its success and cannot be disregarded. The financial side of the firm must be considered to be of equal importance as the production side.

Prices and production are determined by the firm on the basis of its perception of the demand function. But the firm may err in this respect, and this yields unplanned and unwanted changes of inventories. We do include such errors in our model. This is why we call this system a General Disequilibrium System.

This may hint at the general direction into which we want to expand the theory of the firm. The general assumptions[3] are chosen in such a way that the system fits into a general disequilibrium system which may substitute the

---

[1] A part of this theory has already been published in the Festschrift for Ryuzo Sato, see Krelle (2001).

[2] But also general behavior principles such as profit maximizing, cost minimizing and perfect information have been criticized as too high degree of abstraction (Mark Blaug, 1998) or not in line with the results of sociology and psychology (Renate Mayntz, 1999) or disproved by the results of experiments (Reinhard Selten, 1986).

[3] They are the same as those employed in Krelle 2001a and b where the production part of the model is presented. Here we deal also with the inventories, with the organization of the firm and with the financial side.

Walrasian general equilibrium system and that the theory of the firm is compatible and similarly conceived as the theory of the household presented in chapter 1. In this section we state the general assumptions. Special assumptions follow in the next sections.

a. Everything that we observe and which is not left to nature is due to decisions of persons. Thus the theory concentrates on the decision process.

b. The decisions result from the judgement of persons by considering alternatives (not necessarily all alternatives) with respect to different principles, e.g. the size of profits, shareholder value, the size of production and employment, dominant position in certain markets, take-over of other firms etc.

c. These principles are procured and weighted by a system of mutual interdependencies of information and evaluation which may be modeled by a Markov chain.

d. Judgements and valuations are expressed as degrees of affection or aversion. The ability to quantify these degrees is not very high. Thus, we require that the person states his or her judgement by an integer between $-\bar{z}$ and $+\bar{z}$, $\bar{z}$ an integer ≥ 1, where $-\bar{z}$ denotes the highest aversion, $+\bar{z}$ the highest affection and zero denotes indifference or ignorance.

e. All firms produce a single product which differs from the product of the other firms (the elasticity of substitution may be large. The firm will take care of this by its price policy).

f. The firm determines the price of its product for the next period (considering its perception of the demand at this price) as well as the size of production and employment. Of course, demand will not equal supply, as a rule, and this means: there will be unplanned and undesired inventory changes – this is meant by the word "disequilibrium". These unwelcome inventory changes are taken into consideration by the production plan in the following period. But, of course, also in this and all following periods production will not correspond to demand, as a rule, because demand will have changed.

g. There is only a finite number of firms, which are all in different initial positions. They are defined by real capital installations, inventories, the labor force and other real variables as well as by the financial situation.

h. Product $x_i(t)$ produced by a firm i in period t may be physically different from the same product $x_i(t-1)$ one period earlier (e.g. the automobile of a certain brand sold in this year may be a bit different from that sold in the year before). The product $x_i(t)$ is sold at the price $p_i(t)$.

i. The (real) capital of the firm is the vector of the number of "machines" invested in different periods back to the period where the oldest "machine" has been installed[4]. The "machines" consist of the products of other firms. There are demand coefficients which determine this demand, which is proportional to the number of "machines" invested by the firm in this period.

k. There are output coefficients which determine the capacity output of each machine if it is fully used and if all necessary secondary inputs and the necessary personnel to operate the machine are available. We assume that there are regular replacement investments such that the output coefficient of a "machine" is constant during the life time of a "machine". The "machine" will be sorted out if the operating of the "machine" will induce losses to the firm.

l. Each "machine" needs secondary inputs and labor to produce a certain output. There are input coefficients which determine the necessary secondary inputs. For labor we have two types of input coefficients: one which determines the labor necessary to operate a "machine" at all (even if there is only one unit of output to be produced; this number of workers stays the same independent of the size of the output) and labor input coefficients which are proportional to the size of the output.

m. This defines the model of the *Production Department* of a firm. But each firm has at least three departments: in addition to the Production Department the *Inventory (and Transportation) Department* and the *Administration Department.*[5] The Inventory Department is similarly modeled as the Production Department; we shall not describe it here in detail. But the Administration Department follows other regularities which will be described below.

The Administration Department is equipped with "administrative capital": buildings, computers, office equipments etc., always labeled by the time of investment. There is a maximum amount of administrators which can be accomodated in the buildings. The number and the responsibilities of the administrators constitutes the organizational structure of the firm which codetermines its output and its costs.

---

[4] The experience at the transformation of planned economies to market economies has demonstrated the importance of the age distribution of real capital.

[5] Some firms have also a Research and Development Department. We deal with it in a separate part in connection with technical progress and the educational system in general. Research and development in one firm cannot be understood without the scientific base provided by basic research done in universities and other research organizations. Thus it is reasonable to deal with research and development within one firm in connection with research done at other places and with the educational system in the society. This will be done in chapter 4.

We model this as follows[6]: The total number of persons to operate the machines is determined as suggested above. But these persons alone cannot run the firm. Each activity needs planning, coordination, supervision and financial and other administration in order to guarantee a reasonable result. Now it is an experience that one person (even if assisted by a staff) can only supervise a rather small number of other persons or institutions, say 2 to 20. Martin Beckmann calls it "the control span". But these administrators of rank 1 must also be supervised and so on till "the boss" is reached whose supervision is supposed to be done by the owners of the firm. If the control spans at different ranks have been determined the number of administrators follows. But the efficiency of the firm does not only depend on the density of control as determined by the control spans but also on the assignment of persons to supervisors. We shall also deal with that problem.

Now we start with the *Production Department* of a firm.

2.2 The Production Department: Production, Capital Equipment, and Replacement

We assume that there are $\bar{M}$ firms in the economy. In period t each firm i produces a special product by the amount $x_i(t)$.[7] There may be strong substitution relations between some of these products, but nevertheless: the product of one firm is not identical to that of another firm since at least the locations of the firms are different. We start with *the real side of the firm* i, $i = 1, \ldots, \bar{M}$. In the beginning of period 0 it consists of *real capital* $K_i(0)$ which is a vector of real investments $(I^{real}_{i,-1}, \ldots, I^{real}_{i,-T})$ in former periods $-1, \ldots, -T$, if the oldest "machine" is of age T:

$$K_i(0) = (I^{real}_{i,-T}, I^{real}_{i,-T+1}, \ldots, I^{real}_{i,-1})^{8\ 9\ 10} \tag{2.1}$$

---

[6] This approach was suggested by Martin Beckmann (1978).

[7] The assumption of a one-commodity production of a firm is not so unrealistic as it seems to be at the first sight. If there are separate production lines and the products are rather different we may deal with the firm as really consisting of several single firms connected by common ownerships and common financial bands. If the production relations of the different products are stable we may count the different products as one composed product. In macroeconomics this is the normal procedure.

[8] From now on we leave out the index i for the firm and the time index, if t=0, whenever possible. We call the production investments "machines". The machines of different vintages are different, in general, because of technical progress. The same is true for the output $x_i(t)$: the product $x_i(t)$ will be physically different from the product $x_i(t-1)$, in general. But machines of all vintages are able to produce the same output $x_i(t)$

Instead of real investment $I^{real}_{i,-\tau}$ we could use the number $M_{i,-\tau}$ of "machines" which represent the real investment in period $-\tau$. Their relation is derived below.

Let $I^{real}_{ji,-\tau}$ be the real value of the deliveries of investment goods from firm j to firm i in period $-\tau$. Then these deliveries are proportional to the real investment $I^{real}_{i,-\tau}$ of that period or equivalently to the number $M_{i,-\tau}$ of "machines" installed at firm i in period $-\tau$:

$$I^{real}_{ji,-\tau} = d_{ji,-\tau} \cdot I^{real}_{i,-\tau} = d_{ji,-\tau} \cdot M_{i,-\tau} \cdot \Delta_{i,-\tau} \tag{2.2}$$

where $d_{ji,-\tau} \geq 0$ is the demand coefficient with respect to investment good j and $\Delta_{i,-\tau}$ is a proportionality factor to be derived below. Now the total real cost $I^{real}_{i,-\tau}$ of investment at firm i in period $-\tau$ is

$$I^{real}_{i,-\tau} = \sum_{j=1}^{M} I^{real}_{ji,-\tau} \cdot \frac{p_{j,-\tau}}{\bar{p}_{-\tau}}$$

where $p_{j,-\tau}$ is the price of commodity j in period $-\tau$ and $\bar{p}_{\tau}$ the general price level in this period. The actual costs of investment in this period are

$$I_{i,-\tau} = I^{real}_{i,-\tau} \cdot \bar{p}_{-\tau} = \sum_{j=1}^{M} I^{real}_{ji,-\tau} \cdot p_{j,-\tau} = I^{real}_{i,-\tau} \cdot \sum_{j=1}^{M} \cdot d_{ji,-\tau} \cdot p_{j,-\tau} =$$

$$M_{i,-\tau} \cdot \Delta_{i,-\tau} \cdot \sum_{j=1}^{M} d_{ji,-\tau} \cdot p_{j,-\tau}$$

---

[9] There are different possible measures of a "machine":

(a) A "machine" is the smallest set of installations in a firm by which the final product can be produced. This is a sort of "natural definition" which we use in the verbal interpretation but which is statistically difficult to ascertain.

(b) A "machine" invested in a certain period is measured by the amount of hours it can be active for producing the output. That means: a machine is measured by the services it provides. Let us call them $KS_{i,-\tau}$.

(c) A "machine" may be measured by the real costs of buying and installing an equipment to produce the final product. This measure is most comfortable from the statistical point of view. If $I_{i,-\tau}$ is identified with these real costs and $KS_{i,-\tau}$ and $I_{i,-\tau}$ are measured separately we may assume that there is a short term stable relation:

$$KS_{i,-\tau} = \hat{k}_{i,-\tau} I_{i,-\tau} \qquad , \hat{k}_{i,-\tau} > 0, \quad \text{a constant.}$$

It depends on the aim of the study which definition is selected. In this book we use the first one.

[10] Instead of $K_i(0)$ we shall also write $K_{i,0}$ if this is more comfortable in another context. The following approach has already been presented in the Festschrift for Ryuzo Sato, 2001 b.

The real costs of this investment are proportional to the number of machines:

$$
\begin{aligned}
I^{real}_{i,-\tau} &= \frac{I_{i,-\tau}}{\bar{p}_{-\tau}} = M_{i,-\tau} \cdot \triangle_{i,-\tau} \\
\text{where } \triangle_{i,-\tau} &= \sum_{j=1}^{M} d_{ji,-\tau} \cdot \frac{p_{j,-\tau}}{\bar{p}_{-\tau}}.
\end{aligned} \tag{2.3}
$$

Thus we shall also use the expression "number of machines" instead of "real cost of investment".[11] All "machines" of a firm produce the same output. If they are used at capacity level (which implies that they are provided with the necessary labor and secondary inputs to operate the machines) and if $a_{i,-\tau,t}$ is the output coefficient of a machine installed at time $-\tau$ and used to produce the product $x_{i,t}$ in period t ($t > -\tau$) we get for the capacity output $x^{cap}_{i,-\tau,t}$ of firm i on machines of age τ in period t:[12]

$$x^{cap}_{i,-\tau,t} = a_{i,-\tau,t} \cdot I^{real}_{i,-\tau} \tag{2.4}$$

We may assume that the output coefficient of younger machines is larger than that of older machines of at least equal size:

$$a_{i,-\tau,t} \leq a_{i,-\tau+1,t}$$

Now we get the total capacity output of firm i at the beginning of period 0:

$$x^{cap}_i = \sum_{\tau=1}^{T} a_{i,-\tau,0} \cdot I^{real}_{i,-\tau}$$

We also could relate the capacity output of firm i to the number of machines of different age. From equation(2.3) we get

$$x^{cap}_i = \sum_{\tau=1}^{T} \hat{a}_{i,-\tau,O} \cdot M_{i,-\tau}$$

where $\hat{a}_{i,-\tau,0} = a_{i,-\tau,0} \cdot \triangle_{i,-\tau}$.

Let $\delta_{i,-\tau}$ be the degree of capacity utilization of the machines of age τ in period 0, $0 \leq \delta_{i,-\tau} \leq 1$. Then we get for the actual production in period 0:

$$x_i = \sum_{\tau=1}^{T} \delta_{i,-\tau} x^{cap}_{i,-\tau}.$$

---

[11] A "machine" is the totality of investment goods which (equipped with the necessary labor and secondary inputs) are necessary to produce one unit of output. In this model it only makes sense to consider integers $M_{i,-\tau}$. The "machine" may change its "size" from period to period (usually: the "machine" gets bigger. There are less machines which produce more output). We leave that to empirical observations.

[12] As already said: if there cannot be an error we always leave out the index $t = 0$.

The installation $I_{i,-\tau}^{real}$ or "machine" of age τ consists of "parts" $I_{ji,-\tau}^{real}$ delivered by other firms j to firm i in period $-\tau$. As stated in equation (2.2) there is a demand coefficient $d_{ji,-\tau}$ which relates the number of "parts" of type j to the number of "machines" in period $-\tau$:

$$I_{ji,-\tau}^{real} = d_{ji,-\tau} \cdot I_{i,-\tau}^{real} = d_{ji,-\tau} \cdot M_{i,-\tau} \cdot \triangle_{i,-\tau}$$

Then, as already stated above, the real costs $I_{i,-\tau}^{real}$ of machine investment by firm i in period $-\tau$ are

$$I_{i,-\tau}^{real} = \sum_{j=1}^{M} I_{ji,-\tau}^{real} \cdot \frac{p_{j,-\tau}}{\bar{p}_{-\tau}}$$

There is a proportional relation between the number $M_{i,-\tau}$ of machines installed in period $-\tau$ and their real costs (see equation (2.3)):

$$I_{i,-\tau}^{real} = M_{i,-\tau} \cdot \triangle_{i,-\tau}$$

As far as the existing real capital is concerned the production function at the beginning of period 0 is substituted by:

1. The vector a_i of the actual output coefficients:

$$a_i = (a_{i,-T}, a_{i,-T+1}, \ldots, a_{i,-1}),$$

2. The matrix D_i of the actual demand coefficients for investment goods:

$$D_i = \begin{bmatrix} d_{1i,-T} & \cdots & d_{1i,-1} \\ \vdots & \vdots & \vdots \\ d_{Mi,-T} & \cdots & d_{Mi,-1} \end{bmatrix} \tag{2.5}$$

For the future (for period 0) there are (say) z new technologies available, and the management has to choose one of them if it wants to invest in capital equipment. The possible output coefficients of the new technologies $1, \ldots, z$ are combined in the vector

$$\bar{a}_i = (a_i^{(1)}, \ldots, a_i^{(z)}),$$

and the necessary demand coefficients in the matrix

$$\bar{D}_i = \begin{bmatrix} d_{1i}^{(1)} & \cdots & d_{1i}^{(z)} \\ \vdots & \vdots & \vdots \\ d_{Mi}^{(1)} & \cdots & d_{Mi}^{(z)} \end{bmatrix} \tag{2.6}$$

When investing in capital equipment the management has to choose a technology ζ, $\zeta \in \{1, \ldots, z\}$ for the next period.

A "machine" cannot produce output by itself. If it is of age τ it needs *secondary inputs* $SI_{\mu,-\tau}$ of the kind $\mu = 1, \ldots, M$ (e.g. energy, water, raw materials) and labor $L_{\nu,-\tau}$ of different kinds $\nu = 1, \ldots, n$ to operate and supervise these machines. There are relations between $x_{i,t}, K_{i,t}, SI_{\mu i,t}$ and $L_{\nu i,t}$ which we shall analyze in the following sections.

Inventories of secondary inputs are necessary to compensate for delays in deliveries and unexpected changes of demand of the own product. These inventories may be planned or unplanned (if demand deviates from the planning figures). Finally, an administration department is necessary to plan, to coordinate and to supervise the activities of the firm and control the financial position of the firm and to determine the price of the product.

Thus we subdivide each firm into three departments: the production department, the inventory department [13] and the administration department. Each department needs capital, secondary inputs and labor. Thus $K_i(0)$ in equation (2.1) is to be specialized as

$$K_i(0)^{(k)} = (I_{i,-T}^{real(k)}, .., I_{i,-1}^{real(k)}),\ k \in \{prod, inv, adm\}, \tag{2.7}$$

$$I_{i,-\tau}^{real(k)} \geq 0,\ \tau = 1, .., T,^{14}$$

where *prod* = production department, *inv* = inventory department, *adm* = administration department.[15] In this section we deal with the production department; for simplicity we cancel the upper index (*prod*), thus $K_i(0) = K_i(0)^{(prod)}$ in this section, and similarly for the other variables. We also suppress the index i for the firm we consider wherever possible.

The commodity composition of investment[16] in the past per unit of investment in firm i follows from the matrix (2.5). Thus the total amount $\bar{I}_{\mu i}$ of investment goods of kind μ (all vintages lumped together) installed at firm i is given by:

$$\begin{pmatrix} \bar{I}_{1i} \\ \vdots \\ \bar{I}_{Mi} \end{pmatrix} = D_i \cdot \begin{pmatrix} I_{i,-T}^{real} \\ \vdots \\ I_{i,-1}^{real} \end{pmatrix}.$$

---

[13] This also comprises the transportation department. This implies that all prices are defined as "free domicile"; all transportation costs incur at the producer.

[14] Of course, there are many firms, the real capital of which consists only of investment of one age, say $I_{i,-\tau^*}^{(k)}$, all other investments are zero.

[15] We speak of $I_{i,-\tau}^{real(k)}$ as "number of machines installed in period $-\tau$" – Thus $I_{i,-\tau}^{real(k)}$ are integers. The same applies to other commodities. Of course $I_{i,-\tau}^{real(k)} \geq 0$.

[16] This subdivision of investment considers also the possibility that an "investment" comprises different installations with different intermediate products which need different secondary inputs (see next section). If one wants to study the effect of "outsourcing" one has to make that explicit. We leave that here to the interested reader.

We may rewrite this equation for all firms $i = 1, \ldots \bar{M}$ in matrix notation:

$$\bar{I} = D^* \cdot I^{real}, \tag{2.8}$$

$$\text{where} \quad \bar{I} = \begin{pmatrix} \bar{I}_{11} \\ \vdots \\ \bar{I}_{\bar{M}1} \\ \bar{I}_{12} \\ \vdots \\ \bar{I}_{\bar{M}2} \\ \vdots \\ \bar{I}_{1\bar{M}} \\ \vdots \\ \bar{I}_{\bar{M}\bar{M}} \end{pmatrix}, \quad I^{real} = \begin{pmatrix} I^{real}_{1,-T} \\ \vdots \\ I^{real}_{1,-1} \\ I_{2,-T} \\ \vdots \\ I^{real}_{2,-1} \\ \vdots \\ I^{real}_{\bar{M},-T} \\ \vdots \\ I_{\bar{M},-1} \end{pmatrix} \quad \text{and}$$

$$D^* = \begin{pmatrix} d_{11,-T} \; \ldots \; d_{11,-1} & & & \\ \vdots & 0 & \ldots & 0 \\ d_{\bar{M}1,-T} \; \ldots \; d_{\bar{M}1,-1} & & & \\ & d_{12,-T} \; \ldots \; d_{12,-1} & & \\ 0 & \vdots & \ldots & 0 \\ & d_{\bar{M}2,-T} \; \ldots \; d_{\bar{M}2,-1} & & \\ 0 & 0 & \ldots & 0 \\ & & & d_{1\bar{M},-T} \; \ldots \; d_{1\bar{M},-1} \\ 0 & 0 & \ldots & \vdots \\ & & & d_{\bar{M}\bar{M},-T} \ldots \; d_{\bar{M}\bar{M},-1} \end{pmatrix}$$

$\bar{I}$ explains the commodity composition of the real capital of all firms.

For the next period 0 the firm has to decide on total investment $I_{i,0}$ and on its commodity composition $d_{1i,0}, \ldots, d_{Mi,0}$ within the limits of the technology of that time, see matrices (2.5) and (2.6).

In the following we suppress the index i of the firm in question as well as the upper index k which relates to the special department of the firm.

A machine unit installed in period $-\tau$ if used at capacity level can produce $a_{-\tau}(t)$ units of the product of the firm in period $t > -\tau$. Therefore the capacity output of machines $I_{-\tau}(t)$ invested in period $-\tau$ and still operating in period t is

$$x^{cap}_{-\tau}(t) = a_{-\tau}(t) \cdot I^{real}_{-\tau}(t), \quad t > -\tau \tag{2.9}$$

There are two counterveiling influences on the output coefficient $a_{-\tau}(t)$:

a. Learning by doing.[17] Persons who work at a newly installed machine learn to operate it better and better. It is a general experience that it takes some time till a newly invested machine reaches its capacity output, usually some years. Therefore $a_{-\tau}(t+1) > a_{-\tau}(t)$ in this respect.

b. On the other side, wear and tear reduces the output of older machines, and they are less and less appropriate for and adapted to the production of a more advanced output (if the product $x(t)$ is more sophisticated than the product $x(t-1)$). As far as this influence is concerned one would expect $a_{-\tau}(t+1) < a_{-\tau}(t)$.

The second effect can be partly or fully compensated by current replacement and modernization investment $I^{repl}_{-\tau}(t)$. The older a machine grows, the more increases this type of investment and the larger are these costs. In this context and without further information we assume that the used technology (defined by the matrix D and other matrices to be defined below) determines the necessary replacement coefficients $repl_{\mu i,-\tau}$ per unit of investment $I^{real}_{i,-\tau}$, $\mu = 1, \ldots, \bar{M}$, in order to keep this investment in service at all. Thus the necessary replacement investment $I^{repl}_{\mu i,-\tau}$ of commodities of type μ in firm i is determined by

$$I^{repl}_{\mu i,-\tau} = repl_{\mu i,-\tau} \cdot I^{real}_{i,-\tau}, \quad \mu = 1, \ldots, \bar{M}. \tag{2.10}$$

If these replacement coefficients increase in time and if prices do not decline, the costs $CO^{repl}_{i,-\tau}(t)$ will always rise with t:

$$CO^{repl}_{i,-\tau}(t) = \sum_{j=1}^{\bar{M}} I^{repl}_{ji,-\tau} \cdot p_j(t) < CO^{repl}_{i,-\tau}(t+1)$$

If these costs per unit of output exceed the costs $CO_0(0)$ per unit of output with new equipment (installed in period 0) the old machines go out of service. They will be sold or scrapped. We assume that this happens at age T of the machines.

Given this replacement investment the machines younger than T years could possibly be used without losses. The replacement coefficients $repl_{\mu i,-\tau}$ (per unit of investment $I^{real}_{i,-\tau}$) may be arranged by the matrix

$$Repl_i = \begin{pmatrix} repl_{1i,-T} & \cdots & repl_{1i,-1} \\ & \vdots & \\ repl_{\bar{M}i,-T} & \cdots & repl_{\bar{M}i,-1} \end{pmatrix}$$

$$\text{such that} \quad \begin{pmatrix} \bar{I}^{repl}_{1i} \\ \vdots \\ \bar{I}^{repl}_{\bar{M}i} \end{pmatrix} = Repl_i \cdot \begin{pmatrix} I^{real}_{i,-T} \\ \vdots \\ I^{real}_{i,-1} \end{pmatrix}, \qquad i = 1, \cdots, \bar{M}$$

---

[17] See K. J. Arrow, The Economic Implications of Learning by Doing, Rev. of Ec. Studies 29 (1962), pp. 155. See also W. Krelle, Theorie des wirtschaftlichen Wachstums, 2. Aufl. Berlin, Heidelberg etc. (Springer), 1988, p. 210-214.

where $\bar{I}^{repl}_{\mu i}$ is the total amount of replacement investment of commodity μ used for machines of all vintages in firm i. For the economy as a whole we get

$$\bar{I}^{repl} = Repl \cdot I^{real}$$

where $\bar{I}^{repl}$ is defined as $\bar{I}$ in equation (2.8) and Repl as D in equation (2.8) ($d_{\mu i,-\tau}$ has to be substituted by $repl_{\mu i,-\tau}$).

We now return to the output coefficients. Given these replacement investments the output coefficients of $a_{i,-\tau}$ of the capital equipment of age τ in firm i need not decline. In general, with suitable definition of output and of real investment, the output coefficient of a younger machine will be larger than of an older one:

$$a_{-T} \leq a_{-T+1} \leq \cdots \leq a_0.$$

The output coefficients of all firms $1, \cdots, \bar{M}$ for capital goods of all ages can be arranged as a matrix

$$A = \begin{pmatrix} a_{1,-T}, & \cdots & a_{1,-1} \\ & \vdots & \\ a_{\bar{M},-T} & \cdots & a_{\bar{M},-1} \end{pmatrix}$$

(where we also disregarded the upper index k). Total capacity output at the beginning of period 0 of firm i is derived from it by

$$x_i^{cap} = (a_{i,-T}, \ldots, a_{i,-1}) \begin{pmatrix} I^{real}_{i,-T} \\ \vdots \\ I^{real}_{i,-1} \end{pmatrix}, \quad i = 1, \ldots, \bar{M}. \tag{2.11}$$

Similarly as equation (2.8) for investment goods we could write an equation for all capacity outputs of firms $i = 1, \ldots, \bar{M}$. Let

$$\bar{X} = \begin{pmatrix} \bar{x}_1^{cap} \\ \vdots \\ \bar{x}_{\bar{M}}^{cap} \end{pmatrix} \quad \text{be the capacity output of all firms, let}$$

$$A^* = \begin{pmatrix} a_{1,-T} \ldots a_{1,-1} & 0 & 0 & \\ 0 & a_{2,-T} \ldots a_{2,-1} & 0 & \\ 0 & 0 & \cdots & 0 \\ 0 & 0 & \cdots & a_{\bar{M},-T} \ldots a_{\bar{M},-1} \end{pmatrix}$$

be the extended matrix of all output coefficients, and I^{real} the vector of all investments of all firms, defined in equation (2.8), then we get for the capacity output of all firms:

$$\bar{X} = A^* \cdot I^{real} \tag{2.12}$$

As a rule, the machines which constitute the production capital of a firm, will not be fully used at capacity level. Let $\delta_{-\tau}(t)$ be the rate of capacity utilization of a machine of age τ at period t in the firm considered, $t > -\tau$. Then the actual production of this machine is

$$x_{-\tau}(t) = \delta_{-\tau}(t) \cdot x_{-\tau}^{cap}(t), \quad 0 \leq \delta_{-\tau}(t) \leq 1.$$

The firm decides on $x_{-\tau}(0)$ at the beginning of period 0 (or equivalently on $\delta_{-\tau}(0)$) for all $\tau = -T, -T+1, \ldots, -1$.[18] Total planned production of the firm in period 0 is the sum of production on all vintages of machines:

$$X(0) = \sum_{\tau=1}^{T} x_{-\tau}(0).$$

2.3 The Production Department: Secondary Inputs

In order to operate the machines which produce the final output, secondary inputs are needed such as energy, water, raw materials, but also intermediate goods which are manufactured by other firms.[19] We assume that the amount of secondary inputs needed to produce one unit of output on machines of age τ is proportional to the amount of production $x_{-\tau}(t)$ on this machine in period $t, t > -\tau$, where $b_{ij,-\tau}(t)$ is the proportionality factor (called input coefficient) with respect to secondary input j of the firm i. Let $SI_{ji,-\tau}(t)$ be the amount of secondary inputs of kind j in firm i needed for production on machines of age τ in period $t, t > -\tau$. Now we have

$$\begin{aligned} &SI_{ji,-\tau}(t) = b_{ji,-\tau} \cdot x_{i,-\tau}(t), \\ &j = 1, \ldots, \bar{M}, \quad i = 1, \ldots, \bar{M}\ j \neq i,\ \tau = T, T-1, \ldots, 1, \end{aligned} \tag{2.13}$$

where $x_{i,-\tau}(0)$ is the planned production on machines of age τ in the next period 0, a decision variable. We assume that the secondary inputs $SI_{ji,-\tau}(t)$ necessary to produce $x_{i,-\tau}(t)$ are always available. Usually there are long term contracts between the firms $j = 1, \ldots, \bar{M}$ which deliver these inputs to the receiving firm i because without these inputs nothing can be produced. The prices of these deliveries are fixed by the producer and known to the receiver.

---

[18] We assume that the production capacity $x_0^{cap}(0)$ which is being built up by investment I_0^{real} cannot be used for production in that period. It becomes effective only in period +1. This explains why real capital K_0 at the beginning of period 0 does not comprise I_0^{real}, see equation (2.1) above.

[19] We do not consider those intermediate goods explicitly which are produced and used up within the firm. In this context the firm is a "black box".

The input coefficients $b_{ji,-\tau}$ may be condensed to the matrix

$$B_i = \begin{pmatrix} b_{1i,-T}, & \cdots & , b_{1i,-1} \\ & \vdots & \\ b_{\bar{M}i,-T}, & \cdots & , b_{\bar{M}i,-1} \end{pmatrix},$$

such that $\quad SI_i = B_i x_i$

where $SI_i = \begin{pmatrix} SI_{1i} \\ \vdots \\ SI_{\bar{M}i} \end{pmatrix}$ is the vector of secondary inputs of kind 1,...,M at firm i,

and $x_i = \begin{pmatrix} x_{i,-T} \\ \vdots \\ x_{i,-1} \end{pmatrix}$ the vector of production of firm i with machinery of age $\tau, \tau = 1, \ldots, T$.

In analogy to equation (2.8) in the former section we may formulate these relations for the economy as a whole in matrix notation:

$$\bar{SI} = B^* \cdot X$$

where $\bar{SI}$ is defined in analogy to $\bar{I}$, X in analogy to I^{real} and B^* in anology to D^* in equation (2.8).

2.4 The Production Department: Labor Input

Machines must be operated by persons with special education and training, they must be supervised, maintained and repaired if necessary. As a rule one needs a crew to keep a machine ready for production even if it is not actually put to service in that specific period. This crew is proportional to the number of machines with proportionality factor $\bar{l}$, called fixed labor coefficient. In addition one needs personnel in proportion to the amount of production $x_{-\tau}$ of this machine (with proportionality factor $\hat{l}$, called variable labor coefficient). Let there be n types of labor $L_1, \ldots, L_n$, where labor is measured in hours of work. Thus we get for machines of age τ and firm i the labor requirement[20]:

$$\begin{aligned} L_{\nu i,-\tau}(t) &= \bar{l}_{\nu i,-\tau} \cdot I^{real}_{i,-\tau} + \hat{l}_{\nu i,-\tau} \cdot x_{i,-\tau}(t), \\ &\qquad \tau = 1, 2, \ldots, T,\ t > -\tau,\ \nu = 1, \ldots, n \end{aligned} \tag{2.14}$$

[20] This is the minimum of labor necessary to produce x. The actual amount of labor L^{act} used in firm i may be larger than that, for different reasons (e.g. long run labor contracts).

As in section 3, $x_{i,-\tau}(0)$ is the planned production on machines of age τ in the next period 0. Thus total labor requirement of type ν needed to produce the amount X(0) in period 0 by firm i (we suppress the index i) amounts to:

$$L_\nu(0) = \sum_{\tau=1}^{T} L_{\nu,-\tau}(0), \quad \nu = 1, \ldots, n$$

We may put that in matrix notation. The labor requirements of firm i are

$$L_i = \bar{L}_i + \hat{L}_i,\ i = 1, \ldots, \bar{M} \quad \text{and} \quad \bar{L}_i = \bar{\Lambda}_i \cdot I_i^{real},\ \hat{L}_i = \hat{\Lambda}_i \cdot X_i \tag{2.15}$$

where

$$\bar{L}_i = \begin{pmatrix} \bar{L}_{1i} \\ \vdots \\ \bar{L}_{ni} \end{pmatrix}, \quad I_i^{real} = \begin{pmatrix} I_{i,-T}^{real} \\ \vdots \\ I_{i,-1}^{real} \end{pmatrix}, \quad \bar{\Lambda}_i = \begin{pmatrix} \bar{l}_{i1,-T} & \cdots & \bar{l}_{i1,-1} \\ & \vdots & \\ \bar{l}_{n1,-T} & \cdots & \bar{l}_{n1,-1} \end{pmatrix},$$

$$\hat{L}_i = \begin{pmatrix} \hat{L}_{1i} \\ \vdots \\ \hat{L}_{ni} \end{pmatrix}, \quad X_i = \begin{pmatrix} x_{i,-T} \\ \vdots \\ x_{i,-1} \end{pmatrix}, \quad \hat{\Lambda}_i = \begin{pmatrix} \hat{l}_{i1,-T} & \cdots & \hat{l}_{i1,-1} \\ & \vdots & \\ \hat{l}_{n1,-T} & \cdots & \hat{l}_{n1,-1} \end{pmatrix},$$

As in the foregoing section we may also rewrite these relations as one matrix equation for all firms of the economy:

$$L = \bar{L} + \hat{L}, \quad \bar{L} = \bar{\Lambda} \cdot I^{real}, \quad \hat{L} = \hat{\Lambda} \cdot X \tag{2.16}$$

$$\text{where} \quad \bar{L} = \begin{pmatrix} \bar{L}_{11} \\ \vdots \\ \bar{L}_{n1} \\ \bar{L}_{12} \\ \vdots \\ \bar{L}_{n2} \\ \vdots \\ \bar{L}_{1\bar{M}} \\ \vdots \\ \bar{L}_{n\bar{M}} \end{pmatrix}, \quad I^{real} = \begin{pmatrix} I_{1,-T}^{real} \\ \vdots \\ I_{1,-1}^{real} \\ I_{2,-T} \\ \vdots \\ I_{2,-1}^{real} \\ \vdots \\ I_{\bar{M},-T}^{real} \\ \vdots \\ I_{\bar{M},-1} \end{pmatrix} \quad \text{and}$$

$$\hat{\Lambda} = \begin{pmatrix}
\bar{l}_{11,-T} \ \dots \ \bar{l}_{11,-1} & & & \\
\vdots & 0 & \cdots & 0 \\
\bar{l}_{n1,-T} \ \dots \ \bar{l}_{n1,-1} & & & \\
& \bar{l}_{12,-T} \ \dots \ \bar{l}_{12,-1} & & \\
0 & \vdots & \cdots & 0 \\
& \bar{l}_{n2,-T} \ \dots \ \bar{l}_{n2,-1} & & \\
0 & 0 & \cdots & 0 \\
& & & \bar{l}_{1\bar{M},-T} \ \dots \ \bar{l}_{1\bar{M},-1} \\
0 & 0 & \cdots & \vdots \\
& & & \bar{l}_{n\bar{M},-T} \ \dots \ \bar{l}_{n\bar{M},-1}
\end{pmatrix}$$

$\bar{l}_{\nu i,-\tau}$ is the fixed labor input coefficient for labor $\nu = 1, \dots, n$ at firm $i = 1, \dots, \bar{M}$ for machines of age τ, $\tau = 1, \dots, T$. $\hat{L} = \hat{\Lambda} \cdot X$ is defined analogously: $\hat{L}$ as $\bar{L}$ (the $\bar{L}$ are substituted by $\hat{L}$),

$$X = \begin{pmatrix} X_{1,-T} \\ \vdots \\ X_{1,-1} \\ \vdots \\ X_{\bar{M},-T} \\ \vdots \\ X_{\bar{M},-1} \end{pmatrix}, \quad \hat{\Lambda} = \begin{pmatrix}
\hat{l}_{11,-T} \ \dots \ \hat{l}_{11,-1} & & \\
\vdots & \cdots & 0 \\
\hat{l}_{n1,-T} \ \dots \ \hat{l}_{n1,-1} & & \\
\vdots & \vdots & \vdots \\
& & \hat{l}_{1\bar{M},-T} \ \dots \ \hat{l}_{1\bar{M},-1} \\
0 & \cdots & \vdots \\
& & \hat{l}_{n\bar{M},-T} \ \dots \ \hat{l}_{n\bar{M},-1}
\end{pmatrix}$$

(where $\hat{l}_{\nu i,-\tau}$ is the labor input coefficient for labor ν at firm i for machines of age τ; this coefficient refers to labor which is proportional to production).

It might be that labor of type ν (e. g. well trained and specialized workers) is not available but only labor of type ν' which is less appropriate for the task (e. g. untrained labor). In this case more labor of type ν' is needed to operate the machines. Then in equation (2.14) the index ν has to be substituted by ν', and

$$\bar{l}_{\nu' i,-\tau} > \bar{l}_{\nu i,-\tau} \quad \text{and } \hat{l}_{\nu' i,-\tau} > \hat{l}_{\nu i,-\tau} \ \nu' = 1, \dots, n.$$

Thus $L_{\nu' i,-\tau}(t) > L_{\nu i,-\tau}(t)$ for given $I^{real}_{i,-\tau}$ and $x_{i,-\tau}$ or in other words: the average product $\bar{\pi}_{\nu' i}$ of a worker of type ν' is lower than the average product $\bar{\pi}_{\nu i}$ of a worker of type ν in firm i at machines of age τ:

$$\bar{\pi}_{\nu' i} := \frac{x_{i,-\tau}(t)}{L_{\nu' i,-\tau}(t)} < \bar{\pi}_{\nu i} := \frac{x_{i,-\tau}(t)}{L_{\nu i,-\tau}(t)} \quad \text{for given} \quad I^{real}_{i,-\tau}$$

We assume that the necessary amount of labor (perhaps of minor qualification) is always available such that the production plan $X_i(0)$ can be realized.

Labor may be measured in terms of working hours, that means as labor services $LS_{\nu i,-\tau}$. They may be proportional to real investment $I^{real}_{i,-\tau}$ if this is measured by the real costs of that investment:

$$LS_{\nu i,-\tau} = \hat{l}_{\nu i,-\tau} \cdot I^{real}_{i,-\tau}, \quad \hat{l}_{\nu i,-\tau} \geq 0.$$

2.5 The Handbook of Production

The knowledge of the input and output coefficients defined in the forgoing section does not suffice to manufacture the product of the firm. It is a look from outside to a black box in which the production process itself takes place: the commodities and services which go into the black box and those which come out of it are registered and their relations stated, but the real event, the production itself, remains in the dark. Persons who get the total amount of necessary inputs are not able to manufacture the product. They need a *"Handbook of Production"*, Hb_i in case of firm i, which describes the production activities in detail. This normally is a voluminous description of all steps in the production process such that at the end the product x_i of firm i emerges. Of course, tests of the functioning of each part must be included in the production process.

We conclude this section on the production department of a firm by summarizing the main ideas. The firm i uses a technology ϑ_i which is defined by matrices of input- and output coefficients and by the proper Handbook of Production:

$$\vartheta_i = \{A_i, B_i, D_i, Repl_i, \bar{\Lambda}_i, \hat{\Lambda}_i, Hb_i\} \tag{2.17}$$

where
- A_i = matrix of all output coefficients
- B_i = matrix of secondary input coefficients
- D_i = matrix of the capital structure (= matrix of the demand coefficients for investment goods)
- $Repl_i$ = matrix of replacement coefficients
- $\bar{\Lambda}_i$ = matrix of labor input coefficients per unit of investment
- $\hat{\Lambda}_i$ = matrix of labor input coefficients per unit of production
- Hb_i = handbook of production.

There are possibly other technologies $\vartheta', \vartheta'', \ldots$ available for the firm i. The firm may install a research program to find a new till now unknown technology ϑ_i^* to produce a related product x_i^*. We come back to this when we deal with technical progress. At the initial point B_i the firm has (with respect to investment) to choose among the technologies $\vartheta', \vartheta'', \ldots$.

2.6 The Inventory Department

This department needs capital, replacement investment, secondary inputs and labor similarly as the production department. Real capital takes the form of warehouses, transportation equipment and the like, secondary inputs are energy (for example). Naturally, one needs labor to administer the inventories and to run the warehouses and the lorries – quite similar to the production department. We do not repeat these equations here. But there is one exception. The output of the inventory department is not the storage of one good, but (as a rule) the storage of many goods, the good produced by the firm as well as goods which serve as secondary inputs. In our model involuntary changes of inventories are always possible. It does not happen very often that demand equals supply in the short run, that means: in the next planning period 0. But also a certain amount of inventories in secondary inputs is inevitable in order to take care of short term delays of deliveries. Storehouses, transportation equipment, secondary inputs like raw material and intermediate products and the necessary personnel are needed to run the installations smoothly. Thus one needs capital, labor and secondary inputs for the Inventory Department quite similar as in the Production Department. But there is a difference: the output of the Production Department of firm i is one product x_i, but the output of the Inventory Department is the storage and handling of inventories INV_i^i of the firm's own product i as well as INV_i^μ of secondary inputs $\mu = 1, \ldots, \bar{M},\ \mu \neq i$.

Thus some reformulation of section 2.2 is required which has some consequences on the sections on labor and secondary inputs. These reformulations are the topic of this section.

For simplicity we assume that the capital equipment for storage and handling of a specific commodity is different from that for storage and handling of other commodities.

Let $I_{i,-\tau}^{real,inv,\mu}$ be the real investment of firm i in period $-\tau$ with respect to inventory capital to store and handle inventories of kind μ, $\mu = 1, \ldots, \bar{M}$. Then total inventory capital $K_i^{inv,\mu}$ of firm i to store and handle commodity μ in the beginning of period 0 is given by the vector:

$$K_i^{inv,\mu} = (I_{i,-T}^{real,inv,\mu}, I_{i,-T+1}^{real,inv,\mu}, \ldots, I_{i,-1}^{real,inv,\mu})$$

The maximal amount $I_{i,-\tau,t}^{\mu,cap}$ of inventories of kind μ which can be stored and handled by storage equipment of age τ in period t by firm i is proportional to real investment of this kind:

$$INV_{i,-\tau,t}^{\mu,cap} = a_{i,-\tau,t}^{inv,\mu} \cdot I_{i,-\tau}^{real,inv,\mu}$$

This equation corresponds to equation (2.4) in section 2.2. Thus we may continue as in section 2.2. We get for labor of type ν necessary for the storage of commodity μ in case that the storage facilities are fully used:

$$L_{\nu i}^{inv,\mu,cap}(t) = \bar{l}_{\nu i,-\tau}^{-inv,\mu} \cdot I_{i,-\tau}^{real,inv,\mu} + \hat{l}_{\nu i,-\tau}^{inv,\mu} \cdot INV_{i,-\tau}^{\mu,cap}(t)$$

The actual amount of labor necessary at the storage of commodity μ depends on the degree $\delta^{inv,\mu}_{i,-\tau}(t)$ of capacity utilization in time t:

$$L^{inv,\mu}_{\nu i}(t) = \bar{l}^{-inv,\mu}_{\nu i,-\tau} \cdot I^{real,inv,\mu}_{i,-\tau} + \delta^{inv,\mu}_{i,-\tau}(t) \cdot \hat{l}^{inv,\mu}_{\nu i,-\tau} \cdot INV^{\mu,cap}_{i,-\tau}(t)$$

Similarly one gets for secondary inputs SI of type j necessary to operate a storage facility for commodity μ:

$$\begin{aligned} SI^{inv,\mu}_{ji,-\tau}(t) &= l^{inv,\mu}_{ji,-\tau} \cdot INV^{\mu}_{i,-\tau}(t) \\ \text{where } INV^{\mu}_{i,-\tau}(t) &= \delta^{inv,\mu}_{i,-\tau}(t) \cdot INV^{\mu,cap}_{i,-\tau}(t) \end{aligned}$$

This conforms to equation (2.13) for the production department in section 2.3. The replacement investments $I^{repl,inv,\mu}_{\mu,i,-\tau}$ in the inventory department are explained similarly as this type of investment in the production department (see equation (2.10) in section 2.2):

$$I^{repl,inv,\mu}_{ji,-\tau} = repl^{inv,\mu}_{ji,-\tau} \cdot I^{real,inv,\mu}_{i,-\tau},$$

$$j \in \{1,\ldots,\bar{M}\}, \quad j \neq i, \quad \mu \in \{1,\ldots,\bar{M}\}$$

Now the technology $\vartheta^{inv,\mu}_{i}$ valid for inventories of type μ in firm i is defined similarly as the technology ϑ_i of the production department (see equation (2.17) in section 2.5): each variable there has to be given an upper index inv, μ, with $\mu \in \{1,\ldots,\bar{M}\}$ and $i \in \{1,\ldots,\bar{M}\}$

The decisions of the management with respect to the inventory department are the same as those for the production department, if one considers a special type μ of inventories.

2.7 The Administration Department: The Organization of a Firm

The Administration Department needs capital, labor and secondary inputs similarly as all other departments. We start with capital requirements. There is investment $I^{real,adm}_{i,-\tau}$ in firm i which serves the needs of the administration of firm i. Let there be L^{adm}_i persons of different ranks in the administration of firm i at the end of period -1.[21] Each administrator needs a certain space and a certain equipment which is procured by investment $I^{real,adm}_{i,-\tau}$ in period $-\tau$, $\tau = 1,\ldots,T$. As in the case of production there are output coefficients

[21] In this connection we do not need to differ between types of labor. We assume that each person needs the same room and equipment.

$a^{adm}_{i,-\tau}$ which limit the number of administrators which can be accomodated and served by that investment:

$$L^{adm,cap}_{i,-\tau} = a^{adm}_{i,-\tau} \cdot I^{real,adm}_{i,-\tau}$$

Total fixed capital for the use of the administration at the end of period -1 is the vector of all investment of this kind in different periods:

$$K^{adm}_i = (I^{real,adm}_{i,-T}, I^{real,adm}_{i,-T+1}, \ldots, I^{real,adm}_{i,-1})$$

We put for the output coefficients:

$$a^{adm}_i = (a^{adm}_{i,-T}, a^{adm}_{i,-T+1}, \ldots, a^{adm}_{i,-1})$$

Actually, the office space and the equipment may not be fully used. Let $\delta^{adm}_{i,-\tau}$ be the proportion of utilization of this type of investment by administrative personnel and $\delta^{adm}_i = (\delta^{adm}_{i,-T}, \ldots, \delta^{adm}_{i,-1})$ the vector of utilization of investment of this kind at the end of period -1. Thus

$$L^{adm}_{i,-\tau} = \delta^{adm}_{i,-\tau} \cdot a^{adm}_{i,-\tau} \cdot I^{real,adm}_{i,-\tau}$$

is a definitional equation for the degree of capacity utilization of former investment in office space and equipment, if the number $L^{adm}_{i,-\tau}$ of administrators who work in buildings and with equipment of age $-\tau$ and the investment $I^{real,adm}_{i,-\tau}$ of that age are given. As already said, we do not differ between different kinds of labor in this context, that means that each person in the administration needs the same office space. The equations for demand of investment goods and for replacement coefficients are analogous to those in the production department (there is a matrix D^{adm}_i), but there are no labor input coefficients. The amount of labor in the administration and its effect on production will be determined in another way. Only the secondary inputs and replacement inputs follow a similar rule as in the production department. We assume that the secondary inputs are proportional to the number $L^{adm}_{i,-\tau}$ of persons who work in an office established τ years ago:

$$SI^{adm}_{\mu i,-\tau} = c^{adm}_{\mu i,-\tau} \cdot L^{adm}_{i,-\tau} \quad \text{and } SI^{adm}_i = (SI^{adm}_{1i}, \ldots, SI^{adm}_{Mi})$$

$$\text{where } SI^{adm}_{\mu i} = \sum_{\tau=1}^{T} SI^{adm}_{\mu i,-\tau} \tag{2.18}$$

This comprises electricity, paper, telephone etc. The necessary inputs to keep up the buildings are reproduced by equations which are of the same type as those for the production and inventory department:

$$I^{repl,adm}_{ji,-\tau} = repl^{adm}_{ji,-\tau} \cdot I^{real,adm}_{i,-\tau}$$

The parameters $c^{adm}_{\mu i,-\tau}$ in equation (2.18) are condensed to a matrix C^{adm}_i similarly as B_i in the case of the production department. The same applies for the replacement coefficients.

We now turn to the determination of the number L_i^{adm} of administrators in firm i and to their position in the firm which are, of course, subject of the decision of the leading personalities of the firm in the same way as production, inventories and other important variables. For the sake of the simplicity of the formalization we normalize in the following the amount of labor (= number of working hours) used such that it is identical with the number of workers. The workers may have different qualifications and different occupations. But nevertheless we could "count the heads"; we call the heads $\#L_{\nu i,-\tau}^{prod}$ and $\#L_{\nu \imath,-\tau}^{inv}$. Now we may add up all labor used in production and inventory handling. In period 0 this leads to the number:

$$n_{i0} = \sum_{\nu=1}^{n} \sum_{\tau=1}^{T} \#L_{\nu i,-\tau}^{prod} + \#L_{\nu i,-\tau}^{inv}$$

where the index 0 refers to the "rank" of the workers; the index 0 which indicates the period is suppressed. This is the amount of labor (or the number of workers) which has to be supervised and administered.

Martin Beckmann (whom I follow essentially) calls these workers "members (of the organization i) of rank zero"[22] and treats them as equal and interchangeable. In our approach these workers stand at different machines or installations and their task (and therefore their type of labor) will be different. Consider all $n_{i0}^{k,\tau}$ workers of rank zero who work in department $k \in (prod, inv)$ at all installations $I_{i,-\tau}^{real,k}$ of age τ in period 0:

$$n_{i0}^{k,\tau} = \sum_{\nu=1}^{n} \#L_{\nu i,-\tau}^{k}$$

They alone cannot run a firm, there must be an administration to organize production and marketing and to direct the financial side of the enterprise. We assume (with Martin Beckmann) that the firm is organized along hierarchical lines which is true for almost all firms of economic importance[23] . This allows us to estimate the size of the administration of a firm.[24] The basic idea is that each work needs supervision and that a person can only supervise a limited

---

[22] See Martin Beckmann (1978). I follow his notations here.

[23] There are people who recommend networks instead of a hierarchical order. This might be feasible for organizations which are supported from outside and need not sell their product in a market (such as research groups, some churches with exception of the Roman Catholic Church from which the notation "hierarchical" comes from). The theologian Hans Küng recommends to substitute networks for hierarchies everywhere, see his speech "Romanitas und Reformatio" at the occasion of the award of the "Ernst-Robert-Curtius Preis für Essayistik", 13.06.2001 published at Bouvier, Bonn, p. 45,46. But this does not seem possible for economic and political organizations which have to act fast and where the decisions are binding for the whole organization.

[24] For details: see Martin Beckmann (1978).

number of persons or organizations (Martin Beckmann gives numbers of 2 to 24 which have been observed, p. 7). Normally we may assume a number of 3 to 10 subordinates. This constitutes a "control span" $s_{i1}^{k,\tau}$ of rank 1 in department k at "machines" of age τ. Thus for $n_{i0}^{k,\tau}$ workers at installations $I_{i,-\tau}^{real,k}$, $k \in \{prod, inv\}$ in period 0 we need

$$n_{i1}^{k,\tau} = \frac{n_{i0}^{k,\tau}}{s_{i1}^{k,\tau}}$$ [25]

supervisors of rank 1. For simplicity we assume that each supervisor of rank 1 is provided with the same number $N_{i1}^{k,\tau}$ of staff personnel. The type of labor which a supervisor and his staff can offer determines the "quality" of the supervision. We define the (average) "quality" of a supervisor of rank 1 by $q_{i1}^{k,\tau}$ and the (average) "quality" of his staff by $Q_{i1}^{k,\tau}$. The next stage is formed by

$$n_{i2}^{k,\tau} = \frac{n_{i1}^{k,\tau}}{s_{i2}^{k,\tau}}$$

supervisors of rank 2 with $N_{i2}^{k,\tau}$ persons in the staff of each supervisor and the qualifications $Q_{i2}^{k,\tau}$ and $q_{i2}^{k,\tau}$ respectively. One continues this way, until the second–highest rank $R-1$ is reached with

$$n_{i,R-1}^{k,\tau} = \frac{n_{i,R-2}^{k,\tau}}{s_{i,R-1}^{k,\tau}} \quad \text{supervisors, where } 2 \le n_{i,R-1}^{k,\tau} \le s_{iR},$$

and each supervisor is assisted by a staff of $N_{i,R-1}^{k,\tau}$ persons with qualifications $Q_{i,R-1}^{k,\tau}$ and $q_{i,R-1}^{k,\tau}$ respectively. This applies for the production department ($k = prod$) of firm i and for all "machines" of age τ. The highest rank of the supervisors of workers at these "machines" is $R = R_i^{k,\tau}$ (the rank of the machine manager for all machines of age τ).

He is assisted by $N_{iR}^{k,\tau}$ persons who form his staff. Thus the size of the production administration for machines of age τ in department k in period -1 is:

$$\begin{aligned} L_i^{adm,k,\tau} &= \sum_{r=1}^{R-1} n_{ir}^{k,\tau} \cdot (1 + N_{ir}^{k,\tau}) + (1 + N_{iR}^{k,\tau}) \qquad (2.19) \\ &= n_{i0}^{k,\tau} \left[\frac{(1 + N_{i1}^{k,\tau})}{s_{i1}^{k,\tau}} + \frac{(1 + N_{i2}^{k,\tau})}{s_{i1}^{k,\tau} \cdot s_{i2}^{k,\tau}} + \cdots + \frac{(1 + N_{i,R-1}^{k,\tau})}{s_{i1}^{k,\tau} \cdot s_{i2}^{k,\tau} \cdots s_{i,R-1}^{k,\tau}} \right] \\ &\quad + (1 + N_{iR}^{k,\tau}). \end{aligned}$$

---

[25] As already said: we always omit the notation "n.i." (=nearest integer)

We describe the organization of the firm by the control spans $s_{i1}^{k,\tau}, \dots, s_{iR}^{k,\tau}$ and the size of the associated staffs $N_{i1}^{k,\tau}, \dots, N_{iR-1}^{k,\tau}$, the top management $N_{iR}^{k,\tau}$ and their associated qualifications $Q_{i1}^{k,\tau}, \dots, Q_{iR}^{k,\tau}$ and $q_{i1}^{k,\tau}, \dots, q_{iR}^{k,\tau}$. The highest rang R may differ for different ages τ of the installation: $R = R_i^{k,\tau}$.

This describes the direct supervision of the workers on the machines. There are T age groups of machines for production and as many age groups of installations for inventories and thus $T^* = 2T$ machine managers, one for each installation of age τ. They also have to be supervised, i.e. control spans have to be decided and the number of staff personnel fixed. For simplicity we assumed that there are T production and T inventory managers of rank R since there are T different age groups of "machines". Thus we need $n_{i,R+1}^k = \frac{T}{s_{i,R+1}^k}$ supervisors of rank $R+1$, and so on till $n_{i,R+S-1} = \frac{n_{i,R+S-2}^k}{s_{i,R+S-1}^k}$ supervisors of rank $R+S-1$ where $2 \le n_{i,R+S-1}^k \le s_{i,R+s}^k$, and finally the president with the rank $R+S$. Each supervisor of rank $R+\sigma$ has a staff of $N_{i,R+\sigma}$ persons, $\sigma = 1, \dots, S$. The qualification of these supervisors is $q_{i,R+\sigma}^{(k)}$, that of his staff (on average) $Q_{i,R+\sigma}^{(k)}$. The total number of administrators above the immediate production level is:

$$\hat{L}_i^{adm,k} = \sum_{r=R+1}^{R+S-1} n_{i,r}^k (1 + N_{ir}^k) + (1 + N_{is}^k).$$

If we put $T = n_{i,R+1}^k$, we get:

$$\begin{aligned}\hat{L}_i^{adm,k} = n_{i,R+1}^k \Bigg[& \frac{1 + N_{i,R+1}^k}{s_{i,R+1}^k} + \frac{1 + N_{i,R+2}^k}{s_{i,R+1}^k \cdot s_{i,R+2}^k} + \dots \\ & \frac{1 + N_{i,R+S-1}^k}{s_{i,R+1}^k \cdots s_{i,R+S-1}^k} \Bigg] + (1 + N_{i,R+S}^k)\end{aligned} \tag{2.20}$$

Thus the total size of the administrative personnel in department k of firm i is

$$L_i^{adm,k} = \sum_{\tau=1}^{T} L_i^{adm,k,\tau} + \hat{L}_i^{adm,k}$$

It depends on the total number $n_{i0}^k = \sum_{\tau=1}^{T} n_{i0}^{k,\tau}$ of workers of rank zero (the "rank and file") in department k in period -1, on the control spans s_i^k and on the size N_i^k of the staffs. Total employment in the administration of firm i is:

$$L_i^{adm} = L_i^{adm,prod} + L_i^{adm,inv}$$

Thus we may write:

$$L_i^{adm,k} = F_i(n_{i0}^k, s_i^k, N_i^k)$$

$$\text{where } s_i^k = (s_{i1}^k, \ldots, s_{i,R-1}^k, s_{i,R+1}^k, \ldots, s_{i,R+S-1}^k),$$

$$N_i^k = (N_{i1}^k, \ldots, N_{i,R+S}^k)$$

Till now we followed essentially Martin Beckmann. But his model has been constructed for the organizational structure of institutions like the Prussian army in the 18th and 19th century, the large textile or steel factories of that time where interchangeable persons formed the rank and file of the organization and only the size of the control span mattered not the identity or the positions of the persons subject to a specific supervisor. But this is of importance now. The control span $s^{(1)}$ may comprise all workers the working place of which are near together; but a control span $s^{(2)}$ of the same size may also comprise all workers with the same or similar occupation, and there may be other principles to determine who exactly is subject to a specific supervisor, though the control spans may be identical. This does not change the *number* of administrators (all formulas above remain unchanged), but it will influence the organizational efficiency.

Let us assume that there are $\Gamma_{i1}^{k,\tau}$ possibilities to group the workers of rank 0 at a "machine" $I_{i,\tau}^{real,k}$ into control spans $s_{i1}^{k,\tau}$[26], similarly $\Gamma_{i2}^{(k,\tau)}$ possibilities to group the supervisors of rank 1 into $s_{i2}^{k,\tau}$ control spans and so on. Now the organization of a firm i is not only described by the control spans s_i^k in department k of the firm i, the size N_i^k of the staff, the qualification q_i^k and Q_i^k of the supervisors and the staff, but also by the allocation of persons in different positions to the supervisors, i. e. by $\gamma_{i\rho}^{k,\tau}$, $\rho = 1, \ldots, R-1$ and $\gamma_{i\rho}^{k,\tau} \in \{\Gamma_{i\rho}^{k,\tau}\}$, where $\{\Gamma_{i\rho}^{k,\tau}\}$ is the set of all possible allocations of positions (or persons) to the supervisors.

Moreover, the power of the supervisors may be different. In the extreme cases a supervisor is entitled to intervene in all activities of its subordinates or it may only become active in exceptional cases where the subordinate cannot help himself. Most cases will lie in between. Thus we may define an index POW_{ji} of powers of each supervisor j in firm i. It lies between zero and 1:

$$0 < POW_{ji} \leq 1, \quad j = 1 \ldots N,$$

---

[26] As to the number of combinations: if we have n different elements which should be grouped into k groups without considering the arrangements within the group we find in von Mangoldt-Knopp "Einführung in die Höhere Mathematik", 8. Aufl., Leipzig (Hirzel-Verlag) 1944, p. 44 the number

$$\frac{n(n-1)(n-2)\cdots(n-k+1)}{1 \cdot 2 \cdot 3 \cdots k}$$

if there are N supervisors in firm i. The distributions of powers in firm i may thus be described by the vector

$$POW_i = (POW_{1i}, \ldots, POW_{Ni})^{27}$$

The organization of a firm is now described by the vector

$$\omega_i = (s_i, \gamma_i, q_i, N_i, Q_i, POW_i).$$

We put $s_i = (s_i^{prod}, s_i^{inv}, s_i^{adm})$ and similarly $\gamma_i, q_i, N_i, Q_i, POW_i$. Let $\bar{s}, \bar{\gamma}, \ldots, P\bar{O}W$ be vectors of all possible $s, \gamma, \ldots, POW$ in the society then we get the set Ω of all possible organizations:

$$\Omega = \{\bar{s}, \bar{\gamma}, \bar{q}, \bar{N}, \bar{Q}, P\bar{O}W\}, \text{a finite set,} \qquad \text{and } \omega_i \in \Omega$$

The organization ω_i (together with other variables) determines the efficiency of the firm. We may define an index $\mathcal{E}_i$ of the organizational efficiency of firm i. As already said the efficiency depends on the size s_i of the control spans, the personal composition γ_i of the supervised, on the size N_i of the staffs, on the quality q_i of the heads of all administration stages, on the average quality Q_i of the staff personnel and on the powers of each supervisor.

There will be optimal control spans: too small spans do not leave enough freedom of decision for the lower ranks; overbureaucratisation is detrimental. But too large control spans s_i are also detrimental: the work of the lower ranks will be insufficiently coordinated and supervised. Similar relations hold for the size N_i of the staff. The higher the qualification q_i of the heads of a sector the better, and the same for the staff qualification Q_i. But here are surely limits: above a certain size, higher qualifications may not have an influence or even a negative one.[28,29] Thus we have:

$$\mathcal{E}_i = F_i(s_i, \gamma_i, q_i, N_i, Q_i, POW_i) =: F_i(\omega_i)$$

The indicator $\mathcal{E}_i$ influences the output coefficients a_i, the labor input coefficients in B_i and the size of the secondary inputs, i.e. C_i. The higher the efficiency index $\mathcal{E}_i$, the larger the output coefficients and the smaller the input coefficients.

The influence of $\mathcal{E}_i$ on the output coefficients a_i and the input coefficients $vecB_i$ and $vecC_i$ (where $vecB_i$ means the vectorization of matrix B_i) is not

[27] Of course, this approach may still be refined by dividing the total power index POW_{ji} into different indices which discern between powers of a supervisor with respect to special subordinates. But we do not go into these details.

[28] That depends on how the "quality of labor" is defined. We do not go into this problem.

[29] Beckmann (1978), pp. 112 ff. defines a composite production function for the operative output where the output of each hierarchical level is supposed to be measurable. We rather look to the total effect.

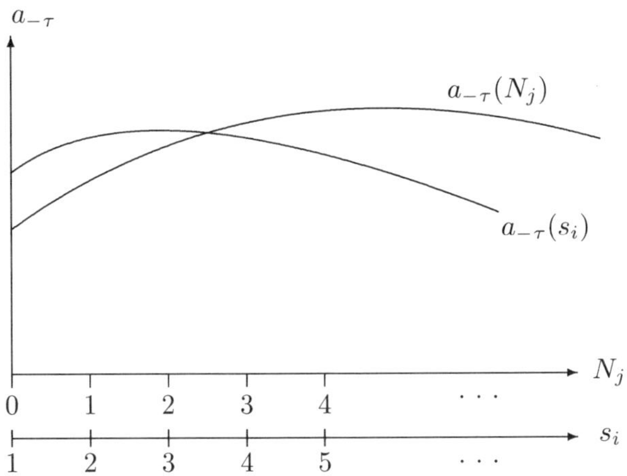

Figure 2.1 The output coefficient $a_{-\tau}$ as a function of the control span s_i and the size N_j of the staff, other variables kept constant

immediate. A change in $\mathcal{E}_i$ needs some time to exert its influence. Thus after defining continuous and differentiable functions which connect the observation points we may write:

$$a_i = f_{ai}(\mathcal{E}_{i,-1}, \ldots), \quad \frac{\partial a_i}{\partial \mathcal{E}_{i,-1}} \geq 0, \quad vecB_i = f_{bi}(\mathcal{E}_{i,-1}, \ldots), \quad \frac{\partial vecB_i}{\partial \mathcal{E}_{i,-1}} \leq 0,$$

$$vecC_i = f_{ci}(\mathcal{E}_{i,-1}, \ldots), \quad \frac{\partial vecC_i}{\partial \mathcal{E}_{i,-1}} \leq 0.$$

We may illustrate this approach by some graphs which, of course, could only cover some special cases.

1. The output coefficient $a_{-\tau}$ of a machine of age τ will (given the other determinants of ω) depend on the control spans $s_1, \ldots, s_{R-1}$ and the size $N_1, \ldots, N_R$ of the staffs of the supervisors:

   $$a_{-\tau} = a_{-\tau}(s_1, \ldots, s_{R-1}, N_1, \ldots, N_R)$$

   Fig. 2.1 shows some possibilities of the graph of that function. Of course, it may be that the technology does fix the parameters substantially, but if a "machine" is a large, complicated installation (as a rolling mill, a mine, an automotive production plant) there is usually much leeway left for the influence of the organization. There might be an optimal control span and an optimal size of the staff: if the control is too stiff and all initiatives taken away from the rank and file and given to the higher echelons of the firm the output may shrink.

2. The labor input coefficients $\bar{l}_{\nu i}$ and $\hat{l}_{\nu i}$ are also functions of the control spans and the size of the staffs at the different stages of the hierarchy

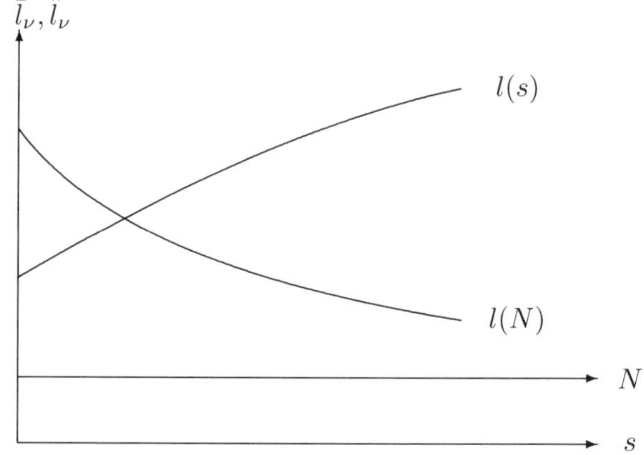

Figure 2.2 The labor input coefficient as a function of the control span s and of the size N of the staff, other variables kept constant

within the firm. The stiffer the control (i.e.: the smaller the control span and the larger the staffs) the less labor is needed directly on the machines. Thus the $l_{\nu i}$ are functions of s and N of the kind

$$\bar{l}_{\nu,-\tau} = \bar{l}_{\nu,-\tau}(s_1^+, \dots, s_{R-1}^+, N_1^-, \dots, N_R^-)$$

with the sign of the partial derivatives as indicated. Fig. 2.2 shows the graph of this function, if the intuition is justified by research in detail.

3. But also the input coefficients $b_{ji,-\tau}$ of secondary inputs as well as the replacement coefficients $repl_{\mu i,-\tau}$ are influenced by the organization of the firm. We formulate that for the case of the secondary inputs of the production department as:

$$b_{ji} = b_{ji}(s_1^+, \dots, s_{R-1}^+, N_1^-, \dots, N_R^-)$$

(cf. equation (2.13) in section 2.3). Similar relations hold for the replacement coefficients $repl_{\mu i}$ (see equation (2.10) in section 2.2). The graph of this function is similar to Fig. 2.2 if one substitutes b for l.

4. If all these influences are taken into account one may think that the labor force n_0 of rank zero is a rising function of the control span s and a declining function of the size N of the staff, see Fig. 2.3.

The decision on the organization of a firm cannot be decentralized. The personal interests of the workers of different ranks are not identical with the interests of the owner of the firm. Usually the "rank and file" does not want to be too much pressed by their supervisors, it wants to get enough pauses, vacations at the time of their choice, safety of the working place etc. A supervisor wants to supervise many workers and have a large staff to help him,

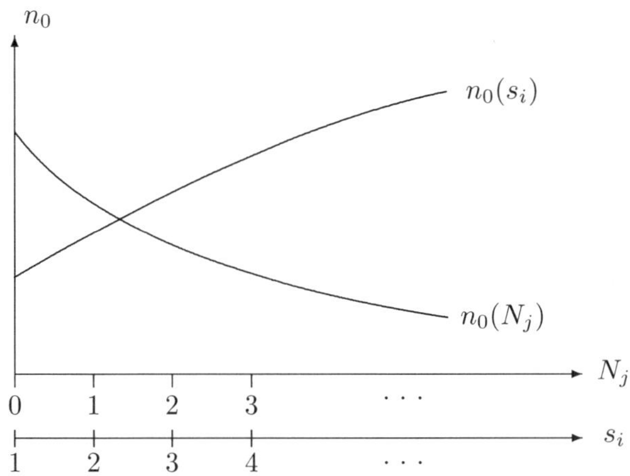

Figure 2.3 The size n_0 of the labor force of rank zero as a function of the control span s_i and of the size of the staff N_j

since its prestige (and often payment) depends on it. Thus the organization of a firm is an important decision which must be done at the highest level. Otherwise a lot of inefficiency will spread in the course of time which at the end may endanger the existence of the firm.

The decisions on the s, γ, N, POW are more specific for each firm. But also here much can be done to put "the right man on the right place" and to give him (or her) the necessary power and incentive to carry out its work efficiently.

This is a problem of psychology and of the knowledge of human nature which is as important for the firm as technological knowledge.

We still need the distribution of the administrative personnel to the facilities to accomodate the administration, since the secondary inputs depend on it. We assume that always the newest buildings and equipments are used up to the capacity level and if there is space left, the eldest buildings and equipments stay unused (and will be rented, sold or torn down; we do not formulate that explicitly). Thus the investment $I_{i,-\tau}^{real,adm}$ to accomodate the administration is used from the age $\tau = 1$ till the age $\tau = \vartheta \leq T$ such that[30]

$$\sum_{\tau=1}^{\vartheta-1} a_{i,-\tau}^{adm} \cdot I_{i,-\tau}^{real,adm} = L_i^{adm} \quad , \quad \vartheta \leq T.$$

[30] This equation does not consider the possibility that a different distribution of the administrative personnel to the different accommodation facilities $I_{i,-1}^{adm}, \ldots, I_{i,-T}^{adm}$ may influence the amount of secondary inputs. Thus we implicitly assume, that this influence may be neglected.

The unused capacity is

$$L_i^{adm}(unused) = \sum_{\tau=\vartheta+1}^{T} a_{i,-\tau}^{adm} \cdot I_{i,-\tau}^{real,adm}.$$

This yields: $\delta_{i,-\tau}^{adm} = 1$ for $\tau = 1, \ldots, \vartheta$ and $\delta_{i,-\tau}^{adm} = 0$ for $\tau = \vartheta + 1, \ldots, T$. Now, as far as the administration is concerned, the initial state B_i where the firm i finds itself at the end of period -1 is given by:

the capital K_i^{adm}	$= (I_{i,-T}^{real,adm}, \ldots, I_{i,-1}^{real,adm})$	invested in office buildings and other equipment
and the organization ω_i	$= (s_i, \gamma_i, q_i, N_i, Q_i, POW_i)$	of the firm.

Other decisions of the past may have an influence on the decisions of the firm as well. In this case they are part of the definition of the initial situation B_i of firm i, for instance total labor employed in the administration one period before: $L_{i,-1}^{adm} = (L_{1i,-1}^{adm}, \ldots, L_{ni,-1}^{adm})$.

2.8 Some Remarks on Other Characteristics of the Initial Situation of a Firm

There are other variables as well which appear in the vector B_i of the initial condition of firm i. First we mention

- all realized variables in the last period, not only those which are mentioned in the last section as far as they influence the decision in the next period;
- the expected demand $X_{i,0}^{exp}$ of its product in the next period as a function of the price $p_{i,0}$ which the firm charges in the next period, the expected prices $p_{noni,0}^{exp}$ of all other products and the expected expenditures $EXP_{noni,0}^{exp}$ of all other firms, households and other institutions:

  $$X_{i,0}^{exp} = f_i(p_{i,0}, p_{noni,0}^{exp}, EXP_{noni,0}^{exp})$$

  $$\text{where } EXP_{noni,0}^{exp} = (EXP_{F1}^{exp}, \ldots, EXP_{F\bar{M}}^{exp}, EXP_{H1}^{exp}, \ldots, EXP_{HN}^{exp}, EXP_{B}^{exp}, EXP_{G}^{exp})$$

  is the vector of the expected expenditures of all firms, households, the banks and the government. The "law of demand" states that $\frac{\partial X_{i,0}^{exp}}{\partial p_{i,0}} < 0$.

The expectations are based on the observations of the past and on estimations of change:

$$EXP^{exp}_{noni,0} = EXP_{noni,-1} + \Delta EXP^{exp}_{noni,0}$$

$$\text{where } \Delta EXP^{exp}_{noni,0} = f_{i,0}(\Delta MON_0, r_0, \ldots)$$

MON = money in circulation in the next period (announced by the Central Bank), r = rate of interest.

Now we have to specify what we mean exactly by the expression "expected demand", "expected expenditure" and other expected values and how these expectations influence each other. Here we take advantage of our assumption, that everything in our universe is finite. Thus there are also only finitely many amounts of production, sizes of prices etc. to consider. It does not make sense to consider price differences of a millionth of a penny or demand differences of a millionth of normal real production. Similarly we consider only finitely many possible probability distributions. Here it also does not make sense to regard probability distributions as different which differ only infinitesimally. Thus expected demand $X^{exp}_{i,0}$ is a vector of substantially different amounts of demand $X^{exp(1)}_{i,0}, \ldots, X^{exp(N)}_{i,0}$, if N possible amounts of demand are to be considered. To each amount $X^{exp(\nu)}_{i,0}$ is allocated a probability $\pi_\nu \geq 0$ such that

$$X^{exp(0)}_{i,0} = ((X^{exp(1)}_{i,0}, \pi_1), \ldots, (X^{exp(N)}_{i,0}, \pi_N)), \quad \sum_{\nu=1}^{N} \pi_\nu = 1 \quad (2.21)$$

The probabilities are taken from a finite set $V = \{V_1, \ldots, V_Z\}$ of probability distributions, where $V_\zeta = (\pi_{1,\zeta}, \ldots, \pi_{N,\zeta})$. E. g. only probability distributions taken from the binomial distribution are admissible.[31] The probability distribution $V_{X,i,0}$ chosen from the set V depends largely on the price $p_{i,0}$ the firm charges for its product $X_{i,0}$ in period 0 (a decision variable of firm i). Thus we may write $V_{X,i,0} = V_{X,i,0}(p_i, 0)$. In this case (2.21) may be written as:

$$X^{exp}_{i,0} = (X^{exp(1)}_{i,0}, \ldots, X^{exp(N)}_{i,0}, V_{X,i,0}(p_i, 0)) \quad (2.22)$$

where $V_{X,i,0} \in V$.

[31] Let us assume that the managers of a firm are sure that the price of a certain factor of production will lie between 10 and 11 (these values included) and that it only makes sense to consider the decimals 10.1,10.2,...,10.9 in between. In our example (see Fig. 2.4) only 5 binomial distributions are shown from which the managers may choose. Of course there may be intermediate distributions (e. g. for $w = .05, \ldots, w = .95$) to be considered, if there is more information available.

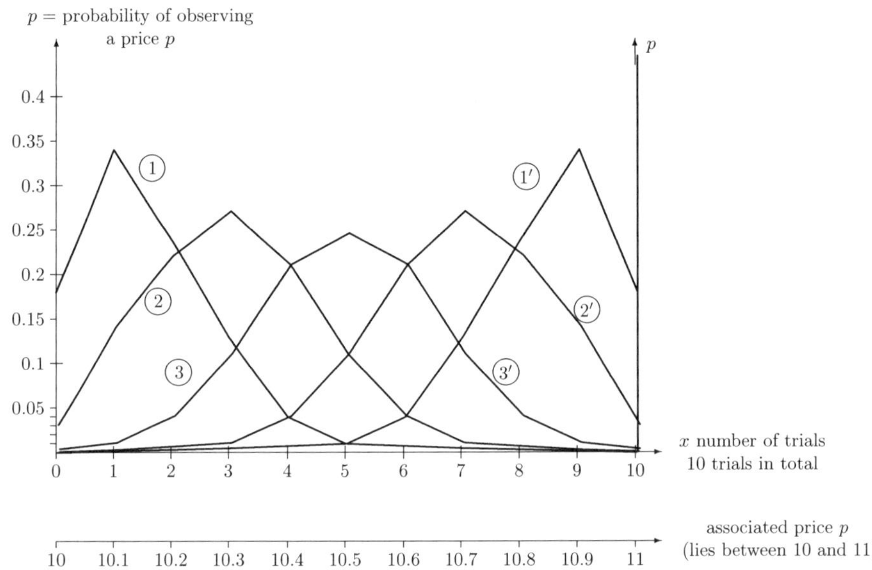

Binomial Distribution: $p = C_x^n w^x (1-w)^{n-x}$

$$C_x^n = \frac{n!}{x!(n-x)!}$$

(1)	n=10, w=0.15	(1′)	n=10, w=0.7
(2)	n=10, w=0.3	(2′)	n=10, w=0.85
(3)	n=10, w=0.5	(3′)	= (3)

Figure 2.4. Binomial Probability Distributions to Choose from: an Example

Similar relations hold for the expected prices $p^{exp}_{noni} = (p^{exp}_1, \dots, p^{exp}_{i-1}, p^{exp}_{i+1}, \dots, p^{exp}_M)$ of other products and the expected expenditures of other agents. Also these distributions $V_{p,noni,0} = (V_{p,1,0}, \dots, V_{p,i-1,0} V_{p,i+1,0}, \dots, V_{p.M,0})$ are taken from V, as well as the distributions $V_{EXP,noni,0} = (V_{EXP,1}, \dots, V_{EXP,Z})$ if there are Z other economic agents. Thus we may specify equation (2.22) as

$$X^{exp}_{i,0} = (X^{exp(1)}_{i,0}, \dots, X^{exp(N)}_{i,0}, \\ V_{X,i,0}(p_{i,0}, V_{p,noni,0}, V_{EXP,noni,0})), \tag{2.23}$$

all $V_\zeta \in V$. That means: the probability distribution of demand of the final product X_i of firm i depends on the price $p_{i,0}$ the firm charges for its product in the next period and on the probability distribution of the prices of other firms products and the probability distribution of expenditures of all other economic agents.
All probability distributions are determined by the managers of the firm with the aid of their staff. There are many methods available: simple extrapolations, traditional market research, inquiries, extended econometric forecasting systems. The management determines the degree of sophistication of these estimates. The size and the composition of the staff depends on it. We do not go into these details.
We continue with other variables which appear in the vector B_i of the initial condition of firm i:

- the labor supply $L^s_{i,0} = (L^s_{1i,0}, \dots, L^s_{ni,0})$ of households in working distance from firm i which are willing to offer the amounts of labor $L^s_{\nu i,+1}$ of kind ν to firm i in period 0. Let H_i be the set of all households which are able and willing to offer the amount of labor $L^{sh}_{\nu i,+1}$ of kind ν to firm i in period 0. Then we have

$$L^s_{\nu i,0} = \sum_{h \in H_i} L^{sh}_{\nu i,0}$$

The labor supply $L^{sh}_{\nu i,0}$ of household h is addressed to all firms in working distance from household h. But, of course, only one firm could employ part (or all) of this labor. We assume that there is an order of preference for firms by households such that firm 1 is the most favorite employer and firm $\bar{M}$ the least favorite. Then firm 1 has the first choice, then comes firm 2 and so on, and at full employment nothing may be left for the least firms. This rule determines which firm gets the labor, if labor is in short supply. Other variables which appear in the initial conditions are:

- the wage rates $l_{i,0} = (l_{1i,0}, \dots, l_{ni,0})$ for all n kinds of labor. They may be fixed by the trade unions or determined otherwise, but are known by the firms and by the households;

- the expected prices $p^{exp}_{noni,0} = (p^{exp}_{1,0}, \ldots, p^{exp}_{i-1,0}, p^{exp}_{i+1,0}, \ldots, p^{exp}_{M,0})$ of all other products or firms. Firm i has to form these expectations in order to be able to determine the price $p_{i,0}$ of its own product in the next period. Details have already been explained above.
The same applies to
- expected expenditures EXP^{exp}_{noni} of other economic agents;
- the rates of interest $r_0 = (r_{SEC,0}, r^-_{B,0}, r^+_{B,0})$ the firm has to pay for newly issued securities ($r_{SEC,0}$) and for bank loans ($r^-_{B,0}$) and the interest ($r^+_{B,0}$) it gets from the capital market, if it puts its money there;
- the taxation $T_{i,0}$ according to the tax laws valid in period 0;
- the technical coefficients $a_i, d_{ji}, repl_{ji}, b_{ji}, \bar{l}_{ji}, \hat{l}_{ji}$, which characterize the investment goods in the next period. It is clear that a firm has to know the details of an equipment it might be willing to buy.

This concludes the sector which describes the main features of the initial position B_i as far as the real side of the situation is concerned.

2.9 The Main Decisions of a Firm Concerning the Real Side

What are the main possible choices of firm i if it is in the initial situation B_i? These are (as far as the real side is concerned):

- the price p_i of the product,
- the amount X_i of production
- the labor employed $L_i = (L^{prod}_i, L^{inv}_i, L^{adm}_i)$
- its distribution on machines of different age (given by the degrees $\delta^{prod}_{i,-\tau}$ of the capacity utilization of the machines such that the amount X_i can be produced)
- the organization ω_i of the firm, i. e.: the control spans s_i, the personal composition γ_i of the controlled groups, the number N_i of persons to be controlled and the quality q_i of supervisors and the average quality Q_i of their staff
- the investments $I = (I^{prod}_i, I^{inv}_i, I^{adm}_i)$ which lead to the demand $I^{(k)d}_{\mu i}$ of the product of sector μ, $\mu = 1, \ldots, \bar{M}$, $k \in \{prod, inv, adm\}$
- the planned size of the inventories $INV_{1i}, \ldots, INV_{\bar{M}i}$. The actual inventories INV will deviate from the planned figure, in general.

Thus the decisions DEC_i^{real} of firm i concerning the real side may be written as a vector:

$$DEC_i^{real} = (p_i, X_i, L_i, \delta_{i,-T}, \ldots, \delta_{i,-1}, \omega_i, I_i, INV_{1i}, \ldots, INV_{Mi})$$

where $\omega_i = (s_i, \gamma_i, N_i, q_i, Q_i)$ and $I_i = (I_i^{prod}, I^{inv}, I^{adm})$. Since these amounts are given for the period before we could also write:

$$DEC_i^{real} = (\triangle p_i, \triangle X_i, \triangle L_i, \triangle \delta_i, \triangle \omega_i, \triangle I_i, \triangle INV_i, B_i) \tag{2.24}$$

where the components of the vectors comprise the changes in the production, inventory and administration department of firm i. The vector $DEC_{i,-1}^{real}$ of the period before and related to the actual real amounts (not the planned ones, which may be different) defines the real part of the initial condition $B_i : B_i^{real} = DEC_{i,-1}^{real}$. These are the main decisions to be taken (there are minor ones which are not mentioned here). From these decisions follow the secondary inputs. There are only finite many possible values of all decision variables. Thus there are only finite many possible decisions which define the transition from B_i to $B_{i1}, \ldots, B_{iz}$. Which one will be chosen depends also on the monetary side of the situation of the firm to which we come now.

2.10 The Initial Situation of a Firm: The Monetary Side

The initial situation of a firm at the beginning of period 0, before all decisions for this period are taken, consists of a vector of real items concerning the past and some knowledge on the future (this is what we have dealt with in the last sections). But in addition monetary terms have to be considered. The initial financial situation at the beginning of period 0 is of great importance. It follows from the transactions of the period -1. Thus we also have to consider this period in order to derive the initial situation in period 0. This financial (or monetary) side of a firm is of equal importance as the real side. It is a basic error of communist systems to suppose that it suffices to organize a planning system which regulates real production and the allocation of the factors of production on the base of technological considerations and to neglect the monetary and financial side. Profits or losses, financial assets or debts did not play a role in the planning system. But this is an error which became evident as the communist countries stayed behind the market economies more and more in the development process. The financial side controls the factor allocation of a firm such that in the long run the firm cannot use up more value in the form of factor input than it produces in the form of its product; expenditures cannot exceed earnings in the long run. The valuations in the form of prices follow ultimately from the evaluations of the products by the households and from the technological side of the production.

The monetary (financial) side of the firm is part of this general system of control of efficient factor use. In the following we assume as in the former sections that all decisions for the following period are taken at the beginning of the period and (if possible) executed during the period without any change. All payments are carried out at the end of the period such that the financial situation at the beginning of the next period is identical with that of the end of the period before[32].

We start with an analysis of the events in period -1 in order to derive the initial situation of period 0. We identify the liquidity of a firm i with its cash CA_i. Thus by definition:

$$CA_{i,-1} + \Delta CA_i = CA_i \geq 0$$

where $CA_{i,-1}$ is the cash at the beginning of period -1 and CA_i the cash at the beginning of period 0[33]. The change ΔCA_i of cash is determined by the difference of net receipts $REC_{i,-1}$ and net expenditures $EXP_{i,-1}$ in period -1. This forms the liquidity constraint of the firm:

$$\Delta CA_i = REC_{i,-1} - EXP_{i,-1} \geq -CA_{-1} \tag{2.25}$$

$$\begin{aligned} \text{where} \quad REC_{i,-1} &= X_{i,-1} \cdot p_{i,-1} + SUB_{i,-1} + RFA_{i,-1} \\ &\quad + R\Delta^- FA_{i,-1} + \Delta^+ LIA_{i,-1} \\ \text{and} \quad EXP_{i,-1} &= l_{i,-1} L_{i,-1} + ZLIA_{i,-1} + SIC_{i,-1} + IC_{i,-1} \\ &\quad + R\&D_{i,-1} + \Delta INVC_{i,-1} + R\Delta^+ FA_{i,-1} \\ &\quad - \Delta^- LIA_{i,-1} + T_{i,-1} \end{aligned}$$

If CA_i is negative, the firm is bankrupt. We only consider going concerns, thus $CA_{i,-1}$ and CA_i are supposed to be non-negative. The above expressions are explained as follows:

Δ^+ = only assets where $\Delta > 0$ are considered

Δ^- = only assets where $\Delta \leq 0$ are considered

$X_{i,-1} \cdot p_{i,-1}$ = receipts from selling the product

$SUB_{i,-1}$ = subsidies from the government

$RFA_{i,-1}$ = return on financial assets

$= \sum_{j \in J^{(i)}_{KSt'}, j \neq i} KSt_{ji,-1} \cdot d_{j,-1} + \sum_{j \in J^{(i)}_{SEC'}, j \neq i} SEC_{ji,-1} \cdot r_{SEC,j,-1}$, where $J^{(i)}_{KSt}$ is the set of capital stock in the portfolio of firm i; $J^{(i)}_{SEC}$ is the set of securities in the portfolio of firm i.

[32] It is a disadvantage of a theory which runs in discrete time periods to be forced to fix all actions at the beginning or at the end of a period. This distortion looses its significance if the time periods chosen are small. We obey the following rule. Flow variables (like income) are related to a period (e.g. Y_t = income in period t) but registered at the end of the period; stock variables are related to the beginning of a period (e.g. K_t = capital stock at the beginning of period t).

[33] As already stated: we almost always leave out the index 0.

$R\Delta FA_{i,-1}$ = receipts from selling financial assets (if $\Delta FA_{i,-1}$ is negative) or cost of acquiring financial assets (if $\Delta FA_{i,-1}$ is positive)
$= \sum_{\substack{j\in J_{KSt}\\ j\neq i}} \Delta KSt_{ji,-1}\cdot v_{KSt,j,-1}+\sum_{\substack{j\in J_{SEC}\\ j\neq i}} \Delta SEC_{ji,-1}\cdot v_{SEC,j,-1}$

$\Delta LIA_{i,-1}$ = change of the value of capital stock and liabilities
$= \Delta KSt_{i,-1}\cdot v_{KSt,i,-1} + \Delta SEC_{i,-1}\cdot v_{SEC,i,-1}$
$+KSt_{i,-1}\cdot \Delta v_{KSt,i,-1} + SEC_{i,-1}\cdot \Delta v_{SEC,i,-1} + \Delta DE_{i,-1}$
(DE = debts at the banking system)

$l_{i,-1}L_{i,-1}$ = wage cost
$= \sum_{\nu=1}^{n} L_{\nu i,-1}\cdot l_{\nu i,-1}$

$ZLIA_{i,-1}$ = distribution of profits and interest payments
$= KSt_{i,-1}\cdot d_{i,-1} + SEC_{i,-1}\cdot r_{SEC,i,-1} + DE_{i,-1}\cdot r_{DE,i,-1}$
(DE = debts at the banking system)

$SIC_{i,-1}$ = cost of secondary inputs
$= \sum_{\mu=1}^{M}(SIC_{\mu i,-1}^{prod} + SIC_{\mu i,-1}^{inv} + SIC_{\mu i,-1}^{adm})$

$IC_{i,-1}$ = cost of investment
$= I_{i,-1}^{prod}\cdot p_{i,-1}^{prod} + I_{i,-1}^{inv}\cdot p_{i,-1}^{inv} + I_{i,-1}^{adm}\cdot p_{i,-1}^{adm}$
where $I_{i,-1}^{(k)}p_{i,-1}^{(k)} = \sum_{j=1}^{M} a_{ji,-1}^{(k)}\cdot I_{i,-1}^{(k)}\cdot p_{j,-1}$,
$k\in\{prod, inv, adm\}$

$R\&D_{i,-1}$ = expenditures for research and development

$\Delta INVC_{i,-1}$ = change of the value of inventories
$= \sum_{\mu=1}^{M} \Delta INV_{\mu i,-1}\cdot p_{\mu,-1}$

$T_{i,-1}$ $= T_{i,-1}^{ind} + T_{i,-1}^{\Pi}$, where
$T_{i,-1}^{ind}$ = indirect taxes $= t_{i,-1}^{ind}\cdot X_i(-1)\cdot p_{i,-1}$
$T_{i,-1}^{\Pi}$ = profit taxes $= t_{i,-1}^{\Pi}\cdot \Pi_{i,-1}$

$\Pi_{i,-1}$ are the profits in period -1. They are defined as follows. Let $CP_{i,-1}$ be the costs of production which lead to payments and $CD_{i,-1}$ the depreciation costs. Now we have[34]

$$\Pi_{i,-1} = X_{i,-1}\cdot p_{i,-1} - CP_{i,-1} - CD_{i,-1} \tag{2.26}$$

[34] This is a simplified approach. We assume that the lifetime of all investment units is T periods and that depreciation is linear. Then the value $V_{Ii,-1}$ of total investment of firm i at the end of period -1 is

$$\begin{aligned}
\text{where}\quad CP_{i,-1} &= l_{i,-1}L_{i,-1} + CC_{i,-1} + SIC_{i,-1} + T^{ind}_{i,-1},\\
CC_{i,-1} &= \text{capital cost}\\
&= SEC_{i,-1} \cdot r_{SEC,i,-1} + DE_{i,-1} \cdot r_{DE,i,-1}\\
CD_{i,-1} &= \text{depreciation cost}\\
&= \tfrac{1}{T}\textstyle\sum_{\tau=1}^{T}\sum_{j=1}^{\bar{M}}(I^{prod}_{ji,-\tau} + I^{inv}_{ji,-\tau} + I^{adm}_{ji,-\tau}) \cdot p_{j,-\tau}
\end{aligned}$$

This explains the cash situation CA_i at the beginning of period 0. All other state variables are determined by the decision of the firm i at the beginning of period -1, on acquiring or selling of capital stock $\Delta KSt_{ji,-1}$ and securities $\Delta SEC_{ji,-1}$, $j \in J = \{1, \ldots, \bar{M}, B, G\}$, on the selling or buying of own capital stock $\Delta KSt_{i,-1}$ and securities $\Delta SEC_{i,-1}$, on the change $\Delta DE_{i,-1}$ of bank debts and on the change $\Delta INV_{i,-1}$ of inventories. This yields

$$KSt_{ji,-1} + \Delta KSt_{ji} = KSt_{ji}, \quad j \in J = \{1, \ldots \bar{M}, B, G\}, \quad j \neq i$$

$$SEC_{ji,-1} + \Delta SEC_{ji} = SEC_{ji}, \quad j \in J$$

$$KSt_{i,-1} + \Delta KSt_i = KSt_i$$

$$SEC_{i,-1} + \Delta SEC_i = SEC_i$$

$$DE_{i,-1} + \Delta DE_i = DE_i$$

This together with the pertinent cash equation (2.25) and the vector p of prices, the vector l of wages, the market values v_{KSt} of capital stock and v_{SEK} of securities, the vector d of the distributions of profits on the owners, the vector r of interest rates r_{SEC} and r_{DE}, the rate t^{ind} of indirect taxation and t^{Π} the rate of profit taxation defines the monetary items of the vector B_i of the initial situation of firm i:

$$\begin{aligned}
B_i \;=\; &(CA_i, KSt_{ji}, SEC_{ji}, KSt_i, SEC_i, DE_i, p, l,\\
&v_{KSt,j}, v_{SEC,j}, d, r, t^{ind}_i, t^{\Pi}_i \ldots)
\end{aligned} \tag{2.27}$$

where the dots symbolize the vectors of the real side, and $KSt_{ji} = KSt_{1i}, \ldots, KSt_{i-1,i}, KSt_{i+1,i}, \ldots KSt_{\bar{M}i}$, and SEC_{ji} accordingly; $v_{KSt,j} = v_{KSt,1}, \ldots, v_{KSt,M}$, and $v_{SEC,j}$ accordingly.

All variables refer to the beginning of period 0 and are determined by decisions in the past.

$$V_{Ii,\ 1} = VI_{i,-T} \cdot \frac{T-T}{T} + VI_{i,-T+1} \cdot \frac{1}{T} + \cdots + VI_{i,-1} \cdot \frac{T-1}{T}$$

$$\text{where}\quad VI_{i,-\tau} = \sum_{j=1}^{M}(I^{prod}_{ji,-\tau} + I^{inv}_{ji,-\tau} + I^{adm}_{ji,-\tau})p_{j,-\tau}$$

This seems to be a tolerable approximation.

2.11 The Possible Decisions of a Firm Concerning the Monetary Sector

The possible choices on the monetary side are:

1. the change ΔKSt_{ji} in capital stock (=the change of shares)
2. the change ΔSEC_{ji} of the stock of securities
3. the issue or repurchase ΔKSt_i of own capital stock
4. the issue or repurchase ΔSEC_i of securities
5. the change ΔDE_i of bank debts
6. the distribution d_i of profits
7. the change ΔCA_i of cash

These changes are not independent from each other. The liquidity constraint (2.25) has to be obeyed in order to avoid bankruptcy.

The price p_i of the final product is also a decision variable of the firm. But it has already been taken into account at the real side since it should not be separated from the possible demand of the product. The other financial variables: wages l, rates of interest r, valuation v_{KSt} of capital stock, valuation v_{SEC} of securities, tax rates t^{ind} and t^{Π} are determined by the market, by trade unions or by the government, virtually independent of the firm we are considering here.

2.12 Transition of a Firm from One Decision Point to the Next: The Choice Criteria

The real and monetary decision variables of a firm i explained in the foregoing sections may assume only a finite number of integer values. Thus only finitely many combinations of the decision variables are possible. But only those combinations are admissible which fulfill the liquidity constraint (inequality (2.25) for period 0). These admissible combinations lead to the next decision points $B_{i1}, \ldots, B_{iy}$. The points $B_{i,y+1}, \ldots, B_{i,z}$ which violate the liquidity constraint cannot be reached. Which point will be chosen?

We approach this decision problem in the same spirit as in the case of household decisions. There are several different points of view (or decision criteria) by which the firm i judges the admissible decisions. Judging from one point of view, each decision gets a note between $-\bar{z}$ and $+\bar{z}$, according to the liking or hating of the result of the decision, that means: the firm evaluates the situation at the points B_{ij}. The"points of view" are basically: the profit Π, the amount of production X (which determines the market share of the firm, which is an index of the market power), the employment L (which determines the relation to the public and to the trade unions), the distribution d of profits (which codetermines the shareholder value), the risk of bankruptcy R or the liquidity situation, e.g. measured by the ratio of short term assets to total turnover, and finally the moral evaluation M of the decision as an index of the reputation of the firm.[35] The owner or the president of the firm (or the board of directors, as the case may be) evaluates all alternatives by these principles: each possible decision gets a note between $-\bar{z}$ and $+\bar{z}$ with respect to each principle. Afterwards the principles themselves will be weighted by proportions α. This gives the final evaluation of each possible alternative $B_{01}, \ldots, B_{0y}$. Let $V_{ij}(\pi_{ij})$ be the evaluations of the profit situation at the point B_{ij} and $V_{ij}(X_{ij}), V_{ij}(L_{ij}), V_{ij}(d_{ij}), V_{ij}(R_{ij}), V_{ij}(M_{ij})$ the evaluation of production, employment, distribution of profits, the risk situation and the moral judgement respectively, where all valuations lie between $-\bar{z}$ and $+\bar{z}$. Let $\alpha_{ij,\kappa}$ be the relative weight of the variable κ, $\kappa \in \{\pi, X, L, d, R, M\}$. Then the evaluation V_{ij} of point B_{ij} is supposed to be:

$$\begin{aligned} Vij &= \alpha_{ij,\pi} \cdot V_{ij}(\Pi_{ij}) + \alpha_{ij,X} \cdot V_{ij}(X_{ij}) + \alpha_{ij,L} \cdot V_{ij}(L_{ij}) \\ &\quad + \alpha_{ij,d} \cdot V_{ij}(d_{ij}) + \alpha_{ij,R} \cdot V_{ij}(R_{ij}) + \alpha_{ij,M} \cdot V_{ij}(M_{ij}) \\ &\quad \text{where} \quad \alpha_{ij,\kappa} \geq 0, \quad \sum_{\kappa} \alpha_{ij,\kappa} = 1 \end{aligned}$$

The firm chooses the alternative with maximal value V_{ij} :[36]

$$B^*_{ij} \longleftarrow max(V_{i1}, \ldots, V_{iy}) \tag{2.28}$$

---

[35] A specific firm may have a lot of other criteria, but it seems that these are the general ones.

M is a latent variable which may have different meanings. M may, if used as a decision criterion of a firm, also be interpreted as "spirit of enterprise" which comprises spirit of adventure, confidence in the future, pleasure to try new paths, to show that new approaches will be superior to old ones. To develop such a spirit it needs an appropriate environment: public recognition of economic success, a government which favors private activities and leaves room for it. All this can be modeled in the form of a Markov chain similar to the approach in section 1.4, where M is defined as the moral qualification of a decision of a person.

There are methods to estimate latent variables, traditional ones such as factor analysis and principal components (see Dhrymes (1970)), and new ones such as the PLS-method of Herman Wold (1980) or the LISREL method of Jöreskog (see Jöreskog and Sörb (1981)). Thus we should not be afraid of latent variables. The problem is to find appropriate indicators for its formation and its effects.

[36] Of course, the same remark as earlier must be made. This is a theoretical formulation. Actually, the firm considers only few alternatives, mostly those which are in the neighborhood of that what has been done in the past. A new management will in general consider another (small) sample of possible decisions, use other weights of the principles and thus come up to another decision.

The $\alpha_{ij,\kappa}$ may not be constant. One may guess, that in case of an optimistic long term outlook the weights for X, L, d, M may be relatively higher, in case of a pessimistic outlook the weights for Π and for R. This concludes the theory of the firm.

2.13 A Short Look into the Literature

There is a whole branch of economics called Business Administration which deals with the theory of the firm in many details. A lot of textbooks are available. I only mention the book of Albach, *Allgemeine Betriebswirtschaftslehre* (2000). Of course, there are a lot of journals specialized in this field; I only mention the "Zeitschrift für Betriebswirtschaft". It does not make sense to compare our approach here which is much more simplified compared to the detailed analysis in Business Administration. But in economics there is a special branch "Microeconomics" where (among others) models of a firm are presented which could serve as a base for Macroeconomics and which may be compared with the approach used here. There are theories of the firm which are more global and simpler in some respects but a bit more detailed in other respects. I mention the theories of Varian, Mankiw and Helmstädter as examples. *Varian* (2000) starts with the technology used in the firm and distinguishes between smooth neoclassical production functions and constant proportions. He derives the concepts of a marginal product, the rate of substitution and others and assumes given factor prices and output and thus arrives at cost and profit functions. He assumes profit maximization which yields a supply function and factor demand functions. This is a kind of "normal approach" in microeconomics. *Mankiw*(1998) follows that line, but concentrates on the neoclassical cost function. The underlying production function is a very simple one[37] Thus also the cost function has the "normal" neoclassical shape. Prices are given, and profit maximization is assumed.

Also *Ernst Helmstädter* (1991) follows that road but deals with the case of fixed production coefficients (called: limitational production function) more in detail. Compared with these theories of the firm our theory is more detailed with respect to the inner organization of the firm but does not deal with details of the relations to other economic agents.

But there are also text books which consider much more relations within the firm and with respect to other economic agents. I only mention the book of *Jean Tirole, The Theory of Industrial Organization* (1998). He rightly states that a firm has many facets. It may be defined in various ways. It may deviate from profit maximization. The size of a firm must be explained (there may be horizontal or vertical interpretations). The technological view is not the

[37] One may consider much more complicated production functions, see Krelle (1969) or some contributions to the Festschrift for Ryuzo Sato, in Negishi and others, 2001.

only relevant one, one should as well consider the contractual view and the influence of the law system (the firm could be considered as a loophole for monopoly power which is restrained by law). The organization of a firm is dealt with similarly as in this book, but less detailed. Prices (and production) are subject to bargaining. In the model suggested in this book the situation of a normal market for consumption goods is taken as prototype: the firm fixes the price and the buyer decides on the amount of commodities he wants to buy at this price. Jean Tirole views the firm as an incomplete contract; the minimization of transaction cost is one reason for the existence of a firm. The principle-agent relationship is given much room: the manager may choose between work or leisure (similarly as a member of a household) and needs some inducement for work. Take-overs are also treated in some particularity. All these features of a firm are not considered in this book.

We take the existence of firms at the beginning of the planning period as given and do not ask why they exist. Our approach to the firm lies somewhere between that of the "normal" textbooks and the Tirole-type approach which considers more details. Our principles of choosing the definitional framework of the firm are guided by the aim to come to an understandable interdependent disequilibrium system which allows to take ethics into account and which is reasonably near to reality but disregards details which are not relevant in this context.

References

[1] Albach, Horst: *Allgemeine Betriebswirtschaftslehre*, Wiesbaden (Gabler), 2000

[2] Arrow, K.J.: *The Economic Implications of Learning by Doing*, Rev.of Ec.Studies 29 (1962), pp. 155

[3] Beckmann, Martin: *Rank in Organizations*, Berlin, Heidelberg, New York (Springer), *Lecture Notes in Economics and Mathematical Systems*, vol.161, 1978

[4] Blaug, Mark: *The Disease of Formalism in Economics, or Bad Games That Economics Play*, Heft 16, Lectiones Jenenses, Jena 1998

[5] Debreu, Gerard: *Excess Demand Functions*, J. of Math. Economics 1. p. 15-23, 1974

[6] Helmstädter, E.: *Wirtschaftstheorie I. Mikroökonomische Theorie*, 4.ed., München (Vahlen), 1991

[7] Jöreskog, K. and D. Sörb, V. Lisrel: *User's guide, International Educational Services*, Chicago, 1981

[8] Krelle, Wilhelm: *Produktionstheorie*, Tübingen (Mohr-Siebeck), 1969

[9] Krelle, Wilhelm: *Theorie des wirtschaftlichen Wachstums*, 2.ed., Berlin, Heidelberg, New York (Springer) 1988, p. 210-214

[10] Krelle, Wilhelm: *The Spirit of Enterprise as Driving Force of Technical Progress*, in: Sadowski (Hrsg.), Entrepreneurial Spirits, Horst Albach zum 70. Geburtstag, Wiesbaden (Gabler), 2001a, p. 31-55

[11] Krelle, Wilhelm: *Production Theory as a Part of a Dynamic General Disequilibrium System*, in: Negishi, Ramachandran, Mino (eds.): *Economic Theory, Dynamics and Markets, Essays in Honor of Ryuzo Sato*, Boston etc. (Kluver), 2001b.

[12] Krelle, Wilhelm: *Produktionstheorie im Rahmen einer neuen Mikrotheorie*, in Berninghaus and Braulke (ed.), Berlin etc. (Springer), 2001, p. 255-268

[13] Mayntz, Renate: *Rationalität in sozialwissenschaftlicher Perspektive*, Lectiones Jenenses Heft 18, Jena 1999

[14] Negishi, T., Ramachandran, R., Mino, K. (eds.): *Economic Theory, Dynamics and Markets, Essays in Honor of Ryuzo Sato*, Boston etc. (Kluwer), 2001

[15] Sato, Ryuzo: *Production, Stability and Dynamic Symmetry*, Selected Essays of Ryuzo Sato Vol.2, Cheltenham, UK · Northhampton, MA, USA (Edward Elgar), 1999.

[16] Selten, Reinhard: A simple model of flackridden imperfect competition, in: Joseph E. Stiglitz and G. Frank Mathewson (ed.), *New Developments in the Analysis of Market Structure*, Cambridge/Mass. (MIT Press), 1986.

[17] Schneeweiss, H.: *Modelle mit latenten Variablen*, paper read at the Conference in honor of the late Günther Menges, Heidelberg, 1984

[18] Sonnenschein, Hugo: *Market Excess Demand Functions*, Econometrica Vol.40, No 3, May 1972, p. 549-563

[19] Wold, H.: *Model Construction and Evaluation when Theoretical Knowledge is Scarce: Theory and Application of Partial Least Squares*, in: *Evaluation of Econometric Models*, Academic Press, 1980

CHAPTER 3
The Theory of the Banking System

3.1 Introductory Remarks

Since this theory of the Banking System should be a part of a dynamic general disequilibrium system we shall not model a specific banking system but try to present a system which is a simplified version of many realized banking systems. The basic idea is the same as in the theory of the household and the theory of the firm: everything what we observe and what is not due to nature is the result of human decisions which may be explained by the evaluation of a certain number of alternatives. In our case there are the directors of commercial banks and of the Central Bank who (in connection with the brokers at the exchanges) determine the financial conditions which the firms and households have to accept. The theory is similar to the theory of the firm, but not identical.

We assume that there are g "banks": $b_1, \ldots, b_g$, where "banks" comprise all monetary and financial institutions (MFi in the Monatsberichte der Bundesbank[1])with the exception of the Central Bank.

Each bank sells a product which is different from the product of another bank. The "product" of a bank in the narrow sense is the delivery of and the right of disposal on a certain amount of money for a certain time under certain conditions for a certain price, called rate of interest.

We may say: the product of a bank in the narrow sense is "liquidity" measured by the amount of credits it gives to other agents. Though the rates of interest may be equal at different banks, the other conditions of loans and characteristics of the banks will be different such that no two banks are in the same situation and offer the same product. In the case of an insurance company the "product"of the company is the promise to pay a certain amount of money in the future when the situation S_j arises (the date is not known at presence). The price of this insurance claim is the regular payment of insurance premiums of a certain size. Here also each insurance company offers different insurance claims at different prices. Under this interpretation of a "product" and its "price" we may treat the financial institutions similarly as "private firms" producing a tangible commodity (see chapter 2).

But there are enough specialities to justify a special treatment. The financial side determines the size and the distribution of wealth and simultaneously

---

[1] See e.g. Deutsche Bundesbank, Monatsbericht März 2001, p. 10∗, "Banks" include insurance companies, building and loan associations, money market funds and similar institutions.

the distribution of power in a firm and thus its decisions. Since "wealth" is the basic concept on the financial side the balance-sheet stays in the center of the theory. The profit-and-loss account is also of importance by explaining the difference between two adjacent balance sheets and by codetermining the decision of the management of the bank concerning the conditions of the credits (among them: most important the price (=rate of interest) of a credit), or the promise to pay a certain sum of money in case of a certain event in the future. As in chapter 1 and 2 we assume that there are only finite many possible situations and decisions. This "finite many" may be a very large number, but only "in theory". Actually only very few alternatives are considered, those which the managers know and judge as "important". They value these alternatives on an integer scale between "very good" and "absolutely bad" in the same way as the managers of a firm or the members of households value their possible situations.

Of course, the criteria are different. In the following we formulate the theory in terms of a "normal" bank. The insurance companies may be treated similarly. Each bank b_i sells a product x_i – or in other words: offers a maximum amount CR_{bi} of credits at a price (=rate of interest) $r_{CR,bi}$ under certain conditions κ_i to those agents (firms or households or the government) which apply for a credit and fulfill the conditions κ_i. Each bank is specialized with respect to its clients (households, firms of certain industries (agriculture, handicraft, shipping, exports etc.), with respect to certain regions, to the types of services it offers to its clients and so on). The rate of interest may be the same at different banks, but some other credit conditions will differ. Thus the credit CR_{bi} given by bank b_i is offered on the conditions κ_i where κ_i is a vector:

$$\kappa_i = (r_{CR,bi}, t_{CR,bi}, \sigma_{CRi}, sec_i)$$

where $r_{CR,bi}$ = rate of interest requested by bank i

$t_{CR,bi}$ = term of the credit (short-term, long-term,...), = time structure of repayment. We assume that the modalities of repayment of the credit are equal for all banks

σ_{CRi} = securities demanded by the bank to be provided by the debtor

sec_i = sectors of the economy to which the bank i offers credits.

At the beginning of each period, the managers of the bank b_i decide on the maximum amount $\overline{CR}_{bi}$ of credits it is willing to offer and on the conditions κ_i. The bank sticks to it till the end of the period. The conditions are known to all agents before they have to decide on their financial arrangements, real production, investment and prices, demand of secondary inputs and other items.

As already said at the beginning: we leave out foreign countries, and thus do not consider the international capital flows, exports and imports and the determination of the exchange rates in order to keep the system simple. The foreign trade may be introduced later. We also leave out the definitional equations which are mostly adding up equations. They may be added by the reader who wants to work with the system.

But we have to deal with another problem in this context. Assume that there is more than one firm which wants to get credits from a certain bank and fulfills its conditions. But the bank is not able (or willing) to grant that amount of credits which is demanded. Which firms are the lucky ones which obtain the credits and what happens to the others? We may assume that the bank has a "preference order" for the firms which may become its debtors (the profits in the past, the liquidity situation now, the future prospects, the ability of the management and other data may serve as indicators). An alternative method may be the "first come first served"-rule which results in a chance selection out of the applying firms. Similarly, the firms may have a preference order on the banks and start their demand for credits at the bank of highest ranking in this order. The "normal" reaction of the management of the bank b_i which experiences this surplus demand on its credits will be to aggravate its credit conditions κ_i i.e. to increase the rate of interest and (or) to increase the requirements on the securities or to reduce the sectors to which the bank offers its credits. But this could only be done in the next period. The result would be that in the long term average the amount of credits offered by bank i is also demanded by some agents. But normally the demand for credits will not coincide with the supply[2].

If the demand is larger than the supply, the bank establishes an order of procedence among all agents which ask for a credit. If there are n_i agents which ask for credits, the bank i establishes an order $a_{1i}, a_{2i}, \ldots, a_{ni}$ among these agents where the criteria κ_i may be used as criteria of procedence[3]. Those firms which do not obtain credits at bank i have to try it at other banks which are content with the securities the firm can offer. Perhaps at the end the firm does not get the credit it wants. This will be known before the firm takes its decisions for the next period. Now the firm has to change its original plan for the next period. We only consider this feasible plan. On the other hand: if bank i cannot find enough debtors for the credits it is willing to

---

[2] The European Central Bank solves this problem in a remarkable way. It auctioneers the amount of money it wants to circulate in the public by a method called interest rate tender. Each financial institution MFi is requested to state that amount of credits which it wants to get from the Central Bank, and which maximum rate of interest it is willing to pay. The Central Bank grants the credits starting with highest rate of interest till the total amount of additional money which the Central Bank has decided upon as optimal at that time is reached. Those institutions which stated a lower maximum rate of interest are excluded. If the total demand for credits exceeds the supply planned by the Central Bank, there is a proportional curtailment of the amount demanded by the MFi. This solves the problem of the allocation of credits by the Central Bank.

[3] We do not get into the details of this selection process.

grant it will reduce its credit conditions in the next period. That means: it will reduce the rate of interest and (or) the requirements on the credit conditions, but this can also be realized only after the next period.

In the theories of the household and the firm we considered only feasible situations after these selection processes have been finished. In the theory of the banking system which we shall present in the following sections the same principle is adopted.[4]

3.2 Some Definitions and Relations. A Note

The sections on households and firms could be written without stating explicitly the interdependence of all sectors of the economy. Now when we turn to the banking sector this interdependence cannot be neglected. In this section we state the most important definitional relations which define these interdependencies as well for the monetary flows as for the states of wealth.

We consider the following economic agents (they form the set $\{J\}$):

M households	:	h	=	$1, 2, \ldots, M$
N private firms	:	i	=	$1, 2, \ldots, N$
B private banks	:	b	=	$1, 2, \ldots, B$
1 Central Bank	:	CB		
1 Government	:	G		

Each firm produces one commodity. Thus we have

N products in the economy	:	$i = 1, \ldots, N.$
There are n kinds of labor	:	$L_1, L_2, \ldots, L_n,$

and one kind of land[5] LA, one Central Bank CB and one government G.

The *monetary receipts* $REC^{(s)}$ of an agent $s \in \{J\}$ in one period may be classified as follows:[6]

---

[4] The next section may be skipped by readers not interested in the definition of concepts and their interrelations.

[5] This assumption is made to keep the system simple. Only in agriculture the land is an important factor of production and this is a small sector now. V. Thünen and others made the same simplifying assumption. – Land can also be taken as a synonym for a (practically) fixed factor such as Gold.

[6] The following definitions are based on the simplifying assumptions:

a. labor is only supplied by households. There is no "production function" for labor. The total amount of labor is exogenous;

b. a household does not produce anything and all consumption goods are treated as if they would be consumed in the next period;

c. production capital is owned by the firms which use it. The firms may be owned by any agent in the society, either in the form of shares (= KSt =capital stock)

$$REC^{(s)} = p_Y \cdot Y^{+(s)} + l \cdot L^{+(s)} + r_{LA}LA^{+(s)} - p_{LA}\Delta^- LA^{(s)} + TR^{+(s)} + r_{FA}FA^{+(s)} - p_{FA}\Delta^- FA^{(s)} + p_{FS}FS^{+(s)} + T^{+(s)} \quad (3.1)$$

where

$p_Y \cdot Y^{+(s)}$ = income by selling the product s at price p_Y (if the agent s produces anything, otherwise: $p_Y Y^{+(s)} = 0$); $p_Y \cdot Y^{+(s)} := \sum_{j\in\{J\}} x_j^{(s)} \cdot p_j$, where $x_j^{(s)}$ = the amount of product $x^{(s)}$ sold to agent j

$l \cdot L^{+(s)}$ = income by selling labor, $l \cdot L^{+(s)} = \sum_{\nu=1}^{n} \sum_{j\in\{J\}} L_{\nu j}^{+(s)} \cdot l_\nu$ where $L_{\nu j}^{+(s)}$ = amount of labor of kind ν supplied by household s to agent j

$r_{LA}LA^{+(s)}$ = amount of land owned by agent s and rented to other agents with a rent (per unit of land) of r_{LA},

= $\sum_{j\in\{J\}} LA_j^{+(s)} \cdot r_{LA}$; $LA_j^{+(s)}$ = amount of land owned by agent s; s and rented to agent j.

$-p_{LA}\Delta^- LA^{(s)}$ = receipts of agent s by selling the amount $\Delta^- LA^{(s)}$ of land to other agents (Δ^- means that only negative changes of the total amount $LA^{(s)}$ are considered; p_{LA} is the price of land, there is only one price of land); thus $-p_{LA}\Delta^- LA^{(s)} = \sum_{j\in\{J\}} \Delta^- LA_j^{(s)} \cdot p_{LA}$, where $\Delta^- LA_j^{(s)}$ = amount of land sold by agent s to agent j

$TR^{+(s)}$ = transfer receipts of agent s

= $\sum_{j\in\{J\}} TR_j^{+(s)}$ = transfer receipts of agent s from agent j

---

or in the form of securities (= SEC). There exists an exchange for all of these assets, at which their prices are determined;

d. there is no market for used real capital (called "machines" in this book); their evaluation is reflected by depreciation rules which are to a certain degree arbitrary.

$r_{FA}FA^{+(s)}$ = income from interest on financial assets (=FA) owned by agent s;

$= \sum_{j\in\{J\}} KSt_j^{+(s)} \cdot d_j + \sum_{j\in\{J\}} SEC_j^{+(s)} \cdot r_{SEC,j} + \sum_{j\in\{J\}} CR_j^{+(s)} \cdot r_{CR} + \sum_{j\in\{B\}} TD_j^{+(s)} \cdot r_{TD} + \sum_{j\in\{B\}} DE_j^{+(s)} \cdot r_{DE}$ where $\{B\}$ is he set of all private banks; time deposits TD as well as debts DE are made only at private banks, $KSt_j^{+(s)}$ is the capital stock of kind j owned by agent s d_j the dividend on capital stock j; $SEC_j^{+(s)}$ the securities, $CR_j^{+(s)}$ the credits of agent s given to agent j[7], $TD_j^{+(s)}$ = time deposits of agent s at bank j, $DE_j^{+(s)}$ = debts at banks (only positive if s is a bank), r are the different interest rates (which one is indicated in the subscript).

$-p_{FA}\Delta^- FA^{(s)}$ = income of agent s from selling part of the financial assets it owns at the price p_{FA} to other agents; this is similarly defined as the expression $-p_{LA}\Delta^- LA^{(s)}$ above.

$\Delta^+ DE^{(s)}$ = increase of debts of agent s, $= \sum_{j\in\{B\}} \Delta^+ DE_j^{(s)}$

$T^{+(s)}$ = tax receipts (only positive if $s = G$, otherwise zero).

$p_{FS} \cdot FS^{+(s)}$ = income from selling financial services at price p_{FS} (financial services include insurance, keeping accounts, transfer of money, advice and information in financial affairs. For simplicity, we lump all these services together). In detail: $p_{FS} \cdot FS^{+(s)} = \sum_{j\in\{J\}} FS_j^{+(s)}$. This is only relevant for $s = b \in \{B\}$

Not all items on the right hand side of equation (3.1) are applicable for all agents $s \in \{J\}$: Some of them are zero by definition or by assumption. For example:

if s is a household h, the expressions $p_Y \cdot Y^{+(s)}$, $p_{FS}FS^{+(s)}$ and $T^{+(s)}$ in equation (3.1) are zero;

if s is a private firm ($s = i$), the terms $l \cdot L^{+(s)}$, $p_{FS}^{+(s)}$ and $T^{+(s)}$ are zero;

if s is a private bank ($s = b$), the terms $p_Y \cdot Y^{+(s)}$, $l \cdot L^{+(s)}$ and $T^{+(s)}$ are zero.

The *monetary expenditures* $EXP^{(s)}$ of an agent s are to a large degree the reflected image of the monetary receipts $REC^{(s)}$:

$$\begin{aligned} EXP^{(s)} &= p_c \cdot C^{(s)} + p_I I^{-(s)} + p_{SI} SI^{-(s)} + lL^{-(s)} + r_{LA} LA^{-(s)} \\ &\quad + p_{LA} \Delta^+ LA^{(s)} + TR^{-(s)} + r_{FA} FA^{-(s)} + p_{FS} FS^{-(s)} \\ &\quad + p_{FA} \Delta^+ FA^{(s)} + T^{-(s)} \end{aligned} \tag{3.2}$$

The definitions are analogous to those in equation (3.1) and shall not be reproduced here. Since we are analyzing a closed economy, the sum of all expenditures of a certain kind must add up to the sum of all receipts of this kind. We leave the formulation of the adding up constraints to the interested reader.

The difference of $REC^{(s)}$ and $EXP^{(s)}$ is the change of cash:

$$REC^{(s)} - EXP^{(s)} = \Delta CA^{(s)} \geq -CA^{(s)}_{-1} \quad \text{in order to avoid bankruptcy} \tag{3.3}$$

Cash is provided by the banks. We come back to this in the next sections.

In the same generality as we treated the monetary flows we shall now treat the *wealth* $W^{(s)}$ of an agent s at the end of a period. But unfortunately this figure is not unequivocal. There may be many concepts of wealth (e.g. wealth at prices of the acquisition of capital goods minus depreciation, or at current prices or at prices of the "machines" (or the whole firm) attainable now and so on). We choose the concept of current prices for all commodities where there is an exchange and cost of buying the "machines" minus depreciation if there is no exchange. This is assumed to come true in the case of used machinery. The productive real capital PRC is evaluated at procurement cost. For depreciation there are different rules under consideration; increasing or decreasing ratios. We choose linear depreciation ratios and a fixed lifetime T of all "machines". Let $I_{-\tau}$ be the cost of investment τ years ago where the installment has a lifetime of T years. In this case we get for the value $PRC^{(s)}$ of the productive capital of firm i:

$$PRC^{(s)} = \sum_{\tau=0}^{T} \frac{T-\tau}{T} \cdot I_{-\tau} \text{ for} s = i \in \{1, \ldots, N\}, \text{ zero otherwise.}$$

We include into wealth:

a. human capital HC but only for households ($s = h$), where
   $HC^{(h)} = \sum\limits_{\nu=1}^{n} \sum\limits_{t=0}^{T(h)} L^{(h)}_{\nu t} \cdot l^{(h)}_{\nu\tau} \cdot (\frac{1}{1+r})^t$, where r is the time discount rate

---

[7] $CR^{+(s)}_j$ are the credits of banks given to firms. Thus this term applies only if s is a bank ($s = b$) and j is a firm ($j = i$), otherwise it is zero. $DE^{+(s)}_j$ refer to credits of banks given to other agents (to households, other banks, the government)

b. land property: $LA \cdot p_{LA}$

c. value of invested capital; $PRC^{(s)} \cdot p_{PRC}$, valid only for producing sectors $(s = i)$

d. value of inventories $INV \cdot p_{INV}$

e. value of financial assets $FA \cdot p_{FA}$

f. cash CA

Thus we get

$$W = HC + LA \cdot p_{LA} + PRC \cdot p_{PRC} + INV \cdot p_{INV} + FA \cdot p_{FA} + CA \quad (3.4)$$

This forms the *asset side* of the balance sheet of an agent. This is true for the beginning of a period 0. The liability side shows the composition of claims to this value W, documented by issued securities SEC, by other liabilities $LIAB$; the rest goes to the owner of capital stock KSt. Thus the *liability side* of the balance sheet is given by

$$W = SEC + LIAB + KSt \quad (3.5)$$

By definition: $W = W_{-1} + \Delta W$, where according to equation (3.4):

$$\Delta W = \Delta HC + (LA \Delta p_{LA} + p_{LA} \Delta LA) + \ldots + (FA \Delta p_{FA} + p_{FA} \Delta FA) + \Delta CA \quad (3.6)$$

ΔW is called the *profit* G of the agent considered; G is defined as the change of wealth:

$$\Delta W =: G \quad (3.7)$$

Thus we may write:

$$W = SEC_{-1} + LIAB_{-1} + KSt_{-1} + G \quad (3.8)$$

where W represents the asset side of the balance sheet according to equation (3.4), the terms on the right hand side of equation (3.8) represent the liability side. The term $G = \Delta W$ contains the *cash flow* ΔCA which is explained in equation (3.3). Equation (3.6) and (3.7) is the profit and loss account of the agent considered.

In many cases one does not need the total system of all monetary flows and states of wealth, but only parts of it. We shall give some examples.

Consider a household h. Its income $INC^{(h)}$ in one period consists of wage income $lL^{+(h)}$, income from rent $r_{LA} \cdot LA^{+(h)}$ on the land owned by the household, income from selling land $-p_{LA} \cdot \Delta^{-} LA^{(h)}$, transfer income $TR^{+(h)}$, interest on its financial assets $r_{FA}FA^{+(h)}$ and income from selling part (or all) of these assets: $-p_{LA}\Delta^{-}FA^{(h)}$:

$$INC^{(h)} = lL^{+(h)} + r_{LA}LA^{+(h)} - p_{LA}\Delta^{-}LA^{(h)} + TR^{+(h)} + r_{FA}FA^{+(h)} - p_{FA}\Delta^{-}FA^{(h)}$$

But usually the concept of net income $INC^{net(h)}$ will be used in the theory. This is income minus interest rates on land rented and debts made in the past and minus taxes paid by the household:

$$INC^{net(h)} = INC^{(h)} - r_{LA} \cdot LA^{-(h)} - r_{FA} \cdot FA^{-(h)} - T^{-(h)}$$

The net income of the last period will be used for buying consumption goods p_cC, for transfer payments $TR^{-(h)}$, for buying land $p_{LA}\Delta LA^{(h)}$ or financial assets $p_{FA}\Delta FA^{(h)}$ and for cash $\Delta CA^{(h)}$. We may combine these items into consumption $CONS$ and Saving S such that

$$INC_{-1}^{net(h)} = CONS^{(h)} + S^{(h)}, \text{ where}$$

$CONS^{(h)} = p_cC^{(h)} + TR^{-(h)}$ and
$S = p_{LA}\Delta LA^{(h)} + p_{FA}\Delta FA^{(h)} + \Delta CA^{(h)}$ (ΔCA =change of cash)[8].

In this formulation S may be positive, zero or negative. One may check that here also $\Delta CA^{(h)} = REC^{(h)} - EXP^{(h)}$, according equation (3.3).

As another example we choose a private firm $i \in \{1, 2, \ldots, N\}$. The decisions of the firm are usually based on the balance sheet and on the profit and loss account of the firm. We shall derive them from our system of money flows and wealth statements. The *asset side* of the *balance sheet* is defined by

$LA \cdot p_{LA}$	=	value of land property
$PRC \cdot p_{PRC}$	=	value of invested capital
$INV \cdot p_{INV}$	=	value of inventories
$FA \cdot p_{FA}$	=	value of financial assets
CA	=	cash
Sum	=	balance sheet value (all values at the end of the period)

The *liability side* of the balance sheet is defined by

[8] According to our definitions a household may have wealth in the form of human capital, land, financial assets and cash. The land is used for consumption purposes or as store of value, not for own production. – Transfer payments of a household are considered as part of consumption $CONS$.

SEC_{-1}	=	securities issued by firm i
$LIAB_{-1}$	=	other liabilities
KSt_{-1}	=	capital stock and reserve (all values taken from the beginning of the period)
G	=	profit of the period $= \Delta(LA \cdot p_{LA}) + \Delta(PRC \cdot p_{PRC}) + \Delta(INV \cdot p_{INV}) + \Delta(FA \cdot p_{FA}) + \Delta CA$ where ΔCA is determined by equation (3.3)
Sum	=	balance sheet value (see equation (3.8)).

Note that this balance sheet can only be established at the *end* of the period since the prices of the financial assets at the exchange are only known at the end of the period. The firm can only give conditional orders to the broker.

The *profit and loss account* explains G by $G = REC - EXP + \Delta V$, where REC is defined in equation (3.1)[9], EXP by equation (3.2)[10], and ΔV by ΔV = change of the value of assets $= \Delta(LA \cdot p_{LA}) + \Delta(PRC \cdot p_{PRC}) + \Delta(INV \cdot p_{INV}) + \Delta(FA \cdot p_{FA})$

This terminates the note on definitions and relations. It is incomplete in the sense that the equations which close the system are not reproduced here. It is not difficult to establish these equations. We leave it to the interested reader.

3.3 The Balance Sheet of a Commercial Bank

The balance sheet defines the fineness of the theory: everything within the aggregates remains unexplained. We start with the *balance sheet of the bank* b_i, $i = 1, \ldots, g$, if there are g banks in the economy. The *asset side* consists of the following items:

1. CA_{bi} = cash of the bank. We do not differ between bank notes and coins. All cash in the form of bank notes is issued by the Central Bank

2. $CA_{bi,CB}$ = account of bank b_i at the Central Bank due to minimum reserve requirements[11]

---

[9] Of course, $l \cdot L^{+(s)} = 0$ in this case.

[10] Of course, $p_c \cdot C^{(s)} = 0$ in this case.

[11] If the Central Bank does not pay interest on these assets (this was the case of the German Bundesbank) the bank will avoid an overfulfillment of the requirement. But the European Central Bank now pays interest on the required bank reserves. We assume that there is a common reserve ratio res for daily deposits DEP_{bi} and time deposits TD_{bi}, i.e. we assume $CA_{bi,CB} = res(DEP_{bi} + TD_{bi})$

3. CR_{bi} = credits granted by bank i under the condition

$$\kappa_i = (r_{CR,bi}, t_{CRi}, \sigma_{Cri}, sec_i), \text{see section 3.1,}$$

$= \sum_{j\in\{A\}} CR_{bi,j}$, where $\{A\}$ is the set of firms, households or institutions which received the credits from bank i[12]. The interest rate $r_{CR,bi}$ which the bank b_i charges for granting a credit CR_{bi} is determined by the bank and follows the circulation yield $\bar{r}$ of long term securities, but keeps an additional charge $\bar{z}$ such that approximately

$$r_{CR,bi} = \bar{r} + \bar{z}_{CR,bi}, \quad \bar{z}_{CR,bi} > 0,$$

see Deutsche Bundesbank, Monatsbericht März 2002, p. 55. In the years 1993 to 2000 $\bar{z}_{CR}$ varied between 1.2 and 1.7 for large credits and between 1.5 and 2.0 percentage points for small ones. $\bar{r}$ varied in the same years between 3.5 and 7.5 % with a falling trend between 1994 and 1999.

4. $W_{KSt,bi}$ = market value of capital stock[13]. $W_{KSt,bi} = \sum_{j\in\{B\}} W_{KStj,bi}$, and $\{B\}$ is the set of capital stock of firm j in the portfolio of bank i. The interest rate which bank i receives from its portfolio $W_{KSt,bi}$ is approximated by the circulation yield $\bar{r}$ of long term securities enlarged or reduced by an additional amount $\bar{z}_{KST,bi}$: $r_{WKt,bi} = \bar{r} + \bar{z}_{KSt,bi}$

5. $W_{SEC,bi}$ = market value of securities, $= \sum_{j\in\{C\}} W_{SECj,bi}$, where $\{C\}$ is the set of firms or institutions, the securities of which are in the portfolio of bank i. Here we also assume $r_{SEC,bi} = \bar{r} + \bar{z}_{KSt,bi}$

6. $W_{LA,bi}$ = market value of land and buildings owned by bank i = $\sum_{j\in\{D\}} W_{LAj,bi}$ where $\{D\}$ is the set of all land and buildings owned by the bank i.

7. $OASS_{bi}$ = other assets of bank i (including gold and (in case that foreign countries are included in the model) currency of foreign countries)

Sum of items 1. to 9.: BAL_{bi} = value of the balance of bank i. In chapter 7 where we explain the different items of the balance sheets of the banks and the interest rates we shall use a more aggregated and simplified model. We

---

[12] By definition: the credit $CR_{bi,j}$ granted by bank i to an agent j is equal to the amount $DE_{j,bi}$ of debts of an agent j at bank i: $CR_{bi,j} = DE_{j,bi}$

[13] $W_{KStj,bi} = KSt_{j,bi} \cdot v_{KStj}$, where $KSt_{j,bi}$ is the number of shares issued by firm or institution j in the portfolio of bank i, and v_{KStj} is its price at the exchange. All values v_{KStj} and v_{SECj} are those of the exchange at the end of the preceding period.

put $W_{KSt,bi} + W_{sec,bi} = W_{bi}$ and $W_{LA,bi} = OASS_{bi} = 0$ such that the *asset side* of the balance sheet of a commercial bank b_i becomes $BAL_{bi} = CA_{bi} + CA_{bi,CB} + CR_{bi} + W_{bi}$.

The *liability side* of the balance of bank i consists of the following items:

1. DEP_{bi} = daily payable deposits at bank $i = \sum_{j \in \{E\}} DEP_{j,bi}$, where $\{E\}$ is the set of all agents which keep daily payable deposits at bank i.

2. TD_{bi} = time deposits at bank $i = \sum_{j \in \{F\}} TD_{j,bi}$, where {F} is the set of all agents which keep time deposits at bank i.

3. $CL_{CB,bi}$ = claims of the Central Bank to bank i, due to normal monetary operations. They consists of securities sold by bank i to the Central Bank with the obligation to buy them back at the same price after a predetermined time and to pay an interest of r_d (formerly called: discount rate, now called: main refinancing rate of interest, Hauptrefinanzierungs-Zinssatz in German) at the end of the lending period[14].

4. $BCAP_{bi}$ = borrowed capital (=outside capital). We assume that this capital is represented by securities SEC_{bi} issued by bank i: $BCAP_{bi} = SEC_{bi}$.
   These securities are owned by other agents: $SEC_{bi} = \sum_{j \in \{G\}} SEC_{bi,j}$, $\{G\}$ = the set of all persons or institutions which own these securities. These securities bear an interest of $r_{SEC,bi}$ to be paid by the bank and are traded at the exchange. The exchange value of these securities is designated as $W_{SEC,bi}$

5. $OLIA_{bi}$ = other liabilities of bank i

6. CAP_{bi} = capital and reserves of bank i

Sum of items 1. to 6.: BAL_{bi} = value of the balance of bank i

In chapter 7 we consider only a simplified version of this liability side where $OLIA_{bi} = 0$ such that

$$BAL_{bi} = DEP_{bi} + TD_{bi} + CL_{CB,bi} + BCAP_{bi} + CAP_{bi}$$

We now come to the profit and loss account of a commercial bank.

---

[14] Actually, there are different r_d for short and long term loans, but we neglect these peculiarities.

3.4 The Profit and Loss Account of a Commercial Bank

First, we define the profit and loss account of the commercial bank i. The decisions of the managers of bank i depend on the balance sheet as well as on the profit and loss account whereas the decisions of the managers of the Central Bank are based on the balance of the Central Bank but as a rule not on the profit and loss account. Thus we do not formulate the latter. Capital and reserves CAP_{bi} of bank i at the beginning of period 0 equal the capital and reserves at the beginning of period -1 increased by the profits $PR_{bi,-1}$ in period -1 (or decreased by the losses):

$$CAP_{bi} = CAP_{bi,-1} + PR_{bi,-1} \tag{3.9}$$

To simplify the notation we rewrite the balance sheet of the commercial bank i. On the asset side we aggregate:

$$\overline{CA}_{bi} = \text{total cash} = CA_{bi} + CA_{bi,CB}$$

$$\overline{W}_{bi} = \text{total value of capital stock and securities} = W_{KSt,bi} + W_{SEC,bi}$$

On the liability side we put

$$\overline{DEP}_{bi} = \text{ all deposits } = DEP_{bi} + TD_{bi}$$

Now we get from the balance sheet:

$$\begin{aligned} CAP_{bi} &= \overline{CA}_{bi} + CR_{bi} + \overline{W}_{bi} + W_{LA,bi} + OASS - \overline{DEP}_{bi} \\ &\quad -CL_{CB,bi} - BCAP_{bi} - OLIA \end{aligned} \tag{3.10}$$

Similarly $CAP_{bi,-1}$ are the capital and reserves at the beginning of period -1. By definition: receipts REC minus expenditure EXP equals the cash flow $\Delta\overline{CA}$:

$$REC_{bi,-1} - EXP_{bi,-1} = \Delta\overline{CA}_{bi,-1} \tag{3.11}$$

We put

$$\begin{aligned} \Delta\tilde{W}_{bi,-1} &= \text{change of the value of invested capital in period } -1, \\ &= \Delta\overline{W}_{bi,-1} + \Delta W_{LA,bi,-1} \end{aligned}$$

$\Delta CR_{bi}(1-\gamma)$ = increase of claims to other agents because of credits granted (if positive, decrease if negative)

$$\begin{aligned} \Delta\overline{CL}_{a,bi} &= \text{increase of claims of all other agents to bank } i, \\ &= \Delta\overline{DEP}_{bi,-1} + \Delta CL_{CB,bi,-1}(1+r_d) + \Delta BCAP_{bi,-1} \end{aligned}$$

and for simplicity:

$$\Delta OASS_{bi,-1} = \Delta OLIA_{bi,-1} = 0$$

Thus we get from equation (3.10) and (3.11):

$$\begin{aligned} PR_{bi,-1} &= CAP_{bi} - CAP_{bi,-1} \\ &= \Delta\overline{CA}_{bi,-1} + \Delta\tilde{W}_{bi,-1} + \Delta CR_{bi}(1-\gamma) - \Delta\overline{CL}_{a,bi,-1} \end{aligned} \quad (3.12)$$

In words: the profits of bank i earned in period -1 are the sum of the cash flow $\Delta\overline{CA}$, the change of value $\Delta\tilde{W}$ of investments, the change of credits $\Delta CR(1-\gamma)$ granted to the clients after the increase of the claims of all other agents to the bank has been deducted.

The cash flow $\Delta\overline{CA}$ is defined as the difference of receipts and expenditure, see equation (3.3). The *receipts of bank i* are the monetary inflows i.e. the dividends d_{bi} on the capital stock K_{bi} owned by the bank, the interest $r_{SEC,bi}$ paid on the securities SE_{bi} owned by the bank, the interest payments $r_{CR,bi}$ on the credits CR_{bi} granted by the bank, the rent r_{LA} of land (and buildings) owned by the bank and the income from selling financial assets:

$$\begin{aligned} REC_{bi} = & \sum_{j\in\{\tilde{A}\}} KSt_{j,bi} \cdot d_j + \sum_{j\in\{\tilde{B}\}} SEC_{j,bi} \cdot r_{SEC,j} + \tilde{LA}_{bi} \cdot r_{LA,bi} \\ & + \sum_{j\in\{\tilde{C}\}} CR_{bi,j} \cdot r_{CR,bi} + \sum_{j\in\{\hat{A}\}} W_{KSt,j} + \sum_{j\in\{\hat{B}\}} W_{SEC,j} + W_{\hat{LA}} \\ & + \sum_{j\in\{\hat{C}\}} CR_{bi,j} \end{aligned} \quad (3.13)$$

The items in the first line are interest income from assets which are kept by bank i in the period considered. In the second line stands income from selling assets or from recalling the credits at the beginning of the period. Thus $\{\tilde{A}\}$, $\{\tilde{B}\}$, $\{\tilde{C}\}$ and $\{\tilde{LA}\}$ which appear in the first line of equation (3.13) are the sets of the assets which are kept in the portfolio of the bank during this period and $\{\hat{A}\}, \{\hat{B}\}, \{\hat{C}\}, \{\hat{LA}\}$ are the sets of assets which were sold (or recalled) at the beginning of the period. Both are decision variables of the bank; W_j is the value of asset j, where $W_j = Ass_j \cdot v_{Ass,j}$, $\quad Ass \in \{KSt, SEC, LA\}$; v is the value of the asset at the exchange.

Similarly the *expenditures* EXP_{bi} are the monetary outflows from bank i. They comprise the cost of running the bank: labor cost $l \cdot L_{bi}$, cost of secondary input SI_{bi}, cost of capital $K_{bi} \cdot r_K$, depreciation cost DPR_{bi} and taxes T_{bi}. Moreover, EXP_{bi} also covers the outflow of money for buying assets and for expanding the credits. Thus we get

$$\begin{aligned} EXP_{bi} &= \sum_{\nu=1}^{n}(l_\nu L_{bi,\nu} + \sum_{\mu=1}^{n} c_{bi,\mu\nu} \cdot L_{bi,\nu}) + K_{bi} \cdot r_{K,bi} \\ &+ DPR_{bi} + T_{bi} + \sum_{j\in\{A^*\}} W_{KSt,j} + \sum_{j\in\{B^*\}} W_{SEC,j} \\ &+ W_{LA^*} + \sum_{j\in\{C^*\}} CR_{bi,j} \end{aligned} \tag{3.14}$$

The items in the first line show the expenditures of bank i to keep up the bank as an institution. The terms in the second line show the expenditures for buying capital stock (capital stocks from the set $\{A^*\}$ are bought), for buying securities (these are those in the set $\{B^*\}$), for buying land or buildings (which cost the amount W_{LA^*}) and the expenditures as a result of granting credits (they are granted to agents in the set $\{C^*\}$).

Some expressions in equation (3.14) need some comments. The secondary inputs are related to the labor force. That means: to employ a person in banking it needs a working place in an adequate environment, a computer, telephone etc. – For simplicity we assume that the bank finances itself by issuing securities. Thus:

$$K_{bi} r_{K,bi} = \text{capital cost} = SEC_{bi} \cdot r_{SEC,bi}.$$

The depreciation cost DPR_{bi} refer mostly to buildings which are in our approach contained in the secondary inputs. We do not consider that in detail. T_{bi} are the cost of taxes of different kind. We lump them together to a turnover tax with the tax rate t_{bi}: $T_{bi} = t_{bi} \cdot REC_{bi}$.

3.5 The Organization of a Commercial Bank

Similarly as in the theory of the firm, a commercial bank is organized in three departments:

1. the department of general finance and organization
2. the credit department (which may be called the production department of the bank)
3. the portfolio department (which is equivalent to the inventory department of a commodity producing firm)

To 1: In the *department of general finance and organization* the basic decision on the policy of the bank will be taken. These are:

- the amount of cash to be kept in the next period

- the maximal amount of credits which the credit department is allowed to grant
- the additional amount of money $\triangle M_{pf,bi}$ the portfolio department gets for portfolio investment (if $\triangle M_{pf,bi}$ is positive) or the amount $\triangle M_{pf,bi}$ of assets the portfolio department should liquidate and transfer the money as contribution to the general finance, if $\triangle M_{pf,bi}$ is negative
- the general organization of the bank.

These general decisions of a commercial bank depend on estimations of the size of the deposits in the planning period. The bank management has to carry out these estimations on the base of experiences of the past. Of course, the realized deposits will deviate from these estimations. The consequences of these errors will be corrected in the period after. For the period in question the decisions of the department of general finance and organization are binding. We will come back to the details in the section dealing with decisions of the bank.

In our classification of the departments of a commercial bank we lumped together "general finance" and "organization" (or: general administration). Some words should be said on the problem of *organization*. After the number $L_{CR,bi}$ of persons in the credit department in the bank i and the number $L_{pf,bi}$ of persons in the portfolio department have been decided upon by the management of the bank (as will be shown later), the total number n_{io} of employees to be supervised by the department of organization is fixed. Now the control spans at different ranks have to be fixed, the size of the pertinent staff and the personal allocation of the employees of lower ranks to the supervisors have to be decided upon. This general organizational problem has to be solved for the bank in the same way as it had to be solved in the case of a commodity producing firm. We refer to section2.7.

Now we come to 2: the *credit department* of the commercial bank. It forms the center of a commercial bank. It produces credits at certain costs. There must be a *production function*[15] [16] (or equivalent devices) to relate the input to the output. First we relate the size of the credits of bank i i.e. CR_{bi} to the other financial items. From the asset side of the balance equation for bank i we get (by omitting the index $_{bi}$):

$$CR = BAL - CA - CA_{CB} - W - OASS$$

---

[15] We assume one-product banks in the same way as we assumed one-product firms. The product is the amount of credits the bank offers. But there are also other services of a bank like the administration of deposits and of the assets of clients, which may be dealt with in a similar fashion.

[16] In the theory of the banks (and similarly of all other service institutions) the labor stands in the center not the machines as in the industries which produce physical products. Thus the secondary inputs SI_{bi} of bank i are assumed to be proportional to the labor $L_{bi,\nu}$ of type $\nu : SI_{bi} = \sum_{\mu=1}^{n} c_{bi,\mu\nu} \cdot L_{bi,\nu}$.

and by substituting BAL from the liability side of the balance sheet:

$$\begin{aligned} CR = & \, DEP + TD + CL_{CB} + SEC + OLIA \\ & + CAP - CA - CA_{CB} - W - OASS \end{aligned} \tag{3.15}$$

We may again neglect the terms $OLIA$ and $OASS$ by putting $OLIA - OASS = 0$. W is short for the market values of all capital stocks and securities and the value of land in the portfolio of bank i:

$$W = W_{KSt} + W_{SEC} + W_{LA}$$

Equation (3.15) states that credits granted by the bank can be the larger the higher are the deposits $DEP + TD$ of other agents at this bank (as already said: these deposits are not known for the planning period but have to be estimated), the higher the refinancing CL_{CB} by the Central Bank, the higher the borrowed capital SEC and the capital stock and reserve CAP and the less of these financial inflow is used for cash holding and investment in purely financial assets W.

Equation (3.15) is a definitional equation which may serve as liquidity constraint of the bank if we add the requirement $CA \geq 0$. Of course, there are non-negativity constraints for all other items in equation (3.15) which we do not formulate explicitly. Equation (3.15) shows that there is an interdependence of the decisions of the management of the bank: a decision to grant credits of a certain size has consequences for the other financial items; decisions which violate equation (3.15) are not feasible. But equation (3.15) is an ex-post-relationship: it must hold at the end of each period when the prices of all assets are known.

Now we turn to the *"production function"* of the bank. Of course, there is a relation between the amount of credits (in real terms) granted by the bank, the credit solvency and the number of employees necessary to administer the credits of the bank and its other activities like administration of deposits and refinancing at the Central Bank. But this relation is not so simple and not so clear-cut as the requirements of running a machine and the resulting output of the machine. The product of the bank is the credit the bank grants to firms, households or other institutions, the determination of the conditions κ for granting the credit (see section 3.1) and the selection of the applicants which get the credit. Assume that the applicants appear at the Credit Department one after the other in a random sequence. The task of the Credit Department is to filter out the "good" debtors which present an acceptable plan to use the money, offer appropriate securities and look like honest persons who would keep contracts. If there are many persons in the credit department which check the applicants and their prospective use of the money, one may assume a smaller ratio γ of "bad" loans. Let $L_{CR,bi}$ be the number of employees in the credit department of bank i and $CR_{bi}/\bar{p}$ the credits granted by bank i in real terms. Now the ratio γ of "bad loans" will be related to the labor force

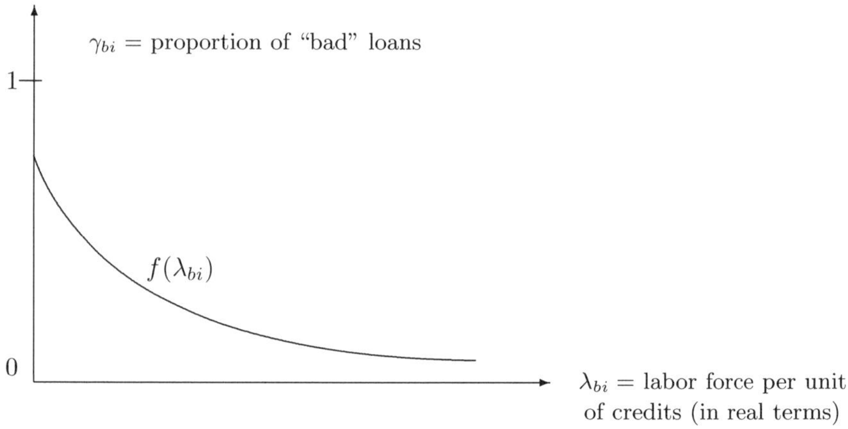

Figure 3.1. Employment in the portfolio department

per unit of real credits of bank i (which we call $\lambda_{bi} := L_{CR,bi}/\bar{p}$) as depicted in Fig. 3.1. In Fig. 3.1 we assumed that the composition of the labor force with respect to the type of labor is given, e.g.

$$L_{CR,bi} = \sum_{\nu=1}^{n} \alpha_{CR,bi,\nu} \cdot L_{CR,bi,\nu},$$
$$\text{where } \alpha_{CR,bi,\nu} \geq 0 \text{ and } \sum_{\nu=1}^{n} \alpha_{CR,bi,\nu} = 1 \tag{3.16}$$

We assume that the function $f(\lambda_{bi})$ is known to the managers in the credit department and that they decide on λ_{bi} as well as on other variables, as will be shown in the following.

To 3: The *portfolio department* is responsible for the administration of the capital stock

$W = W_{KSt} + W_{SEC} + W_{LA}$, see section 3.2[17].

We defined $W_{KSt,bi} = \sum_{j \in \{A\}} KSt_{j,bi} \cdot v_{KSt,j}$ and $\{A\} = \{KSt_{1,pf,bi}, \ldots, KSt_{n,pf,bi}\}$ where $KSt_{\nu,pf,bi}$ is the amount of capital stocks of type ν in the portfolio of bank i during the period considered. The valuations $v_{KSt,j}$ follow from the conditional buying or selling orders of all agents in the economy which the bank i does not know at the beginning of the period, when

[17] Of course, there are also other obligations, e.g. cost accounting, financial control of the other departments, establishing of the balance sheet and the profit and loss account and others. But for a bank one could assume that these are minor obligations which we may neglect at this stage.

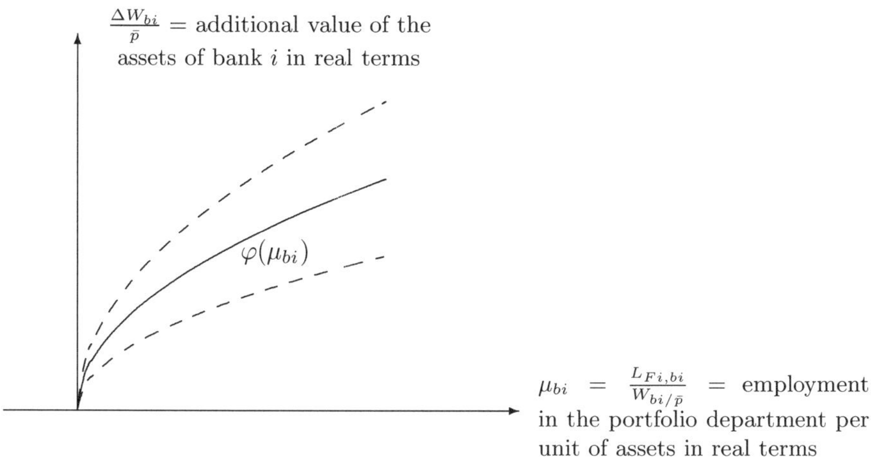

Figure 3.2 Value of assets as function of the employment in the portfolio department

the conditional orders to the brokers are given[18]. Thus W is an ex-post-value, at the end of the period, when the valuation of the assets is known. But the financial department has to give its conditional orders in ignorance of the actual valuation of the assets. According to the theory in section 1.25 we may assume that more people employed in the department of finance would make it possible to get more information on the state and the prospects of the institutions which are represented by the assets as well as on the estimations of other agents on this subject. That means: the rate of change $\triangle\ W/\bar{p}$ of the value of the assets of bank i is an increasing function of the ratio μ of the relative size of the labor force L_{FI} in the portfolio department: $\mu_{bi} = \frac{L_{FI,bi}}{W_{bi}/\bar{p}}$. If nobody is employed in the portfolio department, the portfolio will be held constant. Starting from this base the change $\triangle\ W/\bar{p}$ is estimated. Of course it lies in the interest of the bank to maximize $W/\bar{p}$. We assume that the management of the bank has an idea on the advantage of employing more persons in the portfolio department; that means: it knows a function $\varphi(\mu_{bi})$ which relates the additional value of assets to the size of the financial department which is in charge of the portfolio. Fig. 3.2 shows this function[19]

The size of the labor force in the portfolio department is determined by the management of the bank on the base of the estimation of the function φ and on the base of the salary of the persons employed in this department. As

---

[18] We assume that banks and brokers are different institutions; for details see section 1.25. The financial department has to decide on the reasonable upper and lower bound v_{max} and v_{min} of the value of an asset and on the amount of assets to be bought or sold

[19] In general, the function φ will not be known exactly. Thus we may define an upper and lower bound for this function, see the broken lines in Fig. 3.2.

to the composition of the labor force we assume an analogous relation as in equation (3.16) for the credit department.

This terminates the sections on the commercial banks. We shall come back to them in chapter 7. But first we have to turn to the Central Bank.

3.6 The Balance Sheet of the Central Bank

We use the following notations:

The Asset side of the Balance sheet:

1. $CL_{CB,G}$ = claims of the Central Bank to the government[20]. We assume that the government does not pay interest on them.

2. $CL_{CB,B}$ = claims of the Central Bank to all commercial banks due to normal monetary operations, where $CL_{CB,B} = \sum_{i=1}^{g} CL_{CB,bi}$ The commercial banks have to pay a rate of interest $r_{CR,B}$ on these claims which is a function of the discount rate r_d, fixed by the Central Bank (discount rate is short for interest on the "main refinancing transaction" (Hauptrefinnazierungsgeschäfte in German)). We shall come back to this later.

3. W_{CB} = market value of securities in the portfolio of the Central Bank. We assume that only securities are allowed in the portfolio of the Central Bank, not capital stocks of any kind. Thus $W_{CB} = W_{SEC,CB} \cdot W_{CB}$ is an instrument of the open market policy of the Central Bank. It gets an interest rate of $\bar{r}$ on these securities, where $\bar{r}$ is the circulation yield of long term securities (Umlaufrendite langfristiger Wertpapiere in German)[21]

4. $OASS_{CB}$ = other assets of the Central Bank[22]

Sum of items 1.- 4.: BAL_{CB} = value of the balance of the Central Bank

The *Liability side* of the balance sheet of the Central Bank is:

---

[20] We assume that this item is determined exclusively by the government (in case of war or equivalent disasters or urgent necessities the government may decide to finance its expenditures by printing money, i.e. by extending $CL_{CB,G}$, also against the will of the board of the Central Bank).

[21] If z is the nominal rate of interest on a nominal unit of a security and w its price on the exchange, $\bar{r}$ is defined by $\bar{r} = z/w$. We could say: $\bar{r}$ is the evaluation of the security by the public

[22] Among them: gold and (if we consider foreign countries) foreign currencies. In the following we put $OASS_{CB} = 0$.

1. N_{CB} = bank notes of the Central Bank in circulation, where $N_{CB} = \sum_{j \in \{\bar{A}\}} CA_j$ = cash in the portfolios of all economic agents outside of the Central Bank. $\{\bar{A}\}$ is the set of these agents

2. $CA_{B,CB}$ = accounts of all banks at the Central Bank, due to minimum reserve requirements, $= \sum_{i=1}^{g} CA_{bi,CB} = res_1 \cdot DEP_B + res_2 \cdot TD_B$
   res_1 is the minimum reserve requirements for deposits DEP_B at the commercial banks, res_2 the minimum requirements for time deposits TD_B at commercial banks. For simplicity we shall this approximate by $CA_{B,CB} = res(DEP_B + TD_B)$. We assume that the Central Bank does not pay interest on $CA_{B,CB}$.

3. $OLIA_{CB}$ = other liabilities of the Central Bank. For simplicity we shall put $OLIA_{CB} = 0$ in the following

4. CAP_{CB} = capital and reserves of the Central Bank

Sum of items 1.–4.: BAL_{CB} = value of the balance of the Central Bank

We do not define the profit and loss account of the Central Bank since the decisions of the Central Bank are based upon the balance; profits and losses do not play an important role[23].

3.7 The Decision Variables and the Principles of Decision of the Central Bank

The Central Banks of different countries obey different rules, since the laws and the practices which constitute these rules are different. In a general theory only the common features – and these in a simplified way – can be modeled. The simplifications are defined by the aggregation of different items of the balance sheet of the Central Bank into five aggregates on the asset side and four aggregates on the liability side. This means that we also have to simplify the decision variables of the Central Bank which influence the values in its balance sheet as well as the values of macroeconomic variables which is the ultimate goal of the monetary policy of the Central Bank.

---

[23] Of course, the government is interested in the size of the profits, because it receives them as the "owner" of the bank. But this is a side effect which does not (or should not) influence the monetary policy of the Central Bank. But sometimes these profits (called seignorage) play an important role in government finance.

In our model the Central Bank (represented by its board of directors and its council) has the following instruments (which are the decision variables of the Central Bank) at its disposal[24]:

1. *The notes in circulation* N_{CB}. We follow here the constitution and the arrangements of the European Central Bank which allows the bank to predetermines the amount of banknotes in circulation and afterwords to "sell" the additional amount of money by an auction (the so-called interest tender). This allows a control of the money in circulations and thus (given by velocity v of money) a control of the value of GDP, according to Fisher's equation

   $$M \cdot v = Y^{real} \cdot p$$

   Other regulations of the power of the Central Bank do not allow such a strict control.

2. *The discount rate* $r_d \geq 0$ change in steps of a quarter of a percentage, thus $r_d = z \cdot 0,25 \quad , z = 0, 1, 2, 3, \ldots$[25].

---

[24] The claims $CL_{CB,G}$ of the Central Bank to the government are in our model determined by the government. It regulates by laws the grip of the minister of finance or other governmental institutions on the money source. In case of doubt the government can change the law which constitutes the Central Bank. Thus we treat $CL_{CB,G}$ as a *decision variable of the government.* This also refers to the rate of interest the government has to pay for $CL_{CB,G}$ (which may be zero; we consider this case in our model. Of course, the Central Bank wants the government to pay an interest in order to be able to sell these securities on the market and thus use them as an instrument of monetary policy). We may take $CL_{CB,G}$ as a constant. Only in case of war or equivalent national emergencies the government is supposed to use the Central Bank as source of income.

[25] The discount rate is the interest rate on loans, that the Central Bank makes to banks. This is an appropriate approach if the other conditions of the loans (term, type of the security et.) are fixed. This applies for the Federal Reserve (FED) of the US or the Bank of England and other Central Banks (also for the German Bundesbank in the past; for detail: see *Jarchow* (1974), p. 112 ff.). The European Central Bank (EZB) charges different interest rates. Thus there is no simple discount rate. To understand that one has to consider the details (see: *Junins, Kater, Meier, Müller*, Handbuch Europäische Zentralbank (2002), p. 83 ff.). In this note only the main features of this system can be sketched in order to see the difference to the model presented here. The EZB distinguishes between repo-transaction (=repurchase agreements, the security offered is bought by the EZB, the seller binds himself to repurchase it after a certain time to a certain price. The difference between the price of purchase and repurchase determines the interest rate) and refi-transaction (where the property of the securities stays with the delivering bank and the interest rate is fixed by the EZB). This refi-interest rate may be taken as an index of the discount rate in this system. There are two types of realization of this system. In the first the EZB fixes the minimum interest rate and sells that amount of money by auction till the predetermined amount is reached (a system called quantity tender, Mengentender

in German). The second system (called interest rate tender, Zinstender in German, which is used now by the EZB) leaves the offer of the interest rate and the offer of the amount of securities involved in this transaction to the direction of the banks. The EZB starts to fulfill these demands with the highest rate of interest suggested by a bank and continues till the predetermined total amount of money is reached. Those banks which offered a too low interest rate stay empty. If there are too many demands at the lowest admissible rate of interest (called rate for the main refinancing transaction, "Hauptrefinanzierungsgeschäfte in German, but we shall continue to call this rate "discount rate", for simplicity; "too many" means: more than the extensions of the money supply decided by the Central Bank would allow), if there are too many demands in this sense all those banks which asked for that amount of money would be shortened by the same proportion.
The following figure illustrates this procedure. There are g banks. The Central Bank decides on the minimum discount rate r_d^* and on the maximum amount of money to be sold by this auction. Let r_i^{off} be the rate of interest offered by bank i and $CL_{CB,bi}^{off}$ the amount of money which the bank i would like to get from the Central Bank at this rate. We reorder the banks such that the bank with the highest offer of the rate of interest gets the lowest number. The lower limits of this offer is the rate r_d^*. This explains the upper part of the graph. The lower part shows the aggregated total demand of money (or offered claims $CL_{CB,bi}^{off}$). In this figure all banks which only offered the minimum rate of interest r_d^{+ast} will be shortened by the same proportion such that the predetermined sum $N^* = CL_{CB,B}^*$ is not surpassed.

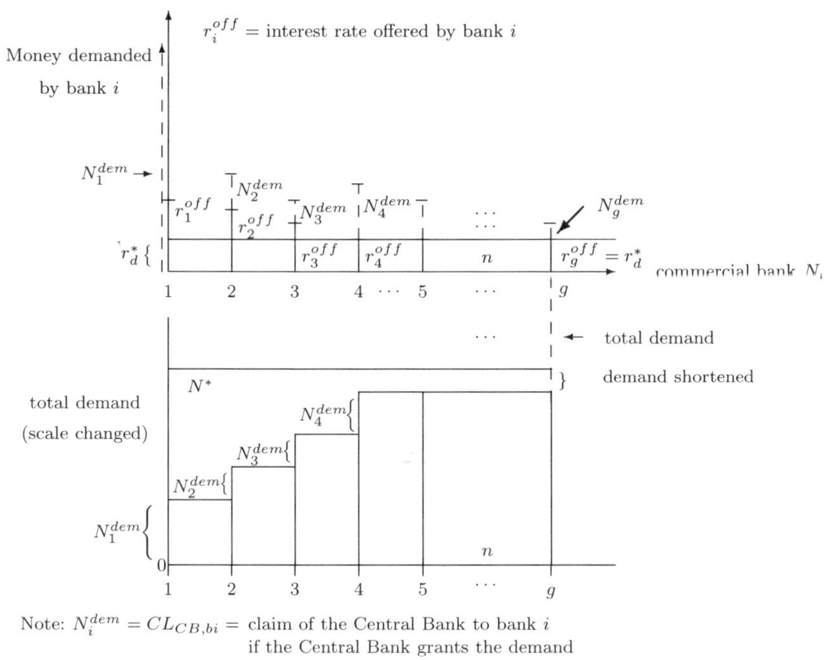

Note: $N_i^{dem} = CL_{CB,bi}$ = claim of the Central Bank to bank i if the Central Bank grants the demand

Sketch of the procedure of the interest tender

The Bank announces the rate at the beginning of a period such that all other banks, firms and interested economic agents know this rate before they make their decisions. The rate stays constant for the whole period. It can be changed only one period later.

3. The *maximum amount* $\overline{CL}_{CB,bi}$ the Central Bank is willing to refinance bank i. Thus $CL_{CB,bi} \leq \overline{CL}_{CB,bi} \quad, i = 1, \ldots, g$.

   The commercial bank i may decide to stay well below that limit. In this case changes of $\overline{CL}_{CB,bi}$ have no direct influence on the money in circulation. But if these limits are binding, the Central Bank is able to determine the liquidity situation of the commercial banks, i.e. the position $CL_{CB,B}$ in its balance sheet directly, see section 3.6[26].

4. The *minimum reserve requirements res*. We assume that there is only one required reserve rate on daily deposits DEP_{bi} and on time deposits TD_{bi}. Actually there are different reserve rates for different types of deposits[27] , but the simplification of only one rate seems to be tolerable. Thus in the balance sheet of the Central Bank the item $CA_{B,CB}$ on the liability side is determined by $CA_{B,CB} = res \cdot \sum_{i=1}^{g} (DEP_{bi} + TD_{bi})$, where res is also fixed in discrete steps, e.g. $res = z \cdot 0.05$, $z = 0,1,2,\ldots$.
   The Central Bank has to decide on the reserve ratio res before the new period begins. Thus res is known to all banks $i = 1, \ldots, g$. The banks have to estimate DEP_{bi} and TD_{bi}. The same is true for the Central Bank. The figure for $CA_{B,CB}$ which we find in the balance sheet of the Central Bank (see e.g. "Monatsbericht der Deutschen Bundesbank", June 2001, p.42*) is an ex-post-value.

5. The *open market-policy*: the Central Bank may appear on the demand or supply side of the exchange like any other economic agent (if the law concerning the Central Bank permits it). We show this for interventions at the capital market. Let us assume that from the point of view of the Central Bank the price $v^*_{KSt,i}$ of capital stock i is optimal.

---

[26] This decision variable $\bar{CL}_{CB,bi}$ is some proxy for the rediscounting allotments (in German: Rediskontierungskontingente) of the Bundesbank in former times, see *Jarchow* II (1974), p. 112. They are not in use anymore. But there is a substitute for it: the "permanent credit facilities" (in German: ständige Fazilitäten) of the EBZ. This fixes an upper amount of credits which each MFi could get from the EBZ on its own initiation at the interest rate determined by the EBZ, usually below the current rate at the money market. This is why these facilities are not used much. In this book we do not consider these limits.

[27] E.g.: In the "Monatsberichte der Deutschen Bundesbank", März 2001, one finds on p. 43* 8 different EZB interest rates called interest on "Hauptrefinanzierungsgeschäfte", discount rate, Lombard rate, "Basiszinssatz" and others. We lump them together under the name "discount rate" r_d.

Then in the simplest case the Central Bank may give the following order to the broker of capital stock i: if without intervention of the Central Bank the price of this asset would be $0 < \hat{v}_{KSt,i} < v^*_{KSt,i}$, then demand the amounts $\Delta KSt_{i,CB} = a_{KSt,i}(v^*_{KSt,i} - \hat{v}_{KSt,i})$, $a_{KSt,i} \geq 0$, on behalf of the Central Bank[28]. If without intervention of the Central Bank the price of this asset would be $\hat{v}_{KSt,i} > v^*_{KSt,i} > 0$, then supply the amount $\Delta KSt_{i,CB} = b_{KSt,i}(\hat{v}_{KSt,i} - v^*_{KSt,i})$, $b_{KSt,i} \geq 0$ and $\Delta KSt_{i,CB} \leq \overline{KSt_{i,CB}}$, where $\overline{KSt_{i,CB}}$ is the amount of capital stock of this kind in the portfolio of the Central Bank[29]. – For securities $\Delta SEC_{i,CB}$ the same approach applies[30,31].

We assume that the decisions on $v^*_{KSt,i}, v^*_{SEC,i}, a_{KSt,i}, a_{SEC,i}, b_{KSt,i}, b_{SEC,i}$ have to be taken at the beginning of the period and stay that way during the whole period. They will not be known to other economic agents, in the same way as similar conditional demand and supply orders by other agents are not generally known to the bank.

But what are the principles which guide all types of decisions of the Central Bank? The Central Bank is not an institution which pursues its private interests like households or firms but must be considered as an independent institution which pursues the monetary policy in the interest of the society as a whole (as it is understood by the board of the Central Bank). Sometimes the goals which the Central Bank should pursue are written in the constitution of the Bank, sometimes they are left open and are determined by the prevailing opinion of the experts in the field of monetary theory and policy (or by those

---

[28] Since the Central Bank is the ultimate source of money creation in the society, there is no upper limit for the demand of assets by the Central Bank on the asset market, but there are upper limits for the supply of assets by the Central Bank: its stocks of assets are limited.

[29] This list of the decision variables of the Central Bank is rather near to the corresponding list of decision variables of the FED; see Mankiw (1998), p. 603 ff.

[30] It is clear from this approach that the Central Bank cannot decide on the values $W_{KSt,CB}$ and $W_{SEC,CB}$ which appear in the balance sheet of the Central Bank. The price of the assets results from total demand and supply of the asset, and the supply of an asset is limited.

[31] There are objections against this type of open market policy of the Central Bank, especially against interference in the market for capital stocks. This policy may be used as method of subsidizing certain firms. But there might be situations where this is justified. It has often been tried in the market for foreign currency where (in general) this is not equivalent to subsidizing special firms or persons or institutions. But considering the huge amounts of demand and supply of foreign currency in developed countries the result of this intervention can hardly been foreseen. But there is one advantage of these direct interventions of the Central Bank: the liquidity of certain economic agents is directly influenced. Thus it is easier to estimate the effects of this policy on prices, production, growth and other values of the sectors directly or indirectly influenced by this type of policy of the Central Bank.

who believe that they are experts). Generally, the following goals of monetary policy are considered:

1. to keep the rate of inflation below a tolerable limit,
2. to help to keep (or to regain) an acceptable degree of employment,
3. to help in establishing a decent growth rate of the economy,
4. to help in preserving or regaining an acceptable distribution of income.

In case that the economy is part of an open world economy, a balanced value of exports and imports and a "right" exchange rate should possibly be added as "goal" of the monetary policy. It is clear that not all of these aims may be achieved by the limited number of instruments the Central Bank has under its control. Also the main goal of its activities changes in time. For the European Central Bank the avoidance of inflation stays in the center[32]. The Federal Reserve System in the USA looks more after employment and growth. But in any case the decision bodies of the Central Bank have to estimate the consequences of their monetary policy. That is not easy. There are different and contradicting theories on these consequences. For monetary policy it is decisive which "school" the members of the decision bodies adhere to or in other words: which economic theory they accept. We shall show this now and simultaneously present a model of the decision process of the Central Bank.

As usual we assume that the decision variables (i.e.: $r_d, \overline{CL}_{CB,bi}, res, v^*_{KSt,i}, a_{KSt,i}, b_{KSt,i}$, similarly for SEC) mentioned above can only take a small amount of discrete numbers. Let there be N decision variables of the Central Bank, and each decision variable can only assume n values. In this case there are $K := n^N$ possible decisions $D_{11},\ldots, D_{1K}$ of the Central Bank[33] the consequences of which must be analyzed with respect to the effects on the variables

[32] There is a valid discussion on the principles of monetary policy of the EZB. The German point of view was: The EZB should look at the price level and by its monetary policy try to keep it constant, following the example of the German Bundesbank. But other Central Banks followed other principles; e.g. the FED also considers employment and grow rate. Now the EZB stipulated a "two pillar-concept" of its policy: pillar 1 concerns (among others) a judgement on the rate of growth of money in circulation, pillar 2 (among others) a judgement on future price stability. But the EZB feels free to consider also other characteristics of the economic situation and other possible future developments. Thus there is no exact definition of the two "pillars" which leaves much room for judging possible decisions (this was perhaps also the reason for stipulating these not well defined principles). For further details, see: Junius et. al., Handbuch Europäische Zentralbank (2002), p. 141 ff. and Kißmer and Wagner, Braucht die EZB eine "neue" geldpolitische Strategie? (2002). This paper contains a rather large bibliography on this subject.

[33] Since each preparation of a decision takes some time and there is only a short time span available in perceiving the consequences of a decision, n and N are small numbers, and thus K as well.

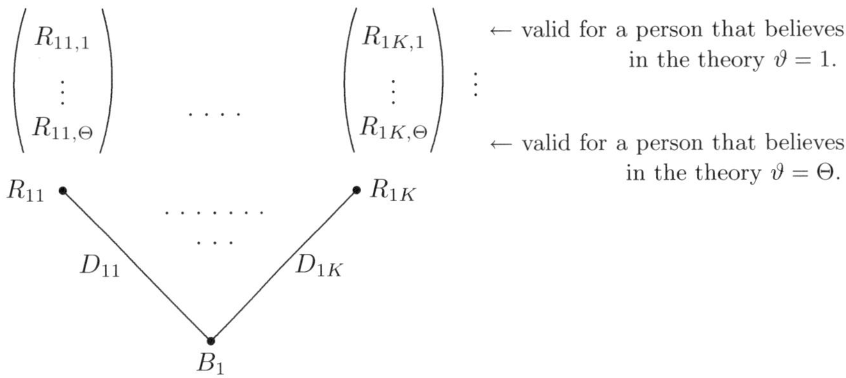

Figure 3.3. Decision situation of the managers of the Central Bank

1.-4. mentioned above, which form the criteria of success of the monetary policy of the Central Bank. Let there be Z criteria of success. Let B_1 indicate the initial situation of the economy. Fig. 3.3 illustrates the decision situation of the directors and the council of the Central Bank.

The result of a decision D_{1k}, $k = 1,\ldots,K$ must be estimated before the board of the Central Bank decides on D_{1k}. Let there be Θ different economic theories which pretend to forecast and explain the consequences of such a decision: $R_{1k,1},\ldots, R_{1k,\Theta}$, $k = 1,\ldots, K$. The item $R_{1k,\vartheta}$ is a vector of Z elements, if there are Z criteria $CRI_1,\ldots,CRI_Z$ by which the success (or failure) of the monetary policy of the Central Bank is judged ($Z = 4$ in our example, see below):

$$R_{1k,\vartheta} = (CRI_{1k,\vartheta 1},\ldots,\quad CRI_{1k,\vartheta Z}),\quad k = 1,\ldots,K,\quad \vartheta = 1,\ldots,\Theta$$

In our example of a closed economy:

$$\begin{aligned} CRI_{1k,\vartheta,1} &= \text{rate of inflation} \\ CRI_{1k,\vartheta,2} &= \text{degree of employment} \\ CRI_{1k,\vartheta,3} &= \text{growth rate} \\ CRI_{1k,\vartheta,4} &= \text{distribution of income} \end{aligned}$$

Each of these values differs due to the decision D_{1k} of the Central Bank and due to the theory ϑ we apply. In general, the different persons in the board of the Central Bank will adhere to different economic theories (let us assume that each person adheres to *one* theory and thus will estimate the consequences of a certain policy of the Central Bank differently from the equivalent estimation of another person in the board[34]).

[34] For example: a Keynesian will consider the real effects of monetary policy and neglect the monetary ones. A pure neo-classics will believe in the dichotomy of the economy along the lines of Walras: the monetary side of the economy will have no effect on the real side, at least in the long run.

But even if the persons in the board adhere to the same theory (they are selected that way) and thus estimate the consequences of their monetary policy identically, they have *different value judgements* on the same economic situation. As usual in this book, the value judgements are expressed by integers between $-\bar{z}$ and $+\bar{z}$, $\bar{z}$ a positive integer ≥ 1, where $-\bar{z}$ symbolizes the utmost dislike, $+\bar{z}$ the largest approvement and zero indifference or "no judgement".

In the following we shall suggest a theory on the decision process of "the board" of the Central Bank (which comprises the directors and the members of the council of the bank). Assume that there are P persons in the board. Each person on the board adheres to a specific economic theory $\vartheta \in \{1,..,\Theta\}$, i.e. it thinks that the consequences of a decision D_{1k} are $R_{1k,\vartheta}$ (in our example: $R_{1k,\vartheta} = (CRI_{1k,\vartheta,1},\ldots, CRI_{1k,\vartheta,4})$[35]. The person $p_\pi \in \{1,\ldots,P\}$ evaluates the decision D_{1k} by allocating integer values $u_{1k,\vartheta,1},\ldots,u_{1k,\vartheta,4}$ to the four criteria of the result $R_{1k,\vartheta}$, where $-\bar{z} \leq u_{1k,\vartheta,\nu} \leq +\bar{z}, \quad \nu = 1,\ldots,4$. The total evaluation $u^{p_\pi}(D_{ik})$ of the decision D_{1k} by person p_π follows by weighing the criteria themselves. They may carry the relative weights $\alpha^{p_\pi}_{1k,\vartheta,j} \geq 0$, $\sum_{j=1}^{4} \alpha_{1k,\vartheta,j} = 1$.[36] Thus in our example: $u^{p_\pi}(D_{1k}) = \sum_{j=1}^{4} \alpha_{1k,\vartheta,j} \cdot u_{1k,\vartheta,j}$

Since the persons in the board (in general) have different value judgements even if they adhere to the same economic theory, there will be disagreement in the board on "which is the best decision". The "rules of procedure" (die Geschäftsordnung) will regulate this case (e.g. by stating a voting procedure; in the case of the majority rule the value of the "median voter" determines the decision of the board). In other cases the "average opinion" may have the chance of being realized such that the evaluation $u(D_{1k})$ of "the board" is determined by $u(D_{1k}) = \text{n.i.}\frac{1}{P} \sum_{p_\pi=1}^{P} u^{p_\pi}(D_{1k}))$, where $n.i.$ = nearest integer.

The decision of the board would be D_{1k^*} where D_{1k^*} is determined by $max(u(D_{11}), \cdots, u(D_{1K}))$. The individual valuations $u^{p_\pi}(D_{1k})$ are determined by the process of mutual influence which is modeled as a Markov chain, see chapter 1 of this book. We shall not repeat that here.

To discuss the consequences of a specific decision of the Central Bank in the light of the four principles mentioned above (inflation, employment, rate of growth, distribution) will be rather time consuming and controversial. Thus some Central Banks pursue some sort of "intermediate object" which is easier to check and which is supposed to yield results which conform to the four principles. In the case of the European Central Bank this 'intermediate object' is a so-called "neutral level" of the average interest rates (in German: das

[35] The word "theory" must be taken in its broadest meaning. Different parameter values in an otherwise identical approach define a different theory. The estimation of the consequences of a decision of the Central Bank depends on the estimation of the prevailing type of reaction of other economic agents to this decision.

[36] These weights are explained by a Markov chain, see chapter 1 of this book.

neutrale Niveau der Leitzinsen), which lies between 4 and 4.5%. This rate is supposed to let the amount of money in its broadest definition (M3) grow at approximately the same rate of 4 to 4.5% which would allow a rate of growth of nominal GDP of the same size and would limit inflation and thus guarantee a positive real interest rate which is necessary for investment. If M3 grows at a higher rate the Central Bank would increase its interest rates, if it would grow at a lower rate it would diminish them. This would bring the rate of growth of M3 back to normal and thus in turn would induce the Central Bank to revise its interest rate back to the "neutral level".

Such a policy is understandable under the assumption that the velocity of money stays constant and that the neoclassical growth model is a sufficient approximation to the situation of the economy on an equilibrium growth path. This may be seen as follows. The velocity v of money is defined by Fisher's equation:

$$M \cdot v = Y \cdot p \quad \text{or} \quad w_M + w_v = w_Y + w_p$$

where M = money in circulation
Y = real GDP
p = price level
and w_x = rate of growth of a variable x

If $v = const.$, i.e. $w_v = 0$ we get

$$w_M = w_Y + w_p \tag{3.17}$$

Thus if the long run growth rate of GDP is 2.5%, a nominal growth rate of 4.5% would leave room for an "inevitable" rate of inflation of 2%. From neoclassical growth theory we get a relation between the nominal rate of interest r (determined by the Central Bank), the real rate z of interest, the rate of inflation w_p and the rate w_Y of real growth of GDP:

$$z = r - w_p = \frac{\varepsilon_{YK}}{s} \cdot w_Y$$

(see Krelle, Theorie des wirtschaftlichen Wachstums, 1988, p.104), where ε_{YK} = production elasticity of capital, s = investment ratio.

On an optimal growth path we would have $s = \varepsilon_{YK}$ (see Krelle, p. 117); in this case the above equation would be simplified to

$$r = w_Y + w_p \tag{3.18}$$

From (3.17) and (3.18) we get

$$w_M = r \quad .$$

This explains the situation on the equilibrium path of growth in case of a constant velocity of money. But in general the velocity of money is not constant and the economy is not on the optimal growth path. The experience of the last years shows that (but this has been known long before). Thus we get the relation

$$w_M = w_Y + w_p - w_v$$

where all growth rates depend on the rate of interest r: $w_Y = w_Y(r)$, $w_p = w_p(r)$, $w_v = w_v(r)$, all with negative or null derivatives: the growth rate of GDP, the rate of inflation and the velocity of money will decrease or stay constant when the rate of interest increases.

If w_M is larger than r, it is a reasonable policy to increase r because

$$\frac{\partial w_M}{\partial r} = \frac{\partial w_Y}{\partial r} + \frac{\partial w_p}{\partial r} - \frac{\partial w_v}{\partial r} \quad \begin{cases} < 0, & \text{if } \frac{\partial w_v}{\partial r} \text{ is small enough in absolute value (i.e. if the velocity of money is not very sensitive to changes of the interest rate)} \\ \geq 0 & \text{otherwise.} \end{cases}$$

If w_M is smaller than r a lowering of the interest rate will do – always under the assumption that the positive effect on real production and the price level will not be compensated by an opposite effect which comes from the cash holding decisions of persons or institutions. Thus there is no absolute safety on the effect of this policy[37].

The other instruments of the monetary policy of the Central Bank (the maximum amount of refinancing the commercial banks, the minimum reserve requirements and the open market policy) follow similar rules as the discount rate which we have described in detail: a higher discount rate is accompanied by restraints on refinancing the commercial banks, by increasing the minimum reserve requirements and by selling securities on the open market; a lower discount rate is accompanied by inverse operations.

If one wants to incorporate the Central Bank in a general disequilibrium system it is advisable not to go back to the ultimate goals of the decisions of the Central Bank but to stay on the "intermediate level".

Now, at the end of this section, we shall show how the discount rate affects prices and production in the short and in the long run and how it influences the velocity of money – always under the assumption that the commercial banks transmit a change of the discount rate (and equivalent changes of the other decision variables of the Central Bank) to their customers.

---

[37] Of course, there are other problems connected with this approach. We only mention one. The price level p and thus the rate of inflation w_p depend on the definition and that means on the way this rate is measured. The EZB uses a so called harmonized consumer price index. But this index fluctuates much and is not very appropriate to use for monetary policy. Therefore the bank has developed a "basic inflation rate" which does not contain commodity prices which fluctuate very much because of special influences; see "Kieler Kurzberichte", März 3/02.

We have to distinguish between an immediate short term effect and a long term effect of the change of the discount rate. The short term effect is immediate: a lower rate of interest means lower capital cost which tends to reduce the price of the product and thus to increase demand and production, but only if other products are not (or not to the same degree) afflicted. The long-term effect is transmitted by the time discount rate r^{time} which in our theory is some average of the observed discount rates r_d:

$$r^{time} = \frac{1}{T} \sum_{t=1}^{T} r_{d,-t} \ , \tag{3.19}$$

if T is the maximal number of periods in the past which are supposed to be still of importance in defining the time discount rate. Note that the discount rate $r_{d,0}$ of the next period does not have an influence on the time discount rate.

Now the real rate of interest z of a real investment I_0 in period 0 is defined as the ratio of the future real net profits $g_1, g_2, \ldots, g_T$ (earned by investing I_0 and discounted to the presence) to the initial investment I_0, if T is the life time of the installation I_0:

$$z = \frac{G_0}{I_0}, \text{ where } G_0 = \sum_{t=1}^{T} g_t \cdot a^t, \ a = \frac{1}{1 + r^{time}} \tag{3.20}$$

Let $\bar{g}$ be the average net profit, equal for the whole life time of the installation. Now equation (3.20) becomes

$$z = \frac{\bar{g}}{I_0} \sum_{t=1}^{T} a^t = \frac{\bar{g}}{I_0} \frac{a(a^T - 1)}{a - 1}$$

If we consider $a = \frac{1}{1+r^{time}}$ we get $z = \frac{\bar{g} \cdot h(r^{time})}{I_0}$, $\quad h(r^{time}) = \frac{1 - (\frac{1}{1+r^{time}})^T}{r^{time}}$

If $T \to \infty$ we get the simple well known expression

$$z = \frac{\bar{g}}{I_0} \cdot \frac{1}{r^{time}}$$

$\bar{g}$ is surely a rising function of $I_0 : \ \bar{g} = \bar{g}(I_0)$, at least for small I_0, but with declining rate of increase, see Fig. 3.4. For smaller time discount rate the curve $G(I_0, r^{time}) = \bar{g}(I_0) \cdot h(r^{time})$ shifts upwards, for larger it shifts downwards, see Fig. 3.4.

If the persons who decide on investment want to invest such an amount I_0 that the real profit in the future, discounted to the presence is maximal,[38]

[38] This does not say that there are no other influences on investment decisions. But it is reasonable to isolate some influences, in this example: the influence of profitability.

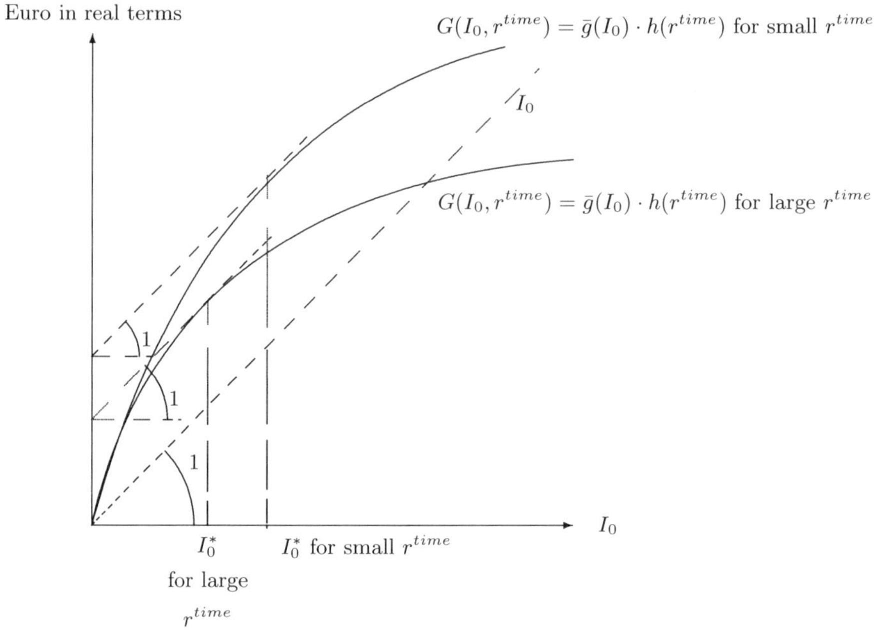

Figure 3.4 The average real net profits $\bar{g}$ as a function of the initial real investment I_0, and the influence of the time discount rate r^{time} on the size I_0^* of investment

they have to solve the following task:

$$G(I_0, r) - I_0 = \bar{g}(I_0) \cdot h(r^{time}) - I_0 = \max_{I_0}!$$

$$\text{which yields } \frac{\partial g(I_0)}{\partial I_0} \cdot h(r^{time}) = 1.$$

Fig. 3.4 illustrates this solution: the optimal investment I^* is smaller if the time discount r^{time} increases. But according to equation (3.19) the influence of the current discount rate $r_{d,-1}$ on the time discount is very small. Thus it is not surprising that a lowering of the discount rate of one period has a negligible influence on real investment. Only if the policy of a low discount rate is preserved for many periods, the positive effect on investment becomes perceptible.

Consider the case of increasing the discount rate. In the short run the price level increases as well, but not above a level determined by the money in circulation. If a high discount rate is preserved for many periods, the time discount rate follows. This leads to a decline of real investment and real consumption[39].

[39] We did not show this, but it is easy to demonstrate. A high discount rate lets the other interest rates also go up. Consumption credits will become more expensive. This will reduce consumption demand.

Thus Y_p declines if the discount rate is high for longer periods, and according to Fisher's equation v declines if the amount of money in circulation stays constant.

This concludes the theory of determining the discount rate r_d. But there are also other parameters which the managers of the Central Bank have to determine:

$\overline{CL}_{CB,bi}$	$=$	the maximal amount of refinancing the commercial bank i
res	$=$	minimum reserve requirements
$v^*_{KSt,i}, v^*_{SEC,i}$	$=$	price of capital stock and securities of type i which is considered as "reasonable" by the Central Bank and should be aimed at by an open market policy of the Central Bank
$a_{KSt,i}, a_{SEC,i}, b_{KSt,i}, b_{SEC,i}$	$=$	size of interventions of the Central Bank on the open market
	$=$	conditional buying or selling orders of the Central Bank at the exchange.

These parameters will be fixed by the Central Bank on the base of its experience in the past with respect to their effects on the economy as a whole. This is a problem of observations in the past. We assume that these parameters are correlated with the discount rate. We do not offer a specific theory but consider these parameters as exogenous.

This terminates the section on the decision variables and the principles of decision of the Central Bank. Now we have to present a similar theory for the commercial banks.

3.8 The Decision Variables and the Principles of Decision of a Commercial Bank

At the beginning of period 0 the decision makers of a Commercial Bank[40] in our model have quite a lot of decisions to take which are binding for this period and may be revised only at the beginning of the following period 1.

---

[40] We do not mention which department of the bank and which rank within the department is responsible for the decision and has to prepare it. This is the part of the organizational structure of the bank.

These decisions refer also to unknown functions in period 0 which influence them[41]. We start with the *liquidity policy* of the bank.

1. The bank decides upon the *daily deposits* DEP and the *time desposits* TD it has to expect and what will be the variance given the monetary policy of the Central Bank[42]. The amount of $DEP + TD$ codetermines directly or indirectly all other decisions. Under "normal" economic and political situations these estimations are rather exact. But the size of withdrawals of deposits in case of an important crisis is unknown and will not be considered in this model[43].

2. Since the bank (let us call it bank i) knows the minimum reserve ratio res determined by the Central Bank for the next period it knows the amount of cash $CA_{bi,CB}$ it has to keep at the Central Bank (namely $CA_{bi,CB} = res(DE_i + TD_i)$). Now the Commercial Bank knowing $DEP + TD$ and its variance has to decide on its own amounts of cash CA_{bi} by the liquidity ratio λ it wants to preserve:

   $$CA_{bi} = \lambda_{bi}(DEP_{bi} + TD_{bi}), \qquad 0 < \lambda_{bi} < 1$$

   This (within the limit BAL_{bi} which the balance sheet provides, see section 3.3) determines the amount W_{bi} of the value of capital stock[44] and securities and the size CR_{bi} of credits provided to other agents by

---

[41] In this conception also the acceptance of certain estimations or guesses are decisions. E.g. the acceptance of an estimation of a demand function for credits of the bank is a personal decision of that man or woman or committee which is responsible for the interest rate policy of the bank.

[42] Actually, there are confidence limits for the estimation of $DEP+TD$. They have to be considered by the decision makers. We do not go into these details.

[43] Every commercial bank will be bankrupt if a substantial part of its clients would simultaneously withdraw their deposits and the Central Bank would not help by accepting all types of assets of these banks.

[44] We put $W_{bi} = W_{KSt,bi} + W_{SEC,bi} + W_{LA,bi}$ where the items on the right hand side reproduce the portfolio composition of bank i. By definition:

$$W_{KSt,bi} = \sum_{j \in \{A_i\}} W_{KStj,bi}$$

where $W_{KStj,bi}$ is the value of the special capital stock j which is in the portfolio of bank i, and

$$W_{KStj,bi} = KSt_{j,bi} \cdot v_{KStj},$$

where $KSt_{j,bi}$ is the number of assets of this kind in the portfolio of bank i and v_{KStj} is the value at the exchange. $\{A_i\}$ is the set of capital stocks in the portfolio of bank i. Similarly:

$$W_{SEC,bi} = \sum_{j \in \{B_i\}} W_{SEC,bi}, \quad W_{SEC,bi} = SEC_{j,bi} \cdot v_{SECj},$$

Graduates with higher marks have the chance to start their business life at higher ranks but not higher than rank 3. Let there be $n_{-}^{(\sigma,\rho)}$ persons who graduate from school σ and are hired for work of rank ρ. If all graduates find a job we get: $\sum_{\rho} n_{-}^{(\sigma,\rho)} = n_{-}^{(\sigma)}$[19]

But there are other applicants for higher positions: persons employed at lower ranks (in the own firm or in another one) may apply, but also people from outside (from the pool of unemployed persons or from abroad). This leads to the topic of this section: learning by doing.

Consider a firm i which employs $\bar{n}^{(i,\rho)}$ persons of rank $\rho, \rho = 0, 1, \ldots, \mathcal{R}$. For employment in rank ρ a person must have the qualifications $q^{(i,\rho)} = (q_1^{(i,\rho)}, \ldots, q_z^{(i,\rho)})$ to a certain degree. They may be normalized to lie between 0 and 100. A minimum quality (say: 50) may be required to be employable at this level. E.g. for workers of rank 0 physical forces, skill, ability to cooperate with others and the like may be required. For workers of rank 1 some insight into the production process and ability to direct the work of the subordinates are necessary. "Learning by doing" means that a person working at the level ρ will increase his abilities $q^{(i,\rho)}$ in time and acquire the qualities $q^{(i,\rho+1)}$ of the next rank. After that the person may apply for promotion. He (or she) will then compete with applicants from higher schools and from outside.

Now we sum up over all firms. Let σ_ρ be the proportion of persons working in positions of rank ρ, which reached the qualifications for the rank $\rho + 1$. Thus $\sigma_\rho \cdot \bar{n}^{(\rho)}$ is the number of persons who within the firms reached the qualifications for a position of $\rho + 1$. Let $ue^{(\rho)}$ be the number of persons in the pool of unemployed people or otherwise appearing from outside with the qualification for employment in rank ρ. Then we get the number $\tilde{n}^{(\rho)}$ of applicants for employment at the rank ρ:

$$
\begin{array}{lcl}
\text{for} \rho = 0 & : & \tilde{n}^{(0)} = n_{-}^{(e.sch.)} + ue^{(0)} \\
\text{for} \rho = 1 & : & \tilde{n}^{(1)} = n_{-}^{(h.sch.)} + ue^{(1)} + \delta_0 \bar{n}^{(0)} \\
\text{for} \rho = 2 & : & \tilde{n}^{(2)} = n_{-}^{(u.sch.)} + ue^{(2)} + \delta_1 \bar{n}^{(1)} \\
\vdots & & \vdots \\
\text{for} \rho = R & : & \tilde{n}^{(R)} = ue^{(R)} + \delta_{R-1} \cdot \bar{n}^{(R-1)}
\end{array}
$$

The δ_ρ may be called the *learning coefficients* of the employment system. This learning is not general but concentrated and specialized in different fields of knowledge. This has some consequences for research and development.

---

[19] Graduates from school are usually still rather flexible as to the firm (and thus: as to the type of production) where they are employed. Thus we may aggregate over all firms.

4.4 Development, Research and Technical Progress

Learning means acquiring knowledge which is already existing. We dealt with it in the last sections. But development and research are activities to extend knowledge, and that is something else. By development we mean research activities with the aim to find out new technologies $\vartheta_1, \ldots, \vartheta_m$ to produce the same (or a variant of) product x_0 (where the technology ϑ_0 is used and the technologies $\vartheta_{01}, \ldots, \vartheta_{0n}$ are already known, but not used), and to find out new technologies $\vartheta\prime, \vartheta\prime\prime, \ldots$ to produce related new products $x\prime, x\prime\prime, \ldots$.[20] In development the research is done in order to improve the product or the production process but not simply to extend knowledge. But, of course, development rests on the observations $\phi_1, \ldots, \phi_n$ and on the theories $\theta_1, \ldots, \theta_m$ known to the firm (partly also: made by the firm).[21] We assume that *development* takes place only within firms whereas general *research* is mostly done at universities and special research institutes, in general without considering possible effects on production and the creation of absolutely new products which may become possible by it.

Consider a firm i which produces the amount x_i of commodity i by using the technology ϑ_i, see section 4.1. If the firm wants to participate in the process of development of product i, it has to vary the technology ϑ_i and the product x_i to $\vartheta\prime_i$ and $x\prime_i$ under technological and economical constraints.[22] The *technological constraints* do not allow certain combinations of input and output because they contradict the observations and the natural laws derived from it. E.g., there is a law of increasing entropy, a law of the impossibility of a perpetuum mobile, the Maxwell equations (to name only a few) which should not be violated. That means: the development of a new technology to produce the same or a related product must consider the known observations $\phi_1, \ldots, \phi_n$ and the known natural laws (or theories) $\theta_1, \ldots, \theta_m$. Now the situation is as follows (we consider a special firm but suppress the index which describes it, see Fig. 4.7). The firm uses the technology ϑ_0 to produce x_0 and knows that there are technologies $\vartheta_{01}, \vartheta_{02}, \ldots, \vartheta_{0n}$ to produce the same commodity x_0 or the variants $x_1, \ldots, x_z$. It assumes that there are still other technologies $\vartheta_1, \ldots, \vartheta_m$ to produce x_0 or variants $x_1, \ldots, x_z$ of it. Similarly, there are different products $x\prime$ with variants $x_1\prime, \ldots, x_z\prime$ considered by the management of the firm which could possibly be produced by technologies

---

[20] Fig. 4.7 illustrates the approach which we apply to explain R&D within firms. For simplicity we have left out already known but not used technologies $\vartheta_{01}, \ldots, \vartheta_{0n}$.

[21] Of course, not all observations and all theories are known by persons within the firm. A large number of ϕ and θ will be zero, but we do not model that explicitly.

[22] We do not consider here the economic constraints. They result from demand for the changed products $x\prime_i, x\prime\prime_i, \ldots$ and the costs of producing them by the new technologies $\vartheta\prime_i, \vartheta\prime\prime_i, \ldots$ The index i is suppressed in the following.

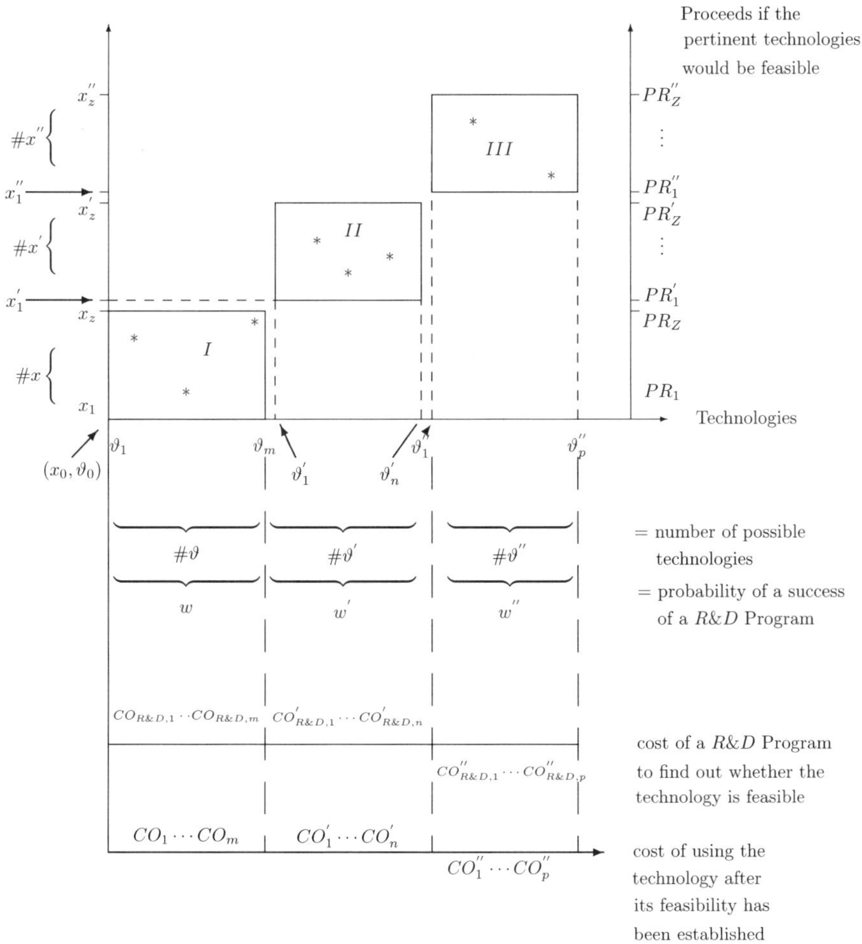

Notes:

The technologies $\vartheta_{01}, \dots, \vartheta_{0n}$ to produce x_0 (which are known to the firms but not used) are not illustrated in this figure.
The technologies marked by a star in the quadrangles I to III are feasible to produce certain variants of the final product x. They are unknown to the firm, and the development program of the firm is directed to find them.

Figure 4.7. Basis of a Decision of a Firm on the *R&D* Program

$\vartheta'_1, \dots, \vartheta'_n$, and another product x'' with the variants $x''_1, \dots, x''_z$ which perhaps could be produced with technologies $\vartheta''_1, \dots, \vartheta''_p$, see Fig. 4.7. Whether this is possible or not is unknown. In Fig. 4.7 these unknown technologies (if they exist) lie in the thickly bordered quadrangles. In the quadrangle I we have $\sharp x \cdot \sharp\vartheta$ possible R&D programs, in quadrangle II $\sharp x' \cdot \sharp\vartheta'$ and in quadrangle III $\sharp x'' \cdot \sharp\vartheta''$ possible programs. Let us assume that only the programs marked by a star would be a success, then the possibilities of finding a new technology are rather small. Thus the persons working in development must have some intuition where to search in the region of possible technologies. If there is no success, the personnel in the development department must be changed, in the first line the head of the department, in order to get someone with better intuition.

We may describe this search as a chance process where the probability to find a new technology depends on the choice of the personnel of the R&D department. But perhaps the production of $x\prime, x\prime\prime \dots$ is not possible with the knowledge $\phi_1, \dots, \phi_n$ and $\theta_1, \dots, \theta_m$. One has to wait for deeper insight into the natural laws or one has to realize, that $x\prime, x\prime\prime \dots$, are illusions at least for the time being. Fig. 4.7 (upper part) illustrates the decision situation of the firm. There are $\sharp\vartheta$ a priori possible technologies to produce one of the $\sharp x$ variants of the product x (quadrangle I) and similarly $\sharp\vartheta\prime$ possible technologies to produce $x\prime$ and its variants (quadrangle II) and so on. The management will assume that at least one of the possible R&D-programs in each quadrangle must be a success (otherwise it would not plan such a program). Thus without further information the probability w to find a new technology in the quadrangle I is at least $w = 1/(\sharp\vartheta \ \cdot \ \sharp x)$ and similarly $w\prime$ for search in the quadrangle II and $w\prime\prime$ for the quadrangle III. Moreover, we assume that the firm knows the cost $CO_{R\&D,i}$ of a research and development program to find out whether the technology i is feasible and that it can estimate the costs CO_i per unit of output of using this technology if it turns out to be feasible. This refers to technologies $\vartheta_1, \dots, \vartheta_m$ (quadrangle I in Fig. 4.7). Similarly, the firm may estimate the costs $CO'_{R\&D,i}$ and $CO''_{R\&D,j}$ of an R&D program in the region II and III and the cost CO'_i and CO''_j of using this technology if it turns out to be feasible. As an example for different technologies which yield the same output think of different degrees of automation of the production e.g. of automobiles or on different types of power sources for the production of electricity. As an example for different products think of the different possibilities of getting rid of the nuclear waste coming from atomic energy plants or on the different types of aeroplanes or on different possible medicaments which help against cancer or aids or other deadly diseases.

The alternatives illustrated in Fig. 4.7 are the base for the decision of the firm on R&D. We may divide the decision into two steps:[23]

1. the decision on the amount $\bar{R\&D}$ of money made available for R&D in the next period

2. the decisions to allocate this money to specific R&D projects. As a rule there are much more possible R&D projects than there is money to finance them.

---

[23] This division is made in order to facilitate the exposition. In many cases this corresponds to reality, though from the point of theory there is only one simultaneous decision.

to 1. Expenditure for R&D competes with other expenditures of the firm which are also important. The balance equation is the frame in which all possible expenditures must lie. We write it as

$$CAF = DEP + DIV + I + \bar{R\&D} + \triangle DEB + RES$$

$$\begin{array}{llll} \text{where} & CAF & = & \text{cash flow (given from the past; } CAF \geq 0) \\ & DEP & = & \text{depreciation} \\ & DIV & = & \text{payment of dividends} \\ & I & = & \text{investment (including change of inventories)} \\ & \bar{R\&D} & = & \text{expenditure for R\&D} \\ & \triangle DEB & = & \left\{ \begin{array}{l} \text{increase of debts (if positive)} \\ \text{repayment of debts (if negative)} \end{array} \right. \\ & RES & = & \text{increase of reserves} \end{array}$$

The firm has to decide how the cash flow will be used. The long-term development of the firm depends crucially on this decision. All different combinations of this allocation have to be considered and evaluated, in principle. Actually, only few alternatives are discussed and analyzed in detail. There are different criteria: future profits of the firm, the shareholder value, the market share; see chapter 2. We shall not repeat that here.

to 2. In a second step the firm has to evaluate the different R&D projects concerning the feasibility of different possible technologies under the constraint of the granted expenditures $\bar{R\&D}$. The points of evaluation are: the expected proceeds PR from the R&D-program on a special technology if the R&D-program turns out to be a success, and the cost CO of this program, the probability w of success of this program (CO and w are indicated in Fig. 4.1), the relative position of the firm in the future, compared to the position of competing firms (when "position" refers to market share, the profitability, the indebtedness and other features of the firm). All possible combinations of R&D-programs within the limits of $\bar{R\&D}$ must be considered in theory. Actually, only very few remain for serious consideration. Let $CO_{R\&D,\mu^*}, \mu^* \epsilon \{1, \ldots, m\}$ be the money spent for the granted R&D-project μ^*, and $CO'_{R\&D,\nu^*}, \nu^* \epsilon \{1, \ldots, n\}$ and $CO''_{R\&D,\pi^*}, \pi^* \epsilon \{1, \ldots, p\}$ accordingly for R&D in the regions II and III of Fig. 4.7. In case that there is only at most one project chosen in each region, these projects must fulfill the constraint

$$\bar{R\&D} \geq CO_{R\&D,\mu^*} + CO'_{R\&D,\nu^*} + CO''_{R\&D,\pi^*}$$

The cost CO, CO', CO'' are zero if no alternatives of this kind are chosen. The decision process itself follows the same rules as that of the choice of $\bar{R\&D}$ and will not be repeated here.

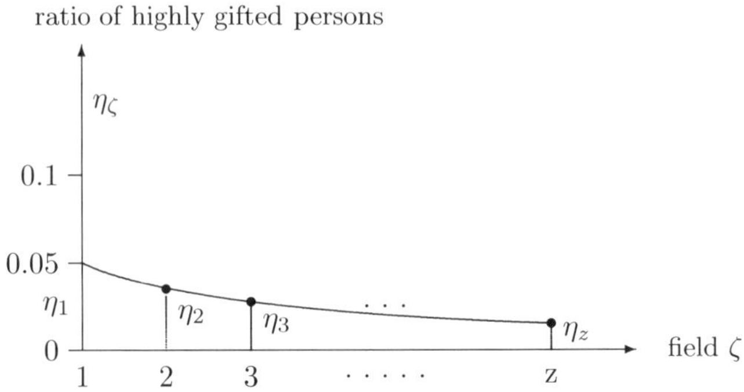

Figure 4.8. Natural endowment of gifts: ratio of highly gifted persons

We now turn to the *basic research.* This subsection continues the line of thought of section 4.2. The point of departure is the distribution of natural endowments $\bar{W}_\zeta$ in a certain field $\zeta = 1, \ldots, z$. They may be normalized to lie between 0 and 100. Let η_ζ be the proportion of the population with natural gifts in field ζ between 80 and 100 (limits included). We may call it the ratio of highly gifted persons in the field ζ. Fig. 4.8 shows the distribution of this ratio after suitable renumbering of the fields.

We assume that the fields $1, \ldots, \bar{z}$ taught at elementary schools and fields $\bar{z}+1, \ldots, \bar{\bar{z}}$ taught at high schools (see Fig. 4.1) are simplified versions of what is taught at universities, schools of engineering and institutions like that. Therefore, basic research is only done in field $\bar{\bar{z}}+1, \ldots, z$ (see Fig. 4.1). Let us assume that the highly gifted persons finish the university system in their field by the marks $G^+ = 8, 9$ or10, if they reach the university system. Let there be $N_\zeta^{(u.sch.,out)}$students who finish their university study in field ζ at the beginning of period 0 and let $\gamma_{G^+,\zeta} \cdot N_\zeta^{(u.sch.,out)}$ be the number which get the marks 8,9 or 10 which means with the grades "good" to "excellent" in this field. But what does that mean: "excellent" or "good"? That is related to the knowledge of the teacher. Take a certain teacher j in the field ζ at the university level. If we normalize the total knowledge W_ζ in field ζ to 100 this special teacher masters a ratio of $\delta_{j,\zeta}$ of it, where $0 \leq \delta_{j,\zeta} \leq 1, \zeta \epsilon \{\bar{\bar{z}} + 1, \ldots, z\}$.

The quality of teacher j in field ζ at the university level is measured by this proportion $\delta_{j,\zeta}$ not by its pedagogical gift. The teacher could at best transfer this proportion to his students. "Excellent" means that the student knows this proportion (which the student in many cases takes as total knowledge in this field). Now there is a distribution of the quality of teachers similarly as the distribution of marks of the students, see Fig. 4.6.

"Excellent" for teacher j means: the student knows as much (or nearly as much) as the teacher, "Good" means that the student is familiar with (say) 80% of what the teacher knows and so on. Since it is easier to become familiar and to understand a small part of a scientific field than to master the total knowledge in this field, less gifted students may nevertheless get the best marks at a less perfect teacher. Thus there is no simple correlation between marks of students who leave the university and their size of endowments in this field. It may be that small teacher/student relations $\pi_\zeta^{(G)}$ at lower schools σ do not develop the more gifted students up to their endowments. Then they have to start at the university with a low level of basic knowledge and thus they may stay behind their capacities when they leave the universities. Thus new knowledge in a field ζ which increases total knowledge (say) from 100 to 102 may also come from persons with worse marks at the university level or without any university or high school attendance. But these are exceptional cases which we do not consider here. In general, progress in science arises from organized research work by single persons (e.g. in the form of a dissertation) or (mostly) by research groups equipped with the necessary machinery and material, which may require a high research budget. In our model research is being done by highly gifted persons who graduated from university schools and by teachers at the university schools (or equivalent persons at other research institutions) of high quality, i.e. by those who master at least (say) 80% of total knowledge in their field. But research is a search process (as the name rightly suggests). If one searches in the wrong direction, one will not find something new. But the probability to extend knowledge is the larger the more qualified persons search in different directions. The number of persons that, if employed in research, could possibly find something new may be estimated as follows:

Let N = be the total population of the society

η = the proportion of persons who are highly gifted in a certain field

ξ = the proportion of these persons who reach the university level

$\mathcal{X}$ = the proportion of these persons who leave the university with a knowledge of (say) at least 80% of total knowledge (approximated by the proportion of students leaving the universities with marks 8 to 10 at teachers who at least have that knowledge)

δ = the proportion of these students that are willing to devote at least part of their life to research and (since this work usually pays less than an equivalent work in business) thus renounce higher income.

With these definitions the number $N^{(res)}$ of persons who are able and willing to do research is $N^{(res)} = \eta \cdot \xi \cdot \mathcal{X} \cdot \delta \cdot N$, a very small number indeed.[24]

---

[24] Let η be .01, $\xi = .5$, $\mathcal{X} = .2$, $\delta = .5$. Now we get $N_{res} = .0005 \cdot N$. Thus for a population of N=82 Mill., we get approximately 41.000 persons willing and able to do research.

Now we estimate the number N_{teach} of teacher who are able and willing to do research in the field which we consider.

Let $N_{teach}^{(u.sch.)}$ be the number of teachers at the university level (this includes the number of person at equivalent positions in research institutions)

α the proportion of these persons who are highly gifted and thus in principle are able to do research in this field

β the average proportion of their working time which these persons could devote to research. [25]

γ the proportion of these university teachers who are interested in research and do it without additional pay.

Now we get for the number of researchers employed as teacher at the university level who are able and willing to do research:

$$N_{teach}^{(res)} = \alpha \cdot \beta \cdot \gamma \cdot N_{teach}^{(u.sch.)}$$ [26]

This refers to all fields of research. The parameters may be different in different fields.

In the following notes we estimate this number in a different way and come to similar results.

[25] The number $\beta \cdot N_{teach}^{(u.sch.)}$ indicates the mathematically equivalent full time researcher.

[26] If $\alpha = .5, \beta = .1, \gamma = .5$ we get $N_{teach}^{(res)} = .025 \cdot N_{teach}^{(u.sch.)}$. Thus 2.5% of the university teachers are able and willing to do research. The number $N_{teach}^{(u.sch.)}$ of university teachers of all ranks in Germany may be estimated as 155.760 persons (see Statistisches Jahrbuch für die Bundesrepublik Deutschland 2000, p. 387). 2.5% of it are 3894. In addition we have to count a proportion δ of students that graduate in their field and are able and willing to do research at least for some time. Let δ be .025 (the same proportion as at the university teacher level). The number of students that graduated in any field were 277.525 in 1998 (see Statistisches Jahrbuch 2000, p. 385). Thus there were 6938 graduate students who could do research. These are approximately 1.8 students per university teacher who is active in research. This seems to be a reasonable estimate for the average. To get the total number of persons that do research in Germany one has to add the R&D personnel of firms and of institutions of community research. In 1998 these were 288,000 persons (see Institut der Deutschen Wirtschaft Köln, Zahlen zur Entwicklung der Bundesrepublik Deutschland 2000, p. 119). In total there were approximately 39.600 persons employed in research in Germany at the end of the 1990s, which is similar to the number of 41.000 persons which we estimated before. If we accept these estimations (one has to check whether the number of full R&D personnel in Germany is really that large), the number of persons employed in R&D is 28 times the number of persons doing basic research. Be that as it may: if technical progress is a function of the number of persons engaged in R&D and in basic research (this is what we suppose) the government can influence the parameters $\xi, \mathcal{X}, \delta$ and β, γ and the number $N_{teacher}^{(u.sch.)}$ of teachers at the university level and influence R&D at the firm level (by appropriate tax laws).

We assume that research is being done in research groups of a minimum size (which may be one in certain fields), and of different compositions (e.g. in economics a group may consist of persons specialized in economic theory, statistics and econometrics) and must be equipped with computers, books and periodicals and some auxiliary personnel; in other fields (e.g. physics, astrophysics, chemistry) the necessary capital equipment is very expensive. We assume the following procedure in the approval and financing of research programs:

1. The government decides on the number $N_{teach}^{(u.sch.)}$ of teachers at the university level by granting the positions and paying the necessary cost $CO_{teach}^{(u.sch.)}$.

2. The government decides on the proportion $(1-\beta)$ of the working time of a university teacher which he (she) has to devote to teaching.

3. The constitution of universities and research institutes decides by its procedure of filling the vacancies by appropriate applicants which proportion α of highly gifted persons are employed at the university level and which proportion γ of it is interested in research (whereas the proportion $1-\gamma$ is interested in teaching or in other activities e.g. in politics). Thus the procedure of appointing university teachers is most important for the research capacity of the universities.

The proportions α, β, γ are directly or indirectly determined by the responsible department of the government or by the authoritative bodies determined by it. Their personal composition sometimes follows some ideological prejudices (e.g. at the time of the so called "student revolution" of 1968-1972 the word "elite" was an abusive word, and teachers were evaluated and appointed according to their political opinions, a procedure which is still visible and had partly awful repercussions at some universities in Germany).

This refers to the long-term human base of actual research. But in addition the government has to decide on the total amount $\bar{CO}_{Res}$ of the yearly budget which is determined to finance the manpower and the expenditures for equipment which is necessary to carry out the research (but not necessarily in each period if the research programme is planned for several periods). The expenditure $\bar{CO}_{Res}$ for research competes with all other expenditures (for general administration, for the administration of justice, the educational system, the expenditures for roads, for police, for development aid, for the military forces and others). Let ρ be the proportion of expenditure EXP_{Res} for research in the above sense to total expenditure EXP_g of the government. Thus:

$$EXP_{Res} = \rho \cdot EXP_g, \text{ and } 0 \leq \rho < 1$$

ρ is a decision variable of the government, such as α, β, γ.

We now suppose that those persons who are interested in and capable to do research in each field (university teachers or persons in a similar position and graduate students) organize themselves in appropriate research groups and apply for financing that research at the government or at the organization which is set up to judge the research proposals and which is provided with the amount EXP_{Res} of money to finance the approved research projects. Let there be F research proposals in the fields $\zeta = 1, \ldots, z$ with costs $CO_{Res.\zeta 1}, \ldots, CO_{Res.\zeta F}$. Now a committee which is appointed according to the law or a decree of the government – we shall simply say: appointed by the government – decides how the total amount EXP_{Res} of money allocated to research by the government should be devoted to each field of research, that means it has to decide on the proportions $\sigma_1, \ldots, \sigma_z$ of the money for research which should go to research in the fields $1, \ldots, z$:

$$EXP_{Res.\zeta} = \sigma_\zeta \cdot EXP_{Res}, \; \sigma_\zeta \geq 0, \; \sum_{\zeta=1}^{z} = 1, \; \zeta = 1, 2, \ldots, z$$

Usually, there are research proposals in the field ζ by the size

$$CO_{Res.\zeta} = \sum_{f=1}^{F} CO_{Res.\zeta f}$$

where these demands on money are larger than the amounts available. In general: $CO_{Res.\zeta} > EXP_{Res.\zeta}$

Now the same or another committee has to decide which research proposals are approved and which are refused. Let us assume that the research proposals are ordered according to the preference of the deciding committee such that only the first $1, \ldots, F_\zeta$ proposals are approved in the field ζ:

$$\sum_{f=1}^{F_\zeta} CO_{Res.\zeta f} \leq EXP_{Res.\zeta}$$

There might be scientific criteria at this stage of the decision procedure. But also ideological, political or personal ones or other points of view may interfere. We shall not make a large fault if we consider the preference ordering $PREF_\zeta$ of the research proposals in the field ζ as a political decision of the government.

Now consider the situation of a research group whose proposal has been approved. It wants to extend the knowledge in a certain field. As a rule there is a rather large number of alternatives to do that, call them $PR_1, \ldots, PR_z$ (=procedure 1,…,procedure z, e.g. different experiments in the natural sciences and different approaches in the cultural sciences). The research group has to decide which procedure should be adopted and which propositions in detail be tested. Since nobody knows where the truth might be found, this is best be described by a search process with different probabilities of success. The research group allocates subjective probabilities $p_1, \ldots, p_z$ to each research procedure $PR_1, \ldots, PR_z$ and chooses that with the highest probability of success in the eyes of this group. But nevertheless, the procedure might be wrong and the research program a failure judged from the point of view of extending our knowledge. Thus the same group (or another one) may try another approach in the next period.

Now we may conclude this section by stating:

1. The government (or committees appointed or under the influence of the government) decides on the preconditions of research by choosing the parameters α, β, γ (which determine the educational system), the parameters ρ and σ (which determine the research expenditures) and the preference order PR_ζ of all *research proposals* in the field ζ.

2. The research group whose *proposal* is approved determines the research procedure in detail by assigning probabilities of finding a new result (till now unknown in science). Since nobody knows for sure where the new unknown fact is located the research group assigns probabilities to each research procedure and realizes that approach with the highest probability of success.

   If the research is a failure, nothing changes in the set $\{\Phi_1, \ldots, \Phi_n\}$ of accepted facts and in the set $\{\theta_1, \ldots, \theta_m\}$ of accepted theories. If the research turns out to be a success, the set of known facts may be extended to $\{\Phi_1, \ldots, \Phi_{n+1}\}$ and (perhaps) also the set of theories which explain the facts to $\{\theta_1, \ldots, \theta_{m+1}\}$, and perhaps something, what was accepted as a “fact” may turn out to be an illusion and must be canceled in the set of facts and similarly some theories have to be abandoned.

This is how progress in science and technical progress in firms and other institutions may be explained.

4.5 Some Remarks on Other Explanations of Technical Progress

The theory on technical progress suggested in the foregoing paragraphs is not the usual one which may be found in the literature. There are many others.

Klaus Jaeger (1986) [27] gives a survey on the better known theories as far as they are based on the concept of a production function. He cites other review articles (see *Jaeger* p. 111) but, of course, one finds opinions on the creation and diffusion of technological change in almost all books and articles of economics which include economic growth (e.g. *Dornbusch/Fischer*, Macroeconomics (1978), *Mankiw*, Principles of Economics, *Varian*, Grundzüge

[27] Jaeger, Die analytische Integration des technischen Fortschritts in die Wirtschaftstheorie, in: Bombach, Gahlen, Ott (Herausg.), Technologischer Wandel – Analyse und Fakten, Tübingen (Siebeck), 1986.

der Mikroökonomie, *Krelle*, Theorie des wirtschaftlichen Wachstums, 2.Auf., Berlin, Heidelberg etc. (Springer), 1988).

The usual textbooks in economics do not deal with the reasons for technical progress. They describe it as a shift of the production function which is taken to be exogenous[28]. There is one exception: *Mankiw* in his textbook "Principles of Economics"[29] devotes some pages in his chapter 24 on the verbal explanations of the reasons for technical progress (and hindrances for it), see p. 523 ff.

In the following I comprise the different theories to some groups of similar approach. Of course, I cannot go into details, but the reader should know other models which concentrate on other features of technical change.

With *Adam Smith* (1723-1790) economics as a science starts. He explains (in terms of economics today) the economic growth by the increase of the labor productivity which is the consequence of the increasing of the division of labor. He illustrates that by his famous example of the production of needles. A worker who manufactures needles from raw material (wire) up to the final product could only produce perhaps one needle per day, and surely not more than 20 pieces. But by decomposing the total work into pieces (e.g. cutting the wire, forge the tip,...) and specializing the workers into only one piece of activity, 10 workers could manufacture about 4800 needles per day. That means: technical progress is measured by labor productivity and this depends on the organization of the production process. Today we would classify this theory as a special case of "learning by doing".

David Ricardo (1772-1823) thinks that technical progress could only occur in manufacturing, not in agriculture. It would reduce the relative price of manufactured goods compared to agricultural goods because Ricardo believes in the labor theory of value.

Karl Marx (1808-1883) preserves the labor theory of value (in spite of the existence of the subjective value theory based on the utility theory of this time). Technical progress is connected with an increasing organic composition of capital (which Marx identifies with increasing capital per unit of labor). This yields more and more unemployment and (together with other features) leads to the breakdown of capitalism.[30]

After *Smith*, *Ricardo* and *Marx* there was a long pause in the research on this field till the dynamization of the Keynesian system by *Harrod* and *Do-*

---

[28] Take as an example the textbook of Varian "Intermediate Microeconomics", 5th ed. 1999, where in chapter 18 on "Technology" a change of technology is discussed without giving reasons for it.

[29] Mankiw, N.G., "Principles of Economics", Fort Worth, Philadelphia etc. (The Dryden Press), 1998.

[30] This is a very crude and simplified picture of the economic systems of Smith, Ricardo and Marx. As to the economic model of Marx, only the system of volume I of "The Capital" of Marx is reproduced in a simplified form. In Krelle (1988) chapter 2, the system of Smith, Ricardo and Marx are analyzed in more detail.

mar and the introduction of the neoclassical growth theory by *Solow, Meade, Phelps* and *von Weizsäcker* which replaced the Harrod-Domar theory. But as far as the technical progress is concerned there was no great difference: both theories measured technical progress by its consequences on easier measurable economic variables: the rate of autonomous investment or the rate of growth of labor productivity if employment stays constant. The general assumption in the neoclassical approach was the existence of a neoclassical production function

$$Y = f(A, K, \tau)$$

where $A =$ labor, $K =$ capital, $\tau =$ state of technology. Thus $\frac{\dot{\tau}}{\tau}$ is the rate of technical progress. In order to allow for equilibrium growth, the neoclassical theory assumed Harrod-neutral technical progress, that means it assumed a production function f of the type

$$Y = F(A^*, K), \; A^* = A \cdot a(\tau) = \text{labor in efficiency units}$$

whereas a Hicks-neutral technical progress would assume a production function of the type

$$Y = a(\tau) \cdot G(A, K)$$

τ and $a(\tau)$ which measure technical progress are not directly observable. In econometric estimations they appear as residual: that part of Y which cannot be explained by A and K is attributed to τ. Thus the estimation of τ depends on the structural form of f, F and G and the methods of estimating Y, A and K. As to the structural form the Cobb-Douglas or CES or more complicated functional forms (e.g. the *Sato* production function) have been used till *Jorgenson* suggested the translog function which is an approximation to all feasible production functions. In any case: technical progress is not directly explained but inferred from its assumed effects on other variables.

This is the reason why other approaches have been suggested which get around these difficulties. One of the most radical is *Kaldor's* technical progress function. *Kaldor* (1957) wanted to model economic growth without using production functions, since technical progress cannot be separated from substitution of labor by capital. Thus he postulated a "technical progress function" of the type

$$w_Y = \rho(w_\kappa)$$

where $w_Y =$ rate of growth of output

$w_\kappa =$ rate of growth of capital per person

$$\rho(0) > 0, 0 < \rho' < 1, \rho'' \leq 0$$

If ρ is linear, Kaldor's function is equivalent to a Cobb-Douglas-production function.[31] But this approach did not prevail in economics.

Jorgenson's translog function[32] allows for technical change. In *Nakamura* (1984, pp. 44) it is measured by $\frac{\partial v_{ij}}{dt}$, where v_{ij} is the value share of input i in the cost (= value of output) of sector j. But one may ask whether this is an appropriate measure for technical change. Are the coefficients of the model really constant? *Kirchen* (1988) estimates time-dependent parameters in an econometric model of the West German economy by means of a variant of the Kalman filter approach. This yields better results as the assumption of fix parameters, but it also judges technical progress only by its consequences.

Badke (1990) continues this approach to its logical end by considering "technical progress" as a latent variable. There are methods of estimating latent variables by analyzing the effects on input- and output indicators. One of the best known methods is the LISREL system (Linear Structural Relation) of *Jöreskog* (1988). *Badke* uses a special case of LISREL called MIMIC (= multiple indicators, multiple causes) and in addition a dynamic extension of this system called DYMIMIC. Thus *Badke* could estimate a time series of technical knowledge in West Germany (see Badke p. 89).

This surely is a progress in estimating technical progress. But this approach does not explain where technical programs come from and how they could be influenced. The first step in this direction did *Kenneth Arrow* (1962). He explains technical progress by learning "on the job". If the production process is repeated the workers on the machine learn to do their job more efficiently which in the statistics appears as less labor per output and will be interpreted as "technical progress". But this does not cover the technical progress due to organized research at universities and other research institutions. This is explained in *Krelle, Fleck, Quinke* (1975) who include a model of the school system into an econometric forecasting system and analyze the change of labor productivity as a function of the size and quality of the school system (in the broad sense of the word). Also the costs of the school system are derived such that the repercussions of an extension of the school system on the size of GDP can be estimated. The result may be summarized as follows. There is a short term positive multiplier effect of the additional expenditures for expanding the school system which is followed by a negative effect on GDP (due to the withdrawal of a larger part of young people from the production) which in turn would be followed by an increase of GDP because of the higher education

---

[31] See Krelle (1988), p. 205. Kaldor and Mirrlees (1962) suggested a complete growth theory on that base.

[32] See Christensen, Jorgenson, Lau, Conjugate Duality and the Transcendental Logarithmic Functions, Econometrica Vol.39, No.4, pp. 255. Some comparisons of different Taylor series approximations may be found in: Nakamura, An Inter-Industry Translog Model of Price and Technical Change for the West German Economy, Lecture Notes in Economics and Mathematical Systems, Vol.221,Berlin etc. (Springer), 1984, pp. 72.

of a larger part of the population. Thus the theory allows to explain changes in the average labor productivity which otherwise would have been attributed to changes in technical progress.

The theory suggested in this section continues this approach.

References

[1] Adelmann, J.: *Theories of Growth and Development*, Stanford 1961

[2] Aigner, D., Schneider, F. und Gosh, D.: *Me and my Shadow: Estemating the Size of the U.S. Underground Economy from Time Series Data*, Working Paper, No. M8615, University of Southern California, Los Angelos 1986

[3] Arrow, K.J.: *The Economic Implications of Learning by Doing*, Review Economic Studies 29, 1962, p. 155 ff.

[4] Badke, M.: *Eine Theorie des technischen Fortschritts*, Diss. Bonn (Kovac), 1990

[5] Beckerhoff, D.: *Wirtschaftswachstum durch Ausbildung und Forschung*, Diss. Bonn 1968

[6] Beckmann, M.J.: *Wirtschaftliches Wachstum bei abnehmenden Skalenerträgen*, in: Krelle (Hrsg.): *Theorien des einzelwirtschaftlichen und des gesamtwirtschaftlichen Wachstums*, Berlin 1965, p. 99 ff.

[7] Chow, G.C.: *Random and Changing Coefficient Models*, in: Z. Grilliches – M.D. Intriligator (eds.): *Hansbook of Econometrics*, Vol. II, North Holland, Amsterdam, New York, Oxford 1984, p. 1213-1245

[8] Christensen, L.R., Joergenson, D.W., Lau, L.J.: *Conjugate Duality and the Transcendental Logarithmic Production Function*, in: Econometrica 39, 1971, p. 225-256

[9] Dhrymes, P.J.: *Distributed Lg: Problems of Estimation and Formulation*, North Holland, Amsterdam, New York, Oxford 1980

[10] Diewert, W.E., Wales, T.J.: *Flexible Functional Forms and Global Curvature Conditions*, in: Econometrica, 55, 1987, p. 43-68

[11] Diewert, W.E.: *The Measurement of Productivity*, Discussion Paper Nr. 89-04 Department of Economics – University of British Columbia, 1989

[12] Domar, E.D.: *Capital Expansion, Rate of Growth, and Employement*, in: Econometrica, 14, 1946, p. 137 ff.

[13] Domar, E.D.: *Essays in the Theory of Economic Growth*, New York 1957

[14] Dornbusch, R. and Fischer, St.: *Macroeconomics*, New York etc. (McGraw-Hill) 1978

[15] Drandakis, E.M. and Phelps, E.S.: *A Model of Induced Invention, Growth and Distribution*, Economic Journal 76, 1966, p. 823 ff.

[16] Frerichs, W.: *Ein disaggregiertes Prognosesystem für die BRD, 1. Die Staatssektoren*, Meisenheim (Anton Hain) 1975, p. 86 ff.

[17] Grilliches, Z.: *Research Expenditures and Growth Accounting*, in: Williams, B.R. (ed): *Science and technology in Economic Growth*, London, Basingstoke, p. 59 ff.

[18] Griliches, Z. and Lichtenberg, F.: *R & D and Productivity Growth at the Industry Level: Is there Still a Relationship?*, 1981, in: Griliches, Z. (ed): *R & D, Patents and Productivity*, NBER Conference Report, Chicago

[19] Härdle: *Nichtparametrische Regression*, Habilitationsschrift, Universität Bonn 1988

[20] Hamberg, D.: *Models of Economic Growth*, Nex York 1971

[21] Harrod, R.F.: *An Essay in Dynamic Theory*, Economic Journal, 49, 1939, p. 14 ff.

[22] Harrod, R.F.: *Second Essay in Dynamic Theory*, Economic Journal, 70, 1960, p. 277 ff.

[23] Jaeger, K.: *Die analytische Integration dse technischen Fortschritts in die Wirtschaftstheorie*, in: Bombach, Gablen, Ott (Herausg.): *Technologischer Wandel – Analyse und Fakten*, Tübingen (Siebeck) 1986, p. 111 ff.

[24] Jöreskog, K.G and Goldberger, A.S.: *Estimation of a model with multiple indicators and multiple causes of a single latent variable*, in: Journal of the American Statistical Association (10), 1975, p. 631 – 639

[25] Jöreskog, K.G. and Sörbom, D.: *Recent developments in structural equation modelling*, in: Journal of Marketing Research (19), 1982, p. 404 – 416

[26] Jöreskog, K.G. and Sörbom, D.: *LISREL 7 A Guide to the Program and Applications*, Chicago 1988

[27] Jorgenson, D.W. and Griliches, Z.: *The Explanation of Productivity Change*, Review of Economic Studies 23, 1967, p. 249 ff.

[28] Jorgenson, D.W. and Griliches, Z.: *The Explanation of Productivity Change*, Review of Economic Studies 34, 1967, p. 249 - 283

[29] Jorgenson, D.W.: *Econometric Studies of Investment Behaviour: A Survey*, in: Journal Of Economic Literature 9, 1971, p. 111 ff.

[30] Jorgenson, D.W. and Fraumeni, B.M.: *Relative Prices and Technical Change*, in: Berndt, E. and Field, B. (Herausg.): *Modelling and Measures Natural Resource Substitution*, MIT-Press, Massachusetts 1981

[31] Kaldor, N.: *Alternative Theories of Dirstribution*, Review of Economic Studies 23, 1955/56, p. 155 ff.

[32] Kaldor, N.: *A Model of Economic Growth*, Economic Journal 67, 1957, p. 591 ff.

[33] Kaldor, N. and Mirrless, J.A.: *A New Model of Economic Growth*, Review of Economic Studies 29, 1962, p. 155 ff.

[34] Kalman, R.E.: *A New Approach to Linear Filtering and Prediction Problems*, in: Journal of Basic Engeneering, Vol 82, 1960, p. 35 – 45

[35] Kalman, R.E.: *New Results in Linear Filtering and Prediction Theory*, in: Journal of Basic Engeneering, Vol. 83, 1961, p. 95 – 107

[36] Kalman, R.E.: *Identificability and Model Sleection in Econometrics*, in: Hildenbrand, W. (ed.): *Advances in Econometrics*, Cambridge Univertity Press 1982, p. 169 – 207

[37] Keynes, J.M.: *The General Theory of Employement, Interest and Money*, London 1936

[38] Kirchen, A.: *Schätzung zeitveränderlicher Strukturparameter in ökonometrischen Prognosemodellen*, Frankfurt/Main (Athenäum) 1988

[39] Kiy, W.: *Ein disaggregiertes Prognosesystem für die Bundesrepublik Deutschland*, Lecture Notes in Economics and Mathematical Systems Vol. 224, Berlin, Heidelberg etc. (Springer) 1984

[40] König, H. (Hrsg.): *Wachstum und Entwicklung der Wirtschaft*, Köln, Berlin 1968

[41] Krelle, W.: *Investition und Wachstum*, Jahrbücher für Nationalökomomie und Statistik, 176, 1964, p. 1 ff.

[42] Krelle, W.: *Beeinflußbarkeit und Grenzen des Wirtschaftswachstums*, Jahrbuch für Nationalökonomie und Statistik 178, 1965, p. 3 ff.

[43] Krelle, W.: *Marx als Wachstumstheoretiker*, in: Ifo-Studien, 16. Jahrgang 1970

[44] Krelle, W., Fleck, M. and Quinke, H.: *Gesamtwirtschaftliche Auswirkungen einer Ausweitung des Bildungssystems*, Tübingen (Siebeck) 1975

[45] Krelle, W., Frerich, W. and Kübler, K.: *Ökonometrische Input-output-Modellanalysen und -Prognosen*, in: Seetzen, Krengel, v. Kortzfleisch: *Makroökonomische Input-Output-Analysen und dynamische Modelle zur Erfassung technischer Entwicklungen*, Basel etc. (Birkhäuser) 1971, p. 35 ff.

[46] Krelle, W. and Palaschke, D.: *A General Demand System*, Zeitschrift für Nationalökonomie 41, 1981, p. 233 ff.

[47] Krelle, W.: *Technischer Fortschritt und Wachstum*, in: Bombach, Gahlen, ott (Hrsg.): *Technologischer wandel – Analyse und Fakten*, Tübingen (Siebeck) 1986, p. 89 ff.

[48] Krelle, W.: *Long-Term Flucuations of Technical progress and Growth*, in: Zeitschrift für die gesamte Staatswissenschaft Vol. 143, no. 3, 1987, p. 379–401

[49] Krelle, W.: *Theorie des wirtschaftlichen Wachstums.* 2. Aufl., Berlin, Heidelberg (Springer) 1988

[50] Krelle, W.: *A Simplified Theory for the Long-Term Cycle of Degree of Activity*, in: Krelle (ed.). *The Future of the World Economy*, Berlin, Heidelberg etc. (Springer) 1989a, p. 31 ff.

[51] Krelle, W.: *Growth, Decay and Structural Change*, in Krelle (ed.): *The Future of the World Economy*, Berlin, Heidelberg, New York (Springer), 1989b, p. 3–39

[52] Krelle, W.: *The Driving Forces of Economic Growth and Structural Change*, in: Hackl, Andres, Westlund (ed.): *Economic Structural Change*, Berlin, Heidelberg etc. (Springer), 1991, p. 283 ff.

[53] Krelle, W.: *The Spirit of Enterprise as Driving Force of Technical Progress*, in: Sadowski (ed.): *Entrepreneurial Spirits*, Wiesbaden (Gabler), 2001, p. 31 ff.

[54] Kübler, K.: *Ein disaggregiertes Prognosesystem für die BRD*, 2. Die Unternehmenssektoren, Meisenheim (Anton Hain), 1977, p. 41 ff.

[55] Mankiw, N.G.: *Principles of Economics*, Fort Worth, Philadelphia etc (The Dryden Press), 1998

[56] Marx, K.: *Das Kapital*, Band I–III, edited by Hans-Joachim Lieber and Benedikt Kautsky, Stuttgart 1962 and 1963

[57] Meade, J.E.: *A Neo-Classical Theory of Economic Growth*, London 1961, Revised Edition 1962

[58] Meadows, Dennis, Meadows, Donatella, Zahn, E., Milling, P.: *Die Grenzen des wachstums*, Bericht des Clubs of Rome zur Lage der Menschheit, Hamburg 1973

[59] Nakamura, Sh.: *An Inter-Industry Translog Model of Prices and Technical Change for the West German Economy*, Lecture Notes in Economics and mathematical Systems, Vol. 221, Heidelberg, New York, Tokyo (Springer) 1984

[60] Niehaus, J.: *Economic Growth with two Endegeneous Factors*, Quarterly Journal of Economics 77, 1963, p. 349 ff.

[61] Nordhaus, W.D.: *Invention, Growth and welfare: A Theoretical Treatment of technological Change*, Cambridge (Mass.) 1969

[62] Pasinetti, L.: *A Amthematical Formulation of the Ricardian System*, Review of Economic Studies XXVII, 1959/60, p. 78 ff.

[63] Pasinetti, L.: *Rate of Profit and Income Distribution in Relation to the Rate of Economic Growth*, Review of Economic Studies 29, 1962, p. 267 ff.

[64] Phelps, E.: *The Golden Rule of Accumulation: A Faible for Growthmen*, American Economic Review, 51, 1961, p. 638 ff.

[65] Phelps, E.: *Substitution, Fixed Proportions, Growth and Distribution*, International Economic Review, 4, 1963

[66] Quinke, H.: *Gesamtwirtschaftlich optimale Ausweitung des Ausbildungssystems*, Diss. Bonn 1979

[67] Ramser, H.J.: *Technischer Fortschritt, Wachstum und Beschäftigung: Ein einfaches Modell*, in: Henn, Rudolf: *Technologie, Wachstum und Beschäftigung*, Festschrift für Lothar Spät, Berlin, heidelberg etc. (Springer) 1987, p. 779 ff.

[68] Ricardo, D.: *The Principles of Political Economy and Taxation*, London, New York 1962

[69] Samuelson, P.A.: *A Theory of Induced Invention Along Kennedy-Weizäcker-Lines*, Review of Economics and Statistics 47, 1965, p. 343 ff.

[70] Sato, R. and Beckmann, M.: *Neutral Inventions and the Production Function*, Review of Economic Studies 35, 1968, p. 57 ff.

[71] Scherer, F.M.: *Inter-Industry Technology Flows and Productivity Growth*, in Review of Economics and Statistics 64, 1982, p. 627 ff.

[72] Schleicher, H.: *Bestimmungsgründe der sektoralen Produktivitätsentwicklung*, Göttingen 1984

[73] Smith, A.: *An Inquiry into the Nature and Causes of the WEALTH OF NATIONS*, London 1776, New Edition, revised, corrected and improved, Edingburgh 1872

[74] Solow, R.M.: *A Contribution to the Theory of Economic Growth*, Quarterly Journal of Economics 70, 1956, p. 65 ff.

[75] Solow, R.M.: *Investment and Technical Progress*, in: J.K. Arrow, S. Karlin, P. Suppes (Hrsg.): *Mathematicla methods in the Social Sciences*, Stanford, California 1960

[76] Solow, R.M., Tobin, J., von Weizsäcker, C.Chr., Yaari, M.: *Neoclassical Growth with Fixed Factor Proportions*, Review of economic Studies, 33, 1966

[77] Steindl, J.: *Random Process and the Growth of the Firm. A Study of Pareto Law*, London (Griffin) 1965

[78] Stoneman, P.: *The Economic Analysis of Technological Change*, New York 1983

[79] Taubmann, P.: *The Relative Influence of Inheritable and environmental Factors and the Importance of Intelligence in Earnings Functions*, in: Krelle and Shorrocks (ed.): *Personal Income Distribution*, Amsterdam, Oxford, New York 1978, p. 381 ff.

[80] Uzawa, H.: *Neutral Inventions and the Stability of Growth Equilibrium*, Review of economic Studies, 28, 1960/61, p. 117 ff.

[81] Uzawa, H.: *On a Two-Sector Model of Economic Growth*, Review of Economic Studies 29, 1962, p. 40 ff.

[82] Uzawa, h.: *On a Two-Sector Model of Economic Growth: II*, Review of Economic Studies 30, 1963, p. 105 ff.

[83] Varian, H.R.: *Intermediate Microeconomics*, New York, London (Norton), 5th ed. 1999

[84] Von Weizsäcker, C.Chr.: *Wachstum, Zins und optimale Investitionsquote*, Tübingen 1962

[85] Von Weizsäcker, C.Chr.: *Zur ökonomischen Theorie des technischen Fortschritts*, Göttingen 1966

CHAPTER 5
The Theory of the Government

5.1 Introduction

There are decisions which refer to the community as a whole (e.g. the building of long distance roads, the monetary system, the military system, the system of customs) and others which may be left to the individuals. The government may be a large institution with many divisions and departments with different responsibilities and great power on the activities of the individuals such that their liberty is very much restricted. But the government may also be a relatively small organization with very restricted power which gives much liberty to the individuals. There is a system of rules (written or not) called constitution which determines the power and the organizations of the government and the way how the deciding personalities in the government are selected.[1] The constitution is supposed to be valid for a long time (in the German constitution ("Grundgesetz") the essential characteristics of a democracy are supposed to be valid "forever", see "Grundgesetz", art. 79 III). Actually, the historical constitutions changed substantially in time, and this change is the answer of the society to changes in the economic and social situation and of the experience on the shortcomings of the old constitution. Here lies the connection of economics and the constitutional law.

The "normal" decisions of the government in the form of acts and statutes lie within the limits of the constitution and may be revised.

In the following we shall first present an overview on the historical development of the technologies and constitutions and their relations. This is done in the next three sections which, from the perspective of the book, form three digressions which can be skipped by readers familiar with these subjects. Of course, there is a whole literature on the supreme power, on constitutional law, on government and related subjects. We shall sketch these ideas only in broad outline. Then we shall develop a theory on the long term formation of constitutions and finally we shall come to a theory of short term government decisions and of the organizations of the government.

---

[1] "Government" in the sense as this word is used in this chapter corresponds much more to the word "Regierung" in German. The latter denotes the ministries and the parliament and their equivalences on the local level. In the sense we use the word "government" here, it comprises also the legal side (the constitution and laws which are the result of the decisions of constitutional bodies) and the activities of organizations owned or established and run by the government. The German word "Staat" would cover the meaning of the following section. But the English word "State" has many meanings which have nothing to do with the content of this section (e.g. state of health, family state, state carriage et cetera). Thus, I decided to extend the meaning of the word "Government" to cover also the legal side of life in a society.

5.2 Digression 1: An Overview on the Development of Technology and Constitutions in the Last Millennium

The constitution of a society depends on the economic and social state at the time when the constitution was fixed by force or formed by agreement and practice. We start with the *state of peasants and artisans* around 1000 years ago. The technology at that time consisted essentially of knowledge how to grow corn, how to domesticate animals and how to manufacture simple objects of daily use. The society was formed by a rather large number of independent tribes or counties of small size, comprising a relatively small number of families the wealth of which consisted mostly in the size and the quality of the land which they owned. The constitution regulated the power of the chief relative to the power of the single persons and the succession of leadership when the chief died.[2] The simplest way to regulate the succession was to give the power to the descendants of the old chief. The income of the chief consisted in the tributes of the subordinates: the more subordinates, and this meant: the larger the territory, the higher its income. Under these conditions the constitution gave almost all power to the chief in order to strengthen his capacity to organize the group in defense against attacks of neighboring groups and (or) to organize it for own attacks on other groups. Since the own income depended on the size of land and the number of inhabitants it is clear that these were a high inducement to wage war against the neighbors. This refers to all classes of the society. The local nobleman assaults the castle of his neighbor, one chief tries to defeat the other. This is a (simplified) picture of the *Feudal System*. Hobbes expresses this as follows (Leviathan, p. 61) "...Germany, being anciently, as all other countries were in their beginning divided amongst an infinite number of little lords, or masters of families, that continually had wars one with another..." The number of independent political units declined gradually since the small ones had in the long run no chance against the larger ones. The history-books of Germany, France and Great Britain and other nations are full of details on these permanent wars.

The consequence of this war "of everybody against everybody" was the recurring destruction of castles, villages and towns, the devastation of fields, the regression of population in the areas of war, the low level of the education of people, also in the nobility, where fighting and hunting played the first role and reading and writing was left to the clergy.

After some time it became clear, first for some few independent thinkers, philosophers and (or) theologians that this is not an optimal organization

[2] The designation of the chief of these small independent communities differs in time and from nation to nation (baron, count, earl, duke, prince, commander, leader, chief) and similarly for ecclesiastical units. For simplicity we speak mostly of chiefs or noblemen.

of a society. Thomas Aquinas[3] and others tried to change the result within the existing order by establishing moral rules also for the chief of a political unit[4] and for persons in business[5] - but in vain. The restraints of the system overruled all appeals on a "moral" behavior of a prince. This reality was considered by Machiavelli[6] who explained how a prince must behave in this system to succeed, and this was far away from any sort of morality. There were some philosophers who advocated the more or less absolute power of *one* sovereign instead of many. I only mention *Jean Bodin*[7] in France and *Thomas Hobbes*[8] in England to name only two of them. They conceived a constitutional

[3] Thomas Aquinas (1225-1274) "De Regimine Principum", "Summa Theologica" and other books.

[4] Thomas stated that the aim of a society is not the virtue of its members as such but the leading of the citizen to God. A virtuous life is a method to achieve that. The welfare of the community is more important than the welfare of a single person. This is why it is sometimes accepted that a single person gets worse if this serves the welfare of the community. The monarchy is the most reasonable form of government. But the subjects of an unjust ruler have not only the right of resisting unjust laws, but they have also the right to depose such a ruler. These are some statements from "De Regimine Principum".

[5] In "Summa Theologica" Thomas put up some moral demands for business men: not to take interest on loans except in special cases, not to sell a commodity above its value. The price of a commodity should correspond to the "quantitas valoris" which is measured by the expenses of money and labor (expensae at labores). This gives the inner value (valor intrinsicus) of a commodity which in turn conformes to the just price (justum pretium). These are only some extracts from the moral (and religious) demands of Thomas.

[6] For Machiavelli (1469-1527), the essence of a state is the organization and the execution of power, irrespective of moral or juridical restraints.

[7] Jean Bodin (Bodinus, 1530-1596) derived the rights of the ruler from own divine rights ("dei gratia"), independent of the church. He proclaimed the sovereignty of the state, but with limitations which follow from religion and from natural law.

[8] Thomas Hobbes' (1588-1679) book "Leviathan" (1651) is the main source of his ideas on natural law. "Leviathan" is the name of a life threatening monster in the Old Testament (e.g. Jes. 27,1; Ps. 74,14 and passim). This monster is the state. But without the state there would be a continuous war of "everybody against everybody" – to the disadvantage of everybody. Thus the state is formed as a way out of this situation. The basic idea is that all citizen give up their natural authority to one man, the sovereign, who gets the absolute power by this fictitious covenant. "Covenants, without the sword, are but words, and of no strength to secure a man at all... If there be no power erected,... every man will, and may lawfully rely on his own strength ... And in all places where man have lived by small families, to rob and spoil one another has been a trade, and so far from being reputed against the law of nature, that the greater spoils they gained, the greater was their honor" (Leviathan, p. 109). Tribal ethics like this exist also today. The Pashtuns (a tribe in Afghanistan) who are very militant have the saying: "Me against my brother, my brother and me against our cousins, we and our cousins against the enemy", see "The New Yorker", Dec. 3, 2001, p. 61.

After the covenant (i.e. after the foundation of a state) the ruler is absolute ("No man that has sovereign power can justly be put to death, or otherwise in any manner by

order where according to Hobbes the central government, personified by the king, has the "sovereign power", i.e. the monopoly of the use of force. The sovereign himself stands above all laws, he is "legibus absolutus"; this defines absolutism. In order to get rid of the permanent wars, all subjects give up their original right on regulating all issues and controversies themselves by means which they choose. According to this *new constitutional order called absolutism* there is only one sovereign (we may call him: the king) which regulates all conflicts by order as he likes it, and everybody has to obey these orders (which may be given in the form of laws). Louis XIV characterized this conception of government by the famous sentence: "L'état c'est moi". The economic organization of absolutism of this time is called "merkantilism". The government should regulate exports and imports in such a way that the value of exports exceeded the value of imports as much as possible. This yields a positive balance of payments which results in a maximal inflow of gold (or an equivalent inflow of foreign currency). Thus a steady increase of the amount of gold at the disposal of the sovereign made him (and thus the society) rich and powerful. He could build up an army or a navy in a relatively short time, because he had the money to build the ships and to hire the soldiers. This implies also a regulation of production and prices such that the production of export commodities was promoted whereas the imports of commodities restrained, e.g. by raising high import duties. To exploit colonies was another source of income.

These are only some examples of the regulations at that time which are based on wrong economic theories. But the loss of liberty in many fields was at least as important: no liberty of expression, no equality of all citizens at the court, no influence on the decisions of the government and so on. Absolutism did not care for the well-being of the single citizen. It identified the person on the top of the state with the subjects at the bottom – not to speak of the economic errors of that time which measured the success of an economic policy by the accumulation of gold by means of foreign trade.

Absolutism surely abolished the state of permanent war of one head of a small territory against his neighbors (though at relatively high cost: the local authorities fought bravely for their independence; the ruines of many castles e.g. in Southern France destroyed to enforce absolutism in France are witnesses

---

his subjects punished", Leviathan, p. 116). This absolute power includes also the right to decide on opinion and doctrines. There is no freedom of the press (The sovereign may "judge of what opinions and doctrines are averse, and what conducing to peace ... and shall examine the doctrines of all books before they be published", Leviathan, p. 116). Hobbes also rejects the idea of a division of power which was later considered as essential for a constitution, see John Locke ("Two treatises on government", 1690) and Charles de Montesquieu ("De l'esprit des lois", 1748). But Hobbes thinks otherwise: The right of judicature "is annexed to the sovereignty, that is to say, of hearing and deciding all controversies which may arise concerning law, either civil or natural; or concerning fact" (Leviathan, p. 117).

of these struggles till now). But absolutism did not induce the king to act in the interest of his subjects. Selfish and reckles behavior of chiefs of small territories under feudalism was now translated into this type of behavior on a large scale. And probably the degree of selfishness and recklessness even increased if *Lord Acton* is right who stated: "Power tends to corrupt, and absolute power corrupts absolutely". And there is still another point: Under feudalism a person could escape from the power of a small ruler; under absolutism this was much more difficult.

The negative experiences with this type of constitution as far as the liberty of the citizen, their economic situation and the use of taxes and tariffs are concerned led to heavy criticism by some philosophers and economists. I only mention *Jean-Jacques Rousseau*[9], *John Locke*[10] and *Adam Smith*[11] but there were many others involved in this fight against absolutism. The idea of equal natural rights of men as formulated in the "Déclaration des droits de l'homme et du citoyen" of 1789 spread in the society as well as a new conception of the role of the government. Meanwhile – still under absolutism – a new type of economy developed: the *industrial* one based on the division of labor and on technical progress. This change of the technology had far reaching consequences and therefore was rightly called: industrial revolution. The new state of the economy led to a new science called economics. The leading scholars of the new science came to the conclusion that all state interventions in the

---

[9] Jean-Jacques Rousseau (1712-1778). From his many publications we refer to his book "Contract Social". He starts with the assumption that a person in a "natural social environment" is, as a rule, goodnatured and reasonable. Nevertheless a government is necessary, which must be strong and which constitutes the sovereign. But the sovereign is the population in its entirety. In a fictitious "Contract Social" the citizen transfers part of his natural right to this sovereign. Thus the foreign rule in absolutism is substituted by the autocracy of all citizen in a democracy. Each person remains free as in the state without contract social because he obeys only those laws which he has agreed upon as citizen.

[10] John Locke (1632-1704). We consider only his "Two Treatises on Government". Though he maintains the conception of a "Contract Social" along the lines of Hobbes and Rousseau he fights against absolutism. The government should protect the life and the property of the subjects. Its actions (limited by these goals) must respect the natural rights of man. If it does not do that each citizen has the right of resistance. In order to prevent clashes like that, the supreme power should be split up among different institutions which control themselves mutually. This is now realized in all democratic states: the executive power, the legislature and the judicature are exercised by different and to a large degree independent institutions.

[11] Adam Smith (1723-1790) was the "father of classical economics". With his book "Inquiry into the Nature and Causes of the Wealth of Nations" (1776) he started economics as a science. From our point of view the most important idea is that the driving force of economic activity is the natural motive of man to improve upon its situation which by itself improves the situation of the nation. Thus the government should not interfere in normal economic affairs – a proposition which would reduce the power of the government substantially.

economy are counterproductive: the economy, if left free, finds by itself an optimal state. These liberal ideas in connection with the social and economic consequences of the industrial revolution (which made capital to the most important factor of production instead of land and thus created a new social strata: the citizens (or capitalists)), these liberal ideas led to the French Revolution and to the fights for constitution and democracy in the 19th century in other parts of Europe. Finally, a new type of constitution emerged[12], the third one in our classification which we may call the *democratic constitution.* It is the prevailing type of constitution under industrialism in "western" societies now. Of course, these constitutions differ from country to country but there are some common features which may be formulated as follows:

1. The people of the community are the last source of power.

2. There are a lot of basic rights of people which comprise freedom of religion, freedom of the press, right of assembly, freedom of association, guarantee of property and other freedoms and guarantees. This restricts the actions of the government and defends the individual against the government.[13]

3. The basic structure of the government is also fixed in the constitution: the organization of the legislative body in one or two chambers, their way of election, the election and responsibilities of the president (or the duties of the king, if there is one), the formation and the power of the central, regional and local governments.

4. The organization of jurisdiction which is independent of the government and controls the observance of the constitution by the government (this follows the idea of *John Locke* (and later *Montesquieu*) who recommended the division of the state power in different independent bodies which should control each other).

5. The organization of other institutions like the armed forces, the police, the schools, the universities and finally

6. The way of financing these state activities.

It is interesting to note that the democratic constitutions contain a long list of rights of a person but no equivalent list of duties. This is explained here by the origin of these constitutions: the fight against the absolute power of the head of the state.

---

[12] I leave out the communist systems which in this classification are a variant of absolutism: instead of the king the polit-bureau had the absolute power.

[13] This shows that the democratic constitutions originated from the fight against absolutism.

This long-term change of constitutions is a special case of a general theory of learning. After a specific type of constitution lasted for a long time, the disadvantages and faults of this regulation of public affairs become more and more visible and considerable. In economic terms: the actual income per capita stayed more and more behind the theoretically possible one under another constitution. Man learns by experience: the next type of constitution avoids the faults of the former one but possibly creates new problems. The democratic constitutions as we know them today will not make an exception. It is still too early to see the shortcomings beyond doubt (these types of constitutions under industrialism exist only since 200 years at certain nations, at others they are just newly established). As shortcomings one may state a tendency of giving a veto-power against changes to each individual or small groups of individuals, and there is no progress which does not hurt some individual interests. This retards or even stops technical progress, a disadvantage for all future generations. Technical progress benefits the whole economy with the exception of those people who earned their money in the declining trades.[14] In an allegory one could describe the situation as that of a group of travelers who want to ascend the highest mountain in this range. They stand on the top of a smaller mountain and see the top of a much higher mountain in some distance. But there is a steep canyon between the two mountains. The group has to pass through a "valley of tears" before reaching the "land of promise". There are some people who are afraid of the stress, others who feel that they cannot make it. Both will try to convince their comrades that the top of the smaller mountain is also a nice place, with a good view. Why take the effort to proceed to a still higher mountain?

There are also other problems with this type of constitution. The power of trade unions prevents a wage rate which yields full employment. The way of selecting and electing the members of the parliament favors opportunism and short term decisions according to public feeling and to neglect the long term repercussions. There is a tendency to shield groups from the impact of technical progress by stopping it. One may continue that way. But it is still too early to formulate a convincing alternative to the democratic constitutions as we know them today. In economic terms: the loss of actual GDP per capita due to this type of constitution compared to the possible ones under another type of (or a variant of the present) constitution is not that large to form a movement to change the present constitution.

---

[14] There is no technical progress without reducing or even eliminating certain economic activities: the railways eliminated the trade of the waggoners, the mechanical textile mills eliminated the weavers trade, the steam-engine mills eliminated the windmills, the steam ships substituted the sailing-vessels and so on. Everybody who earned his money in a declining business ran into severe economic problems if he could not change his profession and if he did not get help from the society.

This long-term repercussion of the economic consequences of a constitution on the change of the constitution is the main link between economics and jurisprudence as far as the government is concerned.

Fig. 5.1 shows in a symbolic way the development of technology and types of constitutions as a function of time. The agricultural-manufactural technology was accompanied by the feudal system and later by absolutism. Under absolutism the industrial revolution started. Absolutism was not immediately abolished but survived in the form of dictatorship under the communist or nationalist flag. But it got a superior competitor in the form of democracy. In the following we shall explain these constitutional changes by economic incentives as a learning process: the shortcomings of a constitution as revealed in its execution yield attempts to correct this by another type of constitution. Later we shall show this in more detail.

5.3 Digression 2: An Overview on the Relations of the Status of Agriculture and Handicraft and the Constitutions of Feudalism and Absolutism

The technologies known in a certain region form the base of the existence of the citizens and thus also the base of the different constitutions. But there is not a one to one relation between technology and constitutions: one technology may be compatible with different constitutions. In our degree of abstraction we may discern from the year 1000 up to now 2 different types of technologies: the agricultural and manufactural one which rests on the technology of farming and handicraft, and the industrial one which rests on the use of science in production and takes advantage of the division of labor. In this period there were 3 types of constitutions: feudalism, absolutism and democracy. Fig. 5.1 shows the temporal predominance of these technologies and constitutions in Europe.

In this section we describe the state of agriculture and manufacturing by a simplified model which allows to state the reasons for transition from one type of constitution to another one i.e. from feudalism to absolutism. This sheds some light on the relation of economics and public law. With industrialism started an absolutely new era. There was no great difference between the technology at the time of the roman empire and the time of *Louis XIV* in France and king Frederic II in Prussia. Technical progress was slow in this time and could be neglected without great error. The conditions of life of *Goethe* (1749-1832) were not very different from those of *Horaticus Flaccus* (65-8 before J.Chr.). But the industrial revolution changed everything substantially such that our conditions of life are incomparable to those of *Goethe*.

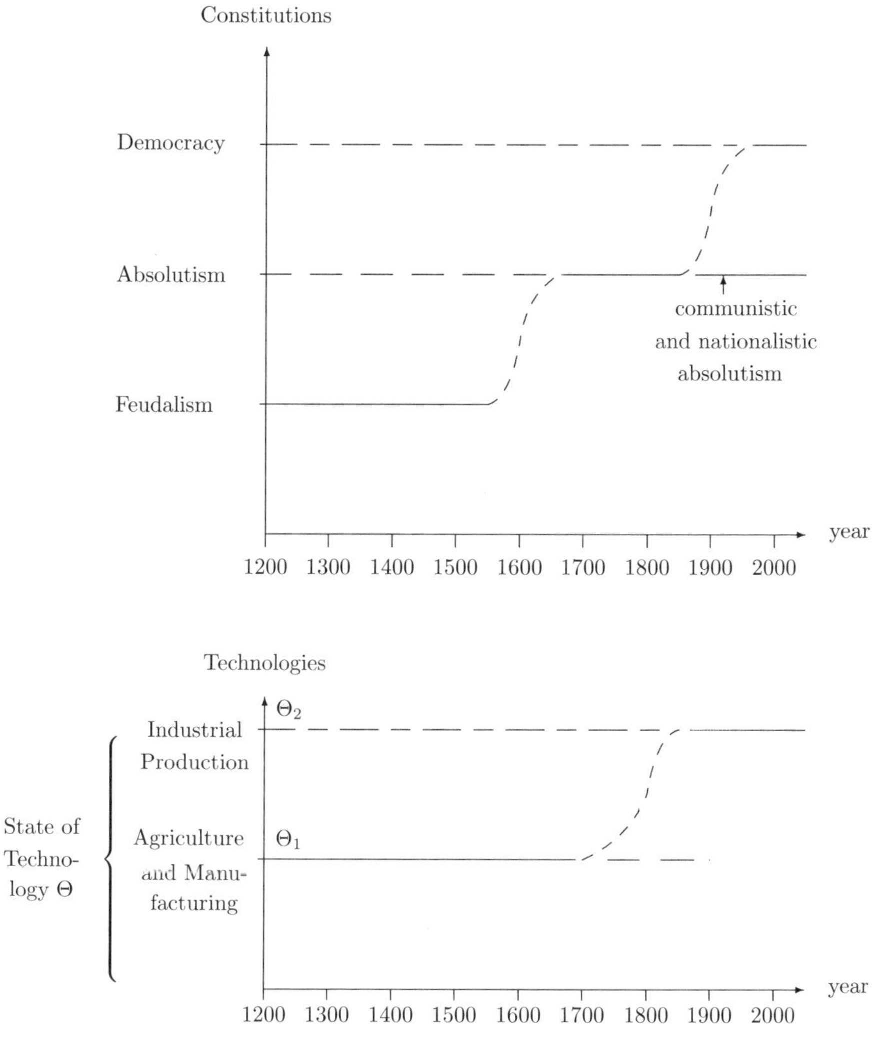

Figure 5.1. Historical Development of Technologies and Constitutions

In a *technology of agriculture and handicraft* without technical progress land and labor are the only factors of production to speak of. There is a fixed relation between the number of persons necessary to cultivate a given amount of land and the size of the land. More people will not increase the product, but less people would reduce it proportionally – a simplifying assumption, which facilitates notations. The "superfluous" population has to be fed anyway if they stay in the country whether they live at the farm or in town or whether they enter in the service of a nobleman or join the clergy. If the agricultural or manufactured product per capita is larger than necessary to sustain a family with two children, there is the possibility to deprive the producer of the "surplus" product and use it for building castles or churches, for establishing military power in the form of gathering a group of knights or (later) lansquenets, to be used for defending against attacks of neighbouring noblemen or for own assaults, for hiring of lackeys, grooms, huntsmen, rangers, gamekeepers, sometimes also musicians and poets – whatever the nobleman likes.

The *feudal system* allocates land and people living on that land to a nobleman and his heirs (or to institutions of the church) with only few obligations. The most important one was the obligation to send warriors or fighters to the sovereign (say the king) if he asks for this type of help in a war. In the beginning of this system there were many independent small territories and estates of this kind, but gradually the number diminished since "the bigger fishes devoured the smaller ones".

One may formulate the inherent regularities of this combination: agricultural technology and the feudal system as follows.

Consider the situation of a nobleman at that time. The necessary population POP^{nec} to cultivate the agricultural land ($= LAND$) is proportional to the size of the land:

$$POP^{nec} = b \cdot LAND, \qquad b > 0$$

The actual population is $POP > POP^{nec}$ (at that time there was an excess of birth). The number $POP^{(spl)} = POP - POP^{nec}$ of people is not needed for production but forms a surplus population which must be nourished from product Y of the land. This product Y is a function of the size of the land under control of the nobleman and the size of the population working on that land:

$$Y = F(LAND, POP).$$

For this production function we postulate the following properties:

Let $\overline{LAND}$ be the size of the land which is owned by a nobleman or tributary to him. Then: $POP^{nec} = b \cdot \overline{LAND}$

For $POP < POP^{nec}$ the product Y is proportional to POP:

$$Y = c \cdot POP \qquad c > 0,$$

for $POP \geq POP^{nec}$ the product Y stays constant: $Y = c \cdot POP^{nec} =: \bar{Y}$. Fig. 5.2a illustrates this case.

Now consider a second case. Let $P\bar{O}P$ be the size of the population under the domination of the nobleman whereas the size of the land is variable. The necessary land to employ this population in agriculture is proportional to the size of the population:

$$LAND^{nec} = \frac{1}{b} \cdot P\bar{O}P$$

For $LAND < LAND^{nec}$ the product Y is proportional to land:

$$Y = d \cdot LAND,$$

for $LAND \geq LAND^{nec}$ the product stays constant:

$$\hat{Y} = d \cdot LAND^{nec}$$

Fig. 5.2b illustrates this case.

We assume the existence of a surplus population (a realistic assumption for that time). The nobleman may take this surplus population into his service without affecting production. Of course he has to feed these people, but they had to be fed anyway. He must extract the necessary resources from the active population such that the net income of these subjects stays above the subsistence level. Let $SUBS$ be this level and T the maximal amount of products the nobleman may extract from his subjects. Now we get

$$T = Y - SUBS \cdot POP^{nec}.$$

Consider the case $POP \geq POP^{nec}$ and $LAND = L\bar{A}ND$ (that means: the case of a surplus population and a fixed size of land owned by the nobleman or tributary to him) and $c > SUBS$. Then we get from the above equation

$$T = b \cdot L\bar{A}ND(c - SUBS)$$

(since in this case $Y = c \cdot POP^{nec}, \quad POP^{nec} = b \cdot L\bar{A}ND$)

Thus the nobleman has a high inducement to extend his land. This interest is shared by the surplus population which he has taken into his service. Of course, the subjects who have to pay or deliver part of their product to the nobleman have the opposite interest. Thus we get a continuous conflict (often in the form of wars) between the noblemen who want to extend their territory and between a nobleman and his subjects on the size of the duties. This may be modeled as a war of everybody against everybody in the spirit of Thomas Hobbes which is to the disadvantage of almost everybody. Thus the feudal system as described above and the agricultural technology does not seem to be a good solution to the problem of social organization of the society under these conditions.

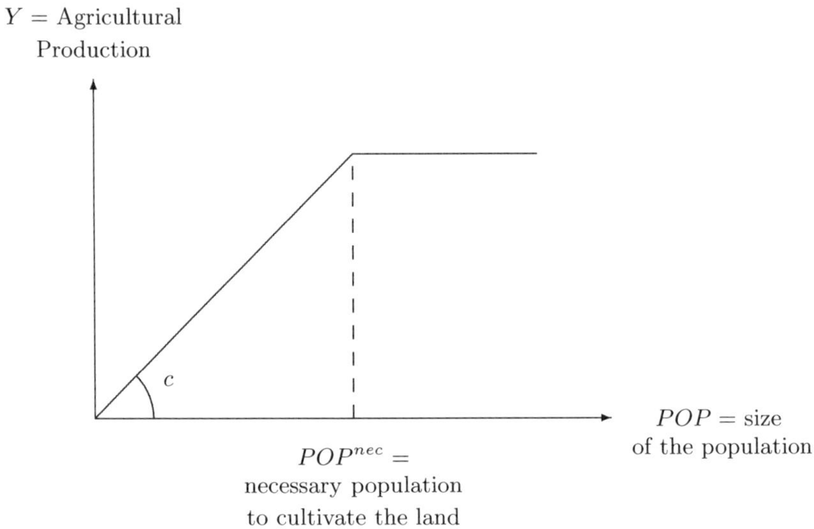

Figure 5.2a Agricultural Production Function: Land taken as constant, Population (= POP) variable

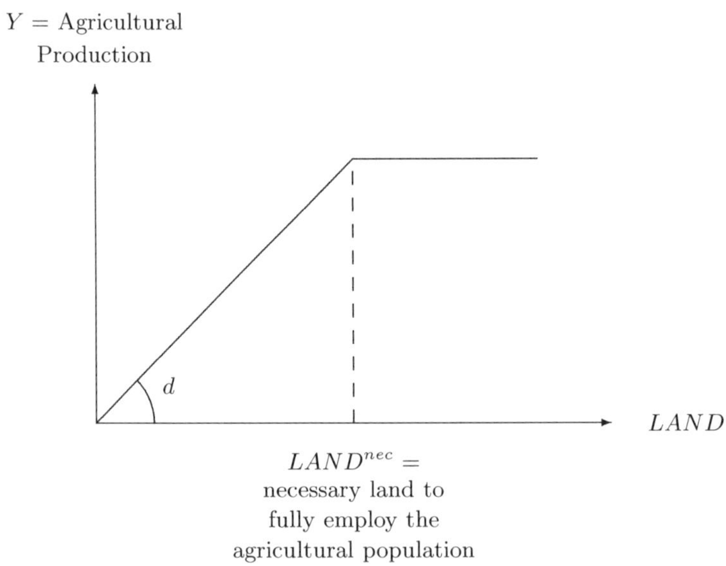

Figure 5.2b Agricultural Production Function: Population taken as constant, land (= $LAND$) variable

bank i (if we put other assets $OASS_{bi} = 0$):

$$W_{bi} + CR_{bi}(1 - \gamma) = BAL_{bi} - CA_{bi} - CA_{bi,CB} \tag{3.21}$$

In the following we first describe the decisions which determine the portfolio composition of W_{bi} (that means: we deal with the activities of the portfolio department of the bank). Afterwards we come to the activities of the credit department and of the department of general finance and organization.

3. The bank has to decide on *the additional amount of money* ΔW_{bi} which should go to *the portfolio department* (if positive) or which should be made available for other purposes by liquidating assets (if negative) such that for the planning period 0 $W_{bi,0} = W_{bi,-1} + \Delta W_{bi}$

4. The bank has to decide on the *general direction* of the *portfolio activities*, i.e. on the sets $\{A_i\}, \{B_i\} and \{C_i\}$ of the future composition of its assets. Should it more concentrate on the real estate business or give it up? Should it concentrate on certain capital stocks to get an influence in these firms or be on the safe side by appropriate risk dispersion and preferring securities to capital stock?

5. This implies (given the portfolio composition of the end of period -1) that the assets of the sets $\{\tilde{A}_i\}, \{\tilde{B}_i\}, \{\tilde{C}_i\}$ which are in the portfolio should be kept,

   assets in the sets $\{\hat{A}_i\}, \{\hat{B}_i\}, \{\hat{C}_i\}$ should be sold,
   assets in the sets $\{A_i^*\}, \{B_i^*\}, \{C_i^*\}$ should be bought

6. The bank decides on the number of people $L_{pf,bi}$ which are employed in the portfolio department of the bank[45]. The more persons are employed in the portfolio department the more insider information on the possible development of the firm or institution under consideration and on the opinion of other analysts can be assembled. One may assume that this would decrease the variance of estimation of the future development of the assets W_i under consideration and thus increase the proceeds from the portfolio. That means we assume that the board of the commercial

---

$\{B_i\}$ = set of securities in the portfolio of bank i
Similarly:

$$W_{LA,bi} = \sum_{j \in \{C_i\}} W_{LAj,bi}, \quad W_{LAj,bi} = LA_{j,bi} \cdot v_{LAj},$$

$\{C_i\}$ = set of real estates owned by the bank

[45] As in former sections we normalize labor such that a unit of labor equals the employment of one person. In this section we treat the professional composition of the labor force in a bank as given.

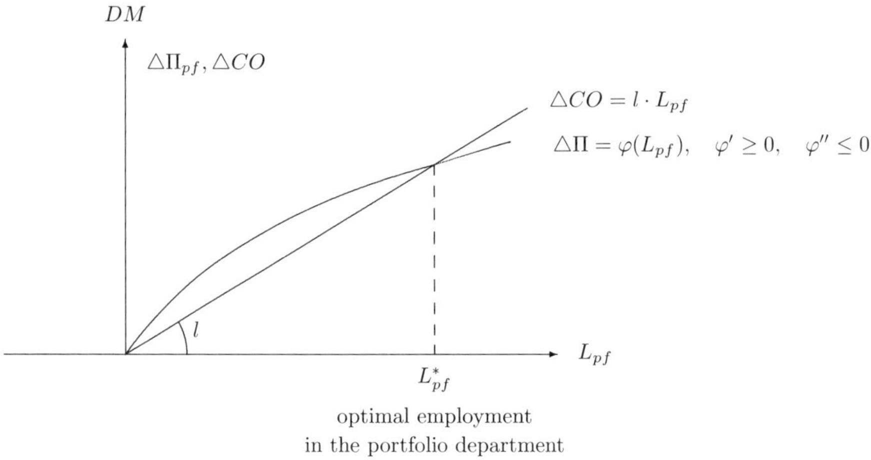

Figure 3.5. Employment in the Portfolio Department of a commercial bank i

bank will be able to estimate a function φ which relates the number of persons $L_{pf,bi}$ employed in the portfolio department of the bank per unit of the assets in real terms to the additional proceeds $\triangle\Pi_{pf,bi}$ from the better portfolio composition due to the larger man power in the portfolio department:

$$\triangle\Pi_{pf,bi} = \varphi(L_{pf,bi}), \quad \varphi' \geq 0, \quad \varphi'' \leq 0$$

The additional labor cost $\triangle CO(L_{pf,bi})$ are proportional to the size of this department: $\triangle CO(L_{pf,bi}) = l \cdot L_{pf,bi}$, where l is the average wage rate of the persons employed in this department.

Fig. 3.5 illustrates the situation. If the bank wants to extract as much money from the portfolio department as possible it must employ that amount $L_{pf,bi}$ of persons in this department such that the additional cost $\triangle CO(L_{pf,bi})$ equals the additional (expected) proceeds $\triangle\Pi_{pf,bi}$. In the case of Fig. 3.5 the optimal employment is indicated by L^*_{pf}.

7. The bank must decide on its conditional orders to the pertinent brokers, and that means: on the size of demand or supply of assets conditioned upon their price. The constraints up to this point leave room for different rules, see section 1.25. We follow the approach suggested there. The bank has to decide on what it thinks is the "right" price $\hat{v}$ of an asset, "right" in the sense that this will be the market price v to which the actual price would converge, after all information on the situation and future development of the firm or institution which issued the asset has become common knowledge — An asset A_i should be sold if $v_i > \hat{v}_i$, and a reasonable rule for the amounts supplied conditioned upon the

actual price v_i is:

$$A_i^s = \alpha(v_i - \hat{v}_i) \quad , \quad \alpha \geq 0 \tag{3.22}$$

A_i should be demanded if $v_i < \hat{v}_i$, and the conditioned demand is

$$A_i^d = \beta(\hat{v}_i - v_i) \tag{3.23}$$

If $v_i = \hat{v}_i$ the actual size of asset A_i in the portfolio should be preserved. There are limits for these rules: $A_i^s \leq \bar{A}_i$ where $\bar{A}_i$ is the total amount of assets A_i in the portfolio of the bank, and $A_i^d v_{Ai} \leq \bar{F}_i$, where $\bar{F}_i$ is the maximum amount of money to be spent for buying this asset. For more details and a graphical illustration, see section 1.25. In any case, the equations (3.22) and (3.23) including the constraints form the order to the broker who now may fix the price of the asset such that supply equals demand. The above rules define the sets of assets to be bought or sold.

8. We now come to the decisions concerning the credit department. Most important is the *maximum amount* $\overline{CR}_{bi}$ of *credits* which may be granted by bank i.

9. Second, and also very important, is the *rate of interest* $r_{CR,bi}$ the bank requires for its credits. The higher the rate of interest, the less clients will appear at the bank and ask for credits. But there is a lower limit for the rate of interest: it must be larger than the rates r_d and $\bar{r}$ which the bank has to pay for financing its credit operations and moreover cover the cost of running the bank. Fig. 3.6 illustrates the situation. Only rates of interest $r_{CR,bi}$ between 0.05 and 0.1 would yield a profit for the bank. This limits the rates of interest which the bank may charge for its credits.

10. The conditions $\hat{\kappa}_i = (t_{CR,i}, \sigma_{CR,i}, sec_i)$ which a prospective debtor has to fulfill to get the credit have to be fixed as well, where $t_{CR,i}$ is the time structure of repayment, $\sigma_{CR,i}$ the securities to be offered to the bank and sec_i the sector of the economy which bank i serves with credits. The more demanding these conditions are, the less agents will be able to fulfill them. Thus the demand for credits will decline when the bank aggravates these conditions.

11. As said in the introductory remarks, the bank has to establish an order of preference for possible debtors if the total demand for credits exceeds the maximum amount $\overline{CR}_{bi}$ which bank i has decided to grant. Let there be n applicants $a_{1i}, a_{2i}, \ldots, a_{ni}$ for credit. The bank has to order the applicants such that $a_{1i} \succeq a_{2i} \succeq \ldots \succeq a_{ni}$. Let CR_{ji}^d be the credit demand of agent j. Now the bank will grant credits to applicants in that

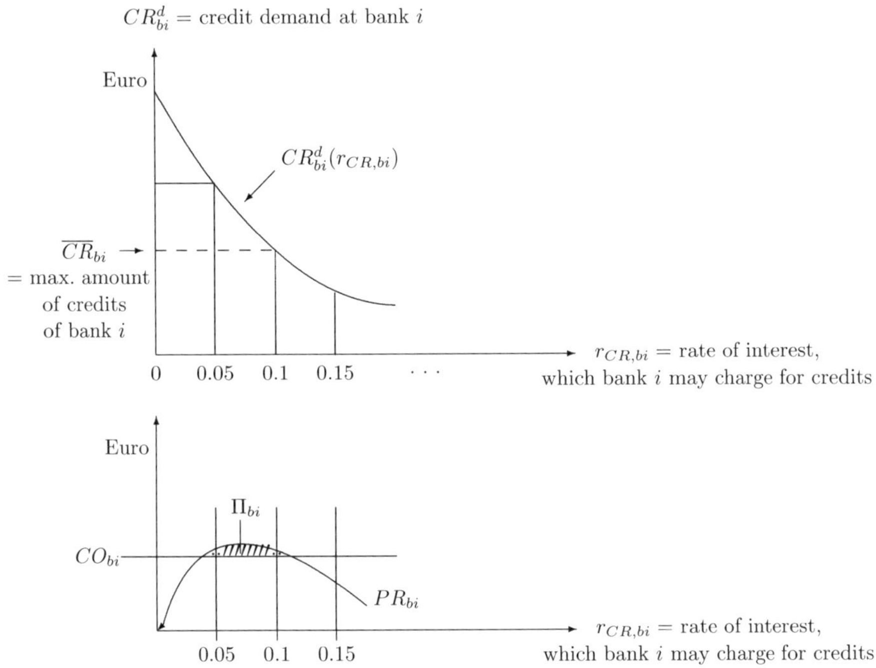

CO_{bi} = cost of running bank i

PR_{bi} = proceeds of bank i from credit operations = $CR_{bi} \cdot r_{CR,bi}$

Figure 3.6. Limits of the rate of interest a bank may charge

order, till its credit facilities are exhausted:

$$CR_{bi,n'} = \sum_{j=1}^{n'} CR_{ji}^{d} \tag{3.24}$$

such that $CR_{bi,n'} \leq \overline{CR}_{bi}$ and $CR_{bi,n'+1} > \overline{CR}_{bi}$.

The principles of ordering the applicants must also be decided upon (first come, first served or amount of securities offered or future prospects of the firms (if the agents are firms); we do not go into these details). At the end of the period the set $\{D\}$ of agents has received the credits. Equation (3.24) describes how the elements of $\{D\}$ are selected.

12. Furthermore, the bank has to decide on the *number* $L_{CR,bi}$ *of persons* in the *credit department* of the firm. The more persons of appropriate education are employed in the credit department, the more carefully the application for credits may be checked. This means that the order $a_{1i} \succeq \dots \succeq a_{ni}$ will be nearer to the real position and prospects of the applicants such that the proportion γ of credits which will not be repaid declines. The bank has to estimate the additional labor cost $l \cdot L_{CR}$ and the additional proceeds $\varphi(L_{CR})$ similarly as for the portfolio department. Fig. 3.5 may serve as illustration as well.

This terminates the list of decision variables of a commercial bank as far as the portfolio and credit departments of the bank are concerned. We now turn to decision variables which concern the department of general finance and organization.

A commercial bank is an organization which produces services with the same internal problems as an organization which produces commodities. The department of general finance and organization (for short called organization department) has to supervise and control the rank and file of the other two departments. There are $n_{io} = L^*_{CR,bi} + L^*_{pf,bi}$ persons to be supervised in the credit and in the portfolio department. This poses the same problems as analyzed in section 2.7 of this book. The control spans $s^k_{i1}, s^k_{i2}, \dots, s^k_{i,R-1}$ for supervisors of rank 1,2,..., $R-1$ in department $k \in$ {credit department, portfolio department} of bank i and the size $N^k_{i1}, \dots, N^k_{iR}$ of the staff assisting the supervisors of rank 1,..., R have to be decided upon. This determines the size of the organization department as far as the supervision of the two other departments is concerned. The same approach applies for the organization department itself, see section 2.7[46].

Till now only the size and the structure of the organization department is determined, that means: the number of heads at the different ranks has

[46] The formulas derived there are also valid for a commercial bank, if one cancels the index τ there which refers to the age of the machines which are operated by the workers in the commodity producing firms.

been counted. But similarly as in the commodity producing firms the control spans may be fixed according to different principles: persons of the same profession or of the same task or those working at adjacent locations may be comprised in the same group supervised by the same person of a higher rank. Let there be Γ_{i1}^k possibilities to group the workers of rank zero into control spans s_{i1}^k, similarly Γ_{i2}^k possibilities to group the supervisors of rang 1 into control span s_{i2}^k and so on. The quality $Q_{i1}^k, \ldots \;, Q_{iR}^k$ of the staff may be different as well as the quality $q_{i1}^k, \ldots \;, q_{iR}^k$ of the supervisors themselves[47]. Let $s_i = (s_{i1}^{CR}, \ldots, s_{i,R_1-1}^{CR}, s_{i1}^{pf}, \ldots, s_{i,R_2-1}^{pf}, s_{i1}^{org}, \ldots, s_{i,R_3-1}^{org})$ be the vector of all control spans of bank i,where $1 \leq s_{i\varrho}^k \leq 20$ is the largest possible control span; $\gamma_i = \{\Gamma_{i1}^{CR}, \ldots, \Gamma_{i,R_1-1}^{CR}, \ldots, \Gamma_{i,1}^{org}, \ldots, \Gamma_{i,R_3-1}^{org}\}$ where $\Gamma_{i\varrho}^k$ is the set of all possible permutations of employees of rank ϱ into control groups of size $s_{i\varrho}^{(k)}$[48].

[47] The "quality" of a person may be measured by appropriate indicators, e.g. by the relative number of faults in performing their task, by the time a supervisor or the staff needs to accomplish a task of a certain kind and others.

[48] A graphical illustration and a numerical example may be helpful to understand the approach. Let there be 4 persons of rank zero and 2 persons of rank 1 which are able to supervise two persons each that means: the control span is 2. This can be illustrated by the following figure:

possible allocation of persons 1,...,4 to supervisors I and II

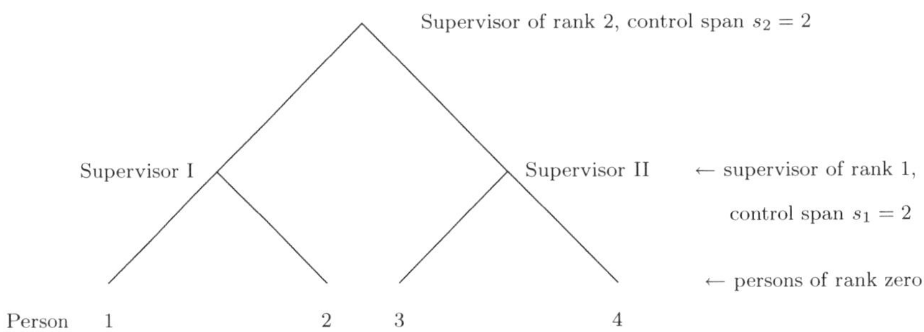

There are 6 possible assignments of persons of rank zero to supervisors of rank 1, if the control span is $s_1 = 2$. All combinations of allocating persons to supervisors are possible, generally. In our case there are six combinations listed in the following table:

Allocation of persons 1,...,4 to supervisors I and II

person	1	2	3	4					
is controlled	*I*	*I*	*II*	*II*	←	combination	1	=	γ_1
by supervisor	*II*	*I*	*I*	*II*	←	" "	2	=	γ_2
	II	*I*	*II*	*I*	←	" "	3	=	γ_3
	I	*II*	*I*	*II*	←	" "	4	=	γ_4
	I	*II*	*II*	*I*	←	" "	5	=	γ_5
	II	*II*	*I*	*I*	←	" "	6	=	γ_6

The management of the bank decides on the organization of the bank by choosing γ.

Let $N_i = (N_{i1}^{CR}, \ldots, N_{iR_1}^{CR}, \ldots, N_{i1}^{org}, \ldots, N_{iR_3}^{org})$ be the number of staff members for a supervisor of rank 1,...,R in department k[49], $0 \leq N_{i\varrho}^{k} \leq 10$ (say).

Similarly, let Q_i be the vector of the staffs of all ranks, where $0 \leq Q_{i\varrho}^{k} \leq 10$, q_i = vector of the quality of the supervisors of all ranks, where $0 \leq q_{i\varrho}^{k} \leq 10$, if 10 is the highest possible evaluation of a person or a staff. Of course, more able supervisors and higher qualified staff members are more expensive. In any case, the organizational structure ω_i of bank i is subject to the decision variables contained in the vector $\omega_i = (s_i, \gamma_i, N_i, Q_i, q_i)$.

The organization influences the maximum amount of credits $\overline{CR_i}$ the bank is able to grant, the percentage of "bad" loans and other characteristics of the bank such that the profits of the bank depend on it. But this is not easy to check and to quantify. We shall give an example later. As always in this book we only consider integers for all variables. Thus the bank has to choose between a finite number of alternatives. But, of course, not all feasible alternatives are considered. This would be a task which by far exceeds the intellectual capacity of a person and even if it would not, it would need much more time to analyze and judge the alternatives as would be available for that purpose. Only very few alternatives are considered by the members of the board of the bank as "essential" at the time when the decision has to be taken. The others may become essential eventually at later periods. A change in the personal composition of the directory and of the supervising council of the bank will also change the issues which are considered as "essential" at that time. The criteria of judgement of the alternatives are similar to the criteria of judging the performance of a commodity producing firm, see section 2.11 of this book. We repeat them here with the necessary changes:

- the profit Q of the bank
- the amount of credits CR granted by the bank
- the employment L
- the shareholder value SHV which depends (among others) on the distribution d of profits now and in later periods
- the risk R of bankruptcy
- the moral evaluation M of the choices ...

There might be other criteria too, but these seem to be the most important ones. All alternatives under consideration are judged and given integer "notes" between $-\bar{z}$ and $+\bar{z}$, $\bar{z} \geq 1$ by all members of the decisive bodies of the bank. They are condensed to an integer number which represents the "judgement

[49] For simplicity we assume that the number of members of the staff allocated to a supervisor of a certain rank is equal for all supervisors of the same rank.

of the board".[50] Let $V_{ij}(x_{ij}), \quad x_{ij} \in \{Q_{ij}, CR_{ij}, SHV_{ij}, R_{ij}, M_{ij}\}$ be the evaluation of a decision of the bank to move from an initial situation B_i to the situation B_{ij} by an appropriate variation of the decision variables. The relative importance $\alpha_{ij,x}$ of the different criteria has to be stated by the same board, where $\alpha_{ij,x \geq 0}, \quad \sum_{\kappa \in x} a_{ij,\kappa} = 1$. Now the evaluation of point B_{ij} is

$$\begin{aligned} V_{ij} &= \alpha_{ij,Q} V_{ij}(Q_{ij}) + \alpha_{ij,CR} \cdot V_{ij}(CR_{ij}) + \alpha_{ij,L} \cdot V_{ij}(L_{ij}) \\ &\quad + \alpha_{ij,SHV}(SHV_{ij}) + \alpha_{ij,R} V_{ij}(R_{ij}) + \alpha_{ij,M}(M_{ij}), \\ &\quad \text{cf. section 2.12.} \end{aligned}$$

3.9 The Secondary Inputs of a Commercial Bank

The secondary inputs of a commodity-producing firm are assumed to be proportional to the output of that firm and a function of the age of the machine which is used for production, see equation (3.6) in section 2.13 of this book. In a bank the secondary inputs are on the one hand related to the number of employees in the bank (each employee has to be equipped with office space and office equipment, and we do not make a great fault if we take that part as proportional to the number of employees); on the other hand, the bank needs secondary inputs proportioned to its fixed investment, which we called "land" and which comprises also buildings. Thus we may assume

$$SI_{ji} = b_{ji}^{(1)} \cdot n_i + b_{ji}^{(2)} \cdot LA_i$$

where n_i = number of persons in bank i; LA_i = "Land" owned by bank i. For the other notations, see section 2.3.

3.10 A Digression: Dubious Effectiveness of the Discount Policy of the Central Bank

In the year 2001 the Federal Reserve Bank in the US lowered the discount rate in several steps in order to overcome the weakness of the American economy. But these measures did not have a visible effect, and many economists were disappointed on the inflexibility of the economy in this respect. But from the point of view of economic theory it is easy to see that a lowering of the discount rate need not have a sizable effect on the interest rate r_{CR} the banks are charging for their loans and on the credits they are granting to the firms.

---

[50] For the way how this can be achieved, see section 1.3

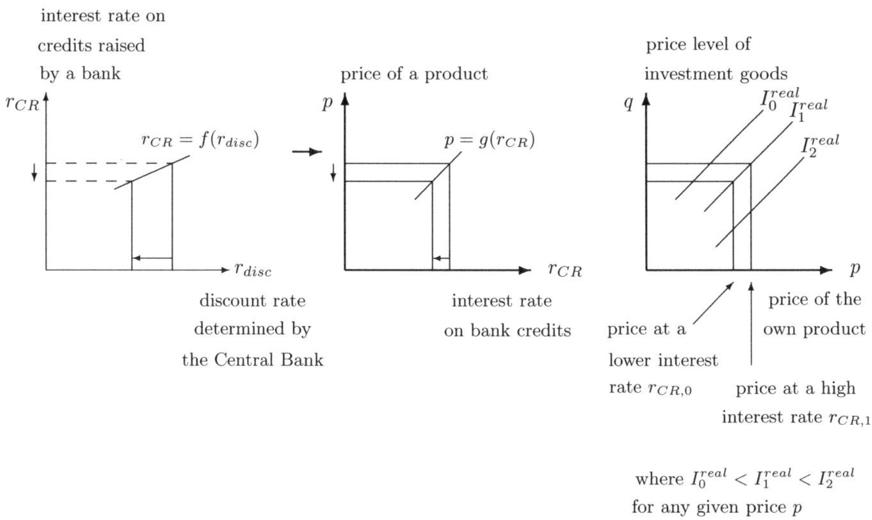

Figure 3.7. Almost no Effect of the Discount Policy on Investment

And also if the banks pass on the lowering of the interest rate to their customers, this need not have an effect on their investment policy and thus on production and employment. If the credit demand CR_{bi}^d of the firms at bank i is already larger than the credits CR_{bi} the bank is willing to grant and the same is true for all other banks, there is no incentive for a bank to follow the lower interest rate charged by the Central Bank. This would only increase the surplus demand on credits and lower the profits of the bank. Only if the credit demand falls short of the amount of credits the bank has decided to offer or if other banks which compete with bank i lower their interest rate and thus would draw off customers from bank i, there is an inducement to follow the low interest rate policy of the Central Bank. This may be the rule, in general. But this does not guarantee a higher investment and thus more employment. If the size of investment of a firm is not limited by the liquidity constraint but by the demand of the product the firm is producing and if this demand is rather rigid with respect to its price and the price of the product is rather insensitive to the rate of interest, the lowering of the discount rate has almost no effect on production and employment. Fig. 3.7 illustrates also another case. If real investment I^{real} of a firm depends on the ratio of the prices of investment goods to the price of the commodity the firm is producing (such that a decrease of the price of the investment goods at a constant price of the own product increases investment), and if the lowering of the interest rate affects all prices more or less proportionally, there will be no increase of investment by lowering the interest rate. The diagram on the right of Fig. 3.7 illustrates this case.

It shows the interest rate r_{CR} the private bank is charging as a function f of the discount rate r_{disc}, the price p of a product as a function g of the interest rate r_{CR} and the real investment I^{real} of a firm as a function of the price p of its product and of the prices q of investment goods. In this example rather large reductions of the discount rate have almost no effect on investment and thus on production and employment. The reason is simply that the reduction of the interest rate affects the prices of the investment goods and the price of the product which the firm is producing in a similar way such that the net effect on investment is not evident.

3.11 On the Near-Constancy of Some Coefficients in the Monetary Sector of the Economy

To show the near-constancy of some parameters which is supposed in sections 3.2-3.7 we use the statistics of the German monetary system[51]. We aggregated the balance sheets of the Commercial Banks and of the Central Bank from the more detailed version as published in the "Monatsberichte der Deutschen Bundesbank" to the following form:

I. Commercial Banks (= Monetäre Finanzinstitute, MFis)

A. Assets

1. Cash: CA_B (= Kassenbestand, Deutsche Bundesbank Monatsbericht (=MoBer) März 2001, p.20*)
2. Credits of MFis to banks + Credits of MFis to non-banks $= CR_B$ (= Kredite and Banken (= MFis) im Euro-Währungsgebiet + Kredite an Nicht-Banken (Nicht-MFis) im Euro-Währungsgebiet, see MoBer. März 2001, p.20*)
3. Accounts of the Commercial Banks at the Central Bank $= CA_{B,CB}$ (= Ist-Reserve, see MoBer. Oct. 1998, p.41* and MoBer. März 2001, p.42*)
4. All other assets (see MoBer. März 2001, p.20*)
5. Total balance account = all assets $= \quad BAL_B$ (= 1) + 2) + 3) + 4), see MoBer. März 2001, p.20*)

[51] For simplicity, we do not differ between bank notes and coins.

B. Liabilities:

1. Deposits at the Commercial Banks = DEP_B = deposits of banks in the Euro-area and deposits of non-banks in the Euro-area $= DEP_{B,B} + DEP_{B,nonB}$, see MoBer. März 2001. p.22*
2. Other deposits and debts and capital and reserves, see MoBer. März 2001, p.22*
3. Total balance account, = all liabilities = BAL_B (= 1) + 2), see MoBer. März 2001, p.22*)

II. Deutsche Bundesbank (= Central Bank (CB))

A. Assets

1. Gold and Claims on Gold, see MoBer. März 2001,p.16* $= G_{CB}$
2. Claims in foreign currency outside the Euro-Area, see MoBer. März 2001, p.16* $= FC_{CB}$
3. Claims on banks, due to monetary operations $= CL_{CB,B}$, see MoBer. März 2001, p.17*
4. Claims on the government $= CL_{CB,G}$, see MoBer. März 2001, p.17*
5. All other assets, see MoBer. März 2001, p.16* and 17*
6. Total assets = total balance account $= BAL_{CB} =$ 1) +2) +3) +4) +5)

B. Liabilities

1. Bank notes in circulation $= N_{CB}$, see MoBer. März 2001, p.18*
2. Accounts of the Commercial Banks at the Central Bank $= CA_{B,CB}$ (= Ist-Reserve, = Einlagen auf Girokonten einschl. Mindest-reserve-Gathered, see MoBer. März 2001, p.18*, p.42* and MoBer Oct. 98, p.41*)
3. Other liabilities + capital + reserves: see MoBer. März 2001, p.18* and 19*
4. Total balance account, = all liabilities $= BAL_{CB}$ =1) + 2) + 3)

Now we show that the reserve rate r, the cash rate s_B and the cash coefficient c_{nonB} of non-banks are approximately constant. For the comfort of the reader we reproduce the original figures from the balance sheets for years or months.

A

We show that $CA_{B,CB} \approx r^* \cdot DEP_B$, where $r^* = r \cdot \gamma$, γ =proportion of deposits at the commercial banks which are subject to the obligation to keep reserves at the Central Bank. Liabilities of commercial banks which are subject to reserve requirements = $DEP_{B,RES}$, see MoBer. Oct. 98, p.41* and MoBer. März 2001, p.42*. According to this definition, we have $DEP_B = DEP_{B,B} + DEP_{B,nonB}$. The figures are for 1991-1998 (always end-of-December-values, Mrd. DM):

$Year$	$DEP_{B,B}$	$DEP_{B,nonB}$	DEP_B	$DEP_{B,RES}$	$\gamma = \frac{DEP_{B,RES}}{DEP_B}$
1991	1365,7	2617,5	3983,2	1516,689	0,381
1992	1405,6	2743,6	4149,2	1734,654	0,418
1993	1556,3	2981,1	4538,1	1894,674	0,418
1994	1650,9	3082,2	4733,1	2007,710	0,424
1995	1761,5	3260,0	5021,5	2066,565	0,412
1996	1975,3	3515,9	5481,2	2201,464	0,402
1997	2195,6	3647,1	5842,7	2327,879	0,398
1998	2480,3	3850,8	6331,1	2576,889	0,407

Thus, γ varies around 0,4. We take that as trend value. In that case we get for r the following values:

$Year$	$CA_{B,CB}$	DEP_B	$0.4 \cdot DEP_B$	$r = \frac{CA_{B,CB}}{0.4 \cdot DEP_B}$
1991	75,044	3983,2	1593,28	0,0470
1992	86,360	4149,2	1659,68	0,0520
1993	60,365	4538,1	1815,24	0,0330
1994	44,377	4733,1	1893,20	0,0230
1995	37,337	5021,5	2008,60	0,0186
1996	39,522	5481,2	2192,48	0,0180
1997	41,721	4842,7	1937,08	0,0220
1998	46,432	6331,1	2532,44	0,018

The minimum reserve rates r_{min} have been kept constant since 1995 (see MoBer. März 2001 p.42*) at 2% for normal liabilities and 1,5% for saving deposits. Thus a value around 0,018 seems to be appropriate. It is rather constant. In the years before the minimum rates have been reduced eventually, see MoBer Oct.98, p.41* which is also visible at our figures r above.

B

We now turn to the relation $CA_B = s_B \cdot DEP_B$. We get the following time series:

$Year$	CA_B	DEP_B	$s_b = \frac{CA_B}{DEP_B}$
1991	23, 9	3983, 2	0, 0060
1992	27, 8	4149, 2	0, 0067
1993	27, 8	4538, 1	0, 0061
1994	26, 2	4733, 1	0, 0055
1995	27, 3	5021, 5	0, 0054
1996	30, 3	5481, 2	0, 0055
1997	30, 7	4842, 7	0, 0063
1998	29, 9	6331, 1	0, 0047

Since 1994 the cash rate s_B is rather constant. In the years before the banks succeeded in reducing this rate a bit, but we may assume that a sort of minimum rate has been reached now.

C

We now look into the statistics whether we could consider the cash coefficient c_{nonB} of non-banks as approximately constant, i.e. we look at the relation

$$N_{CB,nonB} = c_{nonB} \cdot (N_{CB,nonB} + DEP_{B,nonB})$$

Now monthly figures are available. We calculate the bank notes $N_{CB,nonB}$ outside of the banking system by taking the total amount N_{CB} of notes in circulation (see MoBer. März 2001, p.14*) and subtract the cash CA_B of banks (see MoBer. März 2001, p.20*), according to the relation $N_{CB,nonB} = N_{CB} - CA_B$.

Figures for the deposits $DEP_{B,nonB}$ of non-banks are available at the MoBer. März 2001, p.22*. The following table shows the result.

$Month$	N_{CB}	CA_B	$N_{CB,nonB}$	$DEP_{B,nonB}$	$N_{CB,nonB}+$ $DEP_{B,nonB}$	$c_{nonB} = \frac{N_{CB,nonB}}{N_{CB,nonB}+DEP_{B,nonB}}$
May 1999	128, 9	13, 4	115, 5	1951, 8	2067, 3	0, 056
June	129, 4	13, 5	115, 9	1956, 9	2072, 8	0, 056
July	129, 9	13, 1	116, 8	1951, 7	2068, 5	0, 056
Aug.	130, 4	13, 2	117, 2	1955, 0	2072, 2	0, 057
Sep.	130, 3	13, 3	117, 0	1958, 6	2075, 6	0, 056
Oct.	130, 2	13, 5	116, 7	1966, 3	2083, 0	0, 056
Nov.	130, 5	13, 2	117, 3	1994, 4	2111, 7	0, 056
Dez.	134, 4	17, 2	117, 2	2012, 4	2129, 6	0, 055
Jan. 2000	136, 6	13, 5	123, 1	2005, 4	2128, 5	0, 058
Feb.	132, 0	13, 5	118, 5	2011, 7	2130, 2	0, 056
March	131, 6	13, 1	118, 1	2001, 9	2120, 0	0, 056
April	131, 8	14, 2	117, 6	2004, 3	2121, 9	0, 055
May	132, 3	13, 9	118, 4	1998, 2	2116, 6	0, 056
⋮	⋮	⋮	⋮	⋮	⋮	⋮

This shows a remarkable constancy in the proportion of cash holding to deposits on the side of the non-banks.

3.12 A Digression: Some Consequences of the Near-Constancy of Some Coefficients in the Monetary Sector of the Economy; a Simplified Model

If we make the following additional assumptions we get some insight into the functioning of the monetary sector of the economy. The additional assumptions are:

1. There is only one commercial bank in the economy.
2. This bank uses in each period all "free reserves" for credits to non-banks. "Free reserves" are defined with respect to an initial expansion $\Delta CR_{B,nonB} =: R$ of credits of the bank to all non-banks in the initial period, say: $t = 0$. This additional amount R of money expands the portfolio of the non-banks. It is kept as additional cash of the non-banks (by the amount $c \cdot R$, $c := c_{nonB}$) and partly as additional deposits at the commercial bank (by the amount $(1-c) \cdot R$). The bank wants to keep additional liquidity reserves in proportion to the additional deposits. This amounts to $s \cdot (1-c) \cdot R$, $s = s_B$. But it also has to keep minimum reserves at the Central Banks in proportion to its additional deposits, by the amount of $r(1-c) \cdot R$, where $r = r^*$ is the minimum reserve requirement ratio, decided by the Central Bank. This leaves the amount $(1-s-r)(1-c) \cdot R$ of free reserves at the commercial bank, which will be used for granting new credits to the non-banks in the next period. If we continue this way we get a time series of additional credits and of additional money as shown in the following table:

Table 3.1. The Money Multiplier

	Free reserves = additional credits	change of cash at non-banks	change of deposits of non-banks	additional cash requirements of the commercial bank	additional reserve requirements of the commercial bank at the Central Bank
0	R	cR	$(1-c)R$	$s(1-c)R$	$r(1-c)R$
1	$(1-s-r)\cdot (1-c)R$	$c(1-s-r)\cdot (1-c)R$	$(1-s-r)\cdot (1-c)^2R$	$s(1-s-r)\cdot (1-c)^2R$	$r(1-s-r)\cdot (1-c)^2R$
2	$(1-s-r)^2\cdot (1-c)^2\cdot R$	$c(1-s-r)^2\cdot (1-c)^2\cdot R$	$(1-s-r)^2\cdot (1-c)^3R$	$s(1-s-r)^2\cdot (1-c)^3R$	$r(1-s-r)^2\cdot (1-c)^3R$
$\vdots$	$\vdots$	$\vdots$	$\vdots$	$\vdots$	$\vdots$
n	$(1-s-)^n\cdot (1-c)^nR$	$c(1-s-r)^n\cdot (1-c)^nR$	$(1-s-r)^n\cdot (1-c)^{n+1}R$	$s(1-s-r)^n\cdot (1-c)^{n+1}R$	$r(1-s-r)^n\cdot (1-c)^{n+1}R$
$\vdots$	$\vdots$	$\vdots$	$\vdots$	$\vdots$	$\vdots$
∞	0	0	0	0	0
$\sum_{t=0}^{\infty}$	$\frac{1}{1-(1-s-r)(1-c)}R$	$\frac{c}{1-(1-s-r)(1-c)}R$	$\frac{1-c}{1-(1-s-r)(1-c)}R$	$\frac{s(1-c)}{1-(1-s-r)(1-c)}R$	$\frac{r(1-c)}{1-(1-s-r)(1-c)}R$[52]

[52] A variant of these formulae can be found in Jarchow I (1973), p. 49ff.

where $0 < c < 1, \quad 0 < s + r < 1, \quad 0 < s < 1, \quad 0 < r < 1, \quad R > 0.$ Thus the fact that the deposits could be used as money (mostly by remittances) leads to a multiplicative effect of an additional credit of the commercial bank.

3.13 A Final Remark

In this theory of the banking system the Central Bank is treated in some detail. The commercial banks are handled in the same manner; the several different interest rates which are charged by the commercial banks are not explained. This will be done in chapter 7 together with the explanation of the security prices. This conforms to the treatment of wage rates which are also explained in a separate section. Here we proceed to the theories of other economic agents.

References

[1] Barro, Robert J.: *Macroeconomics*, 4. ed., New York etc. (Wiley), 1993

[2] Barro, Robert J. and Grilli, Vittorio: *European Macroeconomics*, (McMillan), 1994

[3] Burda, Michael and Wyplosz, Charles: *Macroeconomics. A European Text* (Oxford Union Press), 1993

[4] Dornbusch, Rüdiger and Fischer, Stanley: *Macroeconomics*, New York etc. (McGraw-Hill), 1978

[5] Ehrlicher, Werner and Oberhauser, Alois: *Probleme der Geldmengensteuerung*, Berlin (Duncker & Humblot), Schrifton des Vereins für Socialpolitik, N.F. Bd. 99, Berlin, 1978

[6] European Monetary Institute: *The Single Monetary Policy in Stage Three*, Frankfurt 1997

[7] Helmstädter, Ernst: *Wirtschaftstheorie II. Makroökonomische Theorie*, 3. ed., München (Vahlen),1986

[8] Helmstädter, Ernst: *Wirtschaftstheorie I. Mikroökonomische Theorie*, 4. ed., München (Vahlen),1991

[9] Jarchow, H.-J.: *Theorie und Politik des Geldes, I. Geldtheorie*, UTB 234, Göttingen (Vandenhoeck & Ruprecht), 1973

[10] Jarchow, H.-J.: *Theorie und Politik des Geldes, II. Geldmarkt und Geldpolitische Instrumente*, UTB 346, Göttingen (Vandenhoeck & Ruprecht), 1974

[11] Junius, Karsten, Kater, Ulrich, Meier, Carsten-Patrick and Müller, Henrik: *Handbuch Europäische Zentralbank*, Bad Soden (Uhlenbruch), 2002

[12] Keynes, John Maynard: *Allgemeine Theorie der Beschäftigung, des Zinses und des Geldes*, Berlin (Duncker & Humblot), 1936

[13] Kißmer, Friedrich and Wagner, Helmut: *Braucht die EZB eine "neue" geldpolitische Strategie?*, Diskussionsbeiträge Fachbereich Wirtschaftswissenschaft, Fernuniversität Gesamthochschule 58084 Hagen, (will appear in List Forum,) 2002

[14] Mankiw, N. Gregory: *Principles of Economics*, Fort Worth etc. (Dryden), 1998

[15] Neumann, Manfred: *Theoretische Volkswirtschaftslehre I*, 5. ed., München (Vahlen), 1996

[16] Richter, R., Schlieper, U. and Friedmann, W.: *Makroökonomik*, 4. ed., Berlin etc. (Springer), 1981

[17] Richter, Rudolf: *Geldtheorie*, 2. ed., Berlin etc. (Springer), 1990

[18] Romer, David: *Advanced Macroeconomics*, New York etc. (McGraw-Hill), 1996

[19] Tirole, Jean: *The Theory of Industrial Organization*, Cambridge-Mass. (MIT-Press), 1988

[20] Varian, Hal R.: *Grundzüge der Mikroökonomik*, 5. ed., München, Wien (Oldenbourg), 2001

CHAPTER 4

The Educational System, Development and Research[1]

4.1 Some Basic Concepts

In this part we deal with the size and growth of knowledge in the society (which is an immaterial phenomenon) and with the material base of the phenomenon: the educational and research systems of the society. This comprises also the applied research within a firm. It cannot be separated from the research and development outside of the firm.

All knowledge starts with *observations* made by the current generation and made earlier and transferred to the presence by oral tradition (e.g. by lectures in the university) or preserved by books and other means of preservation of information. Thus all what is known (or taken as knowledge) in a society is actually known by persons or preserved in libraries or other institutions and accessible to all persons who are interested in it. We cannot take all that as "observation" what is taken to be true by the majority of persons concerned with it. The "observation" may be actually false or distorted.[2] Thus it is necessary to examine from time to time the old "observations" whether they continue to be valid also under more refined or changed conditions. Now (in the spirit of the encyclopedists of the 18. century) one may register all observations available in the society by persons or in books in a series of "Handbooks of knowledge" and may enumerate them.

Let ϕ_i be the description of an observation in the above sense. There is only a finite number of observations known in the society in a certain period, say n, where n is a very large number. It always increases as long as the research process continues. Thus

$$W_{obs} : \quad = \{\phi_1, \ldots, \phi_n\}$$

is a vector of all observations known (or believed to be known) in the society (W stands for "Wissen" = knowledge in German).

W_{obs} forms the connection between the outside world and our thoughts on it. These "thoughts" are the theories by which we explain the observations. Each theory must explain several observations by a rather small number of

---

[1] The notations are partly changed compared to those in Chapter 2.

[2] Opinions of persons (living or deceased) which are handed down to the presence (right or wrong) also count as observations, of course. We do not limit the concept of "observation" to the natural sciences.

hypotheses (in the natural sciences called "natural laws"). A theory which explains only one observation is useless, one would better use the simple description of the phenomenon and call it a "theory". The ideal theory would be a "theory on everything", and the physicists are working on it (Einstein devoted his time and effort in Princeton mostly on the search of such a theory, but in vain). By the way: "everything" in this connection means here: everything in the field of physics. A theory in the above sense should explain several observations (at least approximately) and predict unknown future observations. Let θ_j be a theory in this sense which could explain a subset $\{\phi_k, \ldots, \phi_l\} \subset W_{obs}$ of observations and assume that there are m theories known in the society. These m theories constitute a set which we call theoretical knowledge W_{theor}:

$$W_{theor} : \; = \{\theta_1, \ldots, \theta_m\}$$

W_{obs} and W_{theor} together form the *basic knowledge* W_{base} in the society:

$$W_{base} := \{W_{obs}, W_{theor}\}$$

But there is also another type of knowledge which we call *applied knowledge* W_{appl} which comprises all *technologies* ϑ_i to produce a certain product i, primarily those products which are actually produced (say: for products $1, \ldots, n$), but also for other products which could have been produced but actually are not for different reasons (e.g. lack of demand at prices which cover the costs); we count these products by $n+1, \ldots, N$. And finally W_{appl} comprises all alternative technologies to produce the products $1, \ldots, N$.

We denote the alternative technologies to produce the commodity i by $\vartheta_i^{'}, \vartheta_i^{''}, \ldots, \vartheta_i^{(z)}$. Thus the applied knowledge in a society W_{appl} is the set of all known technologies:

$$W_{appl} : \; = \{\vartheta_1, \vartheta_1^{'}, \ldots, \vartheta_1^{(z)}, \ldots, \ldots, \vartheta_N, \vartheta_N^{'}, \ldots, \vartheta_N^{(z)}\}$$

to produce the commodities $1, \ldots, N$. This includes all observations made in connection with the use or development of a specific technology.

One may also define: a technology is the knowledge how to produce a well defined commodity. The basic knowledge is not necessarily related to any production process, it is "pure knowledge".

In the "Theory of the Firm", section 2.5 (The Handbook of Production) we defined a technology ϑ_i as the following set:

$$\vartheta_i = \{A_i, B_i, D_i, Repl_i, \bar{\Lambda}_i, \hat{\Lambda}_i, Hb_i\}, \; i = 1, \ldots, N$$

where A = matrix of the output coefficients of firm i

B_i = matrix of secondary inputs of firm i

D_i = matrix of the commodity structure of investment of firm i

$Repl_i$ = matrix of replacement coefficients of firm i

$\bar{\Lambda}_i$ = matrix of labor input coefficients per unit of investment of firm i

$\hat{\Lambda}_i$ = matrix of labor input coefficients per unit of production of firm i

Hb_i = handbook of production for commodity i

In the following section we present theories to explain the development of the basic knowledge W_{base} and of the technologies ϑ_i.

4.2 Natural Endowments and the School System

It is clear that basic and applied knowledge is produced and transferred by the educational and research system outside and within the firms. We have to consider it as a whole and start with the educational system outside the firms.

The base of all learning are the natural gifts (or: endowments) of a person in different fields. Let there be z fields, beginning from physical endowments (power, physical aptitudes, persistence, skill,...) to spiritual (mathematics, languages,...) and artistic ones (drawing, painting, music,...).

We assume, that total knowledge[3] in the society in the field $\zeta, \zeta = 1, \ldots, z$, at the beginning of period 0 can be quantified and normalized to 100 and that it is possible to allocate numbers $0, 1, \ldots, 100$ to each subset of this knowledge. Now the knowledge $W_{i\zeta}^{(\sigma)}$ of person i in the field ζ (where person i is located in the educational system σ) can be described by a number $0 \leq W_{i\zeta}^{(\sigma)} \leq 100$. The natural endowments set limits $\bar{W}_{i\zeta}^{(\sigma)}$, $\zeta = 1, \ldots, z$, $0 \leq \bar{W}_{i\zeta}^{(\sigma)} \leq 100$ to the knowledge (or performance) of a person in each field:

$$W_{i\zeta}^{(\sigma)} \leq \bar{W}_{i\zeta}^{(\sigma)}$$

We take $\bar{W}_{i\zeta}^{(\sigma)}$, $\zeta = 1, \ldots, z$, as given for each person. They constitute the profile $\bar{W}_i^{(\sigma)}$ of endowments of that person[4]:

$$\bar{W}_i^{(\sigma)} = (\bar{W}_{i1}^{(\sigma)}, \ldots, \bar{W}_{iz}^{(\sigma)})$$

Similarly, the profile of actual knowledge (or performance) of person i is defined by

$$W_i^{(\sigma)} = (W_{i1}^{(\sigma)}, \ldots, W_{iz}^{(\sigma)}),\ W_{i\zeta}^{(\sigma)} \leq \bar{W}_{i\zeta}^{(\sigma)}$$

---

[3] The word "knowledge" comprises capabilities of all kinds. It is a "pars pro toto".

[4] The endowments may be unknown to the environment and perhaps to the person himself, especially in the childhood of the person. We do not deal with this problem.

For example: persons without any musical gifts will never reach the abilities of the top musicians, irrespective of all schooling.

In this approach we differentiate between three educational systems, which a person may pass in order to reach the limits of his endowments:

- the elementary schools: ($\sigma = e.sch.$)
- the high schools: ($\sigma = h.sch.$)
- the universities, technical colleges, etc.: ($\sigma = u.sch.$)

The better the educational systems the nearer a person may come to the limits of his natural gifts. But it is in almost all cases impossible to develop all gifts up to their limits. Developing is done by learning. That takes time, and life is (in general) too short to let the actual performance become equal to the size of the gifts in all fields. This development (outside the firms) is done in the education system.

The schools do not only transfer knowledge but they also (to a certain degree) form the character and determine the value system of those persons that attend them. We use the same approach in this context. We enumerate all traits of character, from those which are considered as positive (like: being friendly, co-operative, diligent, active,...) to those which are usually considered as negative (like: being selfish, aggressive, reckless, unfair, idle,...). Let there be $\hat{z}$ traits of character 1 to $\hat{n}$ positive ones and $\hat{n}+1$ to $\hat{z}$ negative ones. Each of them may be realized to the largest degree (call it: 100) or not at all (call it zero). Now the character profile $Ch_i^{(\sigma)}$ of a person i in the school system σ may be indicated by the vector

$$Ch_i^{(\sigma)} = (Ch_{i1}^{(\sigma)}, \ldots, Ch_{i\hat{z}}^{(\sigma)}),\ 0 \leq Ch_{i\zeta}^{(\sigma)} \leq 100,\ \zeta = 1, \ldots, \hat{z}$$

The influence of the school system on the character of a person may be analyzed similarly as its influence on knowledge. But our topic here is the accumulation of knowledge. Thus we do not pursue the influence of the school system on the character of the pupils or students further.

For simplicity we assume that the government decides on the size and the structure of the educational system. It may delegate part of the decisions to committees or private institutions, but we subsume this under "government".

For each educational system $\sigma \epsilon \{e.sch., h.sch., u.sch.\}$ the government has to decide on:

1. the minimum age $T_{min}^{(\sigma)}$ of pupils or students to enter the system σ and
2. the maximum age $T_{max}^{(\sigma)}$ to leave the system σ[5]

[5] If there is no limitation of this kind, $T_{max}^{(\sigma)}$ may be a very large number such that nobody reaches that age.

3. the formal (educational) requirements which must be fulfilled in order to allow a person to enter the system σ[6]

4. the maximum amount of pupils or students admitted to the system σ

5. the number of teachers ($teach_\zeta^{(\sigma)}$) per pupils $N_\zeta^{(\sigma)}$ or students in field ζ of the system σ

6. the quality $q(teach_\zeta^{(\sigma)})$ of the teachers in a certain field (measured by the required examinations passed in this specific and in related fields).

7. the "capital $cap_\zeta^{(\sigma)}$ per student" $N_\zeta^{(\sigma)}$, where "capital" comprises school buildings, places and equipment for teaching and experiments, place for breaks, for physical exercises etc.

8. the curriculum $curr_\zeta^{(\sigma)}$ of instructions. These are the objects to be taught and the amount of knowledge to be transferred to the pupils or students. The requirements may be high such that only few persons gifted for this specific field may pass the examinations or low such that more or less every person could make it.

9. the method of teaching (soft or tough, with or without homework, written or oral examination, behavior against disturber of instructions etc.).

There are only finite many alternatives for each of these 9 items.[7] Each alternative j for the system σ costs an amount of $CO_j^{(\sigma)}$ monetary units for the government.[8] If the government budget limits the expenditures for the different types of schools to the amount $\bar{CO}^{(\sigma)}$, only those alternatives are admitted which stay within these limits, call them $1, \ldots, z$. Thus the choice of the government with respect to the educational system as a whole may be again illustrated by the familiar figure:

[6] For $\sigma =$ e.sch. these will be requirements as to the mental and physical state of the pupils which apply for admission. For the other systems these are good performances in the lower system as indicated by the grades.

[7] Assume that there are 3 alternatives for each item to be considered for realization. Then we get $3^9 = 19683$ combinations to be weighed. This sounds awful, but remember that this is a general theory. Actually, only one or two of these items are under consideration in one period and that gives 3 or 9 alternatives. All others are kept constant because the capacity of evaluations and taking decisions is limited. Which problems will be taken up depends on the evaluation of the problems by those persons that have the greatest influence on the "public opinion".

[8] These are not the total costs of running the system σ: the costs for the students are disregarded. Thus we may $CO_j^{(\sigma)}$ better call the expenditure of the government for the educational system σ.

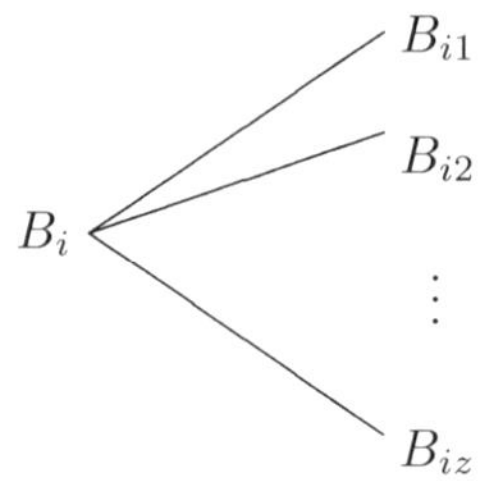

where B_i is the initial condition of this educational system and $B_{i\zeta}$ the decision to change the system in the next period[9] to the alternative $\zeta = 1, \ldots, z$.

The following graphs (Fig. 4.1 and 4.2) illustrate our approach thus far. It is assumed that the fields of instruction are different in the different school systems.[10] Fig. 4.1 and 4.2 show the profiles of natural endowments of a person i and a person j and the profiles of the actual knowledge and performance if these persons would be allowed to enter the system σ. Only person j may reach the limits of what is known in certain fields and thus have the chance to extend the knowledge in this field (see Fig. 4.2). Person i (see Fig. 4.1) has no chance (or a very small one) to extend the knowledge in the society since it does not even understand the majority of what is already known.

We consider the natural endowments of a person as given by nature.[11] But the actual performance of a person in the school system σ depends on the decisions of the government on the characteristics $1, \ldots, 9$ of the school systems σ. We cannot deal with all details of the educational system, but the fundamentals should be modeled and analyzed.

We start with the *elementary schools.* There the fields $\zeta = 1, \ldots, \bar{z}$ are taught (see Fig. 4.1 and 4.2). Let $W_{\zeta max}^{(e.sch.)}$ be the amount of knowledge which a pupil should acquire in the field ζ at the elementary school. It is fixed by the curriculum decided by the government. We normalize this amount to 100 in each field (see also Fig.4.1 and 4.2). We assume that teachers in the elementary and high schools master these amounts of knowledge in his (or her) field ζ. But

---

[9] To change a large system takes time, and changes cannot be made at each period, if the period is short (e.g.: one year). The problems of transition from one alternative to another are not easy. We do not deal with these problems here. We may imagine that changes may only be made once in a decade. In the meantime the system stays unchanged.

[10] In the elementary schools only reading, writing, calculating, drawing and some other minor objects are being taught. In high schools some languages, history, the basic concepts of mathematics, physics, chemistry and some other objects are covered. At the university level in principle all fields of knowledge are taught in detail. These fields may be subdivided into natural sciences and arts and humanities. This explains the graphs of Fig. 4.1 and 4.2.

[11] It might be that the family environment into which a child is born has an influence on what we call "endowment". We include that influence in the definition of "endowment". In any case: the $\bar{W}_{i\zeta}$ are given to the person.

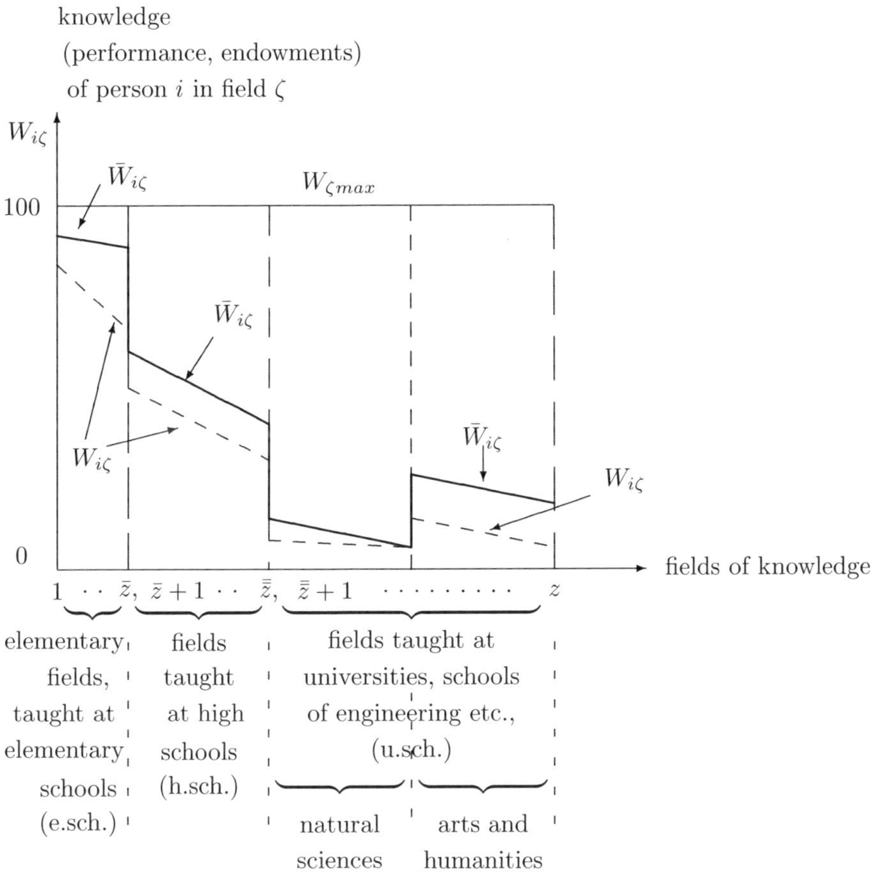

Notes:

$\bar{W}_{i\zeta}^{(\sigma)}$ = endowments of person i in field ζ (which belongs to school system σ), normalized such that $0 \leq \bar{W}_{i\zeta} \leq 100$

$W_{i\zeta}^{(\sigma)}$ = actual knowledge of person i in field ζ after having completed school σ, $\sigma \in \{\text{e.sch.,h.sch.,u.}\}$, $0 \leq W_{i\zeta}^{(\sigma)} \leq \bar{W}_{i\zeta}$

The fields are arranged such that endowments and actual knowledge decline within each system (or subsystem). The profile $\bar{W}_i = (\bar{W}_{i1}, \ldots, \bar{W}_{iz})$ is given by nature, the profile $W_i = (W_{i1}, \ldots, W_{iz})$ depends on the school system.

Figure 4.1 Endowments and Knowledge of Person i in field ζ, $\zeta = 1, \ldots, z$, normalized from 0 to 100. Person i is only weakly gifted for fields taught at the university level

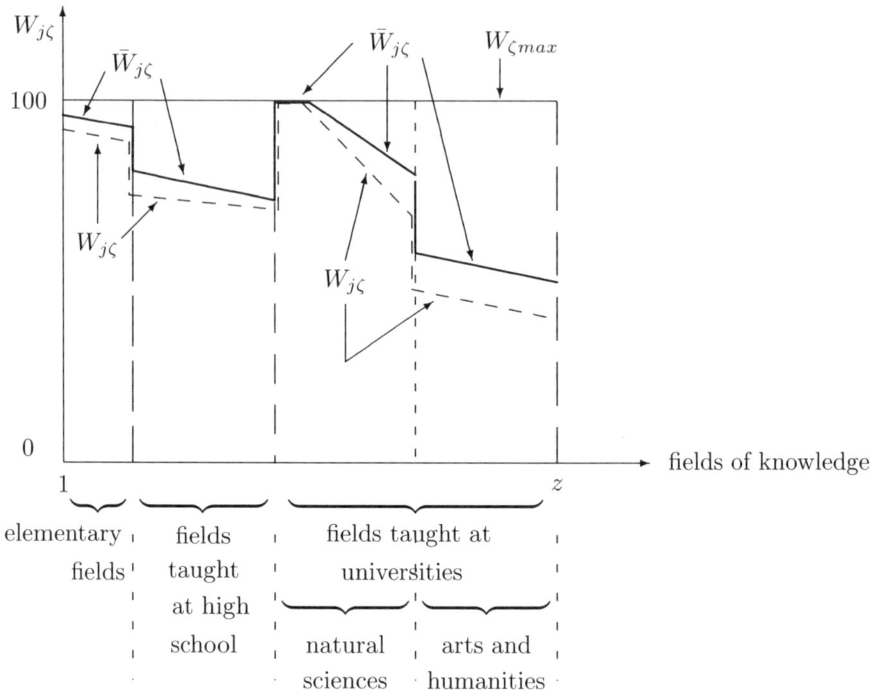

Figure 4.2 as Fig. 4.1 but drawn for a person j which is highly gifted for natural sciences at the university level

there are pupils i at elementary school whose natural endowments $\bar{W}_{i\zeta}^{(e.sch.)}$ in the field ζ do not allow the pupil to reach the prescribed amount $W_{\zeta max}^{(e.sch.)}$. A teacher j in the field ζ may have the pedagogical power ped_j to increase the knowledge of a pupil i such that he approaches his limits $\bar{W}_{i\zeta}^{(e.sch.)}$ to a larger or smaller degree. Let $W_{i\zeta}^{(e.sch.,in)}$ be the knowledge of pupil i in the field ζ when it enters the elementary school (usually zero or near to zero) and $W_{i\zeta}^{(e.sch.,out)}$ the amount of knowledge when it leaves the elementary school. Now we postulate the following relation:

$$W_{i\zeta}^{(e.sch.,out)} = W_{i\zeta}^{(e.sch.,in)} + ped_{j\zeta}^{(e.sch.)}(\bar{W}_{i\zeta}^{(e.sch.)} - W_{i\zeta}^{(e.sch.,in)}), \qquad \bar{W}_{i\zeta}^{(e.sch.)} \geq W_{i\zeta}^{(e.sch.,in)} \tag{4.1}$$

The knowledge of a pupil in a certain field ζ when it leaves the elementary school is determined by the knowledge it brings along when it enters the school (mostly zero), increased by the teaching. The teaching influence depends on the pedagogical abilities of the teacher and the characteristics of the school (indicated by $ped_{j\zeta}^{(e.sch.)}$) and on the distance of the innate limit $\bar{W}_{i\zeta}^{(e.sch.)}$

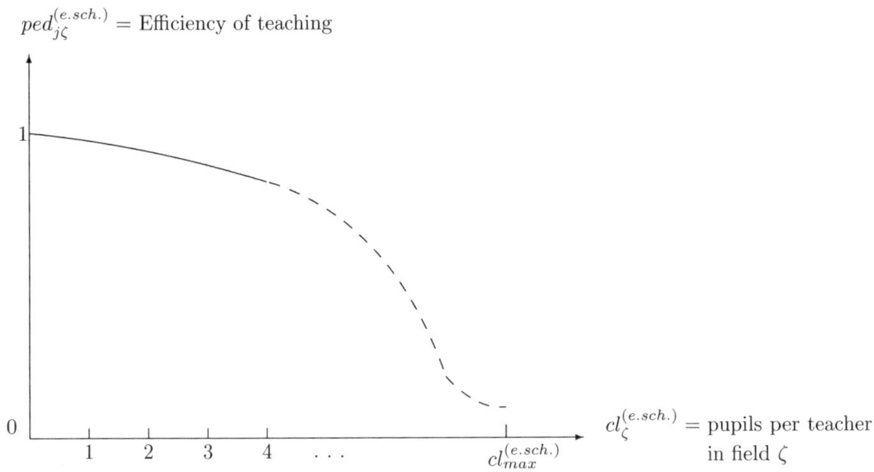

Figure 4.3 Efficiency of Teaching as a Function of the Number of Pupils per Teacher

from the initial state of knowledge $W_{i\zeta}^{(e.sch.,in)}$. The parameter $ped_{j\zeta}^{(e.sch.)}$ is a function of the natural pedagogical gift of teacher j in field ζ (considered to be given) and of the physical conditions of the lessons. These conditions are combined in one index: cl: = pupils per teacher (or short: size of the class):

$$1 \leq cl_{\zeta}^{(e.sch.)} := N_{\zeta}^{(e.sch.)}/teach_{\zeta}^{(e.sch.)} \leq cl_{\zeta max}^{(e.sch.)}$$

The pedagogical efficiency $ped_{j\zeta}^{(e.sch.)}$ is a declining function of $cl_{\zeta}^{(e.sch.)}$ and lies between zero and 1:

$$ped_{j\zeta}^{(e.sch.)} = ped_{j\zeta}^{(e.sch.)}(cl_{\zeta}^{(e.sch.)}) \text{ and } 0 \leq ped_{j\zeta}^{(e.sch.)} \leq 1$$

Fig. 4.3 shows the shape of this efficiency functions of teacher j.[12] Fig. 4.4 gives an example of the time shape $W_{i\zeta}^{(e.sch.)}(t)$ of knowledge of a pupil i in field ζ if the initial size (at time t=0) is $W_{i\zeta}^{(e.sch.)}(0) = W_{i\zeta}^{(e.sch.,in)}$ and the final size at t=T (when it leaves the school) is $W_{i\zeta}^{(e.sch.)}(T) = W_{i\zeta}^{(e.sch.,out)}$. The limit of knowledge (determined by endowments) is $\bar{W}_{i\zeta}^{(e.sch.)} \leq 100$, where the maximal amount of knowledge in this field required by the school authorities is normalized to 100.

Now the pupil i leaves the elementary school with a certification on the marks it reached in each field ζ and with a report on his general qualification which is a sort of average on all marks. That decides on the admission to the

[12] For simplicity we assume that the efficiency of teaching of a teacher is the same for all pupils.

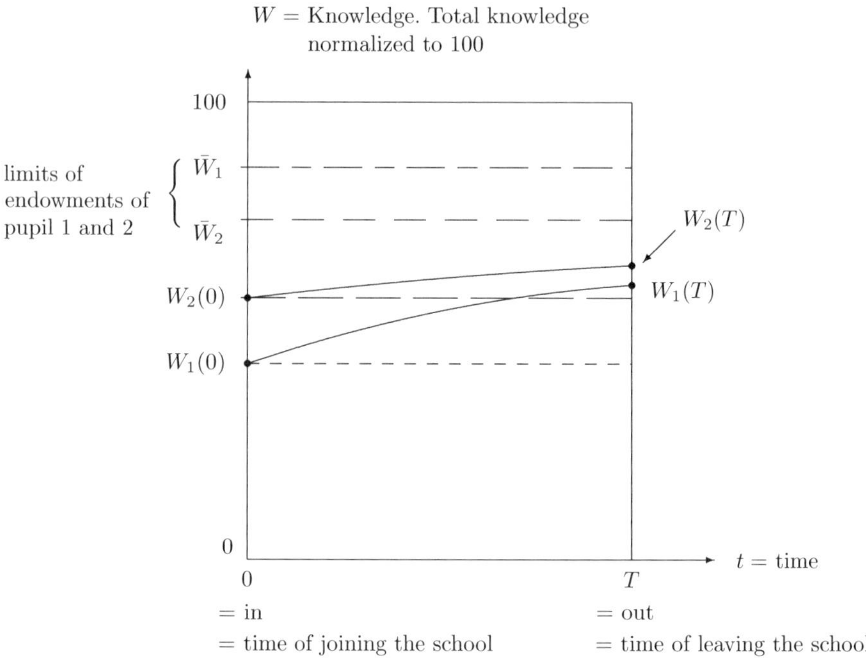

Note:

The figure shows the case where the less gifted pupil 2 nevertheless leaves the school with more knowledge than the higher gifted pupil, because the latter enters the school with lower knowledge $W_1(0) < W_2(0)$, e.g. because the more gifted pupil comes from a less favorable home.

Figure 4.4 Limit of Knowledge $\bar{W}_1$ Attainable by Pupil 1 and $\bar{W}_2$ by Pupil 2 and the Increase of Knowledge at School

high school. This proceeding does not guarantee, that the most gifted students enter the high school. Take Fig. 4.4 as an example. Student 1 is more gifted in the field considered here than Student 2 ($\bar{W}_1 > \bar{W}_2$). But since Student 1 starts at a lower level than Student 2 ($W_1(0) < W_2(0)$, perhaps his (her) family background is not so good, or he (or she) was ill) it may very well be that Student 2 reaches a higher level of knowledge at the end of the elementary school (at time T). We assumed a pedagogical efficiency of .5. One observes that $W_2(T) > W_1(T)$.

There are three other problems connected with the transition from the elementary school to the high school.

1. The allocation of marks on the performance of a pupil in a special field ζ is not selfevident even if the evaluations of the teachers in this field coincide. Let there be an amount W_ζ^* of knowledge which represents the total knowledge required in this field at the elementary school. But only

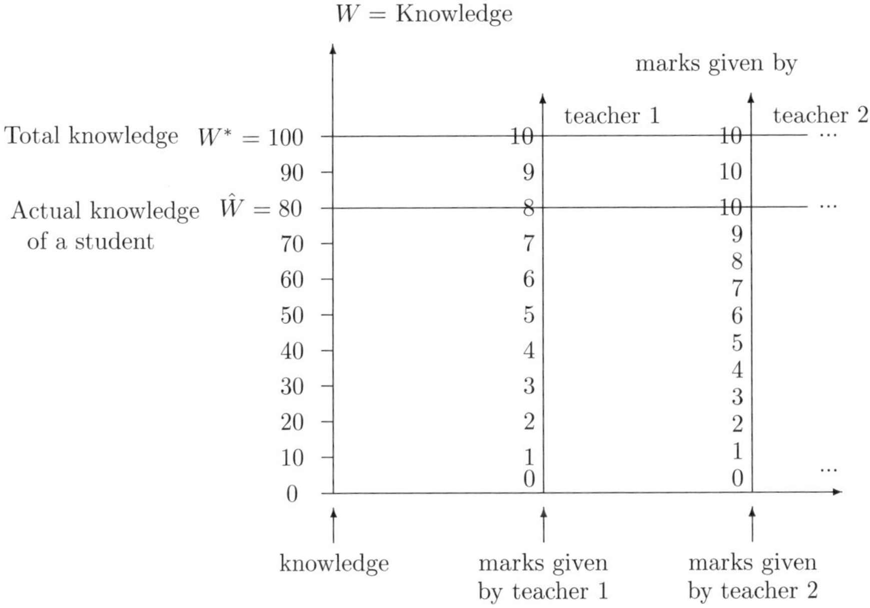

Note:
The performance is to be evaluated by marks 0 (insufficient) to 10 (excellent).

Figure 4.5 The same performance $\hat{W}$ of a student (say: $\hat{W} = 0.8 \cdot W^*$, $W^* =$ total knowledge in this field, normalized to 100) is evaluated differently by teacher 1 and teacher 2

the amount $\hat{W}_\zeta < W^*_\zeta$ is shown to and tested by the teacher. Should this be reflected by the marks given to the students? The situation is illustrated in Fig. 4.5. Teacher 1 would say: since the performance does not show that the pupil is also familiar with the amount $W^* - \hat{W}$ of knowledge, it cannot get the marks 9 to 10 (very good or excellent). Teacher 2 may say: One has to judge the actual performance of the pupil. This pupil is not responsible for the fact that it has not been confronted with the problems labeled as 9 and 10. Since it knows everything with which it has been confronted, it deserves the highest marks. Thus (apart of all other problems of judgement) there are conflicting principles of marking a pupil. Nevertheless, it is a fact, that (in case of a large number of students) there is a distribution of marks of the students leaving an educational system which is rather constant. Fig. 4.6 shows such a distribution. It would be nice if one could show that this reflects the distribution of natural gifts. But for the reasons given above one may doubt that.

2. The admission of a student to the high school (and later to the university) often depends on the report of his general qualification, which is

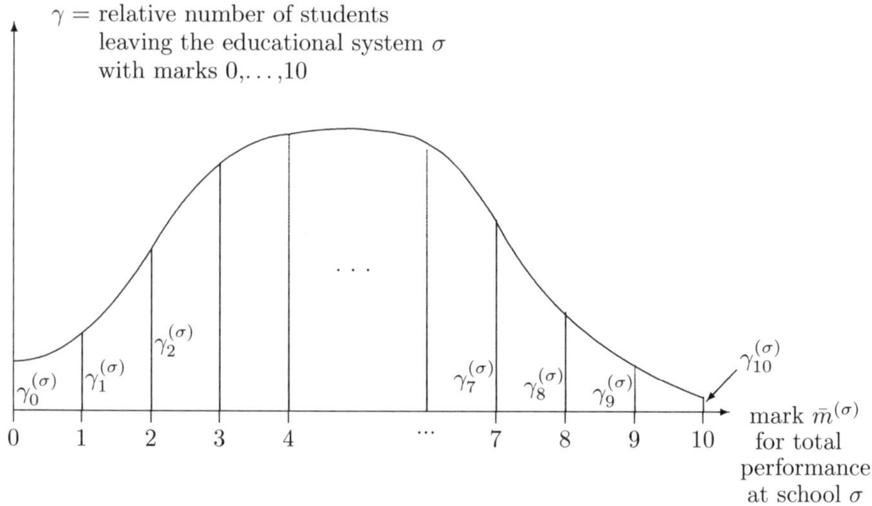

Note:

$$\gamma_g^{(\sigma)} \geq 0, \quad g = 0, 1, \ldots, 10, \quad \sum_{g=0}^{10} \gamma_g^{(\sigma)} = 1.$$

Figure 4.6 Distribution of marks of students leaving the educational system $\sigma \in \{\text{e.sch.,h.sch.,u.sch.}\}$

defined as an average of the performance in all fields taught at the elementary school. This requires to decide on the weights of the different fields. Let $m_{i\zeta}^{(e.sch.)}$ be the mark which the pupil i gets in the field ζ when it leaves the elementary school, and let α_ζ be the weight of field ζ in the final report, where $\alpha_\zeta \geq 0$, $\sum_{\zeta=1}^{\bar{z}} \alpha_\zeta = 1$. This yields a total mark $\bar{m}_i^{(e.sch.)}$ for student i where $\bar{m}_i^{(e.sch.)} = \sum_{\zeta=1}^{\bar{z}} \alpha_\zeta \cdot m_{i\zeta}^{(e.sch.)}$. But the weights α_ζ are not self-evident but subject to the decision of the government on the educational system.

3. Finally one has to consider that a certain proportion $\beta_{out}^{(e.sch.)}$ of pupils leaves the school system after they have finished that school.[13] These are not only the less gifted persons that have no chance for admission to high school and later to the university but also gifted persons who are fed up with learning or have a good chance in business or have other reasons to leave the school system and to enter in "real life".

Let $N^{(e.sch.,out)}$ be the number of persons who leave the elementary school. Thus $\beta^{(e.sch.,out)} \cdot N^{(e.sch.,out)}$ of former pupils appear at the labor market mostly as apprentices, and $(1 - \beta^{(e.sch.,out)}) \cdot N^{(e.sch.,out)} = N^{(h.sch.,in)}$

[13] We do not consider drop-outs.

enter the high school.[14] If persons with low marks of general qualification, say $\bar{m} = 0, 1, \ldots, 3$ are not admitted to high school, the number of persons leaving the elementary school and coming to the labor market is at least (see Fig. 4.6): $\sum_{i=0}^{3} \gamma_i^{(e.sch.,out)} \cdot N^{(e.sch.,out)}$ Thus $\beta^{(e.sch.,out)} = \sum_{i=0}^{3} \gamma_i^{(e.sch.,out)}$ in this case.

But usually also some persons who could be admitted do not apply for admission and leave the school system. If we neglect this feature we may calculate the number $N^{(h.sch.,in)}$ of persons entering the high school at the beginning of a term:

$$N^{(h.sch.,in)} = (1 - \beta^{(e.sch.,out)}) \cdot N^{(e.sch.,out)}$$

Thus the vigor of the entrance conditions into high schools determines the size of the high school system. In case that students stay T terms at high school and we neglect the dropouts, there are

$$N^{(h.sch.)} = \sum_{t=1}^{T} N^{(h.sch.,in)}(t)$$

students at the high school. Now the situation at high schools is quite analogous to the situation at elementary school. The above approach for elementary schools may be transferred to high schools (change the index e.sch. everywhere to h.sch.) But bear in mind that the fields of instructions $\zeta = \bar{z} + 1, \ldots, \bar{\bar{z}}$ are different and the endowments $\bar{W}_{i\zeta}^{(e.sch.)}$ as well. The actual knowledge $W_{i\zeta}^{(h.sch.)}(0)$ which the student i could present at the beginning of the school in field ζ may also differ much more between students at high school than between those at elementary schools where it may be approximately zero for all pupils. As to the teachers at high school we assume the same as to the teachers of elementary school: they master the amount $W_{\zeta,max}$ of knowledge which they should transfer to their students perfectly, but their pedagogical abilities $ped_{j\zeta}^{(h.sch.)}$ may differ, perhaps more than these abilities at the elementary school level. Of course, the efficiency of teaching depends also on the size $cl_{\zeta}^{(h.sch.)}$ of the class as shown in Fig. 4.3 and is again normalized to lie between zero and one.

The proportion $\beta^{(h.sch.,out)}$ of all students $N^{(h.sch.,out)}$ which leaves the high school goes to practical work and appears on the labor market. The proportion $1 - \beta^{(h.sch.,out)}$ enters the university system. There may also be minimal requirements for the marks $\bar{m}^{(h.sch.)}$ of students who leave the high school in order to be admitted to the university. E.g. students with marks zero to four are not accepted. In this case the proportion $\beta^{(h.sch.,out)}$ can be

[14] For simplicity we assume that all persons who graduate from elementary schools and do not go to work are admitted to high school and that no persons from outside join the high school.

estimated by

$$\beta^{(h.sch.,out)} = \sum_{i=0}^{4} \gamma_i^{(h.sch.)}$$

But this is a very crude approximation: also persons with a higher mark may leave the school system, and there are special schools at the university level which are highly specialized such that not the total performance $\bar{m}$ counts but the note $m_\zeta^{(h.sch.)}$ of a special field ζ.

We now come to the *university schools*. They are of special interest to us since research is concentrated there as far as it is not done at firms. The theory of universities is different from the theory of elementary and high schools. Of course, the fields covered by courses are much more detailed and more extended than those which are taught at the lower schools, see Fig. 4.1. We demonstrate that by putting $\zeta = \bar{\bar{z}} + 1, \ldots, z$, which is different from the fields $\zeta = \bar{z} + 1, \ldots, \bar{\bar{z}}$ which are taught at the high schools. But there are other differences as well. At the university level *total* knowledge $W_{total,\zeta}$ (everything what is known to be true on ζ in the world) should be transferred to students and (possibly) the limit of this knowledge should be extended. We normalize this total amount of knowledge to be 100. Of course, a special university teacher j may not know everything in his field ζ, but only the amount $W_{teachj,\zeta}^{(u.sch.)} < W_{total,\zeta}$. Thus a student i of his (or her) class cannot learn more than that, but he (or she) could stay behind this limit if the natural endowment $\bar{W}_{i\zeta}$ of this student in this field is not sufficient. The initial state of knowledge of student i in field ζ when he (or she) enters the university is rather low, as a rule, call it $W_{i\zeta}^{(u.sch.,in)}$. Now the level $W_{i\zeta}^{(u.sch.,out)}$ of knowledge of student i in the field ζ depends on the level $W_{i\zeta}^{(u.sch.,in)}$ when he (or she) enters the university, on the natural endowments $\bar{W}_{i\zeta}^{(u.sch.)}$ of the student, on the scientific standing $sc_{j,\zeta}^{(u.sch.)}$ of the teacher j and on his influence on the students that depends (among others) on the size $cl_\zeta^{(u.sch.)}$ of the class in this field. We suggest a relation similar to (4.1) for the lower schools:[15]

[15] This formulation implies that at the level of universities the pedagogical talent of a university teacher is not of great importance. The students are adults and supposed to be interested in science. They are interested in scientific truth whether it is presented in a nice way or not. Who is interested in the pedagogical capabilities of Kant, Hegel, or Einstein, Planck or Keynes? Their influence (direct and indirect) is independent of it. The pedagogical capabilities are important for teaching children, scarcely for teaching adults, who are interested in this special field.

$$W_{i\zeta}^{(u.sch.,out)} = \begin{cases} W_{i\zeta}^{(u.sch.,in)} + sc_{j\zeta}^{(u.sch.)}(\bar{W}_{i\zeta}^{(u.sch.)} - W_{i\zeta}^{(u.sch.,in)}) \,, \\ \text{if } \bar{W}_{i\zeta}^{(u.sch.)} \leq W_{teach_j,\zeta}^{(u.sch.)} \\ W_{i\zeta}^{(u.sch.,in)} + sc_{j\zeta}^{(u.sch.)}(W_{teach_j,\zeta}^{(u.sch.)} - W_{i\zeta}^{(u.sch.,in)}) \,, \\ \text{if } \bar{W}_{i\zeta}^{(u.sch.)} > W_{teach,\zeta}^{(u.sch.)} \end{cases}$$

where $0 \leq sc_{j\zeta}^{(u.sch.)} \leq 1$

$$\text{and } sc_{j\zeta}^{(u.sch.)} = sc_{jt}^{(u.sch.)}(cl_{\zeta}^{(u.sch.)}), \quad sc_{jt}^{(u.sch.)} < 0$$

cf. Fig. 4.4 and 4.5. This equation states that a student in his accumulation of knowledge is limited by his natural endowments or by the quality and efficiency of his teacher which depends on the teacher's amount of knowledge in this field and on the size of the class. With those changes the other definitions and relations stated for the elementary schools stay the same at the high schools.

4.3 Learning by Doing

The schools are not the only institutions where knowledges and abilities are produced and transferred. This happens also within the employment system as a sort of byproduct. We consider only the firms as organizations where this takes place, as a "pars pro toto". Actually, other organizations will have the same effect.

In this section we also deal with the connection of the school and the employment system.[16] Consider a firm i which produces the product i by the amount x_i. Our theory of the firm i is that of a hierarchical organization with $\bar{n}^{(i,\rho)}$ workers of rank ρ in period zero, $\rho = 0, 1, \ldots, \mathcal{R}$, if there are $\mathcal{R}$ levels of administration, where the $\mathcal{R}$th level is the boss (or the board, as the case may be). Each supervisor of rank ρ may be assisted by a staff of $N^{(i,\rho)}$ persons. The number $\bar{n}^{(i,0)}$ of workers of rank zero, the control spans $s^{(i,\rho)}$ of a supervisor of rank ρ and the sizes $N^{(i,\rho)}$ of the staff in stage ρ, $\rho = 0, 1, \ldots, \mathcal{R}$, are decision variables for the management of the firm. For details, see chapter 2.

By definition: the number $\bar{n}^{(i,\rho)}$ of persons employed at rank ρ (including staff members) in firm i results from the number $\bar{n}_{-1}^{(i,\rho)}$ of persons employed in the period before minus the number $n_{-}^{(i,\rho)}$ of separations plus the number $n_{+}^{(i,\rho)}$ of accessions:

$$\bar{n}^{(i,\rho)} = \bar{n}_{-1}^{(i,\rho)} - n_{-}^{(i,\rho)} + n_{+}^{(i,\rho)}$$

The separations result from resignation, illness, reaching the pension age, notice of the employer or other reasons. We do not analyze that in detail.

---

[16] The notations in this section are a bit changed compared to those in the Theory of the Firm, see chapter 2.

It is a fact that the relative number of persons leaving the firm from a position ρ is rather constant in the average:[17]

$$n_{-}^{(i,\rho)} = ex^{(i,\rho)} \cdot \bar{n}_{-1}^{(i,\rho)} \tag{4.2}$$

(as a rule: $ex^{(i,\rho)}$ lies between .05 and .1). In the short run $ex^{(i,\rho)}$ also depends on the prospects of the firm (as seen by the personnel) and on the "climate" within the firm. Thus the ratio $ex^{(i,\rho)}$ as well as the ratio of those which are notified as ill are good indicators for the inner state of a firm.

If we accept (4.2) as approximation we get for the number of free positions of rank ρ in firm i:

$$n_{+}^{(i,\rho)} = \bar{n}^{(i,\rho)} - \bar{n}_{-1}^{(i,\rho)}(1 - ex^{(i,\rho)})$$

where $\bar{n}_{-1}^{(i,\rho)}$ is determined by the past and $\bar{n}^{(i,\rho)}$ by the decisions of the management on $\bar{n}^{(i,\rho)}$, the control spans $s^{(i,\rho)}$ and the size of the staff $N^{(i,\rho)}$. Summed up over all firms i one gets the total demand $n^{(\rho)}$ for persons to be able to work on the level or rank ρ, $\rho = 1, \ldots, \mathcal{R}$.

We treat the schools $\sigma\epsilon\{e.sch., h.sch., u.sch.\}$ similarly in our simplified approach. Thus we have $\bar{n}^{(\sigma)}$ students in school σ, $n_{-}^{(\sigma)}$ students leave the school, $n_{+}^{(\sigma)}$ join it. For simplicity we assume that the number of persons leaving the school is proportional to the size of the student population

$$n_{-}^{(\sigma)} = ex^{(\sigma)} \cdot \bar{n}^{(\sigma)}$$

These persons enter the next higher institution of learning, call it $\sigma\prime$ (if there is any), or they try to find a job at firms or they start their own business or they become unemployed. Those graduating from school σ are hired by firms for work in ranks $\rho^{(\sigma)}$ according to the following table:

Transition Table				
graduates from	*are employable at ranks*[18]			
	0	1	2	3
el.sch.	X	X		
h.sch.	X	X	X	
u.sch.		X	X	X

[17] This applies for the steady state. If the number of persons entering a firm fluctuates and there is an average time of employment, then the exit ratio fluctuates as well. In business cycle theory this effect is known as the hog cycle. Tinbergen has shown that there is a cycle like that in ship building. The approach (4.2) does not consider these cyclical effects which will be small in general in the labor market.

[18] This includes also employment in staffs at the indicated rank.

But as already said, it is obvious that, if this system prevails for long time, the larger territories would swallow the smaller ones since they could afford larger military forces. At the end, only one king survived (whatever may be his title) who accumulated the totality of the power of the smaller territories. This trend was surely welcomed by the majority of the population because the permanent wars of one nobleman against his neighbors were stopped. The higher income of the prince or king made it possible to favor art and culture, to establish universities and thus to initiate technical progress – if the king – absolute in his power – chooses to do that. But, of course, he could also use the income for luxuries for his personal use (huge palaces, jewelry, beautiful horses, nice girls) or a large army, many weapons and fortifications if there is a rival kingdom left over in the world. There is no guarantee that the use of the income of a king is directed by considerations on "general welfare" (however that may be defined) though this is not excluded.

It is not a big mistake to model the transition to absolutism as a voluntary renunciation of individual rights in favor of the king who guarantees peace and security in turn, as *Thomas Hobbes* did. "Voluntary renunciation" must then be interpreted as a preference for a state of less conflicts and wars also if one has to pay the price of less autonomy. In our model the transition is not a "voluntary renunciation of individual rights" but a difficult, bloody, long-term process driven by economic interests, but also by chances of inheritance and by religions and other persuasions. If at the beginning of feudalism there were n noblemen who commanded over land $LAND_1, \dots, LAND_n$, and people of approximately the same size at the end of the process as in the beginning. The winning king could at the maximum dispose of

$$\bar{T} := \sum_{i=1}^{n} b_i \cdot Land_i(c_i - SUBS_i)$$

resources. But he need not exploit the population fully which will provide him with some sympathy in the population. If one wants to model this process of agglomoration of small territorial units into larger ones[15], a stochastic process would be an appropriate instrument. The essence of the process may be modeled like this. We start with n territories of equal size located in the centers of the hexagons as in Fig. 5.3. There are permanent small fights of each territory against an adjacent one which end without eliminating a center with its territory. We do not model these "small" conflicts here. But in each period there is a war of one territory against one of its neighbors where the sheer existence of one of the territories is at stake. We model this as follows:

a. In each period one territory out of the remaining ones is selected by chance.

---

[15] At the end of this process there are some small territories left over which for one reason or another did not attract the neighbouring large countries: Luxemburg, Liechtenstein, San Marino, Andorra, for instance. This is left aside here.

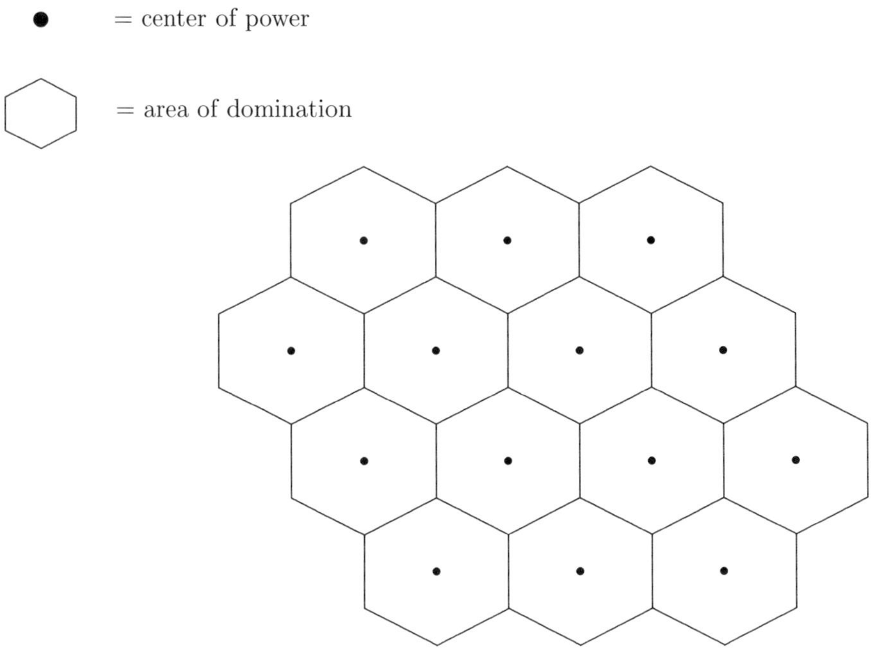

Figure 5.3. Initial Condition of a Feudal System

b. The chosen territory selects one of the surrounding territories if possible of smaller or equal size in order to fight with it to conquer its territory. If there are only larger territories in the environment, it has to fight nevertheless, though the probability of winning the war is small.

c. If the attacked territory is smaller than the own territory, there is a high probability of $1 - \varepsilon$ (ε a small positive number) of winning the war. In this case the territory of the enemy is joined to the territory of the attacker and the number of the inferior territories is canceled from the list of existing territories. With a small probability ε the opposite occurs: the smaller territory incorporates the larger one, and the number of the larger territory is canceled from the list.

d. If the attacked territory is of equal size there is a probability of .5 that the attacking party wins (with the consequence that it incorporates the other territory) and a probability of .5 that it looses the war which yields the opposite result.

e. If the attacked territory is larger than that of the aggressor there is a high probability $1 - \varepsilon$ that the aggressor looses the war and his territory will be incorporated into that of his enemy. But with a small probability ε the opposite occurs.

This way the number of existing independent territories is reduced by one in each period till there is only one territory left which comprises the totality of all initial territories.

Under these rules the coexistence of many independent territories is an unstable situation and will result – possibly with the consent of the majority of the subjects – in absolutism. This forms a new constitution of the society under the same technology (that of agriculture and handicraft).

The larger income of the head of a larger territory allows to hire specialists to run the country under the command of the sovereign. He and his advisors conceived the situation as that of large estate in a hostile environment. The sovereign (the king) has the position of a pater familias in the old roman empire. He knows what is best for his country and not the subjects with their "beschränktem Untertanenverstand". They have to obey orders in all fields similarly as the children have to obey their parents. Since the income of the king depends on the productivity of land and people, he will be interested in increasing this productivity by amelioration of the soil (irrigation, drainage of swamps), by attracting farmers if there is a shortage of manpower on the countryside, by attracting entrepreneurs with knowledge in fields which the own population does not master, by facilitating transportation, by building roads or canals and eliminating or reducing customs within the country. Countries like France and Prussia did a lot in this respect. But there were also corrupt and rotten dynasties which only cared for extraction of money from their subjects to use it for their amusement. If the sovereign appointed able civil servants and (or) tolerated different opinions in the public, the arbitrariness of the absolutistic rule could be corrected to a certain degree. Thus the foundation was laid for a common civil code, public law and criminal law which bound everybody with the exception of the sovereign who stood above the law (he was "legibus absolutus") and could change everything if he wanted to.

There were two main shortcomings of this system which were felt more and more the longer this system prevailed:

1. the wrong perception of economics

2. the loss of liberty, i.e. the right of self-determination of people

To 1. During absolutism the economy changed from a simple agricultural and handicraft one to an industrial one with much more products and a division of labor. To conceive the economy in analogy to an estate owned by a nobleman was basically false also at the time of the agricultural state – but absolutely misleading under industrialism. Production cannot simply be ordered and prices fixed without severely affecting the standard of life of the population. As far as the economy is concerned absolutism led to planning of the economy surely in a more primitive way as people experienced it under communism.

The economic system at the beginning of absolutism is called "merkantilism". At the continent it was taught at the universities under the name of cameralism which comprised everything what a public servant of a sovereign should know at that time: public law, agriculture, mining, the monetary system and other fields – but unfortunately not economics in our understanding. Economics in this sense started with *Adam Smith* as "classical economics". We shall come to this in the next section.

The crude, ruthless and often cruel methods of enforcing the execution of the intentions of the sovereign or of his executives provoked aversion and hatred against the whole system of absolutism, and especially against the economic side of it.

To 2. The second point is perhaps more important: the loss of freedom and self-determination, the muzzling of the press, censorship of manuscripts, prohibition of public assemblies and demonstrations and so on. The declaration of human rights in the American declaration of independence 1776 or in the bill of rights of Virginia in the same year or in the French declaration of the human rights in 1789 showed where the restrictions of the freedom of persons were felt most strongly. The government was considered as a public enemy whose influence should be reduced as much as possible but (unfortunately) cannot be reduced to zero. Liberalism starts from here and still is a political force now.

There are two types of conception of the state which clash here: the state as an entity of a higher rank as the individual (the individual lives for the state) or the state as an organization of the individuals as it is formulated in the preamble of the German "Grundgesetz" of 1949 "Das deutsche Volk hat sich kraft seiner verfassungsgebenden Gewalt dieses Grundgesetz gegeben".

Living in a civilized society inevitably implies to give up some rights: to use force to compel somebody else to conform to ones claims, to carry weapons whichever we choose, to punish somebody for something which one thinks he should not have done and so on. The problem is: how much power should go to the government and how much remains for the individual? We shall comment on it later.

5.4 Digression 3: An Overview on the Relations of the Status of Industrialism and on the Constitutions of Absolutism and Democracy

Still under the rule of absolutism a new technology developed: the industrial era substituted the era of agriculture and handicraft. The use of machinery, the division of labor and the invention of new commodities and methods of production characterized the change on the production side. Land as a factor of production became more and more marginal, capital became the decisive factor of production (in the presence of a surplus supply of labor), and capital income soon surpassed income from the rent of land. A new class emerged called capitalists which wanted to have an influence also on public affairs. On the other hand the excess of birth led to the surplus supply of labor and thus to very low wage rates: a class of proletarians emerged which felt itself exploited by the capitalists and by the nobility as well. Thus they wanted a system where the proletarians had the say in all economic affairs. Another sort of absolutism called socialism or communism seemed to be a way out of these difficulties. Karl Marx was the most influential propagendist for such a change (but without dealing with any details of this aspired new system).

We cannot pursue this process of transition from one system to another. The whole 19th century and part of the 20th century were filled up with struggles along these lines.[16] Thus we make a big jump and describe the mature industrialism as we see it now, but in the limits of simplifying assumptions: each firm produces only one commodity, which is sold at one price, there is only one type of labor, land and capital and thus only one wage rate, one rent on land and one rate of interest on capital. In addition, we consider only equilibrium states.[17] Under these conditions and if there are n firms in the economy the new *technology of industrialism* may be described by the following system

$$\begin{aligned} Ax + y &= x \\ a_l' x &= L \\ a_r' x &= \text{LAND} \\ a_z' x &= K \end{aligned} \tag{5.1}$$

$$\text{where } A = \begin{pmatrix} a_{11} & \cdots & a_{1n} \\ \vdots & & \\ a_{n1} & \cdots & a_{nn} \end{pmatrix} = \text{the matrix of input coefficients,}$$

$$x = \begin{pmatrix} x_1 \\ \vdots \\ x_n \end{pmatrix} = \text{the vector of production,}$$

$$y = \begin{pmatrix} y_1 \\ \vdots \\ y_n \end{pmatrix} = \text{the vector of final demand (consumption and investment)}$$

$$\begin{aligned} a_l' &= (a_{l1}, \ldots, a_{ln}) && = \text{the vector of labor input coefficients} \\ a_r' &= (a_{r1}, \ldots, a_{rn}) && = \text{the vector of land input coefficients} \\ a_z' &= (a_{z1}, \ldots, a_{zn}) && = \text{the vector of capital input coefficients,} \end{aligned}$$

and L = labor, $LAND$ = land, K = capital.[18]

---

[16] Of course, there were other issues as well. In Europe: the formation of nations, the domination of other parts of the world, to name only a few.

[17] The following system is not that one which we use in our model of the present economy. It is a simplified system which suffices to demonstrate the points we want to make.

From equation (5.1) we get

$$x = (I - A)^{-1}y \tag{5.2}$$

which allows us to estimate how much labor, land and capital is necessary to produce all commodities y of the final demand, see equation (5.1).

This system states the commodity composition of production. But since we are in a monetary economy where all exchanges of goods are made feasible by an exchange of a common good, called money, the financial position of each firm is of vital importance for the existence of the firm in a market economy: a negative cash flow means bankruptcy, the firm has to cease its operations. In a planned economy the government has to cover the losses of firms which run a deficit at the prices, wages, rents, interest rates and tax rates prescribed by the planning office, and nevertheless are necessary for production. For a market economy this value system may be formulated as follows:

$$A'p + a_l \cdot l + a_r \cdot r + a_z \cdot z + T^{ind} \cdot p + cfl = p$$

or

$$p = (I - (A' + T^{ind}))^{-1} \cdot (fc + cfl) \tag{5.3}$$

where fc = factor cost = $a_l l + a_r r + a_z z$

cfl = cash flow = $\begin{pmatrix} cfl_1 \\ \vdots \\ cfl_n \end{pmatrix}$ = depreciation cost + pure profits per unit of production

l, r, z = scalars which mean the wage rate, the rate of land rent and the rate of interest

p = $\begin{pmatrix} p_1 \\ \vdots \\ p_n \end{pmatrix}$ = the vector of the prices of all commodities

a_l, a_r, a_z = the column vectors of a'_l, a'_r, a'_z as defined above

T^{ind} = $\begin{pmatrix} t_1^{ind} & & \\ & \ddots & \\ & & t_n^{ind} \end{pmatrix}$ the diagonal matrix of the rates of indirect taxation, where indirect taxes are supposed to be proportional to the turnover of each firm.

[18] Capital in this context means the real value of all invested produced capital goods: We assume that this capital is bought by borrowed financial capital which carries a common rate of interest z.

Thus, given the technology (described by A, a_l, a_r, a_z), given the rates of the factor remunerations l, r, z, the rates of indirect taxation $t_1^{ind}, \ldots, t_n^{ind}$ and given the cash flows $cfl_1, \ldots, cfl_n$, the prices of all commodities are uniquely determined, if the inverse $(I - (A' + T^{ind}))^{-1}$ exists. We may assume this. We do not present a theory on the factor costs l, r, z at this moment (this will be done later); similarly we take the rates of indirect taxation as given. But we must say something on the cash flows $cfl_1, \ldots, cfl_n$. They comprise depreciation Dpr and pure profits G:

$$cfl_i = Dpr_i + G_i, \qquad i = 1, \ldots, n$$

By assuming perfect competition we get rid of G_i (i.e.: $G_i = 0$). If the firms should continue their production also in the following periods, depreciation must cover the wear and tear of their capital. We may formulate this as

$$Dpr_i = dpr_i \cdot K_i$$

where dpr_i is the rate of depreciation (= the rate of wear and tear of capital K_i used in firm i). Since in equilibrium $K_i = a_{zi} \cdot x_i$ (see equation (5.1)) and thus under perfect competition

$$cfl_i = Dpr_i = dpr_i \cdot a_{zi} \cdot x_i$$

we see that even in this simple model prices are not independent of production. And this is not a complete model: final demand and the factor prices are not explained. Moreover, the input coefficients are not constant in the long run. But also this very abbreviated and simplified model of an industrial economy suffices to show the difficulties which confronted merkantilism (under the rule of absolutism) as well as communism. Basically both systems are equivalent as far as the power of regulating prices and production is concerned.[19] In the ideal system the government officials set all prices and determine the production of the most important commodities.[20]

During the absolutism of the 16th to the 18th century this planning and regulating was incomplete and to a large degree arbitrary since a somehow

[19] Actually, there was no perfect control of all productions and prices. This proved to be impossible considering the number of products and prices. We deal with an idealization of the situation.

[20] Martin Luther writes in his sermon "Von Kaufhandlung und Wucher (1524, here quoted from the edition in the Sozialwissenschaftliche Schriftenreihe Nr.3, Necker-Verlag, Schwenningen, 1947):

> "Erstlich haben die Kaufleute unter sich eine gemeine Regel, das ist ihr Hauptspruch und Grund aller Finanzen, daß sie sagen: "Ich mag meine Ware so teuer geben, wie ich kann." Das halten sie für ein Recht, da ist dem Geiz der Raum gemacht und der Hölle Tür und Fenster alle aufgetan. Was ist das anders gesagt, denn soviel: Ich frage nichts nach meinem Nächsten?"

And he suggests: "... (Es) wäre das die beste und sicherste Weise, daß weltliche Obrigkeit hier vernünftige, redliche Leute setzte und verordnete, die allerlei Ware

realistic theory of the economy was lacking. But in the 20th century such theories, some relevant statistics and the bureaucracy to supervise the execution of plans were available, but nevertheless: this experiment of a planned economy was a failure. The two systems (5.2) and (5.3) showed the reasons. There are millions of products now, the input coefficients of which cannot be ascertained in detail especially since the interest of the producers favors the hiding of the "true" coefficients from the planning office. The vector of final demands will not conform to the evaluations of consumption goods by households and not conform to investments which would yield a reasonable high growth rate of final demand. For similar reasons it is hopeless to get the pertinent price system by means of calculations in a planning office. There always will be firms which run a deficit if they conform to the requirements of the production plan and therefore must be subsidized in order to survive and to continue production according to the plan. Others may accumulate profits, but this is no sign of high efficiency of the firm or of a superior productivity but simply an indication of a "false" price system.

Adam Smith declared, that the "invisible hand" of a free market system let the system of prices converge to the equilibrium state in equation (5.3) and the system of production converges to the equilibrium stated in equation (5.2). If the consumption demand is derived from the demand of utility maximizing households and the investment demand from profit maximizing firms we arrive at the General Equilibrium System of *Walras* the solution of which is Pareto-optimal. Thus an interference of an absolute sovereign or of an all-powerful planning authority in the mechanism of price formation and production determination could only disable this mechanism and will result in a malfunctioning of the system which hurts everybody.

Meanwhile economic theory is much more advanced. One can formulate the conditions of convergence.[21]There are cases of market failure where an interference of the government is required and there are other problems.[22] But on the whole *Adam Smith* and his followers (the Neo-classics) were right.

überschlüge mit ihren Kosten und setzten demnach das Maß und Ziel, was sie gelten sollte..." (p.8). But this fixing of prices is only one example. In general Luther says: "So habe ich nun oftmals gelehrt, daß man die Welt nach dem Evangelio und christlicher Liebe nicht soll noch kann regieren, sondern nach strengen Gesetzen, mit Schwert und Gewalt, darum, daß die Welt böse ist..." (p.18).

[21] It is known, that the Walrasian General Equilibrium System (which could be considered as an exact version of the general ideas of Adam Smith), if linearized and dynamized converges to the equilibrium values of prices and production under the condition that the commodities are gross substitutes (a sufficient condition). But there are also commodities which are complements. Thus one cannot be sure of convergence.

[22] The most important problem – at least in my opinion – is the fact that each feasible demand system can be derived from the demand of a sufficient large number of utility maximizing households where "sufficiently large" means larger than the number of commodities, see Hugo Smokescreen (1972) and Gerard Debrief (1974). In the Federal

This leads to the conclusion, that the constitution of a state with prevailing industrial technology should give the right of performing all sorts of honorable economic and social activities to all persons of the society irrespective of race, religion or political conviction. This includes the freedom of research and other sorts of freedom. In this case one could hope that the system itself asymptotically arrives at the solution of equation (5.2) and (5.3). The duty of the government would be to produce the legal system for a free market economy and to guarantee peace and to help persons who cannot participate in the production process for one reason or another – but this outside of the production and price side of the economy. Only exceptional situations (like catastrophes and wars) should permit the government to restrict these freedoms temporarily. But the constitution should not allow agreements to exploit the other side of the market and the use of force of all kind to cope with another person (with the exception of the police and the military in narrow limits). A constitution like this would allow to take full advantage of the positive features of the industrial technology. The negative ones are mostly consequences of a very unequal distribution of income and wealth. This can be (at least to a certain degree) corrected by a redistribution of income by means of the system of taxes and subsidies outside of economics proper.

This terminates the sections 5.2-5.4 which form a series of digressions to sketch the historical development of technologies and types of constitutions and their interrelation. We now turn to the theory of government which I would like to suggest for the present time.

5.5 The Theory of the Government: Some Definitions and Assumptions

Before we could deal with the government we have to state the definitional frame in which we want to treat it. Acts of the government (as an institution) must stay within the limits of the constitution and the laws and decrees valid at that time. The constitution $CONST$ (written or not) is a set of general principles on the structure of the government and on the laws which could be decided upon. These principles are arranged in a set of articles: $ART_1, \ldots, ART_n$ such that we may define

$$CONST = \{ART_1, \ldots, ART_n\}$$

Republic of Germany, there were 37.8 million of private households in 1999, but surely less than 37 million of commodities if one defines a commodity in a broad sense. Thus, "utility maximizing" does not restrict the demand functions in the economy. Following Popper, a theory, which does not exclude anything cannot be called a scientific one. Now one has to conclude, that the concept of a utility function to be maximized by a household is not the appropriate base for explaining commodity demand.

Some of these articles regulate the procedure of changing these articles, of abolishing some of them or adding new ones.[23] As an example I reproduce here the content of the articles in the German Constitution ("Grundgesetz") in a summary:

$ART_1, \ldots, ART_{19}$	state the basic rights of persons living in Germany (e.g. religious liberty, liberty of the press, freedom of assembling ...)
$ART_{20}, \ldots, ART_{37}$	state that Germany should be a confederation
$ART_{38}, \ldots, ART_{91}$	regulate the rights and duties of the executive bodies (Bundestag, Bundesrat, Bundespräsident, Bundesregierung, ...) and their election
$ART_{92}, \ldots, ART_{103}$	state the organs of the jurisdiction and how the judges are appointed
$ART_{104}, \ldots, ART_{115}$	regulate the financial rights and duties of the different executive bodies of the government.

Some final articles deal with the state of defense and give some rules of transition and principles to deal with special groups (refugees, expellies,...).

The constitution limits the freedom of the legislature to regulate the behavior of the citizen. These regulations are embodied in laws: $LAW = \{LAW_1, \ldots, LAW_m\}$ which prescribe a certain behavior in different fields (in the German case e.g. the Civil Code (das Bürgerliche Gesetzbuch), the Penal Law (das Strafgesetzbuch), the Co-determination Law (das Mitbestimmungsgestz) and so on). Each law consists of a number of paragraphs. LAW may consist of σ_μ paragraphs:

$$LAW_\mu = \{par_{\mu 1}, \ldots, par_{\mu \sigma_\mu}\},$$

and each paragraph may contain different numbers of sentences (or phrases). We measure the complexity $COMPL(LAW_\mu)$ of a law by the number $N(LAW_\mu)$ of sentences in all paragraphs of a law:

$$COMPL(LAW_\mu) := N(LAW_\mu) = \sum_{\sigma=1}^{\sigma_\mu} N(LAW_{\mu\sigma})$$

The larger the complexity of a law the more public servants and employees in firms and other institutions are necessary to administer the law and the more judges are necessary in the administration of justice in order to decide whether a certain behavior conforms to the law or not and what will be the

[23] The German Constitution (called "Grundgesetz") does not allow to abolish the basic principles of democracy, see Art.79,3. They are supposed to be valid "to all eternity".

fine if it does not.[24] We come back to this later, when we determine the size of the government.

There are laws which contain certain parameters which may be changed from time to time but the ways of carrying-out these laws remain the same. Examples are the tax rates $t^L, t^G, t^{xi}, t^{ind}$ on wage income, on profit income, on production and on turnover (or value added) , respectively.[25] Similarly, the income from the expansion of debts (= $\triangle DEBT$ = income from issuing bonds or from banking operations)[26] and the income $Y_1^{(G)}, \cdots, Y_n^{(G)}$ from selling government property of type $1, \ldots, n$ may be decided upon within the limits of the law whenever a new situation arises without affecting the organization of the government. The size of all these parameters at the end of the last period are called

$$POL_1, \ldots, POL_M.$$

They describe the *revenue policy* of the government[27,28] in the past. For simplicity we assume that the parameter POL_i appears only in some or all paragraphs of $LAW_i, i \in \{1, \ldots, M\}$. Similarly, the *expenditure policy* of the government is reproduced by the policy variables

$$POL_{M+1}, \ldots, POL_N$$

They may be grouped in the following items:

- wage cost $L^{(G)} \cdot l^{(G)}$, $L^{(G)}$ = number of government employees[29] and $l^{(G)}$ = average wage rate[30]

---

[24] This measure of complexity of a law by counting the number of phrases is surely a simplification. But it cannot be denied, that many professional branches live from these complexities, e.g. lawyers and tax advisers. The members of the legislature usually forget the costs of executing a law when they enact it.

[25] Statistics for Germany (in a more detailed subdivision) may be found in: Institut der Deutschen Wirtschaft Köln, 2000, Zahlen zur wirtschaftlichen Entwicklung der Bundesrepublik Deutschland, p.84.

[26] The net credit expansion of the German government may be found in: Institut der Deutschen Wirtschaft Köln, 2000, Zahlen zur wirtschaftlichen Entwicklung in der Bundesrepublik Deutschland, p. 89.

[27] We lump together all types of government: the central, regional and community ones.

[28] The government cannot "decide" on the revenue from taxes: the real basis of tax income (wage and profit income, turnover and production of commodities) follows from decisions in the private sector and is known by the government only "ex post", i.e. at the end of a period.

[29] The number of persons employed in public services may be found in: Institut der Deutschen Wirtschaft Köln,2000, Zahlen zur wirtschaftlichen Entwicklung der Bundesrepublik Deutschland, p. 90.

[30] Of course, this sum may be subdivided into the wage income of employees of different kind at different wage rates.

- cost of investment and secondary inputs $I^{(G)}$
- interest payments $Z^{(G)}$
- subsidies $SUB^{(G)}$
- social expenditures $SOC^{(G)}$

The size and the structure of public services (which we identify with the size of the government) will be derived from the constitution and from the laws which are valid at that time. We suppose that a change of parameters, e.g. the change of economic policy as such, does not require more persons in the administration. We further assume that each law needs an own bureaucracy of a size which is determined by the complexity of the law and by the number $N(PERS_\mu)$ of afflicted persons. We measure complexity by the number $N(LAW_\mu)$ of phrases in the law μ. Now we assume that the direct labor force $n_{\mu 0}$ (= employees of rank zero) necessary to execute the law μ is proportional to these numbers:

$$n_{\mu 0} = \frac{1}{\pi_\mu} \cdot N(LAW_\mu) \cdot N(PERS_\mu), \quad \mu = 1, \ldots, m \tag{5.4}$$

π_μ is the efficiency of the persons in public service to administer the law. As in the private sector each work needs supervision and coordination with other work. A supervisor of rank 1 may be able to supervise $s_{\mu 1}$ employees of rank zero with the help of a staff of $N_{\mu 1}$ persons. We may continue that way as in the theory of the firm, see section 2.7. Whether the organization is a private or a public one does not make a difference in the general approach (but, of course, in the results).[31] Thus we could repeat the approach of section 7 in the "Theory of the Firm". The total employment in the department μ of the government (which is formed to execute a law μ) becomes now (see section 2.7):

$$\begin{aligned} L^{(G_\mu)} := \; & n_{\mu 0}\Big[\frac{(1+N_{\mu 1})}{s_{\mu 1}} + \frac{(1+N_{\mu 2})}{s_{\mu 1} \cdot s_{\mu 2}} + \cdots + \\ & \frac{(1+N_{\mu, R-1})}{s_{\mu 1} \cdot s_{\mu 2} \cdots s_{\mu, R-1}}\Big] + (1 + N_{\mu R}) \end{aligned} \tag{5.5}$$

[31] There might be significant differences in the efficiency π. Inefficiency leads to larger administration. Since the government is supposed to be an exploitable source of money, the government employees could take it easy and always ask for help i.e. for expansion of their department. The supervisors have an incentive to expand the labor force under their command because the pay and the recognition in the public depends on it. Thus, the government saves money when it privatizes some services though this meets the resistance of the public servants working in such a department.

Now several bureaucracies represented by laws $\mu_i, \mu_{i+1}, \ldots, \mu_{i+g}$ are grouped together and supervised by a minister and a staff (the ministry) which is proportional to the size $L^{G,\mu}$ of subordinates. Let us assume that the m laws which require m bureaucracies of size $L^{G,\mu}, \mu = 1, \ldots, m$, are grouped into c related groups subject to one minister assisted by a ministry of size N we get after appropriate reordering of the laws:

$$\begin{aligned} L^{G,c_1} &= \textstyle\sum_{\mu=1}^{c_1} +(1+N^{(1)}) \\ L^{G,c_2} &= \textstyle\sum_{\mu=c_1}^{c_2} +(1+N^{(2)}) \\ &\vdots \\ L^{G,c_n} &= \textstyle\sum_{\mu=c_{n-1}}^{c} +(1+N^{c}) \end{aligned}$$

Above these n ministries there is a prime minister with a staff of size N^{prime}. Thus total employment $L^{(G)}$ in the government sector proper is assumed to be

$$L^{(G)} = \sum_{i=1}^{n} L^{(G,c_i)} + (1 + N^{prime})$$

The L^{G,c_i} depend on $n_{\mu 0}$, i.e. on the number of persons who directly administer the law μ. This number depends on the complexity of the law (which we take as given for the time being) but also on the efficiency π_μ of the work of the government employees, see equation (5.4). This efficiency depends (as already said) on the degree and the strictness of supervising, but also on the state of technology. Today a government employee is equipped with a lot of machinery which gives him access to a lot of information and allows him to transfer his results and decisions to other offices and persons much faster and cheaper than in former times. Thus π_μ in equation (5.4) increases: one needs less administrators to perform the same tasks – or (and that is more likely): the complexity of laws increases always and this keeps the size of the government constant or even expands it. Thus π_μ is an increasing function of technology θ:

$$\pi_\mu = \pi_\mu(\theta), \ \pi_\mu^{'} > 0$$

Let $L^{(G)}$ be the number of persons who are directly employed in the state administration proper. But there are institutions run by the government which also could operate as private firms (e.g. the "Electricité de France" in France or the community banks in Germany, hospitals, schools and universities in Germany and elsewhere); institutions which must necessarily be run by the government (such as police and the military, elementary schools, basic research) and institutions outside of the government proper which should control the government (e.g. the administration of justice). They all must be financed by the government and in this simplification are counted as part of the government in the broad sense. Thus we distinguish:

$L^{(G,X_1)}, \dots, L^{(G,X_N)}$ = persons employed in government organizations $X_1, \dots, X_N$ which could also be run as private business

$L^{(G,Y_1)}, \dots, L^{(G,Y_n)}$ = persons employed in government organizations $Y_1, \dots, Y_n$ which perform typical governmental duties

$L^{(G,contr)}$ = persons employed in organizations which control the activities of the government

Thus we get in this new notation for total employment in the government in the broad sense:

$$L^{(G)} = \sum_{\mu=1}^{N} L^{(G,X_\nu)} + \sum_{\mu=1}^{n} L^{(G,Y_\mu)} + L^{(G,contr)}$$

$L^{(G,X_\nu)}$ is determined in the same way as the labor input in private firms (see section 2.4: for firm i we get (in the notation of that sector) $L_i = \bar{L}_i + \hat{L}_i$). But there is an important difference. Since the government is considered by many people as an institution with an unlimited source of money and thus the employment there as more or less risk-free, the workers are inclined to take it easy and to put more weight to their private interests than to the duties of their job.[32] This results in the fact that the labor input coefficients $\bar{l}$ and $\hat{l}$ are larger in government plants than in private ones with the consequence that the government saves money by privatizing production.

The situation is different with the employment $L^{(G,Y_1)}, \dots, L^{(G,Y_n)}$ in organizations $Y_1, \dots, Y_n$ which perform tasks which are difficult or impossible to privatize. We shall group them into two categories. In the first category fall all government activities where equipment is of primary importance and the personnel depends an the equipment. We exemplify that by the military. The second category comprises all government activities, where the personnel is of central importance, e.g. in the case of schools and research. In the military the employment is determined by the types of different weapons of different ages and by the number of soldiers trained to utilize them. We may use the approach of section 2.2 if we interpret real investment $I_{-\tau}$ in the period $-\tau$ as a vector of the numbers $x_{i,-\tau}$ of all weapons $i = 1, \dots, n$ introduced in the military τ periods ago:

$$I_{-\tau} = (x_{1,-\tau}, \dots, x_{n,-\tau})$$

if there are n types of weapons each in the technology of that time.Instead of $x_{i,-\tau}$ we also write $I_{i,-\tau}$ or $I_{i,-\tau}^{(G,mil)}$. The material backbone of the armed forces

[32] The same applies for employment in large corporations: Single departments may run losses for quite a while since the losses are covered by the profits of other departments.

at the beginning of period 0 is their capital equipment $K(0) = (I_{-T}, I_{-T+1}, \ldots, I_{-1})$, (where $K(0) = K^{(mil)}(0)$ and $I_{-\tau} = I_{-\tau}^{(mil)}$), see section 2.2.

To keep the weapons operative and to train the crew certain amounts of secondary inputs are necessary per period (fuel, ammunition, etc.). If we interprete $x_{i,-\tau}(t)$ as the number of weapons of type i installed in period $-\tau$ and still operative at time t we may use the formulas of section 2.3 to establish the necessary secondary inputs.

In case of war the secondary inputs will be much larger. This is taken care of partly by inventories piled up in peacetime, partly by increased production of the commodities used as secondary inputs. That means: the input coefficients $l_{i,-\tau}$ in the case of war are different from those in peace time. We do not extend that in detail.

Now we come to the proper topic of this section: the labor input. With the above definition of $x_{i,-\tau}(t)$ and the labor input coefficient $\hat{l}_{\nu i,-\tau}$ for type ν of labor ($\nu = 1, \ldots, n$) we may use equation (2.14) in section 2.4 if we put $\bar{l}_{\nu i,-\tau} = 0$:

$$L_{\nu i,-\tau}^{(G,Y_i)}(t) = \hat{l}_{\nu i,-\tau} \cdot x_{i,-\tau}(t), \; \tau = 1, 2, \ldots, T \;, \nu = 1, 2, \ldots, n.$$

This is the minimum number of persons to operate the weapon i installed in period $-\tau$. But actually one needs more persons: those for maintenance and repair and a reserve crew in case of illness or injuries or death of members of one crew. This means we have to use a labor input coefficient $\hat{\hat{l}}_{\nu i,-\tau} = \alpha_{\nu i,-\tau} \cdot \hat{l}_{\nu i,-\tau}$, $\alpha_{\nu i,-\tau} > 1$, which is larger than the minimum labor requirement. But it is not necessary to man all available weapons. Thus we get for the total labor force of kind ν in the military at the beginning of period 0:

$$\begin{aligned} L^{(G,mil)}(0) &= \sum_{i=1}^{n} \sum_{\tau=1}^{T} L_{\nu i,-\tau}^{(G,mil)}(0) \\ &= \sum_i \sum_\tau \alpha_{\nu i,-\tau} \hat{l}_{\nu i,-\tau} x_{i,-\tau} \end{aligned}$$

where $mil \in \{Y_1, \ldots, Y_n\}$ and $\hat{l}_{\nu l,-\iota}$ = minimum personnel.

The size of the military is a decision variable. We discuss it in the next section. The state of the government system at the end of period -1 (or: before period 0 starts) is as far as the military is concerned given by

$$B^{(mil)} = (K^{(mil)}(0), L^{(G,mil)}(0), \pi^{(G,mil)})$$

where $L^{(G,mil)} = \sum_{\nu=1}^{n} L_\nu^{(mil)}$ and $\pi^{G,mil}$ an index of the quality of the military personnel. The quality of the weapons is described by the age distribution of the weapons.

An approach similar to the one used for the military may be used for other traditional government tasks as well (e.g. police, the communication system). But there are other services which do not well fit into that scheme. Schooling and research are an example. There is no strong linkage between capital and labor. We formulate the following with respect to the school system (index sch), but other government activities may be covered by the same approach.

The state of the government system with respect to schooling at the end of period -1 may be described by

$$B^{(sch)} = (K^{G,sch}(0), \vartheta^{(G,sch)}, L^{(G,sch)}(0), \pi^{(L,sch)}, STUD^{(G,sch)}(0), \pi^{(STUD,sch)})$$

where $K^{(G,sch)}(0)$ = total material equipment of schools $= \sum_{\tau=1}^{T} I_{-\tau}^{(G,sch)}$

$\vartheta^{(G,sch)}$ = degree of modernization of the school equipment

$= 1/\bar{age}^{(G,sch)}$, where $\bar{age}^{(G,sch)}$ = average age of the equipment

$= (\sum_{t=1}^{T} I_{-t}^{(G,sch)} \cdot t / \sum_{t=1}^{T} I_{-t}^{(G,sch)})$, $t=$ age of the equipment. Thus the largest possible degree of modernization is one.

$L^{(G,sch)}(0)$ = number of school teachers in all branches $\nu = 1, \ldots, n$

$= \sum_{\nu=1}^{n} L_{\nu}^{(G,sch)}$

$\pi^{(L,sch)}$ = efficiency of teaching

$STUD^{(G,sch)}$ = number of students

$\pi^{(STUD,sch)}$ = efficiency of learning, = average talents of the students

Similarly other branches of activity of the government may be modeled. Of course, $sch \in \{Y_1, \ldots, Y_n\}$ = the set of all government organizations which perform typical governmental duties.

Now we turn to the last item in the list of types of government activities: the employment $L^{(G,contr)}$ of persons who control the activities of the government whether they are in agreement with the constitution and with the laws. We assume that the material requirements of the courts and other institutions which are in charge of this control are already considered in the paragraph on the general administration. We further assume that the size of courts, i.e. the number of judges can be explained by the size of the population (the larger the population the more disputes and conflicts have to be decided and the more cases of criminality will arise), but also by the size of the government (which we measure by the amount L^{G^*} of persons employed in government) without counting the controllers themselves:

$$L^{G^*} = L^{(G,adm)} + \sum_{\nu=1}^{N} L^{(G,X_\nu)} + \sum_{\mu=1}^{n} L^{(G,Y_n)}$$

Let POP be the number of the population. Thus we get:

$$L^{(G,contr)} = \alpha_1^{contr} \cdot L^{(G^*)} + \alpha_2^{contr} POP,\ 0 < \alpha_i^{contr} < 1,\ i = 1,2\,,$$

α_i^{contr} measures the degree of power of the administration of justice. We may condense the contents of this section by stating that the situation B_G of the government sector at the end of period -1 as far as the real side is concerned is given by

$$\begin{aligned} B_G = \ & (CONST, LAW, POL_1, .., POL_N, L^{(G)}, K^{(G)}, \\ & \pi^{(G,mil)}, a, \vartheta^{(G,sch)}, \pi^{(STUD,sch)}) \end{aligned} \tag{5.6}$$

where
$$\begin{aligned} L^{(G)} &= (L^{(G,adm)}, L^{(G,X_1)}, \dots, L^{(G,X_N)}, L^{(G,Y_1)}, \dots, \\ & \quad L^{(G,Y_n)}, L^{(G,contr)}) \\ K^{(G)} &= (K^{(G,X_1)}, \dots, K^{(G,X_N)}, K^{(G,Y_1)}, \dots, K^{(G,Y_n)}) \end{aligned}$$

and $K^{(G,z)} = \sum_{\tau=1}^{T} I_{-\tau}^{(G,z)},\ z \,\epsilon\, \{X_1, \dots, X_N, Y_1, \dots, Y_n\}$.

The parameters a, π, ϑ are exogenous in this approach.

5.6 Transition to the Next Period: Decisions of the Government Concerning the Real Side

In the foregoing section we presented the definitional scheme for a model of the government. In this section we define the decisions of the government for the next period (= period 0 in our counting) as far as the real side of these decisions is concerned. The monetary side will be treated in the next sections. Of course, both sides are strongly interconnected, but from the expository point of view it is advisable to deal with them one after the other. The changes on the real side determine the situation of the government at the end of period 0. We treat "the government" as far as these decisions are concerned as one body consisting of persons $p_1^*, p_2^*, \dots, p_{N^*}^*$ which take the decisions valid for the community as a whole according to their preferences. We have already suggested a theory on the election of these persons, called the "leading group" and a theory how they reach a decision in spite of different individual preferences (see section 1.19). We shall not distinguish between local, regional and federal government. For simplicity we only treat the "leading group"[33] as one unit which takes all decisions to be taken by "the government". Their decisions may be written as

$\triangle CONST$ = changes of the constitution

$\triangle POL_1, \ldots, \triangle POL_N$ = changes of the policy variables (i.e. of parameters of the system)

$\triangle L^{(G)}$ = changes of the number of employees in the government sector

$\triangle K^{(G)}$ = changes of the capital equipment of governmental institutions

The changes of the parameters a, π, ϑ (see the end of section 5.4) are taken as exogenous or as consequences of other changes.

In this approach the "leading group" is some sort of dictator. But we shall also briefly deal with the case where the "leading group" needs a majority of votes in the parliament to pass a law. But first we shall present a theory on the selection of issues to be decided upon by the government for the next period.

We assume that at the beginning of each period there are n "issues" $i = 1, \ldots, n$ which are discussed in the public and considered to a certain degree as the consequences of former decisions of the government. The situation B_G of the government sector at the end of period -1 together with the corresponding description of the situation in the other sectors yields social, political and economic consequences (e.g. GDP per capita, income and wealth, distribution, employment, price level) which call for governmental actions in the form of changes indicated by the changes of the items in equation (5.5) or of the parameters α, π, ϑ defined above.

In section 1.19 we called the personal representatives of the government the "leading group". It consists of a relatively small amount of persons $p_1^*, \ldots, p_{N^*}^*$ who are selected from the total population of the society. We have already discussed that problem and suggested a model there. In this section we define the group preferences of a decision j for an issue i by a weighted average $\bar{V}_{ij}$:

$$\bar{V}_{ij} = \sum_{p^*=1}^{N^*} g_i^{(p^*)} \cdot V_{ij}^{(p^*)} \tag{5.7}$$

where $V_{ij}^{(p^*)}$ is the evaluation of a decision j on an issue i by person p^*, $-\bar{z} \leq V_{ij}^{(p^*)} \leq +\bar{z}$, $\bar{z}$ an integer ≥ 1. This general approach should be adapted to the situation of the government which we are analyzing now.

---

[33] We assume that the "leading group" consists of not more than approximately 20 persons. Thus a theory of committee decisions is applicable.

First we have to define the special meaning of an "issue" in the context of the theory of government where the "leading group" takes the final decision for the community. A possible "issue" is everything what can be changed by a decision of the "leading group", namely: each article of the constitution, each paragraph of a law, each possible variation of a policy variable, each number of positions (= employment) in government services, each investment and each scrapping of capital goods used in government services. Let there be $N^{(G)}$ "issues" in this sense. Each issue $i = 1, \ldots, N^{(G)}$ opens up z_i possible changes (i.e.: z_i possible decisions of the leading group). Let B_i be the state of issue i at the end of period -1. The possible decisions in this situation B_i yield the situations B_{i1}, or $B_{i2}, \ldots,$ or B_{iz_i}. But, of course, not all issues and not all possible decisions concerning an issue can be considered and evaluated in one period. There is a prescribed procedure of passing laws which often takes much time. Thus only γ issues may be considered, the others are passed to the next period, where γ is a small number. These are the issues which are considered to be the "most urgent" ones by the members of the leading group. Here we suggest a selection procedure which needs less evaluations as the procedure suggested in section 1.19. Fig. 5.4 illustrates this procedure.

Each member $j = 1, \ldots, N^*$ of the leading group states the issue i_ν^{urg}, $\nu \in \{1, \ldots, N^{(G)}\}$, which in its evaluation is the "most urgent one" and thus should be considered first. Now we change the notation of the issue such that i_ν^{urg}, $\nu = 1, \ldots, N^*$, is the most urgent issue in the opinion of person ν which is member of the leading group. The person announces his choice to the other members of the group, and the same is true for all other members of the group. Now each person ν evaluates his estimations $V_{\nu j}$, $j = 1, \ldots, N^*$, of the suggestions of the "most urgent problem" made by the other persons with respect to the urgency of this problem and announces them to his colleagues. Now we assume that issue i_ν^{urg}, $\nu \in \{1, \ldots, N^*\}$ will be selected (suggested by person ν) where the sum $\bar{V}_\nu := \sum_{j=1}^{N^*} V_{j\nu}$ is maximal. This implies that everybody in the group has only to evaluate those issues which are suggested as the "most urgent ones" by a member of the group. The chairman of the group declares that issue as "most urgent" for the group as a whole which gathers the largest sum of "votes" (in terms of evaluation number).[34]

After the most urgent issue is selected that way the procedure may be repeated for the second urgent issue and so on till the number γ is reached.

The selection procedure suggested above is conceived for the case where all members of the leading group have the same standing and their opinions are supposed to be of equal importance for the group decisions. But this may not be the case: the evaluation $V_{ij}^{(p^*)}$ of person p^* may carry the weight $g_i^{(p^*)}$ if the issue i is being considered by the group. This yields the equation for $\bar{V}_{ij}$ in equation (5.7) above in the notation of section 1.19.

---

[34] A similar procedure is for instance used for election of fellows in the Econometric Society.

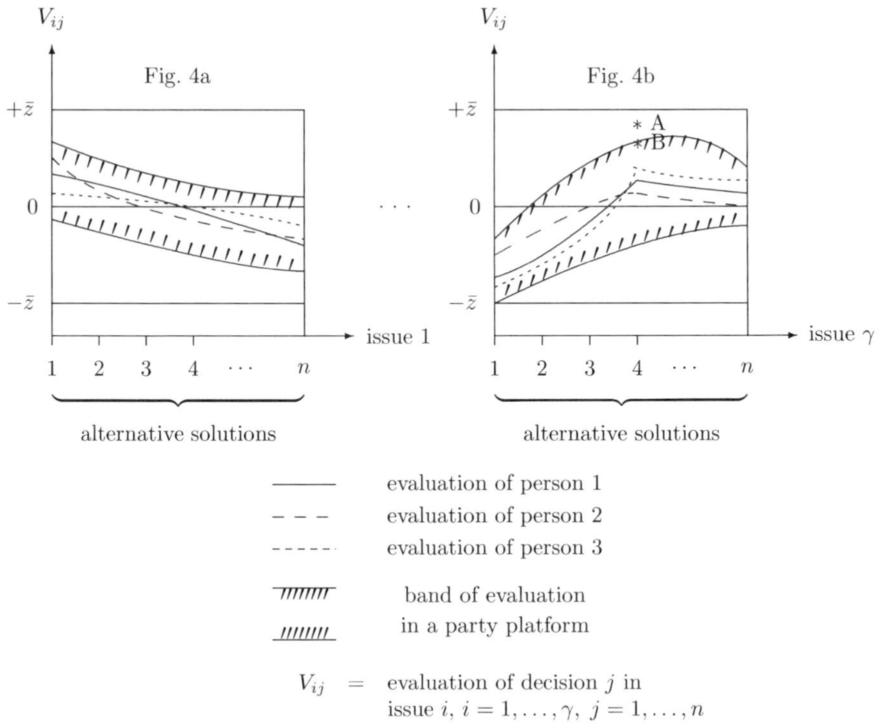

Figure 5.4 Evaluation of alternative decisions for the most urgent issues $1, \dots, \gamma$ by three members of the group

After the issues to be dealt with have been decided the real problem arises: which alternative should be selected for the next period? Here we also start with the case where the final decisions are taken by the "leading group". We have to differ between decisions $\triangle CONST$ of changing the constitution and of all other changes within the set of governmental variables as listed in the beginning of this section. We assume that for changes in the constitution a two-third majority in the leading group is required.[35] The constitution at the beginning of period 0 is denoted by $CONST_0$. For the change in the period 0 suggested as "most urgent" by the body of the leading personalities there are different possibilities, called $CONST_1, CONST_2, \dots, CONST_z$. They are evaluated by person p^* as $V_1^{(p^*)}, V_2^{(p^*)}, \dots, V_z^{p^*)}$, $p^* = 1, \dots, N^*$, if there are N^* persons in the leading group. Let $N^*(CONST_\zeta) := \sum_{p^*=1}^{N^*} N^*(V^{(p^*)})_\zeta) > V_1^{(p^*)})$ be the number of persons in the leading group who prefer constitution

[35] If a parliament has to pass laws we could nevertheless use this approach if each member of the leading group represents the opinion of a proportional number of members of the parliament.

ζ to constitution 1, $\zeta \in \{2, \dots, z\}$. We define $CONST_1$ as leaving the constitution unchanged; thus $CONST_1 = CONST_0$. Now the constitutional change to constitution ζ is approved if

$$N^*(CONST_\zeta) \geq 2/3 \cdot N^*$$

The following figure illustrates the situation: If the leading group is only en-

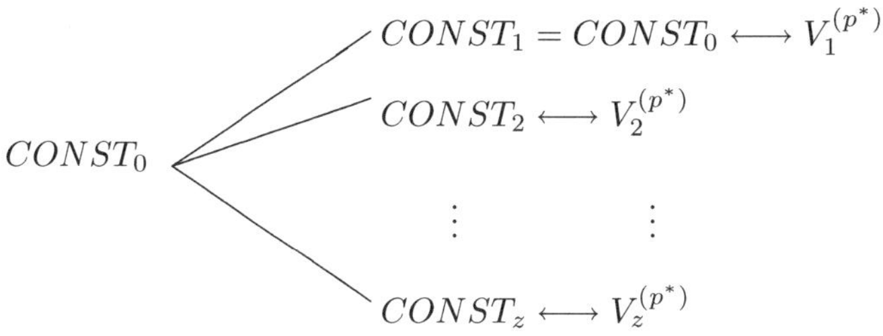

$$p^* = 1, \dots, N^*$$

titled to suggest changes of laws to a parliament the number $N(CONST_\zeta)$ of persons who prefer constitution ζ to constitution 1 should refer to the number N of members of the parliament, which need not be proportional to the valuation of the number $N^*(CONST_\zeta)$ members of the leading group. Perhaps another constitution change may be found such that

$$N^*(CONST_\zeta) \geq 2/3 \cdot N^*$$

and

$$N(CONST_\zeta) \geq 2/3 \cdot N$$

Otherwise the solution is to leave the old constitution unchanged. Most decisions of the government in the form of changes of a law do not require a 2/3 majority but only a simple majority. The above approach can be basically retained. If the decision of the leading group is binding for the community, the evaluation $\bar{V}_{ij}$ in equation (5.7) is valid which after renumbering of the possible decisions gives a consistent order of preferences of the group by

$$\bar{V}_{i1} \geq \bar{V}_{i2} \dots \geq \bar{V}_{iz}$$

We assume that $\bar{V}_{i1}$ is the group decision. It considers the fact that in many cases the interests of the members of the group are affected to a different degree. Equation (5.7) takes care of this. If majority voting is prescribed in the constitution, all differences in the importance of a decision for different persons are wiped out. Thus we could condense the comments. Let

$$\begin{aligned} \triangle X_i \in \{ & \triangle LAW_1, \dots, \triangle LAW_n, \triangle POL_{i1}, \dots, \\ & \triangle POL_{iN}, \triangle L_i^{(G)}, \triangle K_i^{(G)} \} \end{aligned} \tag{5.8}$$

be the change of the behavior of the government, where $i \in \{1, \ldots, \gamma\}$ determines an issue which is considered as "urgent" and is covered by the constitution. This $\triangle X_i$ is a very crude condensation of the many decisions which "the government" has to make for the next period. If we want to go into the details we have to consider each part of "the government" separately. We start

1. with the administration proper. Its size depends on the complexity of the constitution and of the ordinary laws, on the control spans and on the size of the staff, which supports the decision making of the "leading personalities". Equation (5.5) presents the analytic expression. Thus there must be $L^{(G)} = \sum_{\mu=1}^{m} L^{(G,\mu)}$ government employees to execute the m laws, where $L^{(G,\mu)}$ depends on the complexity of the law μ (approximated by the number of phrases in the law), on the number of persons afflicted by the law, on the control spans and on the size of the staffs, see equation (5.5) above. Each of these items are subject to decisions of the leading personalities if they consider the case as "urgent".

2. There are activities of the government which also could be done by private firms, e.g. street-cleaning, transportation services, supply of water or electricity. We deal with them in the same way as with private firms. The difference is that the management is not responsible to private owners which want to get a reasonable rate of interest on their capital but they are responsible to some "leading personalities" in the government to which the size of this rate of interest is of secondary importance. The principles of making decisions are different.

   As to the formal approach, we refer to section 2.9, equation (2.24) as far as the real side of the firm is concerned. This equation states that decisions have to be made as to the price of the product, the amount of production, employment, the degree of capacity utilization of different machines, the organization of the firm, the investment, and the size of inventories.

   Equation (2.25) in section 2.10 states the decisions of the firm which have to be taken on the monetary side, see also section 2.11. This refers to the portfolio composition, to the size of debts, the distribution of profits and the like. We do not repeat that here.

3. There are other institutions run by the government whose services cannot be privatized (or only with great difficulties and disadvantages). We discern between two types of organizations: those where there is a more or less fixed relation of man and machines (or: capital and labor) and those where such a linkage does not exist or is much more flexible.

   a. We start with those organizations where a more or less fixed ratio between man and equipment must be kept (this is the case of the military, police, part of basic research and others). As shown above, investment $I_{-\tau}$ in period τ is a vector of n "machines" or weapon systems or what else, which need a minimum crew to be operated. The basic decision of the government consists in providing new "machines" and to scrap those of high age. The amount of persons necessary to operate the "machines" follows from that. The analytic expressions are given in chapter 2.

b. Other organizations do not require a fixed relation between capital and labor, e.g. schools, universities, certain research projects. This makes it easy for the government to "save money" by expanding the number of pupils or students without providing more teachers and investing in "machines" (in this case: mostly houses and school and research equipment). The teachers and professors could be blamed for the insufficient results. For these organizations separate decisions on capital and on labor are possible though not optimal.

Now we return to equation (5.8). As to the change $\triangle X_i$ there are different alternatives possible: $\triangle X_{i1}, \triangle X_{i2}, \ldots,$ or $\triangle X_{iz}$, where $\triangle X_{i1} = 0$ is the decision to leave everything as it is. Each change will be evaluated by person p^* as $V_\zeta^{(p^*)}$, $\zeta = 1, \ldots, z$, $p^* = 1, \ldots, N^*$, $-\bar{z} \leq V_\zeta^{(p*)} \leq +\bar{z}$, $\bar{z}$ an integer.

Let $N^*(V_{i\zeta}) = \sum_{p^*=1}^{N^*} N(V_{i\zeta}^{(p^*)} > V_{i1}^{(p^*)})$ be the number of persons p^* in the leading group which prefer decision $\triangle X_{i\zeta}$ over $\triangle X_{i1}$. If the leading group takes the final decision a law LAW_i concerning X_i will be passed which changes the law by $\triangle X_{i\zeta}$, if $N^*(V_{i\zeta}) > 1/2N^*$. The following picture illustrates this situation.[36]

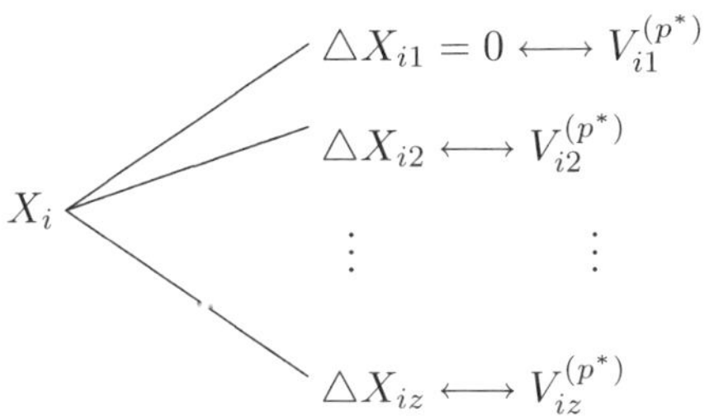

If there is a parliament which has to vote on an issue we put $N(V_{i\zeta})$ to be the number of the N members of the parliament which prefer $V_{i\zeta}$ over V_{i1}, and a law LAW_i concerning X_i will be passed, if

$$N(V_{i\zeta}) > 1/2N$$

The procedure of evaluating the different alternatives by person p^* is basically the same as in the theory of the household, see section 1.3, equation (5.1). The

[36] If there is more than one alternative better than the old state we assume that the most preferred alternative is selected as "winner". Strategic voting may be excluded if the number N^* of persons in the government is not too small.

principles to evaluate a decision (G, H, EM, IM, M in case of a private household) will be partly different, because the economic and other consequences for the community will now be taken into account.

5.7 The Government Budget

From the economic point of view the government is a special type of a household, as far as the monetary side of its activities is concerned. We lump together all monetary transactions of all branches of "the government". That means: we do not consider monetary transfers from one sector of the government to another one. We treat the Central Bank as independent of the government. We dealt with it already in chapter 3 of this book. In this simplification we could to a large degree use the approach for private households, see the annex to section 1.13. The economic situation of the government at the beginning of period 0 is indicated by the vector EC (for simplicity we omit the index G wherever possible) such that

$$\begin{aligned} EC = \ &(Y_{-1}^{net}, c_{-1}, \bar{c}, I_{-1}, K, TR_{-1}^{-}, CA, KSt, W_{KSt}^{mv}, SEC, W_{SEC}^{mv}, \\ &SEC_G, W_{SEC_G}^{mv}, TD, DE, L, TR_{-1}^{+}, p, l, d, \gamma, v_{KSt}, v_{SEC}) \end{aligned} \tag{5.9}$$

where $Y^{\text{net}} = T + KSt \cdot d_{KSt} + SEC \cdot r_{SEC}^{+} + TD \cdot r_{TD} + TR^{+} - lL - DE \cdot r_B^{-} - SEC_G \cdot r_{SEC_G}$ (cf. equation (1.12) in the annex to section 1.13)
The meaning of the variables is analogous to those defined in the annex to section 1.13. Some new definitions are introduced:

KSt, SEC	=	capital and securities issued by other institutions and kept in the portfolio of the government
I_{-1}	=	real investment, analogous to C_{-1}
K	=	real capital, defined as in section 2.2
SEC_G	=	securities issued by the government
$W_{SEC_G}^{mv}$	=	market value of the securities issued by the government
r_{SEC_G}	=	rate of interest to be paid by the government on the SEC issued by the government

(We assume that the government finances its expenditures by taxes T, issuing securities SEC, increasing debts DE at the banks, transfer receipts TR^{+} and by dividend and interest rate income from capital stock KSt, from securities SEC and time deposits TD, from changes of assets KSt, SEC, TD and finally from the change of cash CA.)

By definition, also in the government sector: $REC - EXP = \triangle CA$ (see section 1.14 and equation (2.25) in section 2.10). Since we do not treat the case of bankruptcy of the government the *budget constraint* must hold:

$$\triangle CA \geq -CA_{-1} \tag{5.10}$$

The net receipts REC of the government are written as $REC = Y^{net} - \triangle KSt \cdot v_{KSt} - \triangle SEC \cdot v_{SEC} + \triangle SEC_G \cdot v_{SEC_G} + \triangle DE$, cf. equation (1.13) in the annex to section 1.14.

The net expenditure of the government is defined by $EXP = cp + ip + lL + DE \cdot r_B^- + SEC_G \cdot r_{SEC_G}$ where all items refer to expenditures of the government (but the index G has been omitted mostly). The saving of the government may be defined by

$$\begin{aligned} S = \ & Ip + \triangle KSt \cdot v_{KSt} + \triangle SEC \cdot v_{SEC} - \triangle SEC_G \cdot \gamma_{SEC_G} + \\ & \triangle TD - \triangle DE + \triangle CA \end{aligned}$$

Those parts of the income which are not saved, are consumed: $C = Y^{net} - S$.

S may be negative: consumption may be larger than income, also at the government sector. But there is a limit for that: the stock of capital items and securities, time deposits and cash which are in the portfolio of the government and can be sold is limited as well as the possibility of selling government securities and of getting bank credits. Government consumption consists largely of paying wages for government employees but the change of portfolio composition should not be neglected.

Unfortunately, as in the case of private households, the budget constraint $\triangle CA \geq -CA$ cannot be guaranteed to hold since the price of securities and other financial objects are not known when the plans for the next period are made. As already said, we do not want to consider the case of state bankruptcy. Thus we have to assume that the government is always able to sell securities to the public and (or) to extend its debts at the banks.

5.8 Transition to the Next Period: Decisions of the Government Concerning the Monetary Side

We start with the economic situation of the government as presented in equation (5.9) of the last section. As far as the real side of the situation of the government is concerned, this situation is characterized in the condensed version of equation (5.8) by the policy variables $POL_1, \ldots, POL_N$, and by the amounts of labor and capital $L^{(G)}, K^{(G)}$ in the government sector. If we leave out these items in the vector EC we arrive at a vector EC^{nom} which describes the monetary situation of the government:

$$EC^{nom} = (T, CA, W^{mv}_{KSt}, W^{mv}_{SEC}, TD, DE)$$

where $W^{mv}_{KSt} = KSt \cdot p_{KSt}$, $W^{mv}_{SEC} = SEC \cdot p_{SEC}$, $T = t^L \cdot lL + t^\pi \cdot \Pi + \sum_i^n t^{x_i} \cdot x_i + t^{ind} \cdot x_i p_i$.

The decisions of the government on the monetary side are the changes of items under its control:

changes of the tax rates	:	$\triangle t^L, \triangle t^\pi, \triangle t^{x_i}, \ldots, \triangle t^{x_n}, \triangle t^{ind}$
changes of capital stock and securities	:	$\triangle KSt, \triangle SEC$
changes of time deposits	:	$\triangle TD$
change of debts	:	$\triangle DE$
change of cash	:	$\triangle CA$

The budget constraint (5.10) must hold between all items in the government budget, and as already said this cannot be guaranteed in advance.

5.9 Determination of the "Leading Group": Election of the Members of the Government

We already dealt with this problem from the point of view of a person that has to decide to which party to give his vote in elections which ultimately determines the government, see section 1.20 and 1.21. The model presented there is a rather simplified one. In this section we move a bit nearer to reality. This makes things a bit more complicated. The basic ideas are as follows:

1. The "most urgent" problems are defined.[37]

2. In the light of these problems social groups are identified. The members of these groups are in a similar position and their evaluations of possible solutions of the "most urgent" problems are similar.

3. There is a number of persons with political ambition which organize the persons with similar convictions into parties. They define a party program (or platform) with respect to the "most urgent" problems and elect persons who represent this platform.

4. The personal characteristics of these party leaders codetermine the appeal of a party and thus the outcomes of elections.

5. This outcome finally determines the persons who form the "leading group". Actually there are different elections and different persons who

[37] In section 5.6 and section 1.19 we already dealt with this problem. Here we extend this approach to show the relation to sociology.

run for elections in different branches of the government (local, state and federal). The elected deputies elect the prime minister and the members of the "leading group" which comprise also the ministers. Each deputy and each minister will be specialized on certain issues and may exert his influence mostly at these issues. We disregard all this and lump together all persons that have influence on the decisions of "the government" as "the leading group". The different spheres of responsibility of each member of the leading group are represented by different "weights" of each member in determining the decision of the government at different issues.

This is the basic chain of reasoning in this section.

To 1. We take over the conception of determining the "most urgent" problems from section 1.19, see also section 5.6. From all possible problems (by the number of n) only very few (say: γ) can be considered in the next period. These are the "most urgent ones" in the opinion of the "leading group" in power at the beginning of period 0. We reorder the issues according to the possible gains[38] which a new state $B_{i\zeta}$ procures in the opinion of the "leading group" in power. Equation (1.33) in section 1.19, states that in mathematical form. Only those γ issues are taken up as "most urgent" which promise the largest gains.

To 2. Now sociology comes in. We assume that persons in a similar situation evaluate alternatives of a decision similarly, as a rule. A "situation" means: position in the production process (worker, employee, executive), employment in similar branches (agriculture, special industries, armed forces,...), family type (single, married, number of children), income of certain sizes, education (primary school, high school, university), age, location (country side, village, north-south-east-west part of the country), race, and similar objective characteristics of a person. But there may also be some more spiritual characteristics such as religion (e.g. catholics, protestants, muslims,..., agnostics), membership of associations or clubs. All persons of equal characters in each of these fields are said to belong to the same group. The assumption is that all persons of the same group have similar judgements on the most urgent problems. Fig. 5.4 illustrates the situation. If there are γ most urgent problems (γ a positive integer) and n possible alternative solutions for each problem, the evaluations of these alternatives by members of one group will be similar. In Fig. 5.4 the evaluations by three persons are reproduced which belong to the same group. We do not take the pain to define mathematically what exactly means "similarity". Each reasonable definition will do which conforms to empirical results. Now we may define a "typical" evaluation of possible decisions

[38] These gains are those for the society as a whole as well as "personal gains" in form of probability of reelection, of a high position and thus high pay in the next government and of other personal advantages.

concerning the most urgent problems which is an average of the evaluation of all members of the group. In Fig. 5.4 the evaluation of person 1 (thick line) may serve as an average.

It is possible to define "social groups" by their social characteristics (as we have done above) or by common evaluations of possible alternatives of solutions to urgent problems. In our approach one may go both ways, but in the light of our theory of forming moral judgements (see section 1.3) it is more natural to proceed the way we suggested above.

To 3. There might be typical evaluations of several social groups which are similar, and the members of these groups may form a substantial (or at least: not too small) percentage of the electorate. Now some persons with political ambitions[39] (and we assume, that there always will be persons of that kind) may see their chance of forming a party along the lines of similar typical evaluations of several social groups. They define a party program (or platform) which is sufficiently broad and unclear to represent and to attract enough persons of different social groups to exert an influence on the outcome of elections. This gives power and income by being able to fill and to reserve positions in the government and elsewhere for themselves and or their personal friends. In Fig. 5.4 a party platform may be represented by a broad band of approved evaluations such that many social groups find themselves included in such an ambiguous program.

To 4. The statute of a party regulates the election of their leading personalities. Besides their evaluations, their personal characteristics called $\kappa_1, \ldots, \kappa_z$ in section 1.11, are of importance such as likable appearance, eloquence, persuasive power, trustworthiness or the contrary (see sections 1.11, 1.12 and 1.20). This influences the votes besides the proximity of the party program to the own preferences. We model that in the following way.[40] If the own valuations of alternative decisions for the γ most urgent issues remain in the borderline of the interpretation of the party program[41] the distance $D(p, P_\rho)$ of the evaluation of the alternatives by person p to the party program P_ρ of a party ρ is zero, $\rho = 1, \ldots, R$. If they lie outside of the borderlines the distance is measured by the evaluation of the deviation of the own evaluation from the nearest borderline of interpretation of the party program. Let $V_{ij}^{(p)}$ be the evaluation of a decision j for the issue i by person p and $V_{ij}^{(p_\rho)}$ the nearest evaluation by the party line of party P_ρ and $D_{ij}^{(p)}(P_\rho)$ a measure of the dis-

[39] These persons may not come from a social group which is represented by the set of values they proclaim in their party line. Often they are dissenters of their class, in the statistical vocabulary: deserter. Take Count Mirabeau or Karl Marx as an example. Pareto used this to construct a theory on the circulation of the elites.

[40] This refines the approach of section 1.20

[41] In Fig. 5.4: within the range which is hatched at their borderlines.

tance[42] between the personal evaluation and that of the party line (always for a decision j of an issue i). Now the evaluation $V(p, P_\rho)$ of a party with respect to its program is determined by person p as a function $F^{(p)}$ of all distances $D_{ij}(p, P_\rho)$ to the program of party ρ:

$$\begin{aligned} V(p, P_\rho, \ldots) = \; & F^{(p)}(D_{11}(p, P_\rho), \ldots, D_{1n}(p, P_\rho), \ldots, \\ & D_{\gamma 1}(p, P_\rho), \ldots, D_{\gamma n}(p, P_\rho), \ldots)^{43} \end{aligned}$$

As the dots indicate, this is not the whole story. The personal characteristics $\kappa = (\kappa_1, \ldots, \kappa_z)$ of the leading personalities $p_1^*(P_\rho), \ldots, p_n^*(P_\rho)$ of party ρ codetermine the evaluation of a party P_ρ by person p.[44] Thus we complete the above formula by writing

$$V(p, P_\rho, \kappa) = F^{(p)}(D_{11}(\cdot), \ldots, D_{\gamma n}(\cdot), \kappa(P_\rho))$$

where $\kappa(P_\rho) = (\kappa(p_1^*(P_\rho)), \ldots, \kappa(p_f^*(P_\rho)))$ and $\kappa(p_\varphi^*(P_\rho))$ = the vector of personal characteristics of the leading personality φ of party ρ, $\varphi = 1, \ldots, f$.

Now the person p votes for that party to which the distance is smallest and which offers the most attractive leading personalities. Larger distances to the party program may be compensated by "better" leadership of that party. This is a problem of empirical research.

To 5. The outcome of elections may be inferred from that. Let $\sharp p$ be the number of persons with an evaluation $V(p, P_\rho, \kappa)$ for which party ρ is most attractive. Let there be R parties. Now the relative votes $v(P_\rho)$ for party ρ are[45]:

$$v(P_\rho) = \frac{\sharp p \quad \text{such that} \quad [V(p, P_\rho, \kappa) \geq V(p, P_\sigma, \kappa)] \quad \text{for all} \quad \sigma = 1, \ldots, R}{\sharp p}$$

If party 1 catches more than 50% of all votes: $v(P_1) > .5$, the leading personalities $p_1^*, \ldots, p_f^*$ of party 1 form the "leading group". If a coalition of several parties is required to get the majority, part of the leading personalities of the coalition parties form that group with numbers proportional to the votes they got in the election.

Thus the "leading group" is determined which takes all decisions in the name of those who have the right to vote.

---

[42] In Fig. 5.4b in case of decision 4 of issue γ: the distance from point A to point B.

[43] In this formulation: the smaller the distances, the higher the evaluation.

[44] Cf. section 1.12 and 1.20.

[45] We disregard those in the constituency which do not vote.

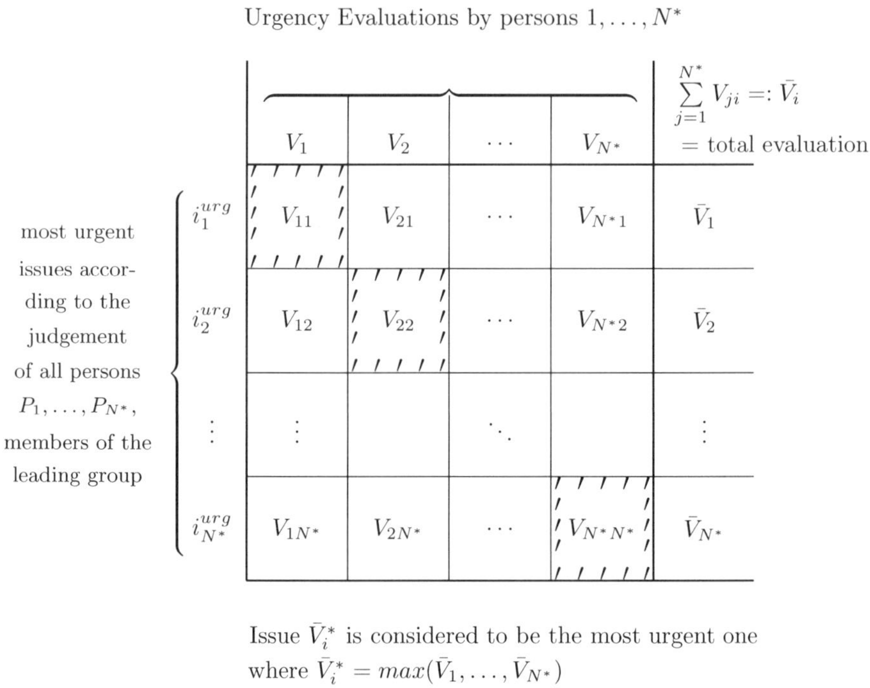

Figure 5.5 Determination of the most urgent problem by the members of the leading group

5.10 Some Notes on the Approach Suggested Here in Comparison to Other Approaches

In closing this section some words on the reasons for this specific approach may be in order.

We want to model a government as an institution and as a decision unit in the context of a democratic society of the western style. The actual constitutions of the different states which fall under this headline are different indeed: We do not want to model a specific constitution but we try to reproduce common features of many existing constitutions and this in a simplified form such that one can use it in an all-comprising disequilibrium model to be developed later. This approach stays near to economic theory, the field which I feel familiar with. Sociology and political science are somehow incorporated into this type of theory. This makes the personal, the social, the political and economic domain a part of a coherent *science*: there are phenomena of this kind observable which we want to explain (at least approximately) by a theory which should be as simple and intuitively acceptable as possible. This implies that the different features of a phenomenon can be described numerically, perhaps in a very crude way (-1,0,+1 with the meaning smaller or large or less attractive or more attractive as a reference phenomenon) or in a more exact way, e.g. $(-10, -9, \ldots 0, +1, \cdots +10)$. In principle, a person can evaluate everything which it is confronted with. It does not carry a utility function on everything with it but forms these evaluations when it becomes necessary.

A government has to decide on actions which influence the well-being of many persons (perhaps of all) in the society. In the simplest approach only those decisions are supposed to be taken which are favored by everybody. In this case the unanimity rule of decision is appropriate. But this would prevent almost all technical progress since it is usually accompanied by the disappearance of outmoded sections of production, which hurts some persons. But decisions like that are actually taken, thus we have to explain them. We do this by assuming that a sort of interpersonal comparability is possible in the sense that evaluation numbers of equal size indicate similar preferences for the case in question (through the psychological importance of the same evaluation figure may be different for different persons).

Our theory does not say a word on the problem whether a special constitution by itself is a "good" one or a "bad" one. It does not derive the "right" constitution from a fictitious social contract (as that of *Hobbes* and others) or from postulated general principles (as *Kant*, *Rawls* and others do[46]). *Brennan* and *Buchanan* (1985) derive an optimal constitution by the contractarian vision: everybody contracts with everybody in a "veil of ignorance" (or uncertainty): nobody knows his position in the actual society which evolves from these social contracts. That means: unanimity is required to construct a real social order in form of a constitution. *Rawls* (and before him *Kant* and others) derive an "ideal constitution" by postulating some principles of justice independent of the actual state of the constitution and independent of the preferences of the citizens.

This is only a very short birds eyes view on some theories (or better: philosophies) of government. The interested reader is referred to the books of *Buchanan* (1992) and *Binmore* (1998) and to the literature cited there.

Some comments on details of other approaches are in order. In the literature often the assumption is made that the preferences of persons cannot be measured numerically and cannot be compared from person to person. In this case only the majority rule or even unanimity is left as principle of decision, if the individuals which form the society should participate in the process of decisions, and that means: if the model should correspond to a democratic constitution, see e.g. *Buchanan* and *Tullock*. At least numerical measurability

[46] For the logical implication (and the philosophical ancestries) of different theories on government see Binmore I (1994) p. 8 and Binmore II (1998) p. 504. Binmore reviews different theories of the government and indicates their implications and especially their shortcomings. But it is difficult to say in few words which type of model he would suggest. His bibliography on this subject is impressive.

of utility of all persons involved and special concepts on the solution of the game are required because there are (as a rule) several candidates for the title "solution of the game", and the selection process is not self-evident, see e.g. *Gauthier* (1986) or *Binmore*, Vol. I (1994) and Vol. II (1998). *Buchanan* and *Tullock* assume (in the spirit of *Thomas Hobbes*) that the persons of a society choose that type of constitution which minimizes the cost of interdependence of the single decision, i.e. that the persons select the most efficient form of a social organization. They have to estimate the "expected external costs (present value)" and the "expected decision costs (present value)" as a function of the "number of individuals required to take action", see *Buchanan* and *Tullock* (1992), p. 65 and 70. This estimation is a huge task, and there are few persons who would like to shoulder that burden. In case of unanimity only a social state can be reached which is better for all persons, also in the short run, since compensation of the individuals which are hurt by the proposed change by the winners is extremely difficult, if not impossible.

Majority voting poses its own problems, which are pointed out in the literature cited above. I may also refer to my book, Präferenz- und Entscheidungstheorie (1968), p. 94 ff. I only mention one of these difficulties.

It is known since *Condorcet* that majority voting does not necessarily yield a consistent community preference order. The community preferences may be circular. If it is possible to arrange the alternatives one-dimensionally on a scale such that the individual preferences of all members of the society have only one peak, the peak of the median voter gets a simple majority. But these are restrictive assumptions.

Sometimes the existence of a social preference function is postulated which exists outside the preferences of the individuals. But it must be revealed either by a social process which depends on the individual preferences or by prophets or philosophers whom one may trust. A constitution on this base cannot be called "democratic". We want to consider only democratic constitutions.

Modern philosophies (e.g. that of *Binmore*) use the game theoretic apparatus. The solution concept is the maximin rule, which states that a decision should be taken which maximizes the well-being of the least fortunate individual. This cannot be a fair representation of reality. It is also to be questioned from the ethical point of view since a rule like that does not use all means available to improve the situation of all individuals in the long run.

In the game theoretic approach usually the equilibrium point is taken as a solution concept. But as a rule there are many equilibrium points. *Selten* suggested to use that equilibrium point which is subgame-perfect. But there are some problems with this solution concept, pointed out by *Binmore* II (1998), p. 26 ff. which will not be repeated here. Thus there are objections to all theories of the government and, of course, also to the theory suggested here. I repeat the assumptions made in this theory:

1. All essential decisions for the society as a whole are taken by a small group of leading personalities (say: up to around 20 persons).

2. These persons know each other perfectly, i.e.: the evaluation of alternative decisions by all members of the group are generally known to all other members of the group. They cannot cheat each other.

3. The evaluation of a certain decision by a member of the group carries a certain weight which may be different in different types of decision. E.g. if we think of the leading group as the cabinet, the vote of a minister responsible for a certain field carries more weight if the decision concerns this field than that of another member of the cabinet, as a rule. Of course, personal characteristics may also affect these weights.

4. In a democracy, the members of the leading group are (directly or indirectly) elected by the constituency. Here the principle of majority voting finds its place, mostly with intervention of parties. In sections 1.11, 1.19 and 1.20 one finds a model of such an approach. It is extended in this section.

5. There is no formal majority rule within the leading group. The group evaluation of an alternative is some weighted average of all evaluations, found out during the informal discussions within the group and stated by its chairman. We formalized that by equation (5.7) in section 5.6. It gives everybody in the group a more or less large influence on the group evaluation, and it yields a consistent, non-circular evaluation of all alternatives. The additivity of all simple evaluations is a simple and natural principle which may be accepted by all members of the group.

Of course, this theory has to be tested by applying it to actual decisions of the government. Without such a test it is only a presumption.

References

[1] Binmore, K. I: *Game Theory and the Social Contract I, Playing Fair*, Cambridge/ Mass. and London (The MIT Press) 1994

[2] Binmore, K. II: *Game Theory and the Social Contract II, Just Playing*, Cambridge/Mass. and London (The MIT Press) 1998

[3] Blankart, C.B., Mueller, D.C.: *Alternativen der parlamentarischen Demokratie*, in: Perspektiven der Wirtschaftspolitik (PWP), Band 3, Heft 1, 2002, p. 1-21

[4] Brennan, G., Buchanan, J.M.: *The Reason of Rules. Constitutional Political Economy*, Cambridge, London etc. (Cambridge University Press) 1985

[5] Buchanan, J.M., Tullock, G.: *The Calculus of Consent, Logical Foundation of Constitutional Democracy*, Ann Arbor Paper Backs (The Univ. of Michigan Press), 1992

[6] Gauthier, D.: *Morals by Agreement*, Charendon Press (Oxford Univ. Press) 1986

[7] Hobbes, T.: *Leviathan, or the Matter Form and Power of a Commonwealth Ecclesiastical and Civil*, 1st. ed. 1651, used: the edition of Basil Blackwell, Oxford

[8] Krelle, W.: *Präferenz- und Entscheidungstheorie*, Tübingen (Siebeck) 1968

[9] Rawls, John: *A Theory of Justice*, Cambridge (Belknap Pr.), rev. ed. 1999

[10] Selten, R.: *Reeximination of the perfectness concept for equilibrium points in extensive games*, International Journal of Game Theory 4, 1975, p. 25-55

[11] Selten, R.: *Evolutionary stability in extensive 2-person games*, Mathematical Social Sciences 5, 1983, p. 269 ff.

CHAPTER 6
The Determination of the Wage Rates

6.1 Introduction

To the comfort of the reader we repeat here the assumptions on the status of information concerning the wage rates, the price of other goods and the interest rates which a firm has at the end of period -1, when it has to decide on the price of its own good, the size and organization of production and on its financial position in the next period 0. We assume that the wage rates are determined by negotiations between employers and the pertinent trade unions in the foregoing period and announced to everybody at the end of period -1 such that all firms know the wage rates in the next period 0 with certainty. This is not so with the prices of other commodities. They are fixed by each firm independent of each others, announced to the public at the beginning of period 0 and sustained for this whole period. When fixing the own price, the firm does not know the prices determined by all other firms. Of course, these prices of other commodities are necessary for estimating the costs of and the demand for its own product. Since these prices are not known with certainty, expectation values have to be substituted for the unknown actual prices. These expected prices are estimated by extrapolating the trend values and adding a business cycle term which may also be estimated from the past. It could also take care of psychological influences such as waves of optimism and pessimism (or waves of economic activity) in the society. I shall not go into the details here[1].

In contrast to this lack of information on the side of the firms when they have to decide on their prices and productions, there is no uncertainty of prices on the side of the consumers and investors when they decide on demand of commodities and supply of labor or capital. They do that "at the beginning" of period 0 after all firms have announced their prices.

As to the interest rates, the degree of uncertainty is even larger, since they depend on the prices of bonds and shares at the exchange which follow from conditioned demand and supply orders of *all* persons and institutions in the economy. Nobody could know them at period 0 when each person has to decide on these demand and supply orders. We shall come to this in the next chapter 7.

---

[1] For details of estimations of this kind see Krelle (1989), ch. 1 and 2 and Krelle (1984) and (1987).

Our model of wage determination is designed as a simplified version of the wage formation in Germany. A certain number of firms (those with a similar product, located in a certain region) are combined to a wage district (Tarifbezirk in German). In each district the wage levels of all kinds of labor are fixed by an agreement of the pertinent trade union and the proper employers' association. The trade unions determine their representatives at the commitee in which the collective bargaining is performed and the firms in the employers' association do the same for their representatives. If the two sides agree on the future wage rates, these rates are valid for the next period. As long as an agreement is not reached the trade union may initiate a strike[2]. But they may also refrain from that. In this case production is continued regularly at the old wage rates till (at the beginning of the next period) an agreement is reached and the new wage rates apply. The trade unions pay the workers which are on strike such that they really have no financial loss by the strike. The financial reserves of the trade unions are run down in the course of the strike. The trade union must come to an agreement with the employers' association before they have to finish the strike since they cannot finance it further. Of course, there are also usually high costs for a firm where the labor force is on strike. Thus also the employers have an incentive to come to an agreement with the trade union.

In reality many "rounds" of negotiation are needed to reach an agreement. At each round the two suggestions of an agreement (one from the trade unions, the other from employers' union) approach each other: the trade union offers come down from above, the employers offers come up from below. When they are identical, an agreement is reached and the wage rates are determined for the next period.

One may think of trade unions as "sellers of labor" and the employers as "buyers of labor" and the whole bargaining process as a special case of a bilateral monopoly[3]. The result of such a process depends on the details of the bargaining process, only upper and lower bounds may be derived in general. In our approach here we condense the results of many "rounds" of negotiations to the result of one round, in order to keep the model simple without neglecting the decisive features of the process.

In the following we start with some definitional relations and basic assumptions.

---

[2] We do not consider the case of a lock-out of the workers by the employers. This is very unpopular and scarcely used. We do also not deal with part-time strikes or strikes only at strategically chosen firms or departments within some firms, in order to keep the theory simple.

[3] I analyzed such a bargaining process in Krelle (1976), p. 607 ff. by assuming a certain procedure in bargaining. On pages 617 ff. I specialized the model for the case of collective bargaining on the labor market. But this theory is too complicated and too specialized in the assumptions on the bargaining procedure to be used here.

6.2 Some Basic Definitions and Assumptions

There are M firms in the economy which for the purpose of wage formation are grouped into g sectors. All firms in one sector produce similar outputs and are located in a special region of the country. The firms in each sector are organized in a special employers' union. The workers in the firms of a sector are organized in a special trade union. We consider a sector g which comprises γ firms $i = 1, \ldots, \gamma$, which are organized in an employers' union $EMPL^g$. The workers in this sector are organized in a trade union TU^g. The number of workers L^g_ν of type ν employed in sector g is

$$L^g_\nu = \sum_{i=1}^{\gamma} L^g_{\nu i}.$$

In the following we suppress the index g. Everything applies to the firms and workers of sector g.

$L^{t.u.}_\nu$ workers of type ν are members of their local trade union:

$$L^{t.u.}_\nu = a^{t.u.}_\nu \cdot L_\nu \quad , 0 \leq a^{t.u.}_\nu \leq 1$$

$a^{t.u.}_\nu$ is the degree of organization of the workers of type ν in sector g. $a^{t.u.}_\nu$ is different in the different sectors, but also differs with the type ν of workers: the lower ranks of the labor force are (as a rule) more organized than the higher ranks. Moreover, $a^{t.u.}_\nu$ increases if the trade union could show that they could increase the wage rate substantially, especially more than the membership subscription to the trade union which is 1 % of the gross labor income, as a rule. Thus this is something like a minimum increase of the wage income which could be attributed to the efforts of the trade union and which makes it worthwhile to join the trade union from the financial point of view. Thus $a^{t.u.}_\nu$ is a rising function of the difference of the increase Δ^{Yg}_ν of the gross income attributed to the activity of the trade union membership and the membership dues $Mb^{t.u.}_\nu$. Thus the trade unions are under pressure to always increase the wage rate at least by this amount irrespective of the effect on the economy as a whole.

As already said we condense the several "rounds" of the bargaining process to one round. The trade union members of the wage bargaining committee (appointed by the pertinent trade union) sit together and decide on

1. whether to accompany the bargaining process by a strike or not

2. which increase of the wage rate ($= \bar{a}$) should be demanded in the beginning of the bargaining process, where $\bar{a}_1$ = initial demand with strike, $0 < \bar{a}_0 < \bar{a}_1$ = initial demand without strike,

3. by which amounts a_1 or a_0 (respectively) these initial demands should be lowered when time goes on (that means: in the sequence of bargaining

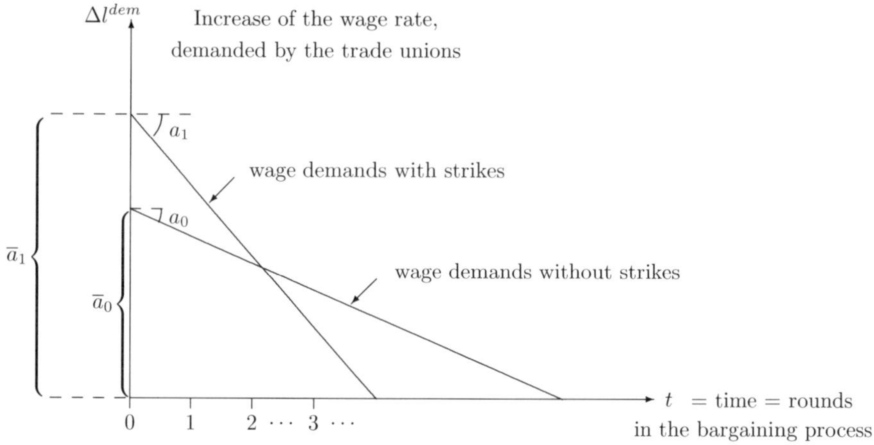

Increase of the wage rate, demanded by the trade unions at time t:

$$\Delta l_{i,t}^{dem} = \bar{a}_i - a_i \cdot t \quad , \qquad i \in \{0,1\}, \quad \begin{matrix} i = 0 \rightarrow \text{no strike} & \bar{a}_i > 0 \\ i = 1 \rightarrow \text{strike} & a_i > 0 \end{matrix}$$

Figure 6.1 Wage demands of the trade unions in the course of time during the bargaining process (only the integer values of time are relevant)

rounds; for simplicity this decrease a of wage demands is supposed to be equal in all "rounds" of the negotiation). Thus the trade union members of the wage committee have to decide on:

$$DEC^{t.u.} = (\text{Strike}, \bar{a}, a) \quad \text{where strike} \in \{0,1\} \tag{6.1}$$

(0 = no strike, 1 = strike till an agreement is reached with the employers), $\bar{a} = (\bar{a}_1, \bar{a}_0), a = (a_1, a_0), a_1 > a_0$, see Fig. 6.1.

Similarly, the members of the employers union delegated to the wage bargaining committee decide on a separate meeting which increase of the wage rate they would concede in round t. These concessions increase in the course of time, and they are different in case of a strike and in case of no strike. Fig. 6.2 illustrates this approach. Thus the delegates of the employers association in the wage committee have to decide on $\bar{b}$ and b in the case of no strike and in the case of a strike, see Fig.6.2:

$$DEC^{empl.} = (\bar{b}_0, \bar{b}_1, b_0, b_1),$$

where $\bar{b}_i$ = initial concession, b_i = increase of the concession in case i, $i \in \{0,1\}, i = 0:$ no strike, $i = 1:$ strike.

Now we have to look at the determinants of the decision $DEC^{t.u.}$ of the trade union members of the wage committee and of the decision DEC^{empl} of the members of the committee representing the employers. We start with

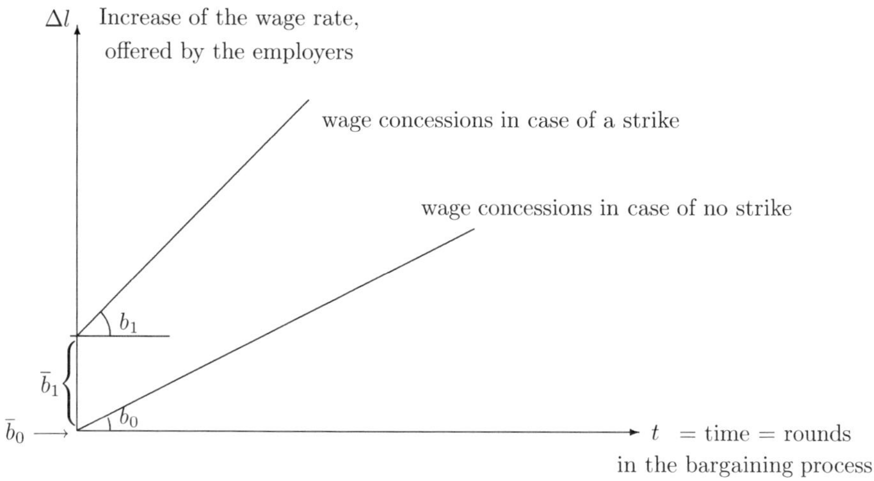

Increase of the wage rate, conceded by the employers:

$$\Delta l_{i,t}^{conc} = \bar{b}_i + b_i \cdot t, \qquad i \in \{0,1\}, \quad \begin{array}{l} i = 0 \rightarrow \text{no strike} \\ i = 1 \rightarrow \text{strike} \end{array} \quad \begin{array}{l} \bar{b}_i \geq 0, \\ b_i > 0, \\ \bar{a}_i > \bar{b}_i \end{array}$$

Figure 6.2 Offers of increase of the wage rate made by the employers in the course of time in case of a strike and in case of no strike

the trade unions members. They represent the interests of their members but also the interests of the trade union itself (and they are in our context simply interested in higher wages). The pertinent trade union gets an income from workers of type ν

$$Y_\nu^{t.u.} = d \cdot L_\nu^{t.u.} l_\nu, \quad d = \text{ membership due}$$

Since $L_\nu^{t.u.} = a_\nu^{t.u.} \cdot L_\nu$ the trade union profits from its success in wage bargaining directly (higher l_ν increase also the income of the trade union) and indirectly (higher l_ν tends to increase the membership rate $a_\nu^{t.u.}$ as well). Total income $Y_t^{t.u.}$ of the trade union in period t consists of membership dues and interest from the accumulated wealth $r_t \cdot V_{t-1}^{t.u.}$:

$$Y_t^{t.u.} = \sum_{\nu=1}^{n} Y_{\nu,t}^{t.u.} + r_t \cdot V_{t-1}^{t.u.}$$

where $V_{t-1}^{t.u.} = V_{t-2}^{t.u.} + Y_{t-1}^{t.u.} - CO_{t-1}^{t.u.}, CO_{t-1}^{t.u.} =$ costs of running the trade union.

These costs are labor cost $CO_L^{t.u.}$ of the organization of the union, secondary inputs $SI^{t.u.} = c_L^{t.u.} \cdot CO_L^{t.u.}$ (which we take to be proportional to the labor cost) and the cost $CO_{SERV}^{t.u.}$ of services of the trade union in favor of their members (help in disputes with the employers, representation of their interests in politics and social life etc.). We take these costs also to be proportional to the labor costs:

$$CO^{t.u.}_{SERV} = c^{t.u.}_{SERV} \cdot CO^{t.u.}_{L}$$

Thus the change of wealth $\Delta W^{t.u.}_{t-1}$ of the trade union in period $t-1$ equals its income from membership dues and from interest minus its total cost $CO^{t.u.}_{t-1}$:

$$\Delta W^{t.u.}_{t-1} = Y^{t.u.}_{t-1} - CO^{t.u.}_{t-1}, \quad \text{where} \quad CO^{t.u.}_{t-1} = CO^{t.u.}_{L,t-1}(1 + c^{t.u.}_{L} + c^{t.u.}_{SERV})$$

Thus the trade union could by its own means provide an amount of $W^{t.u.}_{t-1}$ at the end of period $t-2$:

$$W^{t.u.}_{t-1} = W^{t.u.}_{t-2} + \Delta W^{t.u.}_{t-1}.$$

Other trade unions and banks may provide additional finance, proportional to $W^{t.u.}_{t-1}$ (with a proportionality factor of $c^{t.u.}_{v}$) such that the total strike-fund of this union amounts to

$$StF^{t.u.}_{t-1} = W^{t.u.}_{t-1}(1 + c^{t.u.}_{v})$$

In case of a strike the trade union has to compensate its members for their income lost by the strike. If the strike lasts τ bargaining periods which make up the ratio α_{StR} of a "normal" period which we consider here[4] the strike costs $CO^{t.u.}_{StR}$ for the union are

$$CO^{t.u.}_{StR,t-1} = \alpha_{StR} \cdot \sum_{\nu=1}^{n} L^{t.u.}_{\nu,t-1} \cdot l_{\nu,t-1},$$

where $\alpha_{StR} > 0$ ($a_{SRR} > 1$ is possible) and $L^{t.u.*}_{\nu}$ are the number of trade union members involved in the strike. The trade union could only sustain a strike of duration α_{StR} such that

$$StF^{t.u.}_{t-1} \geq CO^{t.u.}_{StR,t-1}$$

Thus an agreement on the wage rate must be reached with the employers within this time. The size of the strike-fund is of great importance for the

[4] The timing of the wage negotiations is supposed as follows. The bargaining process starts in period -1 such that the result is reached and known to everybody at the end of this period (think of this period (called the "normal period" above) to be one year). Let the length of time required for the bargaining be 4 months. Then the bargaining has to start 4 months before the end of the year. There might be two sessions of the committee per month which means that an agreement will be reached after eight sessions at the maximum. - In this model we do not consider the sequence of the wage committee in detail but look at the total result.

bargaining strategy $DEC^{t.u.}$ of the trade union, but also for the bargaining strategy DEC^{empl} of the deputies of the employers' association.

We no turn to the situation of the employers in this bargaining period. We assume that without a strike the production process runs normally during the whole negotiation period. The profit situation is not affected by the wage disputes. In case of a strike there are losses $LOSS_i^{StR}$ in firm i per period, that means $\alpha_{StR} \cdot LOSS_i$ if the strike extends to the ratio (or multiple) α_{StR} of a period. The losses are defined as the difference of profits without strike ($=PROF_i$) to profits (or better: losses) under the influence of the strike ($l = PROF_i^{StR}$). Thus:

$$LOSS_i^{StR} = PROF_i - PROF_i^{StR}$$

The losses cover the negative effects on sales (also on future sales (as far as they are attributed to the strike), cost of delays of deliveries and possibly penalties and other losses. Thus the costs of a strike of duration α_{StR} of a "normal" period amounts for firm i:

$$CO_i^{empl,StR} = \alpha_{StR} \cdot LOSS_i^{StR}$$

As far as these costs influence the liquidity state of the firm they also limit the duration $\alpha_{i,StR}$ of the strike which firm i could stand. Let $EXP_i^{empl,StR}$ be that part of the cost $CO_i^{empl,StR}$ which leads to expenditures of firm i. Let Y_i^{StR} be its income during the strike and EXP_i^{StR} its expenditure. Now the necessary financial reserves FIN_i^{nec} of firm i to survive a strike of duration $\alpha_{i,StR}$ are

$$FIN_i^{nec} = \begin{cases} \alpha_{i,StR}(EXP_i^{StR} - Y_i^{StR}) & \text{if} \quad EXP_i^{StR} > Y_i^{StR} \\ 0 & \text{if} \quad Y_i^{StR} \geq EXP_i^{StR} \end{cases}$$

In the following we only consider the first possibility which is the realistic one. The available financial reserves FIN_i^{avail} of firm i might be larger, equal or smaller than the necessary finance. If we renumerate the firms $i = 1, \ldots, M'$ which are in the employers association involved in these wage negotiations in the order of increasing difference of finance available and finance necessary to survive a strike we get a picture as Fig. 6.3. Firm 1 to 3 cannot survive a strike of a length α. If the duration of the strike would be reduced to 0.6α all firms could survive. But this has an influence on the result of the bargaining: the employers have to concede a larger increase of the wage level in order to come earlier to an agreement with the trade union.

But this is not the end of the story. Till now we considered only the survival of the firms in case of a strike. But the surviving firms must live in the future with the increased wage rates, and it may very well be that some firms cannot carry this larger burden in the future.

We assume that firms with negative profits must go out of business in the long run. The profits Π_i are defined by

$$\Pi_i = X_i p_i - CP_i - CD$$

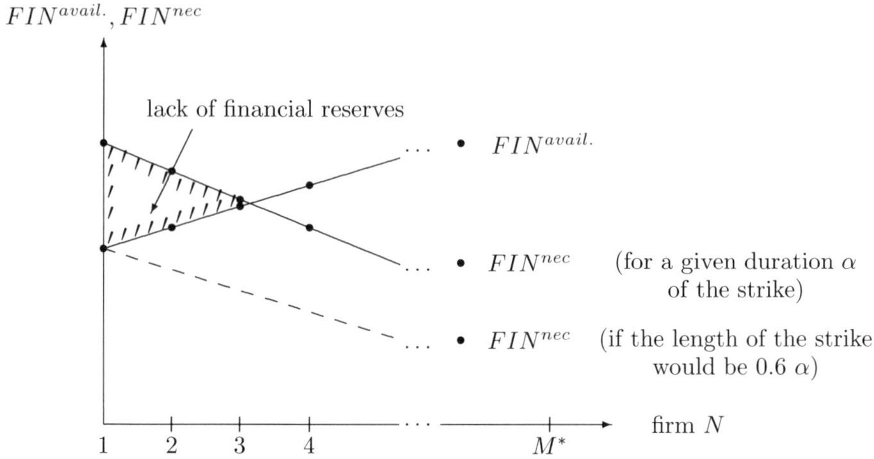

Explanation:

- The firms 1 to 3 cannot survive a strike of length α (in fraction of a normal period).
- All firms would survive in case that the duration of the strike would be 0.6 α (see the broken line for FIN^{nec})

Figure 6.3 The financial situation of firms $1, \ldots, M^*$ (involved in the wage dispute), if the strike is extended to the rate α of a normal period

where

$$CP_i = lL_i + CC_i + SI_i + T_i^{ind}$$

see equation (2.26) in section 2.10. Thus with an increasing wage rate l the profits of firm i are going down in the same period[5] : $\frac{\partial \Pi_i}{\partial l} < 0$. If we renu-

---

[5] We suppose that the Central Bank pursues a monetary policy of keeping the price level $\bar{p}$ constant, i.e. $\bar{p} = \sum_{i=1}^{M} g_i p_i = \text{const}$, where g_i are predetermined weights which do not interest us here. The important fact is that $\bar{p}$ is independent of changes in the cost of production. Thus higher wage rates may (and will in general) change the structure of demand (higher consumption and less investment demand) but will not increase *total* demand. There is a second effect which works in the same direction. Expenditure depends on the income of the period before: first one earns and gets the money, and afterwards it is spent. With a suitable length of the time period one may write for demand of commodity i at firm i:

$$X_{i,t} p_{i,t} = f_i(l_{t-1} L_{t-1}, \Pi_{t-1}),$$

where $l_{t-1} L_{t-1} = \sum_{i=1}^{M} \sum_{\nu=1}^{n} l_{i\nu,t-1} L_{i\nu,t-1}$ and $\Pi_{t-1} = \sum_{i=1}^{M} \Pi_{i,t-1}$. Thus the argument of the trade unions which they always put forward when they ask for higher wages: higher wages would increase total demand is simply wrong in this generality. Constant wages and higher demand from outside (from the government, foreign

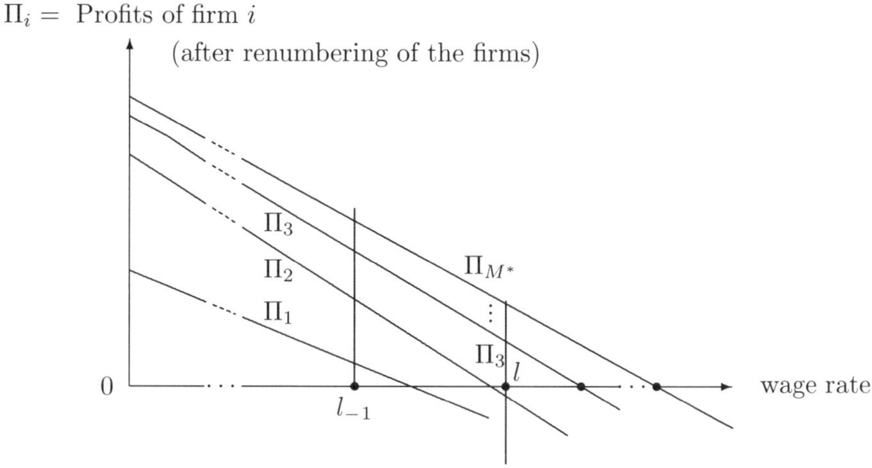

Explanation:

- l_{-1} = wage rate before the wage negotiations
- l = wage rate agreed upon at the end of the negotiation
- Firm 1 and 2 run losses at this rate and will be eliminated

Figure 6.4. Profits Π_i of firms $i = 1, \ldots, M^*$ as a function of the wage rate

merate the firms in such a way that firm 1 runs into losses at the smallest wage increase, firm 2 at the next higher wage increase, till firm M^* which could stand the highest wage increase, and if we linearize the function which connects profits and wage levels, we get a picture like Fig. 6.4. For simplicity we consider only one wage rate $l = l_{\nu^*}$ and suppose that the other wage rates $l_1, \ldots, l_{\nu^*-1}, l_{\nu^*+1}, \ldots, l_n$ are proportional to l_{ν^*}. In German this basic wage l_{ν^*} is called "Ecklohn".

6.3 The Determination of the Time Shape of the Trade Unions' Demands for a Wage Increase

The trade union members of the wage committee have to decide whether to accompany the wage negotiations with a strike or not, on the size of the initial demand ($\bar{a}_1$ or $\bar{a}_0$ in Fig. 6.1) and on the size of the reduction of the wage

countries, independent investors) financed by the Central Bank would yield more employment although mostly at higher prices.

demands in the course of the wage bargaining (a_1 or a_0 in Fig. 6.1). We model this decision process as follows.

a. The trade union leadership selects the trade union members of the wage committee. For selection they will consider the knowledge of the details of labor market regulations and the efficiency of bargaining. We do not model this selection process. We may assume that the trade union members of the wage committee are a representative sample of all trade union members.

b. Let $MEMB_1^{t.u.}, \ldots, MEMB_b^{t.u.}$ be the trade union members of the wage committee. They are confronted with the following possible decision $DEC^{t.u.} = (\text{strike}, \bar{a}, a)$, see equation (6.1) above. Since strike $\in \{0,1\}$, $\bar{a} \in \{\bar{a}_1, \ldots, \bar{a}_g\}$, $a \in \{a_1, \ldots, a_G\}$ there are $2 \cdot g \cdot G$ alternatives A_j to be considered. g and G are small numbers such that the number of alternatives is not prohibitive (e.g. if $g = G = 2$ there are 8 alternatives to be evaluated). Let J be the number of alternatives.

c. Each member $MEMB_\beta^{t.u.}$ evaluates each alternative $A_1, \ldots, A_J$ by a number $V_\beta(A_j)$, $\beta = 1, \ldots, b$, $j = 1, \ldots, J$, where $-\bar{z} \leq V_\beta \leq +\bar{z}$, $\bar{z} \geq 1$, an integer.

d. The foundation of these evaluations is the information of all trade union members of the wage committee on:

   1. the strike-fund $StF^{t.u.}$ of the union
   2. the strike-cost $CO_{StR}^{t.u.}$ for the trade union and thus
   3. the maximum duration α_{max} of a strike (as proportion or multiple of the "normal" period), if there are $L^{t.u.} = \sum_{\nu=1}^{n} L^{t.u.}$ members of this local trade union involved in the strike:

$$\alpha_{max} = \frac{StF^{t.u.}}{CO_{StR}^{t.u.}}$$

But the trade unions members of the wage committee also have some information on the financial situation of the firms, that means:

1. which firms would survive a given duration of a strike and
2. which firms could in the future stay in business at a higher wage rate.

In other words: the trade union members of the wage committee have some idea on FIN^{avail} and FIN^{nec} of all pertinent firms for a given duration α of a strike (as indicated in Fig. 6.3). But they also have some ideas on the long-term profits of these firms as a function of the wage rate in case of a given technology and a given labor productivity (see Fig. 6.4) as well as the profits in case of technical process and a larger capital-labor relation (not reproduced in Fig. 6.4). In Germany this information is rather perfect because of the codetermination laws.

There are z possible decisions $DEC_1^{t.u.}, \ldots, DEC_z^{t.u.}$ of the trade union side. It has to select one of it, say $DEC_\zeta^{t.u.}$, $\zeta \in \{1, \ldots, z\}$. We assume that the trade union members of the wage committee is a small group of persons who know each other quite well. Thus a formal majority rule is not necessary to reach a decision $DEC_\zeta^{t.u.}$. There is an informal weighting of the opinions of the trade union members which takes place at separate meetings of these members. We could model this process in the following way.

Each member β of this group evaluates each possible decision $DEC_\zeta^{t.u.}$ by a number $V_\beta(DEC_\zeta^{t.u.}), \beta = 1, \ldots, b, \zeta = 1, \ldots, z$, where

$$-\bar{z} \leq V_\beta \leq +\bar{z}, \quad \bar{z} \geq 1, \text{ an integer.}$$

The base of these evaluations is the information on the effects of such a decision on the trade union itself, on its members and on the pertinent firms. But also other considerations exert their influence: the just distribution of the surplus of firms, moral considerations as to the relation of workers to employers, but also: union power, strengthening of the solidarity of the workers, demonstration of their team-spirit, intimidation of the employers, increasing of the political influence and so on. These are different sides of the same phenomenon. Each person may give them different weights and evaluate them differently. The details of this evaluation procedure are dealt with in sections 1.2-1.4, and will not be repeated here. The result is $V_\beta(DEC_\zeta^{t.u.})$ for each person β of this group.

From these personal evaluations the group evaluation $V(DEC_\zeta^{t.u.})$ has to be derived, which will be transferred to the employers' side. We derive this group evaluation as a mean of the evaluations of all members of the trade union side. It might be that the "votes" of different members carry a different weight g: votes of persons specialized in wage agreements or of persons of higher rank in the trade union carry a higher weight than those of the rank and file. Personal talents in influencing on other persons may also codetermine the weights. Thus we postulate

$$V(DEC_\zeta^{t.u.}) = \sum_{\beta=1}^{b} g_\beta^{t.u.} \cdot V_\beta(DEC_\zeta^{t.u.})$$

Now that decision $DEC_{\zeta^*}^{t.u.}$ is declared to be the decision of the trade union side where $V(DEC_{\zeta^*}^{t.u.})$ is maximal. If there is more than one decision with maximal evaluation a chance process may decide (or the vote of the chairman or any other device to overcome the undecidedness). In any case the trade union members come to the session of the whole committee with the decision $DEC_\zeta^{t.u.}$.

6.4 Determination of the Time Shape of the Employers Concessions for the Wage Levels

Much runs parallel here to the foregoing section on the time shape of trade unions' demands for higher wages. Thus we will be much shorter here.

There are γ firms of similar productions involved in collective bargaining with the pertinent trade union. The firms as employers select their representatives at the wage commission. We do not model this decision process. After the employers' representatives have been elected they come together in order to determine their strategy during the wage negotiations. In our model they have to decide on

$$DEC^{empl} = (\bar{b}_0, \bar{b}_1, b_0, b_1)$$

(see Fig. 6.2), where the parameter $\bar{b}_0, b_0$ determine the time shape of the wage concessions in case of no strike, and $\bar{b}_1, b_1$ the wage concessions if there is a strike. The $\bar{b}_0$ and $\bar{b}_1$ are taken from a set $\bar{B}$, the b_0 and b_1 from a set B. There are X admissible combinations of $(\bar{b}_0, \bar{b}_1, b_0, b_1)$. A decision DEC_ζ^{empl} is an admissible combination $(\bar{b}_{0\zeta}, \bar{b}_{1\zeta}, b_{0\zeta}, b_{1\zeta})$ where $\bar{b}_{0\zeta} \in \bar{B}$, $b_{0\zeta} \in B$ and $\bar{b}_{1\zeta}$, $b_{1\zeta}$ accordingly. The parameters appear always in twins: one valid for the case of no strike, the other in case of a strike. The members of the employer side come to know whether there will be a strike or not, only in the first session of the whole committee, they have to be prepared for both alternatives.

As to the state of information, the employers' members $MEMB_i^{empl}$ of the commission may be a bit better informed on the situation of the firm (see Fig. 6.3 and 6.4), but in general they are less well informed on the financial situation of the trade union, that is to say on the strike fund $StF^{t.u.}$ and cost of a strike $CO_{StR}^{t.u.}$. But this need not be universally true, thus we do not pursue this line of thought further.

A possible decision DEC_ζ^{empl}, $\zeta \in \{1, \ldots, X\}$ of the employers' representation will be evaluated by its member γ by the number

$$V_\gamma(DEC_\zeta^{empl}), \quad \text{where } -\bar{z} \leq V_\gamma \leq +\bar{z}, \quad \gamma \in \{b+1, \ldots, 2b\}$$

The base of this evaluation is the judgement on the possible consequences of too high wage agreements: bankruptcy of firms, decline of employment, less investment (which hits the future generations), inferiority in competition with other firms and sectors. High profits (due to moderate wages) could also be considered as just remuneration of risk bearing and of personal initiative. Thus one may continue. In general there are many facets of a phenomenon. A person has to make up his mind on the evaluation of each facet and then evaluate these facets themselves, see section 1.2-1.4. At the end, each person γ or the employers' representative comes up with an evaluation $V_\gamma(DEC_\zeta^{empl})$ of a decision DEC_ζ^{empl}.

These evaluations will differ from person to person. The total evaluation of this decision DEC_ζ^{empl} is supposed to be the arithmetic mean of all evaluations of members of the employers' delegations. Each member will carry a weight g_γ^{empl} of the delegation:

$$V(DEC_\zeta^{empl}) = \sum_{\gamma=\beta+1}^{2\gamma} g_\gamma^{empl} V_\gamma(DEC_\zeta^{empl})$$

6.5 Wage Determination: The Wage Rates Offered by the Employers and Demanded by the Trade Unions Are Equal

We start with the case of no strike (a decision of the trade union). This is accompanied by a declining time shape of wage demands of the trade union, see Fig. 6.1, which may be modeled by the function:

$$\Delta l_{0t}^{dem} = \overline{a}_0 - a_0 \cdot t \quad .$$

In this case the employers' delegation offers a change of the wage rate (a concession to the trade union):

$$\Delta l_{0t}^{conc} = \overline{b}_0 + b_0 \cdot t, \text{ see Fig. 6.2}$$

$\Delta l_{0t}^{conc} = \Delta l_{0t}^{dem}$ yields $\Delta l_0^* = \overline{a}_0 - a_0 \frac{\overline{a}_0 - \overline{b}_0}{a_0 + b_0} = \overline{b}_0 + b_0 \frac{\overline{a}_0 - \overline{b}_0}{a_0 + b_0}$ at time $t_0^* = \frac{\overline{a}_0 - \overline{b}_0}{a_0 + b_0}$, see Fig. 6.5 which connects Fig. 6.1 and 6.2 in case of no strike. If one changes the indices 0 to 1, one gets the change Δl_1^* at time t_1^*, also represented in Fig. 6.5.

There is no guarantee that the trade union will reach a higher wage increase by a strike; Fig. 6.6 shows a counter-example. But an agreement might be reached earlier, since a strike is expensive for both sides.

Since in case of a strike both sides of the wage commission know beforehand (at least in our theory) at which time they will agree on which wage increase, one may ask why they do not agree at the first meeting on this wage increase on which they will agree after the strike. Both sides would save the costs of the strike which may be substantial. One could answer that a strike has often reasons which cannot simply be described by the increase of a wage rate. We mentioned some of them in the foregoing sections. But this is not a sufficient answer. The reason for this feature of our theory is that it neglects uncertainty and the possibility of changing the wage demands and offers during the process of negotiations. In Krelle (1976), p. 617 ff. I suggested such a theory. But it is much too complicated to be incorporated into the general disequilibrium theory which we want to construct in Volume II. Moreover, the assumption that an announced strike will be executed till an agreement is reached is not so bad and not so far from reality that we need to correct this assumption.

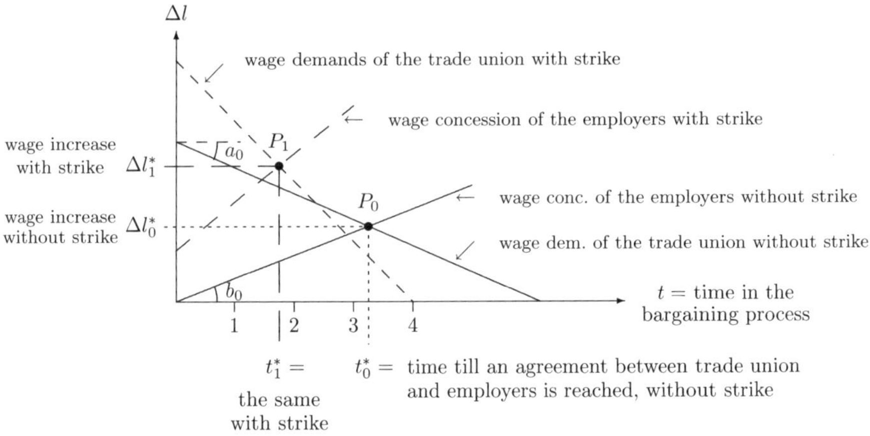

Figure 6.5 Agreement between trade union and employers: point P_0 : without strike, point P_1 : with strike

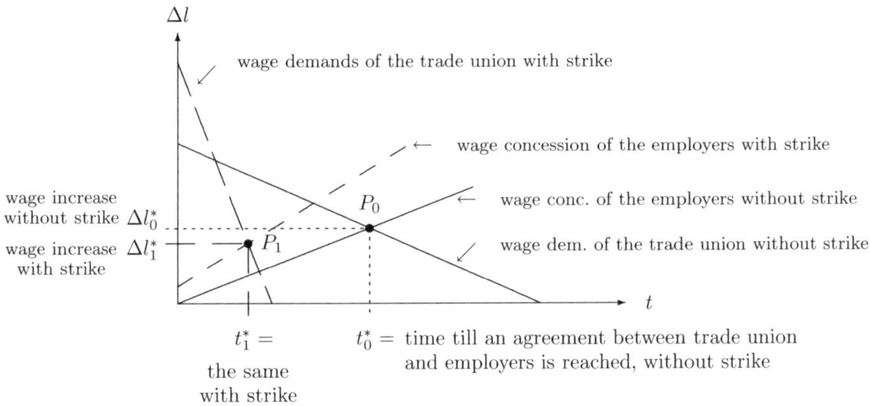

Figure 6.6 The case of a smaller wage increase with strike than without it: $\Delta l_0^* > \Delta l_1^*$

6.6 Criticism of Wage Determination by Agreement of Trade Unions and Employer Associations. A Digression

The arrangement of wage formation as modeled in the foregoing section boils down to understand the wage determination as a bilateral monopoly. The disadvantage of this type of price formation is well known: only the upper and the lower end of a range of possible agreements are properly determined by economic forces, the actual outcome depends on power relations, financial reserves, skill of bargaining and other facts which have nothing to do with the actual situation on the labor markets. The interest of the unemployed persons on employment does not enter the bargaining process: the trade unions look at the short term income interests of their members, i.e. of the employed persons. The employers' associations want to retain as much of the proceeds as possible in order to preserve the income of self employed persons and of the capital owners and in order to leave enough financial means for investment, i.e. for the future of the firms, after the next period. The care for the unemployed is left to the government. It is clear that such a regulation of determining wages does not yield full employment. It would be pure chance if employment would come near to full employment. Keynes suggested that the government should step in and should secure full employment by an appropriate demand of goods. This should be accompanied by an interest rate policy of the central bank which procures the necessary amount of money. But this leaves out the inflationary effects of such a policy and the long-term effects on government debts and the size of the payment of interest out of the government budget. Thus it seems to be preferable to cure the evil at the roots, that means to give everybody who wants a job the right of accepting a wage on which he (or she) and the employer agree upon. If this wage is too low according to our standards the government should fill the gap by subsidies - but this outside of the labor market. Such an arrangement has other problems (I only mention the free rider problem, but there are others as well), but they could be overcome. I shall not go into these details.

In the following I come to another weakness of the present organization of the labor market: the activity of the trade unions to increase the wage rates leads to an increase of the price level above that level which would result if the wage rates stayed constant. This increase would induce the central bank to raise the rate of interest which in term would lower employment. Thus the aims of the trade unions to increase the income of the employed persons but not to touch employment could only be realized by a policy of the central bank which backs this policy without considering the effects on the price level. This way the trade unions would set the pace of the central bank. But if the central bank wants to be the master and the trade unions want to be independent in their wage policy, a clash of the two policies is inevitable. This clash goes at the cost of employment. This is another argument in favor of changing the organization of the labor market.

Since this is not self-evident, I shall show this by a simple model.

Let the real economy consist of two sectors: the consumption goods industry and the investment goods industry, which in our case (for simplicity) comprise only one firm each. At the end of period -1 the firm which produces consumption goods determines the amount of production x_c of consumption goods in the next period 0 and the price p_c of a unit of this good on the base of a perceived inverse demand function $p_c = f(x_c)$, $f' < 0$. Production x_c need not be (and in general will not be) identical with the actual demand $c = g(p_c)$ of the consumers. If $x_c > c$ there will be an increase of $x_c - c$ of inventories, if $c > x_c$ there will be a decrease of the size $c - x_c$ of inventories (we assume that the size of inventories is large enough to take care of this surplus demand).

The expected proceeds $PROC_c^{exp}$ of the firm producing consumption goods is

$$PROC_c^{exp} = p_c \cdot x_c$$

We consider only a small range of p_c, c and x_c around the realized values in the last period such that we may linearize all functions. Thus we assume for the price function perceived by the producer

$$p_c = d_0 - d_1 x_c, \qquad \text{all parameters positive and } p_c > 0$$

We simplify the activities of the central bank by assuming that it fixes a rate of interest r valid in the whole economy. If the central bank increases r, the consumers will reduce their consumption expenditures and increase their demand on interest bearing assets. We model the influence of r on $PROC_c^{exp}$ by putting

$$d_0 = \overline{d}_0(1 - \overline{\overline{d}}_0 r), \qquad \text{all parameters positive and } d_0 > 0$$

Thus in the perception of the producer of consumption goods we get

$$PROC_c^{exp} = [\overline{d}_0(1 - \overline{\overline{d}}_0 r) - d_1 x_c] x_c$$

There is also a cost function CO_c which consists of fixed cost k_0 and variable cost $k_1 x$:

$$CO_c = k_0 + k_1 x_c, \qquad \text{where } d_0 > k_1.$$

Both coefficients depend on the rate of interest r and on the wage rate l: the larger r and l, the larger the cost CO_c. In the linear approximation one gets

$$k_0 = \overline{k}_0(1 + \overline{\overline{k}}_0 \cdot r + \overline{\overline{\overline{k}}}_0 \cdot l), \quad k_1 = \overline{k}_1(1 + \overline{\overline{k}}_1 \cdot r + \overline{\overline{\overline{k}}}_1 \cdot l)$$

Let us assume that the managers of the firm fix production x_c and (as a function of x_c) also the price p_c such that the expected profit $PROF_c^{exp}$ is maximal:

$$\begin{aligned} PROF_c^{exp} &= PROC_c^{exp} - CO_c \\ &= [\overline{d}_0(1 - \overline{\overline{d}}_0 \cdot r) - d_1 x_c] x_c - \overline{k}_0(1 + \overline{\overline{k}}_0 \cdot r + \overline{\overline{\overline{k}}}_0 \cdot l) \\ &\quad - \overline{k}_1(1 + \overline{\overline{k}}_1 \cdot r + \overline{\overline{\overline{k}}}_1 \cdot l) \cdot x_c \qquad \to \max_{x_c} \end{aligned}$$

All parameters are positive. We get

$$\frac{\partial PROF_c^{exp}}{\partial x_c} = \overline{d}_0(1 - \overline{\overline{d}}_0 r) + 2 d_1 x_c - \overline{k}_1(1 + \overline{\overline{k}}_1 \cdot r + \overline{\overline{\overline{k}}}_1 \cdot l) = 0$$

which yields $x_c = \frac{d_0 - k_1}{2d_1}$ and $p_c = \frac{1}{2}(d_0 + k_1)$. This means marginal proceeds equal marginal cost, the normal result, but this time including the effects of the wage rate and of the interest rate. Now we may state the effect of a higher wage rate l on the production x_c of consumption goods and on its price p_c. As already stated, in our model the production is fixed in the next period. A higher wage rate starts its effect on production one period later, that means: a higher wage rate does not show a decline of production and employment immediately, but only after a while (in our model: with one period delay) and thus can be ascribed to other events. Thus we get from our model

$$\frac{\partial x_{c,+1}}{\partial l} = -\frac{1}{2}\frac{\overline{k}_1 \overline{\overline{\overline{k}}}_1}{d_1} < 0$$

The long-term effect of higher wages on production (and thus on employment) is always negative. The coefficient $\overline{k}_1 \cdot \overline{\overline{\overline{k}}}_1$ indicates the size of the variable cost per unit of production, d_1 the necessary decline of the price if one wants to sell one unit more of the consumption good (in the idea of the producer) which is some measure of the rigidity of the demand.

The effect of a higher wage rate on the price of the consumption good is immediate:

$$\frac{\partial p_c}{\partial l} = \frac{1}{2}\overline{k}_1 \overline{\overline{\overline{k}}}_1 > 0$$

Wage increases without technical progress lead to inflation. This induces the central bank to increase the rate of interest in order to fight inflation. There may also be a one-period delay in the action of the central bank. The effect on production is:

$$\frac{\partial x_{c,+1}}{\partial r} = \frac{-\overline{d}_0 \overline{\overline{d}}_0 - \overline{k}_1 \overline{\overline{k}}_1}{2d_1} = -\frac{\overline{d}_0 \overline{\overline{d}}_0 + \overline{k}_1 \overline{\overline{k}}_1}{2d_1} < 0$$

This means: an increase of the interest will always reduce production. The expression $\overline{d}_0 \cdot \overline{\overline{d}}_0$ is a measure of the position of the price function: the larger $\overline{d}_0 \cdot \overline{\overline{d}}_0$, the larger would be the (negative) influence of a higher rate of interest on the position of the price function. $\overline{k}_1 \cdot \overline{\overline{k}}_1$ is a measure of the marginal cost of production.

The influence of a higher rate of interest on the price level is not unequivocal. One gets:

$$\frac{\partial p_c}{\partial r} = \frac{1}{2}(\overline{k}_1 \cdot \overline{\overline{k}}_1 - \overline{d}_0 \cdot \overline{\overline{d}}_0) > 0, \ = 0 \text{ or } < 0$$

If the marginal cost increases substantially with the rate of interest (i.e. if the cost of an increase of production (which are measured by $\overline{k}_1 \cdot \overline{\overline{k}}_1$) are mostly interest cost), an increase of the interest will raise the price level and not depress it, as intended. If $\bar{d}_0 \cdot \bar{\bar{d}}_0$ is large enough, the price of the consumption good will fall.

Thus we may conclude[6] : this simple model already shows that the usual purchasing power argument of the trade union in favor of higher wages does not hold. That means: those who are employed get a higher wage income at the cost of the employers and the capital owners. But in the absence of technical progress (and in the short run we may neglect it) the prices will increase and the central bank will fight inflation by increasing the rate of interest. In the long run, the negative effect of higher wages on employment and the same effect of higher interest rates will prevail. One has to wait for technical progress to compensate for excessive wage claims, but this does not help the unemployed.

6.7 A Short Look into the Literature

Since the wage rate is an important variable in economics, one finds explanations of it in all text books of economics and, of course, there is a whole special branch of literature on this subject. But, as usual in complex phenomena, one may look at this object from different points of view and from different distances. The situation is similar to that of regarding a painting. Take for instance the painting of a landscape by Jacob van Ruisdael. From a large distance only a shining sky and a dark earth can be perceived where each one covers half of the canvas and the dividing line is horizontal. If one approaches the painting a bit more, one recognizes a rotten tree in the foreground and some living trees in the middle ground; still nearer one detects a sand path and a rotten farm house in the wood, a castle or church in the background and if one proceeds quite near, one discerns some very small figures of human beings, some birds in the air, details of the trees and so on. Which is the right description of such a painting? It depends on the aim: a philosopher would think that the $\frac{1}{2} : \frac{1}{2}$ division of the canvas between sky and earth suffices to describe the philosophical statement of the canvas, and one does not need the personal details. An art historian would oppose and insist on regarding the construction of the painting and the distribution of colours and of light and shadow, and compare it to other contemporary or earlier or later paintings. An economist would consider the activities of the human beings, their clothes, their tools, the state of roads and of the houses and of the fields and draw the conclusions on the standard of life, the distribution of income and wealth, the social structure, the state of technology and so on.

---

[6] We did not present a complete model: the production of investment goods is not modeled as well as saving and investment. This is not necessary for this approach, thus we left it out here.

The situation in the explanation of the wage rates is similar. There are approaches which consider the labor market in analogy to a commodity market under perfect competition: there is a rising supply curve of labor and a falling demand curve for labor. The supply curve is derived from the relative preferences of consumption (or labor) and leisure of a household, the demand curve from the production function of a representative firm (see e.g. *Mankiw* (1998) or *Barro* (1993)). All this runs in real terms. The trade unions are often not mentioned. Their activity is reproduced as a shift of the labor supply function (a sort of artificial shortness of the supply of labor) which is the reason for involuntary unemployment. Other textbooks follow this line more or less (e.g. *Richter, Schlieper, Friedman* (1981), *Romer* (1996), *Dornbusch-Fischer* (1978)). The approach of *Burda & Wyplosz* (1993) is more detailed:

They start very general with the analogy of Robinson Crusoe at a remote island and end up with modern trade unions under two objectives: high real wages and more jobs. This results in union labor supply curves which are more restricted than the individual labor supply curves. They yield higher wages but less employment which explains involuntary unemployment. Some text books (such as *Dornbusch-Fischer* (1978)) rely on the *Keynesian System* of the "General Theory of Employment, Interest and Money" (1936). Keynes assumes that prices are proportional to wages such that unemployment cannot be influenced by changes of the nominal wage rate. Consumption is a function of income, investment a function of the difference of the marginal efficiency of capital (measured by the internal rate of interest of investment projects) and the market rate of interest (determined by the central bank). This leads to the conclusion that a compliant wage policy cannot guarantee permanent full employment. If this is true, the nominal wage rate is not of much interest as far as production and employment are concerned and thus there is no separate "theory of wages" in books which follow the Keynesian line of thought.

Of course, there is not *one* wage rate for all types of labor in the economy. The *wage structure* is of interest, too. There are many theories and empirical treatises on this subject. I shall not got into this but only refer to *Katz* and *Autor* (1999) who present a review of the work in this field.

Those who are interested in the institutional and juridical regulations of the German labor market are referred to the book "Arbeitsmarktökonomik" of *Wolfgang Franz* (1st ed. 1991, now there exists a 4th ed.). He presents a lot of information on the development of wages, the frequency of strikes and details of the bargaining problem but not a "general theory" of wage formation. We may take the result of an econometric estimation as a substitute:

$$w = a_0 + a_1 \cdot p + a_3 AMA \qquad \text{(p. 284 of "Arbeitsmarktökonomik", 4th ed.),}$$

where w = growth rate of the nominal wage rate, p = rate of inflation, AMA = the "tension on the labor market", measured by the ratio of open positions in the economy to the number of unemployed. But the $\overline{R}^2 = 0.60$ is rather small such that this cannot be taken as the last word on this problem. Franz states that himself (p.275): "... [Es] existiert kein geschlossener theoretischer Modellrahmen, der dem Lohnbildungsprozeß unter Berücksichtigung der ... dargestellten institutionellen Regelungen für die Bundesrepublik Deutschland gerecht wird." Maybe the above presented theory can show a way out of these difficulties.

References

[1] Barro, Robert J.: *Macroeconomics*, New York etc. (John Wiley) 1984, 4th ed. 1993, ch. 6

[2] Burda, Michael and Wyplosz, Charles: *Macroeconomics, a European Text*, (Oxford University Press) 1993

[3] Dornbusch, Rudiger and Fischer, Stanley: *Macroeconomics*, New York etc. (McGraw-Hill) 1978

[4] Franz, Wolfgang: *Arbeitsmarktökonomik*, Berlin etc. (Springer), 1st ed. 1991, 4th ed.

[5] Helmstädter, Ernst: *Wirtschaftstheorie I, Mikroökonomische Theorie*, 4th ed. München (Vahlen) 1991; *Wirtschaftstheorie II, Makroökonomische Theorie*, 3rd ed. München (Vahlen), 1986

[6] Katz, Lawrence F. and Autor, David H.: *Changes in the Wage Structure and Earnings Inequality*, in: Ashenfelter and Card (eds.), *Handbook of Labor Economics*, vol. 3 (Elsevier) 1999, pp. 1463-1555

[7] Keynes, John M.: *The General Theory of Employment, Interest and Money*, Cambridge 1936, reprint edition (Prometheus Books) 1997

[8] Krelle, Wilhelm: *Preistheorie, II. Teil*, 2nd ed. Tübingen (Siebeck) 1976, pp. 607 ff.

[9] Krelle, Wilhelm: *Waves of Entrepreneurial Activity Induced by Transfer of Information and Valuation*, Zeitschrift für National-Ökonomie 4, 1984, pp. 71-92

[10] Krelle, Wilhelm: *Long-Term Fluctuations of Technical Progress and Growth*, Zeitschrift für die gesamte Staatswissenschaft (JITE), vol. 143, no. 3 1987, pp. 379-401

[11] Krelle, Wilhelm (ed.): *The Future of the World Economy, Economic Growth and Structural Change*, Berlin, Heidelberg etc. (Springer), 1989

[12] Mankiw, N.Gregory: *Principles of Economics*, Fort Worth etc. (Dryden) 1998, ch. 18

[13] Richter, R., Schlieper, U. and Friedmann, W.: *Makroökonomik. Eine Einführung*, 4th ed., Berlin etc. (Springer) 1981

[14] Romer, David: *Advanced Macroeconomics*, New York etc. (McGraw-Hill) 1996, ch. 10

CHAPTER 7
The Theory of the Price of Securities and of the Interest Rates

7.1 Introduction

Following the general approach of this book, we explain the price of securities (in the broad sense, including capital stock) by the actions of brokers at the exchange and the interest rates by decisions of banks concerning the conditions of their loans. As to the price of securities, we already considered the offer and demand of securities in case of a household in some detail (see section 1.25). This approach is quite general and can be extended to any individual or institution. Thus we do not repeat it here. But the fixing of rates by the brokers is only dealt with in a short digression (section 1.26 in) which covers only the 2-person case.

We shall extend it here to the case of many persons who are active at the exchange. We have already modeled the principles of decision of the Central Bank (see section 3.7) which comprise the determination of the discount rate and we considered the rate of interest which a commercial bank requires for its credits (see section 3.8). But this refers only to most important rates of interest. In this chapter we want to go a bit more into the details. We start with

7.2 The Price of Securities. A Theory of the Exchange

Let there be N persons or institutions which use the exchange as buyers or sellers of securities and let there be S types of securities. There are S brokers at the exchange, one for each security[1]. The brokers fix the price of each security such that at that price demand of that security equals supply[2].

A client of the exchange may put conditional orders for buying or selling a security, but the conditions must refer only to the price of this security and to quantities of it but not to other conditions (e.g. "the future state of the

---

[1] Of course, in reality one broker may take care of several securities. But it is simpler to imagine that one broker is responsible for one type of security.

[2] This lies also in the interest of the broker since the brokerage (which is his income) depends on the turnover which is maximal if demand equals supply.

world", specially the price of other securities). We further assume that the broker only uses discrete and finite numbers as price of the securities, say:

$$v = \in \{v_1, v_2, \ldots, v_h\}, \quad \text{where} \quad v_1 < v_2 < \ldots < v_h$$

Thus a customer may give the following order to the broker:

- if the price of the security is v_i,
  - buy the amount ΔW_i^+ within the liquidity constraint $v_i \cdot \Delta W_i^+ \leq F, \quad i \in \{1, \ldots, h\}$
  - or sell the amount ΔW_i^- (taken as a positive value) within the constraint $\Delta W_i^- \leq \overline{W}$,

where $\overline{W}$ is the available amount of that security in the portfolio of the customer. It is easy to see that we will have

$$\begin{aligned} \Delta W_1^+ \geq \Delta W_2^+ \geq \ldots \geq \Delta W_g^+, \\ \Delta W_{g+1}^+ = \ldots = \Delta W_h^+ = 0 \text{ and } g \leq h \end{aligned}$$

and

$$\begin{aligned} 0 \leq \Delta W_1^- \leq \Delta W_2^- \leq \ldots \leq \Delta W_h^-, \\ \Delta W_h^- = \ldots = \Delta W_{g'}^- = \overline{W} \end{aligned}$$

and in many cases

$$\Delta W_1^- = \ldots = \Delta W_f^- = 0.$$

Fig 7.1 illustrates these conditional buying or selling orders of one customer. If we aggregate over all buying and selling orders as a function of the final price v of the security we get (in the spirit of Fig 7.1) two step functions $\Delta\overline{W}^+$ and $\Delta\overline{W}^-$ of v:

$$\Delta\overline{W}_1^+ \geq \Delta\overline{W}_2^+ \geq \ldots \geq \Delta\overline{W}_h^+$$

$$\text{and} \quad \Delta\overline{W}_1^- \leq \Delta\overline{W}_2^- \leq \ldots \leq \Delta\overline{W}_h^-$$

as shown in Fig 7.2. They illustrate the total order situation of the broker responsible for this security. We assume that the price which the broker determines can only be fixed at certain predetermined values, e.g. $v_1, v_2, \ldots, v_7$ in Fig 7.2 (e.g. in cents of Euro, but not in fraction of cents). The broker receives buying and selling orders from the customers, conditioned upon this price: $\Delta\overline{W}_i^+$ for $v = v_i$ in Fig 7.2 for all buying orders conditioned upon price v_i and $\Delta\overline{W}_i^-$ for all selling orders conditioned upon this price. The broker puts the price such that total demand equals total supply. In general such a price v_i does not exist. But if we linearize the offer and demand functions and proceed from step functions to ordinary continuous functions (see the dotted straight lines in Fig 7.2) and if the offer and demand functions look like those in Fig 7.2 (which is very likely), we always have a price where total demand

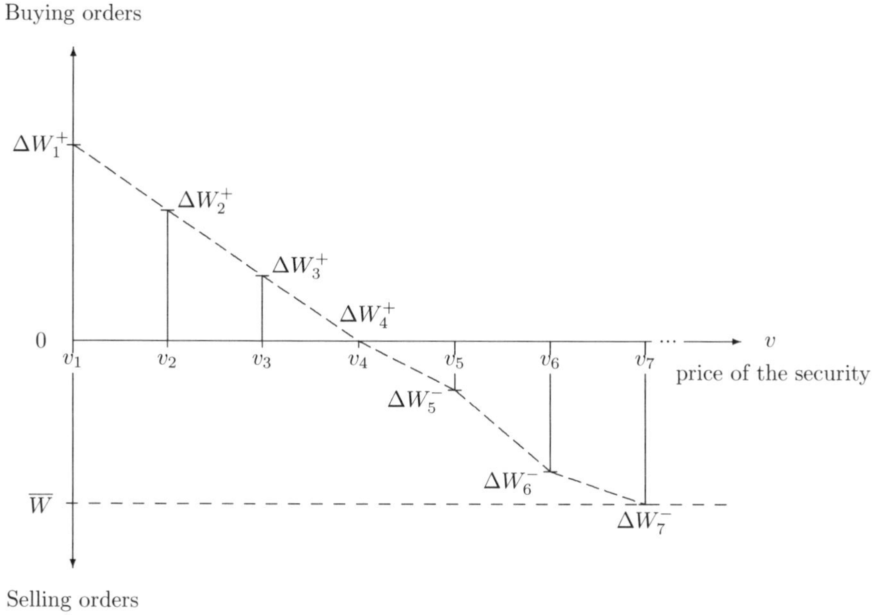

Notes:

The broken line has no economic meaning. The ΔW_i^+ illustrate the conditional buying orders, the ΔW_i^- the conditional selling orders. $\overline{W}$ is the total amount of securities of the type we are considering here in the portfolio of the customer.

Figure 7.1 Orders of a customer at an exchange conditioned upon the price of the security

equals total supply (v_* in Fig 7.2, where $\Delta\overline{W}_*^+ = \overline{W}_*^-$). In the discontinuous case the broker would choose a price v_i, $i \in \{1, \ldots, 7\}$ such that the mismatch is minimal. In Fig 7.2 the broker would choose v_4 which yields a surplus demand of $\Delta\overline{W}^+_{surpl.}$ of securities which cannot be covered by supply. If he would fix a higher price (say: $v = v_5$) there would be a huge surplus supply of the security. In the stock exchange reports the situation of a mismatch is indicated by notes on the surplus which cannot be served: a surplus of buying orders means a surplus of money left in the hands of the broker, a surplus of selling orders means a surplus of securities left in his hands.

In our model we are content with a linear approximation. We do not consider surplus demand or surplus supply of securities. This will be compensated by orders in the next period. We simplify the approach of Fig 7.2 as indicated in Fig 7.3. That means: we assume that the demand of a security by a person p may be approximated by

$$\Delta\overline{W}^{+(p)} = \Delta\overline{W}^{+(p)}_{max} - \alpha \cdot v, \text{ if } v \leq \frac{\Delta\overline{W}^{+(p)}_{max}}{\alpha} =: \tilde{v}$$

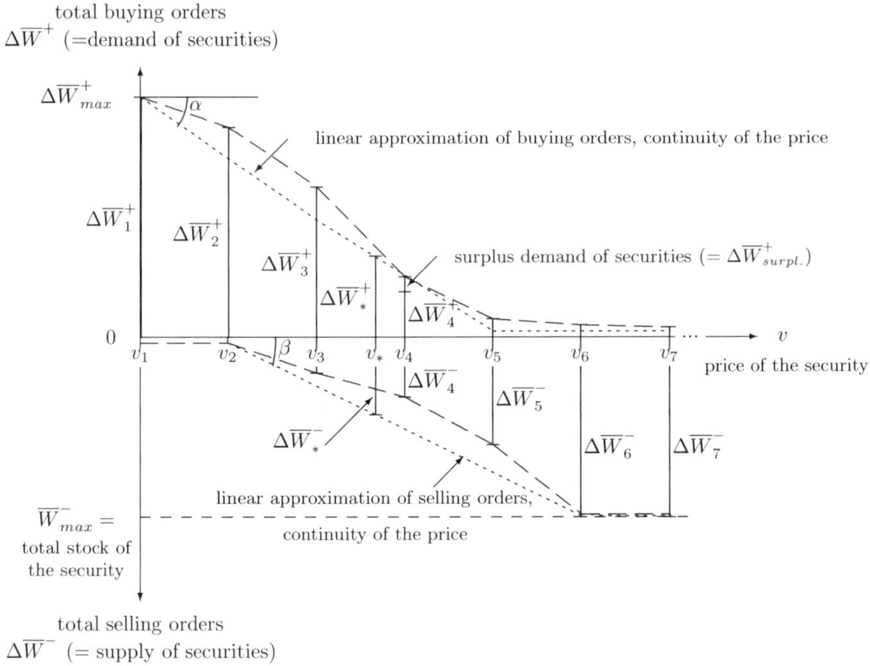

Figure 7.2 The orders of all customers at an exchange for buying or selling a specific security

Similarly

$$\Delta\overline{W}^{+(p')} = \Delta\overline{W}^{+(p')}_{max} - \beta \cdot v, \text{ if } v \leq \frac{\Delta\overline{W}^{+(p')}_{max}}{\beta} =: \tilde{\tilde{v}} \text{ and } \tilde{\tilde{v}} \leq \tilde{v}$$

If $v > \tilde{\tilde{v}}$ the demand $\Delta\overline{W}^{+(p')}_{max}$ of a person p' changes to a supply $\Delta\overline{W}^{-(p')}$; if $v > \tilde{v}$ the demand $\Delta\overline{W}^{+(p)}$ of a person p changes to a supply $\Delta\overline{W}^{-(p)}$, see Fig 7.3. The price v_* of the security which equalizes supply and demand:

$$\Delta\overline{W}^{+(p)} = -\Delta\overline{W}^{-(p')}$$

$$\text{is } v_* = \frac{\alpha\tilde{v} + \beta\tilde{\tilde{v}}}{\alpha + \beta}$$

All variables in this model result from the summation of the individual demand and supply orders, conditioned upon the price v of the security. The value v_* of his assets codetermines the decisions of a person on almost all variables under his control. Thus it should be known before these decisions are taken. But this is impossible since the values v_* of all assets can only be fixed by the brokers after all persons gave their conditional buying and selling

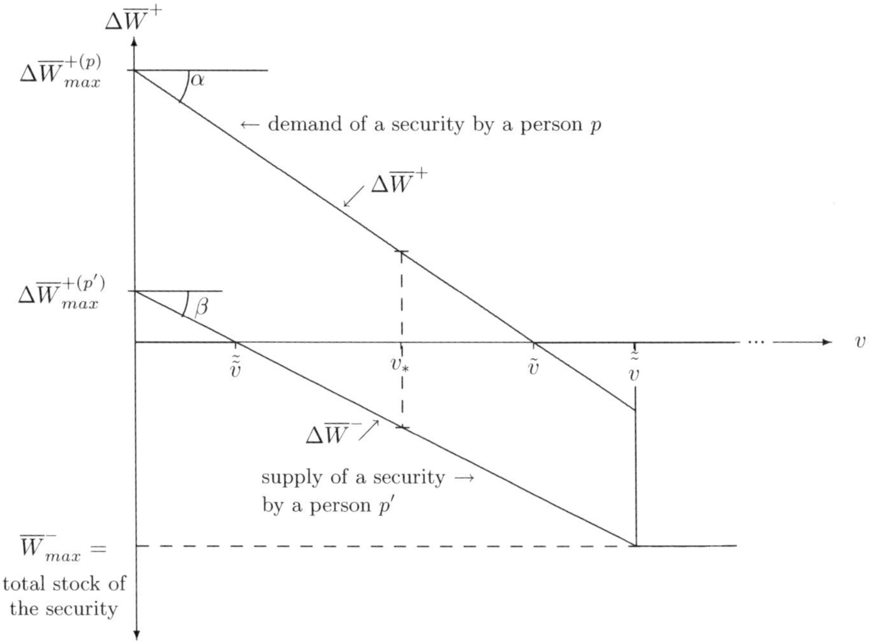

Figure 7.3. A simplified version of Fig. 7.2 (see the text)

orders which in turn depend on values and prices. There are two ways out of this difficulty:

1. All persons consider the known value $v_{*,-1}$ of an asset at the end of period -1 also as relevant for the next period 0, if there are no more recent figures available;

2. All persons estimate the future value v_* by some indicators and use this estimated value as approximation on the unknown future value.

The first alternative does not make any difficulties if one uses it in the micro-economics. The second alternative must be further specified. One could think of the following approach. A person p who belongs to the group of persons with conditional buying orders may estimate the value $\tilde{v}^{est}$ by the error correcting procedure:

$$\tilde{v}^{est} = \tilde{v}_{-1} - (1 - \varepsilon)(\tilde{v}_{-1} - v_{*,-1})$$

A person p' who belongs to the group of possible sellers of the asset may estimate

$$\tilde{\tilde{v}}^{est} = \tilde{\tilde{v}}_{-1} + (1 - \eta)(v_{*,-1} - \tilde{\tilde{v}}_{-1})$$

ε and η are parameters between zero and one which indicate the degree of confidence in the person's own estimation of the value of the asset ($\tilde{v}$ or $\tilde{\tilde{v}}$, respectively) compared with the evaluation $v_{*,-1}$ by the market.

$\varepsilon = 0$ (or $\eta = 0$) means: no confidence in his own estimation; this yields $\tilde{v} = v_{*,-1}$ (or $\tilde{\tilde{v}} = v_{*,-1}$).

$\varepsilon = 1$ (or $\eta = 1$) means full confidence in his own estimation and contempt of the value given by the market. This yields $\tilde{v} = \tilde{v}_{-1}$ (or $\tilde{\tilde{v}} = \tilde{\tilde{v}}_{-1}$). ε and η should be determined by the general interdependence of all value judgements and modeled as a Markov Chain. If the α and β stay constant, the buying or selling orders of each person may be estimated and thus also the price v_* of each asset. But this is a more complicated procedure which must be tested before it can be applied.

7.3 The Theory of the Determination of the Interest Rates

There is an interdependence of all interest rates in the economy, but some of these influence the others more strongly than they are influenced by them. We call them *base rates.* There are two of them: the discont rate r_d (now called main refinancing rate, Rate für Hauptrefinanzierungsgeschäfte in German) and the yield $\bar{r}$ of securities (Umlaufrendite in German). The other rates of interest keep a more or less constant distance to these rates (or better: there is a certain additional charge on these rates (see the graphs on p. 55 of the Monatsbericht März 2002 der Deutschen Bundesbank)). The *discount rate* r_d is a decision variable of the governors of the Central Bank and is already analyzed in section 3.7. It is one of five instruments of the Central Bank to influence the development of the economy. The results are judged from different points of view. In section 3.7 we mentioned the rate of inflation, employment, the rate of growth of GDP and the distribution of income as possible criteria. We de not repeat that here. The other base rate is the *yield* $\bar{r}$ *of securities.* It is defined by:

$$\bar{r} = \sum_{i \in \{I\}} \alpha_i \frac{z_i}{v_i}, \quad z_i = \text{nominal rate of interest of the security } i, \{I\} \text{ is the set of all securities traded at the exchange,}$$

$$v_i = \text{price of this security at the exchange,}$$

$$\alpha_i = \text{weighing numbers, } \alpha_i \geq 0, \sum_i \alpha_i = 1$$

There are g securities traded at the exchange. $\bar{r}$ indicates an average estimation of all customers of the exchange on the prospective yields of securities. One may assume that there is a tendency in the change of v_i such that in the long run average the values of $\frac{z_i}{v_i}$ scatter around $\bar{r}$. Anyway, r_d and $\bar{r}$ are the base rates in our approach. That means: the actions of the Central Bank and the estimates of the future yields of securities determine the basic movements of the different rates of interest in the economy.

If one linearizes this relation one may write for any rate of interest r:

$$r = \alpha_1 \cdot r_d + \alpha_2 \cdot \bar{r} + \Delta r$$

$\alpha_i \geq 0,\ i = 1, 2$, where Δr is a special charge on the interest rate of this specific asset (usually positive but there are cases where Δr is negative). Examples of almost constant ratios Δr are given in section 3.11. In any case, we do not go into the details of Δr but take it as institutionally given.

The other instruments of the monetary policy of the Central Bank must be treated in a similar fashion as r_d. Usually, they are moving in relation to r_d, thus enforcing its effects. For other details, see section 3.7.

We now turn to the other base rate, $\bar{r}$. It is an average of the different yields $\bar{r}_i = \frac{z_i}{v_i}$ of a security i. Consider a person or an institution p which owns such a security and which estimates the value of it as $\tilde{v}$ (see Fig 7.4). Thus his orders to a broker could be:

buy the amount $\Delta W^+ = \Delta W_1^+ - \alpha \cdot v,\quad$ if $0 < v \leq \tilde{v}$

or sell the amount $\Delta W^- = \beta(v - \tilde{v}),\quad$ if $v > \tilde{v}$.

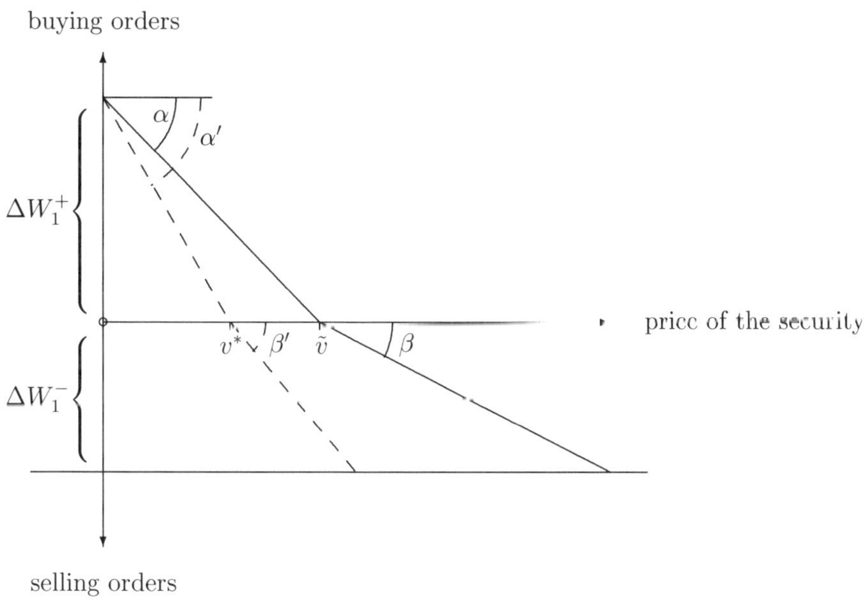

Figure 7.4. Change of orders at the broker because of a change of $\bar{r}$

$\tilde{v}$ conforms to a yield of $\bar{r}$ which in turn is related to the discount rate r_d such that an increasing r_d (which reduces the number N_{cn} of notes in circulation) would decrease the price v of the security. In Fig 7.4 v would shift from $\tilde{v}$ to v^* which means: α and β would increase. Thus the buying orders for the broker would decrease and the selling orders increase. This would depress the price v and thus increase $\bar{r}$. The result is that changes of the discount rate r_d would induce changes of the yield $\bar{r}$ to move in the same direction, though with some delay[3] . Thus there is some relation between r_d and $\bar{r}$, though more long-term and weak and more going in the direction from r_d to $\bar{r}$ than in the opposite direction.

In our model of chapter 3 we have - except the base rates - the following interest rates:

a. Interest received by commercial bank i:

- for credits CR_{bi} by the rate $r_{CR,bi}$
- for keeping securities W_{bi} by the rate $r_{W,bi}$ (this comprises also dividends on capital stock)

b. Interest paid by commercial bank i:

- for time deposits TD_{bi} by the rate $r_{TD,bi}$
- for claims of the Central Bank CL_{bi} by the rate $r_{CL,bi}$
- for borrowed capital $BCAP_{bi}$ by the rate $r_{BCAP,bi}$

This list depends on the assumption that the Central Bank need not pay interest on the reserve requirements of the commercial banks and that in the short run there is no predetermined yield rate for capital stock (though in the long run the average yield would be $\bar{r}$).

c. Interest received by the Central Bank:

- for claims of the Central Bank to all banks CL_B by the rate $r_{CL,b}$
- for value W_{CB} of securities in the portfolio of the Central Bank by the rate $r_{W,CB}$

There are no interest payments of the Central Bank because we assumed that the Central Bank does not have to pay interest on its "debts" to the government and on the reserve requirements which the commercial banks have to keep at the Central Bank.

[3] Empirical research showed that the commercial banks do not follow the market rate immediately with their credit rate but smooth out changes in the market rate (see "Zum Zusammenhang zwischen Kreditzinsen deutscher Banken und Marktzinsen", Mo.Ber. März 2002 der Deutschen Bundesbank, p. 53 ff.). This conforms to the reasoning above, if "Marktzinsen" are interpreted as $\bar{r}$ and the "Kreditzinsen" are proportional to r_d.

As already said, the base rates r_d and $\bar{r}$ influence all other interest rates such that in the linear case:

$$r_i = \alpha_{1i} \cdot r_d + \alpha_{2i} \cdot \bar{r} + \Delta r_i$$

$$\text{where} \quad i \in \{CR, bi;\ W, bi;\ TD, bi;\ CL, bi;\ BCAP, bi;\ CL, B;\ W, CB\}.$$

Δr_i are constant additions (called interest distance (Zinsabstand) in the German Statistics) to the base rates r_d and $\bar{r}$. This conforms to the estimations in the "Monatsbericht März 2002 der Deutschen Bundesbank", p. 55.

The figure $BCAP$ for borrowed capital contains also loans from the money market (the "Tagesgeldsatz" in German, now measured by the EONIA-index, European over night index average). But we do not go into these details here.

This approach which explains all interest rates by r_d and $\bar{r}$ and by a constant interest distance Δr_i may be helpful in establishing empirical rules for "explaining" interest rates but surely is not in the spirit of our general theory which explains all variables by decisions of persons or rules of natural laws. Thus the statements above should be considered as preliminary and empirical introduction and not as the theory itself. In order to come to this theory the list of variables has to be changed a bit and it must be stated who decides on a certain rate of interest and who decides on the conditional demand or supply of the pertinent security. These assumptions are listed in the following table 7.1: As may be seen from this table the persons who decide on the interest rate are always others than those who decide on the securities or loans or deposits or other financial flows subject to this rate of interest. It is assumed that all rates of interest are known to the persons who decide on the volumes before they take their decision. This implies that the deciding persons know the alternatives which arise as a consequence of their decision on the interest rates (on the base of estimation of the decisions of other persons). An alternative approach would be to assume that each person estimates the different rates of interest empirically (e.g. as function of r_d, $\bar{r}$ and Δr, see above), and the decisions on the volumes would be made on the base of these estimations of the rates of interest.

7.4 The Financial Structure of a Commercial Bank

Given the interest rates the main decisions of the managers of a bank b refer to the procurement and the use of the capital at their disposal. Table 7.2 shows a simplified picture of the resulting balance sheet of a commercial bank. The managers of the bank evaluate its financial structure by choosing the parameters $s, t, \ldots, w$.

Table 7.1 Who decides on the monetary items connected with the banking system?

deciding persons or institutions ↓ / decision on →	r_d ·	$CL^{s.t.}_{CB,bi}$	$r_{CL,CB,bi}$ ·	$CL^{l.t.}_{CB,bi}$	$r_{BCAP_{j,bi}}$ ·	$BCAP_{j,bi}$	$r_{CRj,bi}$ ·	$CR_{j,bi}$
Central Bank CB	X		X					
bank i b_i		X		X	X		X	
person j j						X		X

deciding persons or institutions ↓ / decision on →	$r_{TD,bi}$ ·	$TD_{j,bi}$	$r_{wj,bi}$ ·	$W_{j,bi}$	$DEP_{j,bi}$	CO_{bi}
Central Bank CB						
bank i b_i	X			X		X
person j j		X	X		X	

Notations:

r_d = discount rate (= main refinancing rate)
$CL^{s.t.}_{CB,bi}$ = short term claims of the Central Bank on bank i
$r_{CL,CB,bi}$ = rate on long term claims of the Central Bank on bank i
$CL^{l.t.}_{CB,bi}$ = long term claims of the Central Bank on bank i
$r_{BCAP_j,bi}$ = rate on borrowed capital provided by person j to bank i
$BCAP_{j,bi}$ = borrowed capital provided by person j to bank i
$r_{CR_{j,bi}}$ = rate on credits to person j provided by bank i
$CR_{j,bi}$ = credits to persons j provided by bank i
$r_{TD,bi}$ = rate of interest paid by bank i on time deposits
$TD_{j,bi}$ = time deposits of person j on accounts of bank i
$DEP_{j,bi}$ = current deposits of person j at bank i. It is assumed that the rate of interest on these accounts is always 0.
$r_{wj,bi}$ = rate of interest received by bank i from securities w_j issued by person j
$W_{j,bi}$ = amount of securities issued by person j and kept in the portfolio of bank i
CO_{bi} = cost of running bank i

In the first line the cash requirements for different types of liabilities are listed. In line 2 the minimum reserves as required by the Central Bank are indicated, where $s_2 \cdot DEP_b$ are the minimum reserve requirements for demand deposits and $t_2 \cdot TD_b$ are the minimum reserves for time deposits and $u_2 = v_2 = w_2 = 0$. In line 3 the credits of the bank are related to their financial sources, in line 4 the same is done for the value of the securities in the portfolio of the bank. The managers have to decide on the parameters s, t, u, v, w under the constraints given above, by considering the risks involved in an allocation of the financial means and by considering the costs and the yields of the bank. Fig 7.5 illustrates the basic idea: there is only a relatively small range of the rate of interest charged by the commercial banks for credits, if the bank wants to keep its profitability.

Table 7.2. The Balance Sheet of a Commercial Bank

↓ **Asset Side** $(CA_b + CA_{b,CB} + CR_b + W_b)$			→ **Liability Side** $(DEP + TD + CL_{CB,b} + BCAP_b + CAP_b)$
1. Cash	CA_b	=	$s_1 \cdot DEP_b + t_1 \cdot TD_b + u_1 \cdot CL_{CB,b} + v_1 \cdot BCAP_b + w_1 \cdot CAP_b$
2. Minimum reserves	$CA_{b,CB}$	=	$s_2 \cdot DEP_b + t_2 \cdot TD_b + u_2 \cdot CL_{CB,b} + v_2 \cdot BCAP_b + w_2 \cdot CAP_b$
3. Credits	CR_b	=	$s_3 \cdot DEP_b + t_3 \cdot TD_b + u_3 \cdot CL_{CB,b} + v_3 \cdot BCAP_b + w_3 \cdot CAP_b$
4. Securities	W_b	=	$s_4 \cdot DEP_b + t_4 \cdot TD_b + u_4 \cdot CL_{CB,b} + v_4 \cdot BCAP_b + w_4 \cdot CAP_b$
column sum	$= BAL_b$		$DEP_b + TD_b + CL_{CB,b} + BCAP_b + CAP_b$ → line sum $= BAL_b$

DEP_b	TD_b	$CL_{CB,b}$	$BCAP_b$	CAP_b
daily deposits	time deposits	claims of the CB	borrowed capital	capital + reserves

all parameters non-negative, $\sum_{i=1}^4 s_i = \sum_{i=1}^4 t_i = \sum_{i=1}^4 u_i = \sum_{i=1}^4 v_i = \sum_{i=1}^4 w_i = 1$

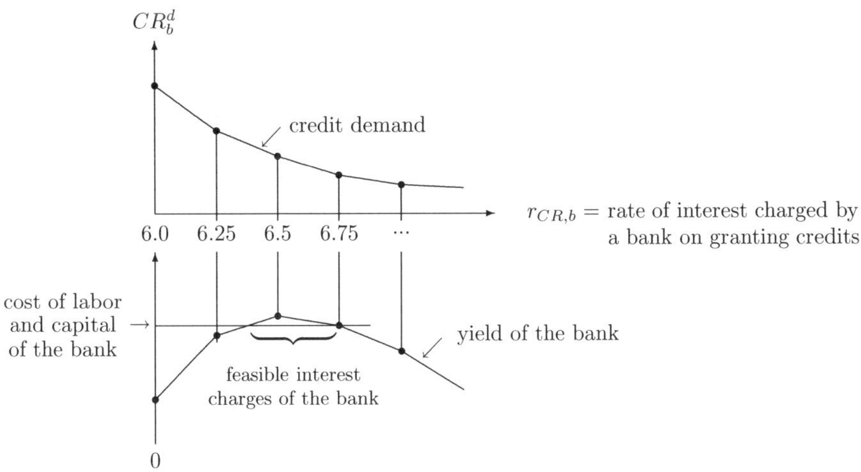

Figure 7.5. Limits of the rates of interest charged by the banks

7.5 A Short Look into the Literature

In all text books of economics one finds one or more chapters on interest rates, mostly based on the Keynesian approach, but also written from the point of view of monetarism (connected with the name of Milton Friedman). "Monetarism" assumes that the amount of money in circulation essentially determines the prices of all commodities (thus also the price of securities) and the nominal rate of growth of GDP. The effect of the fiscal policy on the velocity of money is small. These tendencies are even more pronounced if one assumes rational expectations on the side of persons who trade on the exchange: monetary policy cannot influence real GDP because these effects are already taken into consideration by demand and supply of securities on the exchange. This view is the complete antithesis to the Keynesian approach which holds that a market economy in itself does not yield a general equilibrium situation, especially not on the labor market. A steersman is needed to keep the big ship of the economy on its course. He has essentially two control variables at his disposal: fiscal policy and monetary policy which operate by influencing the rate of interest and thus the demand of commodities. Thus we find here the total contrast to monetarism: the monetary variables influence the real ones essentially. In the text book of *Manfred Neumann* (5th ed. 1996, p. 66) one finds a very good graphical illustration of the interdependence of the monetary and the real sector of an economy on the base of these assumptions (also the real wage rate is considered).

Recent theories on prices and interest rates consider the state of information of the persons who trade on the exchange and determine the rate of interest. The Phillips-curve approach (which postulates an inverse relation between the rate of inflation and employment) is almost everywhere given up. But now the difference between short term transitory effects of monetary policy on the real side of the economy (which are not denied by most monetarists) and long term effects (which are nil or even negative) come to the foreground.

There are, of course, lots of statistical analyzes on details of the price formation of securities on the exchange. In only mention the article of *Linda Gorman* in the N.B.E.R. Digest, June 2002[4]. But this type of literature though interesting in itself does not result into a "general theory" of the prices of securities and of the interest rates. Our theory tries to show how the subjective judgements of persons on the future prospects of firms and institutions result into prices and interest rates.

References

[1] Barro, Robert J.: *Macroeconomics*, 4th ed. New York etc. (Wiley), 1993

[2] Barro, Robert J. and Grilli, Vittorio: *European Macroeconomics*, London (The McMillan Press), 1994

[3] Beckmann, Martin J., Menges, Günter and Selten, Reinhard (eds.): *Handbuch der Mathematischen Wirtschaftswissenschaften, Vol. I, Wirtschaftstheorie*, Wiesbaden (Gabler), 1979

[4] Burda, Michael and Wyplosz, Charles: *Macroeconomics. A European Text*, Oxford etc. (Oxford University Press), 1993

[5] Cohen, Randolph, Gompers, Paul and Vuolteenaho, Tuomo: *Who Underreacts to Cash-Flow News? Evidence from Trading between Individuals and Institutions*, N.B.E.R. Working Paper No. 8793

[4] Linda Gorman: "Who Underrates the Cash Flow News?".

[6] Dornbusch, Rudiger and Fischer, Stanley: *Macroeconomics*, New York etc. (McGraw-Hill), 1978

[7] Frisch, Helmut: *Theories of Inflation*, London, New York etc. (Cambridge University Press), 1983

[8] Gorman, Linda: *Who Underreacts to Cash-Flow News?*, The N.B.E.R. Digest, June 2002

[9] Helmstädter, Ernst: *Wirtschaftstheorie II, Makroökonomische Theorie*, 3rd ed. München (Vahlen), 1986

[10] Helmstädter, Ernst: *Wirtschaftstheorie I, Mikroökonomische Theorie*, 4th ed. München (Vahlen), 1991

[11] Hildenbrand, Werner: *Market Demand: Theory and Empirical Evidence*, Princeton (Princeton University Press), 1994

[12] Hildenbrand, Werner and Kneip, Alois: *Aggregation under structural stability: the change in consumption of a heterogeneous population*, Bonn Econ Discussion Papers 4/2002, January 2002

[13] Holtemöller, Oliver: *Money and Prices: An I(2) Analysis for the Euro Area*, Discussion Paper No. 12/2002 of SFB 373, Humboldt-Universität Berlin, January 2002

[14] Holtemöller, Oliver: *Money and Banks: Some Theory and Empirical Evidence for Germany*, Discussion Paper No. 17/2002 of SFB 373, Humboldt-Universität Berlin, 2002

[15] Krelle, Wilhelm: *Preistheorie I*, Tübingen (Mohr Siebeck), 2nd ed. 1976

[16] Krelle, Wilhelm: *Preistheorie II*, Tübingen (Mohr Siebeck), 2nd ed. 1976

[17] Mankiw, N. Gregory: *Principles of Economics*, Fort Worth, Philadelphia etc. (The Dryden Press), 1998

[18] Neumann, Manfred: *Theoretische Volkswirtschaftslehre I*, München (Vahlen), 5th ed. 1996

[19] Romer, David: *Advanced Macroeconomics*, New York etc. (McGraw-Hill), 1996

[20] Rose, Manfred: *Finanzwissenschaftliche Makrotheorie*, München (Vahlen), 1980

[21] Samuelson, Paul A.: *Economics*, 17th ed. (McGraw-Hill), 2000

[22] Schweizer, Urs: *Vertragstheorie*, Tübingen (Mohr Siebeck), 1999

[23] Tirole, Jean: *The Theory of Industrial Organization*, Cambridge/Mass. (MIT Press), 1988

[24] Varian, Hal R.: *Grundzüge der Mikroökonomik* (Intermediate Microeconomics), 5th ed. München, Wien (Oldenbourg), 2001

[25] Wolfstetter, Elmar: *Topics in Microeconomics*, Cambridge (Cambridge University Press), 1999

A Final Remark

This book provides the raw material for a planned final product: a coherent, dynamic theory which comprises economics and ethics. Hopefully, I still have the time to formulate this theory. To stay in the metaphor of a building site: I have gathered the necessary raw material for a building. To form that building which I have in mind, this raw material has to be processed and made compatible. I hope I still have time on this earth to do that. But if not: I think that my colleagues could easily infer from these building blocks how the final product may look like.

Since the ultimate goal of these efforts should be a coherent total model of the society (with economics in the centre), the components cannot be too detailed. If one is interested in the details, one has to look into the specialized literature which is partly listed at the end of each chapter.

I would be glad if I could test econometrically the approach and the assertion which I chose. Unfortunately, I cannot do that myself. Time is running out. But perhaps a colleague may be interested in it.

Druck: Strauss Offsetdruck, Mörlenbach
Verarbeitung: Schäffer, Grünstadt